AF575748

A GUIDE TO BAROQUE ROME: THE PALACES

Title page: Design taken from the engraving in De Rossi's *Architettura Civile* of the main door of Palazzo del Grillo

Copyright © 2015, 2018, 2020, 2024 by Anthony Langdon
The moral right of the author has been asserted
All rights reserved

All photographs courtesy of Anthony Langdon, except pp. 136 and 227 courtesy of the publisher; p. 239 courtesy of Emanuele (zak mc) and p. 245 courtesy of Anthony Majanlahti under Creative Commons license

All other images courtesy of the publisher, except pp. 61, 62 and 125 courtesy of the Warburg Institute; and pp. 68, 109, 129, 144, 203, 204-5, 209-10 and 225 courtesy of the British Museum

Special thanks to Lisa Adams

ISBN 978-1-84368-253-0

First published 2015 by
Pallas Athene (Publishers) Ltd
2, Birch Close, Hargrave Park, London N19 5XD
Reprinted 2016, 2018, 2020
New edition with revisions 2024

www.pallasathene.co.uk

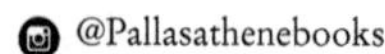 @Pallasathenebooks

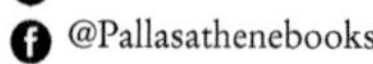 @Pallasathenebooks

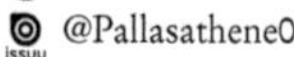 @Pallasathene0

Printed and bound in Great Britain by
TJ Books Limited, Padstow, Cornwall

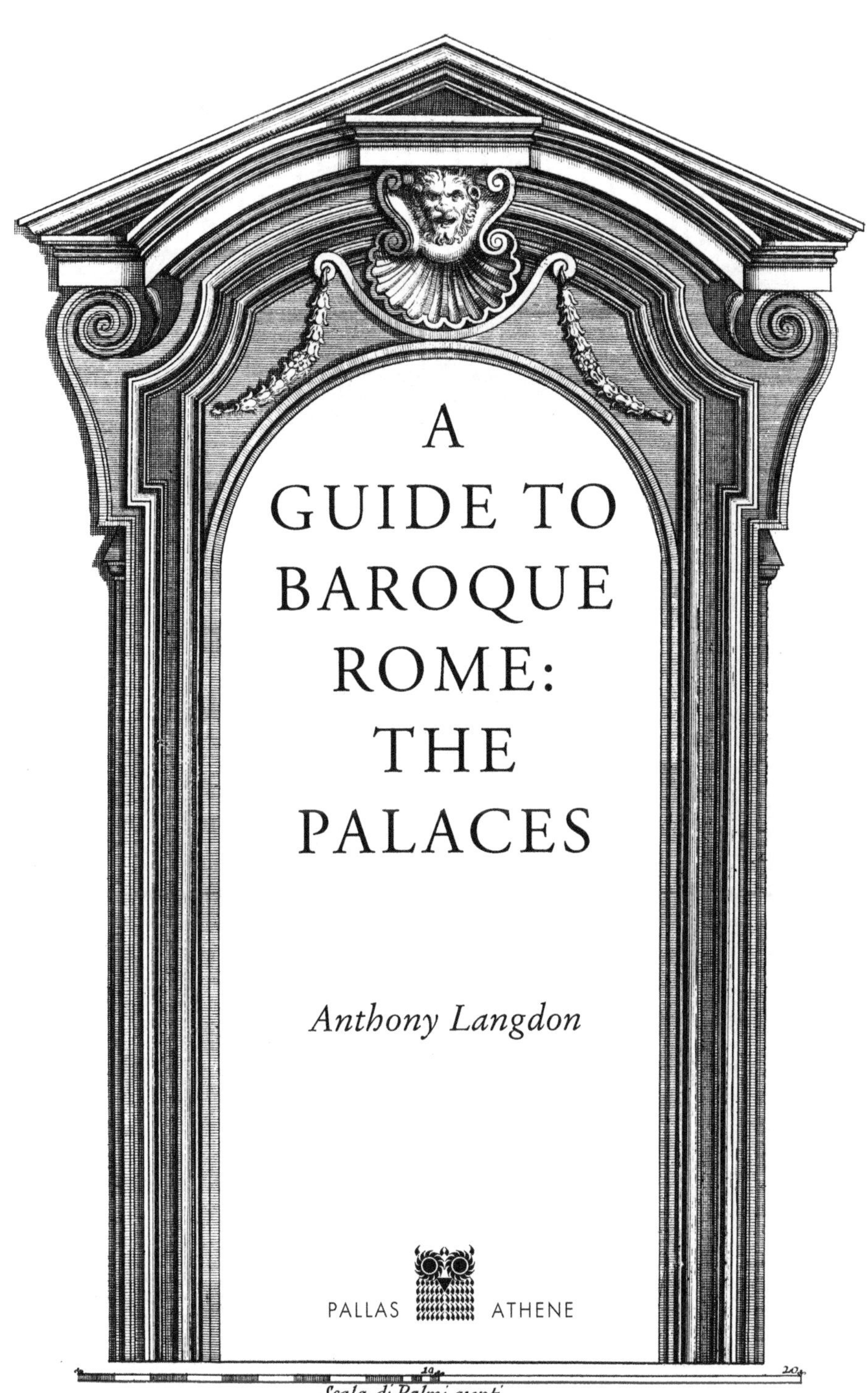

A GUIDE TO BAROQUE ROME: THE PALACES

Anthony Langdon

PALLAS ATHENE

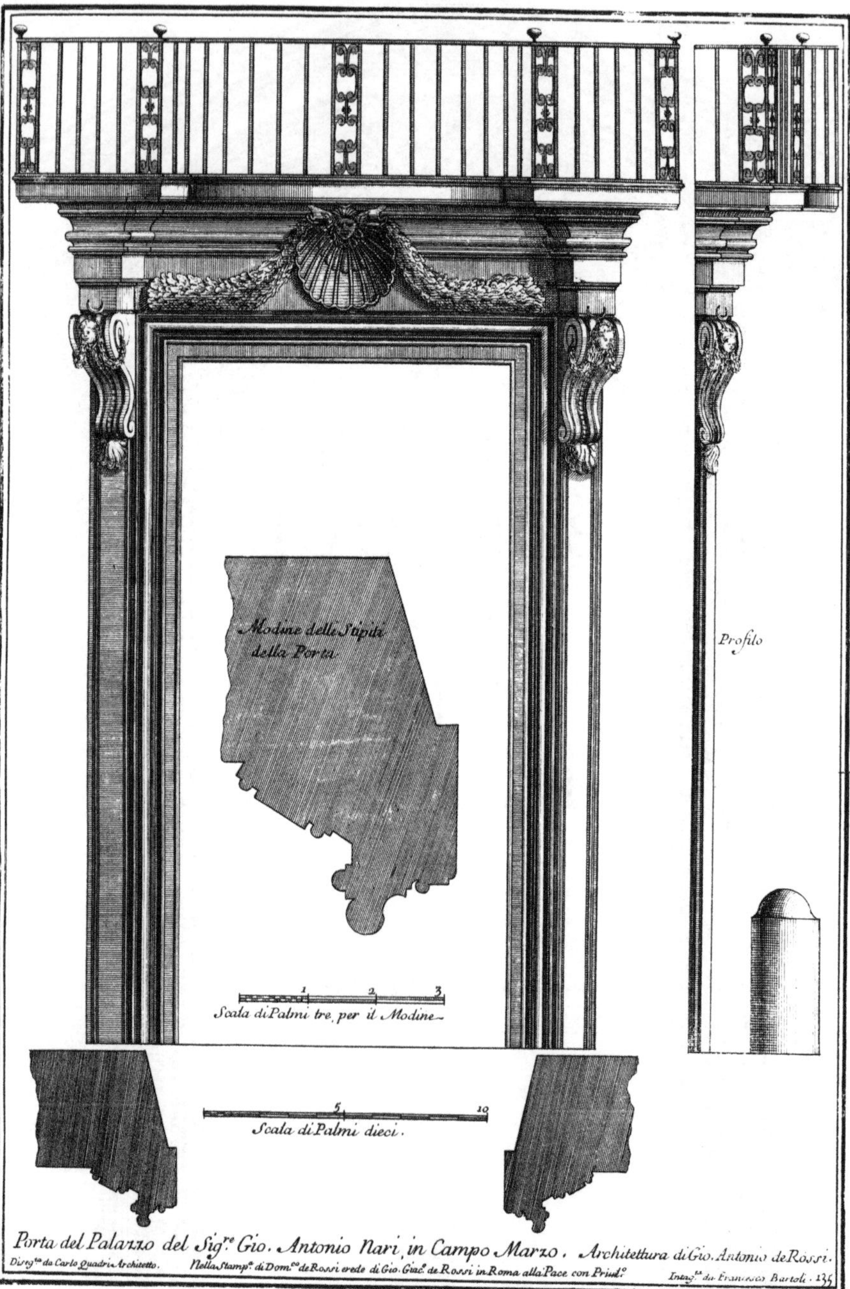
Modine delle Stipiti della Porta
Profilo
1 2 3
Scala di Palmi tre, per il Modine
5 10
Scala di Palmi dieci.
Porta del Palazzo del Sig.re Gio. Antonio Nari, in Campo Marzo. Architettura di Gio. Antonio de Rossi.
Diseg.ta da Carlo Quadri Architetto.
Nella Stamp.a di Dom.co de Rossi erede di Gio. Giac.o de Rossi in Roma alla Pace con Priv.o
Intag.ta da Francesco Bartoli. 135

Contents

Introduction 15

A few practical details
Visiting the palaces 21
Some essential places to see 22
Some possible itineraries 22

A note on the prints used to illustrate this book 27

THE PALACES

Casa degli Agostiniani Scalzi............................35
Palazzo Albani (Mattei, Massimi, Nerli, del Drago)............................36
Palazzo Albertoni (Spinola)............................38
Palazzetto Alibrandi or Alivrandi (Cavalieri)..39
Palazzo Altemps............................39
Palazzo Altieri............................41
Palazzetto Ansellini............................47
Palazzo Antamoro (Strada)............................47
Palazzo Astalli............................48
Palazzo D'Aste (in via di Ripetta)............................49
Palazzo D'Aste (Rinuccini, Bonaparte, Misciattelli)............................49
Palazzo D'Aste (Pericoli, Sterbini)............................53
Palazzo Avila............................54

Palazzo del Banco di S Spirito (Spada, Bennicelli)............................54
Palazzo Barberini ai Giubbonari or Casa Grande ai Giubbonari............................55
Palazzo Barberini............................57
Palazzi Bernini............................74
Palazzo Boncompagni Corcos (Starinci)............................75
Palazzo Boncompagni Ludovisi (Cerasi)............................76
Palazzo Borghese, Palazzo della Famiglia Borghese and Palazzetto Baschenis............................77
Palazzo Bossi............................89
Palazzo Braschi............................90
Palazzo Del Bufalo............................90
Palazzo del Bufalo Ferraioli (Niccolini)............................92

Palazzo della Cancelleria............................93
Palazzo Capizucchi (Troili, Massimo, Gasparri)............................93
Palazzo Capponi (Orsini, Stampa, Pediconi)............................95
Palazzo Capponi ('della Palma')............................96
Palazzo Cardelli............................97
Palazzo de Carolis (Simonetti, Banco di Roma)............................98
Palazzo Carpegna (Baldinotti)............................100
Palazzo Carpegna (Accademia di S Luca)............................100

Opposite: The door of Palazzo Nari in Campo Marzio by the architect G. A. De Rossi. The engraving comes from D. D. De Rossi's Architettura Civile

Palazzo Cavallerini Lazzaroni....................101
Palazzo Celani....................102
Palazzo Celsi....................102
Palazzo Cenci-Bolognetti (Petroni)....................104
Palazzo Centini (Toni, 'dei Pupazzi')....................105
Palazzo Cerri (Gaucci)....................106
Casa dei Chierici Minori....................106
Palazzo Chigi (Aldobrandini)....................108
Palazzo Chigi (Odescalchi)....................111
Palazzo Cimarra....................113
Palazzo del Cinque....................114
Palazzo Colonna....................115
Palazzo della Consulta....................119
Houses at Piazza delle Coppelle, 64 and 66.....122
Palazzo Corsini (Riario)....................123
Palazzo Costaguti (Patrizi)....................124
Palazzo Crescenzi (Bonelli, De Dominicis).....130

Palazzo Donarelli (Ricci)....................133
Palazzo Doria-Pamphili....................134
Palazzo del Drago (Gentili)....................139

Casa del Falco (Casa di Biagio Puccini)....................140
Palazzo Falconieri....................140
Palazzo Farnese....................143
Palazzo Ferrini (Cini)....................146

Palazzo Galloppi (Santovetti, Volpi di Misurato)....................147
Palazzo Gambirasi....................148
Palazzo Ghetti....................152
Palazzo Giangiacomo....................152
and House at via Monserrato, 102
Casa Giannini....................153
Palazzo Giustiniani....................153
Palazzo Gomez (Lepri, Gallo di Roccagiovanine, Silj)....................155
Palazzo Grazioli (Gottifredi)....................156
Palazzo del Grillo (de Robilant)....................157
Palazzo Guelfi Camajani (Montauto, Rovarella, Polidori, Pericoli)....................160

Palazzo Lancellotti....................160
Palazzo Lante (Medici, Lante Della Rovere, Grazioli, Aldobrandini)....................162
Palazzo Lateranense....................163
Palazzo Lazzaroni (Grimaldi)....................164
Palazzetto Lupardi ('Casa dei Ritratti')....................165

Palazzo Maccarani Odescalchi....................166
Palazzo Maccarani Savorgnan di Brazzà....................166
Palazzo Macchi di Cellere (Capranica)....................166
Palazzo Madama....................168
Casa di Carlo Maderno....................170
Palazzo Maffei (Peretti, Sannesi, Ludovisi, d'Este, Acciaioli, Marescotti, del Vicariato)....................170
Palazzo Magnani....................171
Palazzo Malta (del Sovrano Ordine Militare Gerosolomitano di Malta etc)....................171
Palazzo Mancini (Salviati)....................172
Palazzo Mandosi (Castelli-Mignanelli)....................173
Palazzo Manfroni....................174
Palazzo Marescotti....................174
Palazzo Maruscelli (Lepri)....................174
Palazzo Massimo di Rignano (Colonna)....................175
Palazzo Mastrozzi (Graziosi)....................177
Palazzo Mattei di Giove....................179
Palazzo Mellini (Cesi, Salviati, Michiel)....................181
Casa dei Merolli (Partini)....................183
Palazzo del Monte di Pietà....................183
Palazzo di Montecitorio....................186
Palazzo Montoro (Chigi Montoro, Patrizi, Naro, Lepri)....................189
Palazzo Muti Bussi....................190
Palazzo Muti Papazzurri (Savorelli, Balestra)....................193
Palazzo Muti Papazzurri (in Piazza della, Pilotta)....................196

Palazzo Nari (in Piazza S Maria in Campo Marzo)....................199
Palazzo Nari (in via Monterone)....................199
Palazzo Nuñez (Torlonia)....................199

Palazzo Ottoboni Boncompagni....................201

Palazzo Pallavicini Rospigliosi (Bentivoglio, Mazzarino, Pallavicini)....................201
Palazzo Pamphili....................205
Palazzo Panizza....................210
Palazzo Patrizi (Aldobrandini)....................212

Palazzo Patrizi (Clementi)....212
Palazzo Pecci Blunt (Fani, Ruspoli)....212
Palazzo Peretti (Fiano, Ottoboni, Boncompagni Ludovisi, Almagià)....213
Palazzo Perucchi (Campello)....214
Palazzo del Pio Sodalizio dei Piceni (della Naziona Picena, Casa di Sisto V)....214
Palazzo Pighini (Fusconi, del Gallo di Roccagiovine)....214
Palazzo Pio di Savoia da Carpi (Orsini, Righetti)....217
Palazzo Pizzirani (Cesarini, Leoni)....219
Palazzo Pizzirani (in Via di Torrre Argentina)....220
Palazzo Poli....220
Palazzetto di Flaminio Ponzio....221
Palazzo Pulieri (Ginetti)....221

Palazzo del Quirinale....221

Palazzo Raggi....229
Palazzo Rocci (Pallavicini)....229
Palazzo Rondinini or Rondanini (Sanseverino)....229
Palazzo De Rossi....231
Palazzo Ruggeri....232
Palazzo Ruspoli....233
Palazzo S Calisto....234
Palazzo Santacroce....235
Apartment buildings in Piazza di S Ignazio....238
Apartment building in Piazza S Lorenzo in Lucina....240
Palazzo Sciarra (Colonna di Sciarra, Carbognano)....240
Palazzo Serlupi Crescenzi....242
Palazzo Sinibaldi (dei Cavalieri dell'Ordine Teutonico)....243
Palazzo Spada....243
Palazzo di Spagna....247
Palazzo della Stamperia (Cornaro)....248
Palazzetto Sterbini (Boncompagni)....249
Palazzo Strozzi (Olgiati, Besso)....249

Palazzetto 'dei Telamoni'....250
Palazzo Testa Piccolomini....250

Palazzo Valentini (Bonelli, Alessandrino, Spinelli, Imperiali, della Provincia)....250
Palazzo Varese or Varesi (Degli Atti)....252
Palazzo Verospi....253

Unnamed building at via degli Zingari, 55....254
Palazzo Zuccari....255

General Bibliography 259

Select Bibliographies and Notes 263

Glossary 283

Index of artists 285

Index of streets 291

Profilo del Cornicione
della Porta
Profilo
Scala di Palmi due per il Modine
1
2
Modine delli stipiti
della Porta.
Scala di Palmi dieci
5
20

Introduction

As someone from outside the academic community, I am diffident about producing a guide of this sort. When I was in Rome for several months in 2003, however, I was so struck by the lack of an up-to-date general guide to the Baroque palaces that I felt it would not be too presumptuous to try my hand at writing one. After many more visits to Rome, this book is the result.

Before going any further I must say a word about Anthony Blunt's *Guide to Baroque Rome*, which is the default guide for most people, and a much-loved one at that. Nobody could admire Blunt more than I do, but an enormous amount of work has been done on the palaces since his day. Furthermore – as he himself acknowledged* – his treatment of the palaces was perfunctory in comparison with what he had to say about the churches.

For both these reasons, I believe that there is plenty of space for a new effort that does not try to supplant Blunt, but just to provide a practical guide that is genuinely up-to-date and comprehensive. Blunt's *Guide* will always have its own value. My aim has simply been to produce a really accurate summary of the building history of the palaces, drawing on recent material published in English and Italian, and providing for each building a bibliography that has been brought up to date. I have also tried to indicate the main features of each building as clearly as I can, and to convey the feeling of actually looking at it on the spot.

Those who are already well informed may, I hope, at least find it convenient to have a handy summary of what is now known about the authorship and history of the lesser-known buildings. I ask their forbearance for my efforts to summarise quite drastically the extensive literature on the more famous palaces and their builders.

Although I have managed to see the interior of many of the buildings described here, there are also many where I have only been able to see what is visible from the street. In these circumstances there is every chance that one will give too much emphasis to the façade of a building, even if its builders made a conscious decision that it should be conventional and discreet. I have tried to be on my guard about this, but may not always have succeeded.

*Blunt *Guide*, p. ix

Opposite: The door of Palazzo Lancellotti, designed by Domenichino. Engraving from De Rossi's Architettura Civile. *The door was also illustrated by Visentini, see p. 161*

The scope of this guide; the barocchetto; restored buildings; colleges etc

Although I use the word 'Baroque' occasionally in a shorthand way to indicate places, such as Palazzo Barberini and the gardens of Palazzo Borghese, that are always considered to be notably 'Baroque', I have tried to steer well clear of argument about the existence of a Baroque style or what its characteristics might be. I have simply aimed to include notes on most buildings still standing in Rome that have any claim to be called palaces and that incorporate significant parts dating from 1600 to 1750. There are, however, some that are so dull and about which so little is known that I have left them out. I have included a few buildings from before 1600 by architects such as Giacomo Della Porta and Maderno. Beyond the other end of the period I have included a few buildings up to the late 1760s and I follow Blunt in including Palazzo Braschi as an obvious terminal point.

I have also included a handful of buildings that are clearly not palaces, and I need to explain why.

Although some famous noble family palaces (such as those of the Corsini, Doria-Pamphili, Colonna and Rondinini) were built or modified in Rome during the eighteenth century, the emphasis moved steadily towards the construction of buildings designed for multi-occupation. One thing that manifestly had a lot to do with this was the rise in demand from a professional middle class that was growing in importance, partly because of the need to service the bureaucratic requirements of a modern state. But it would be quite wrong to think in simple terms of the nobles living in palaces and the bourgeois in apartment blocks. Many of the purpose-designed new buildings included a range of levels from the humble to the very grand and luxurious. Very often, as at Palazzo Del Cinque, an aristocratic owner occupied only part of his building and, as at Palazzo Pighini, this was not necessarily the most desirable and expensive part. Furthermore, the chapters of churches and other religious communities such as confraternities went into the burgeoning property market and built apartments for rent, sometimes as free-standing independent buildings, sometimes as extensions of their convents.

This blurring of boundaries, with multi-occupation becoming the dominant mode of accommodation, was necessarily reflected in the architecture of the buildings themselves. Overall, there was a strong pull towards a common architectural vernacular, whatever the circumstances of commissioning by lay or ecclesiastical patrons. There were, however, intriguing cross-currents, with palaces (eg Palazzo Boncompagni Ludovisi) adopting the prime characteristics of apartment buildings, and apartment buildings (eg the one at via degli Zingari, 55) imitating the traditional tone and style of palaces.

As regards architectural structure, the main feature of the new buildings was the equality of emphasis given to several storeys, and the expansion of the proportion of the wall that was given over to windows. Small iron balconies (ringhiere) were often employed, both as a facility for the occupants and to provide visual variety in the large flat surfaces that were created. Although some of these buildings were astonishingly functional and austere,* very many of them featured stucco decoration that exploited the qualities of the medium, and this was the defining element of the style that has been given the label 'barocchetto'. Good quality, elegant decoration of windows and doors was routine, and in some cases the most wayward, post-Borrominian shapes were developed for those elements. Another common feature was the 'stacking' together of windows to create uninterrupted vertical bands of stucco framing that articulated the wall surface.

Walking around Rome in connection with this book sharpened my awareness of the extent to which these barocchetto apartment buildings contribute to the urban landscape, what constantly surprising variations on a theme they provide, and how far their characteristics were already beginning to be apparent in many palaces of the later seventeenth century. This was the thread along which domestic architecture developed in Rome during the later Baroque period, and it has hardly been exposed to English readers.

There are so many of these non-palatial barocchetto domestic buildings in Rome that a full list of them would be out of the question for the present book. On the other hand, their typology became so thoroughly co-mingled with that of palaces that ignoring them would lead to a very incomplete idea of the way in which the palace tradition ended. I have therefore chosen just the following six buildings to serve as examples of a far greater number.

The best-known of the six is the group of buildings by Raguzzini in Piazza S Ignazio, which are one of the most famous pieces of 18th century town planning in the city. It seemed to me that this very celebrity distracted attention from the development's purpose as rental property designed to raise money, and that it was worth emphasising this aspect. The building in Piazza S Lorenzo in Lucina is included because it incorporates so many characteristic features that it can serve as the best single example of the class. The Casa del Falco is simply too bizarre to ignore. The Casa degli Agostiniani Scalzi and the Casa dei Chierici Minori are included for their sheer architectural merit. The building at via degli Zingari, 55, has never attracted any scholarly attention so far as I know, but it seems to me to be an interesting example of an apartment building that deliberately mimics the reserved, conservative style of the traditional palace.

A decision was also needed on how many to include of the palaces that have been radically rebuilt, commonly as part of the urban development that took place after Rome became the capital of the united Italy in 1871. I have deliberately been rather lax about this and have included, for example, an entry on the palace of the Cavalieri di Malta because of its exalted history, and very brief notes on several of the rebuilt palaces of the Corso, simply to save readers the time that I myself spent there identifying what was what.

Last, there are many notable colleges and other non-ecclesiastical institutional buildings in Rome but I have had to draw the line somewhere. I have therefore not included them, even though that means excluding buildings such as the splendid Collegio

* See, for example, the convent/apartment building of SS Quirico e Giulitta (now the Hotel Forum) by Valvassori, or the apartments built by Ferdinando Fuga for the chapter of S Giacomo degli Spagnoli at via dei Giubbonari, 29-32.

Fuccioli in the suggestive barocchetto street of via S Agata dei Goti. I have, however, found room for the Monte di Pietà, which I could try to justify because it started life as a family palace, but which I have really included just because the sculpture and polished marble of its chapel is so magnificently enjoyable.

Sources

Substantial books in Italian have now appeared on nearly all the most important palaces. The bulk of them have been devoted to buildings that are owned either by the state or by banks, and have been sponsored by their owners. Those done for banks are a distinct genre of lavish productions for private publication, and, although they are essential reading, they vary greatly in quality and the older ones naturally betray their age in many ways.

In the last two or three decades art history in Italy has increasingly turned towards archival work and there has also been a new interest in urbanism. There has been a steady search for new archival sources, and unprecedented attention has been given to the records of public bodies such as the Maestri di Strade. There have thus been several research monographs on previously neglected Roman palaces (such as Patrizia Cavazzini's work on the Palazzo Lancellotti and Alessandra Anselmi's book on the Palazzo di Spagna) and a steady stream of conference papers and articles about buildings, architects and planning projects. The work by Elisabeth Kieven and Giovanna Curcio on 18th century architecture and urban planning has been particularly important, as has the 'Studi sul Settecento romano' series under the organisation and editorship of Elisa Debenedetti.

The Guide Rionali series, covering every kind of building in Rome, has been produced over a long period and it is therefore inevitable that some material in the earlier volumes has been overtaken by later work. The bibliographies for the main buildings described are extremely useful, however, and the series has tended to become much more detailed as it has progressed.

Ferruccio Lombardi's *Roma; Palazzi, Palazzetti, Case; Progetto per un Inventario, 1200-1850* is a working tool that deserves a special mention. It lists about 750 buildings with photographs and short comments that are always worth taking seriously. The photographs are an excellent record – and a poignant one for those who mourn the old ochre city that has been so ruthlessly scraped, scrubbed and homogenised under recent political leaders.

There are many Italian and English books offering descriptions and pictures of selected Roman palaces, and one or two that purport to be comprehensive. None of them appears to be very precise about its sources, but Giorgio Carpaneto's *I Palazzi di Roma* in the Newton Compton series is worth a mention as a cheap and useful volume to have to hand.

I have not ignored the Strenne dei Romanisti series, now wonderfully available online at http://www.strennadeiromanisti.it. It must be acknowledged that these publications do not include much straight material on building histories etc., but they are a very pleasurable source of miscellaneous contextual material.

The most notable texts published in English since Blunt's time are, I think, Joseph Connors's *Alliance and Enmity in Roman Baroque Urbanism*; Patricia Waddy's *Seventeenth-Century Roman Palaces: Use and the Art of the Plan*; John Beldon Scott's *Images of Nepotism: The Painted Ceilings of Palazzo Barberini*; and Richard Krautheimer's *The Rome of Alexander VII, 1655-1667*.

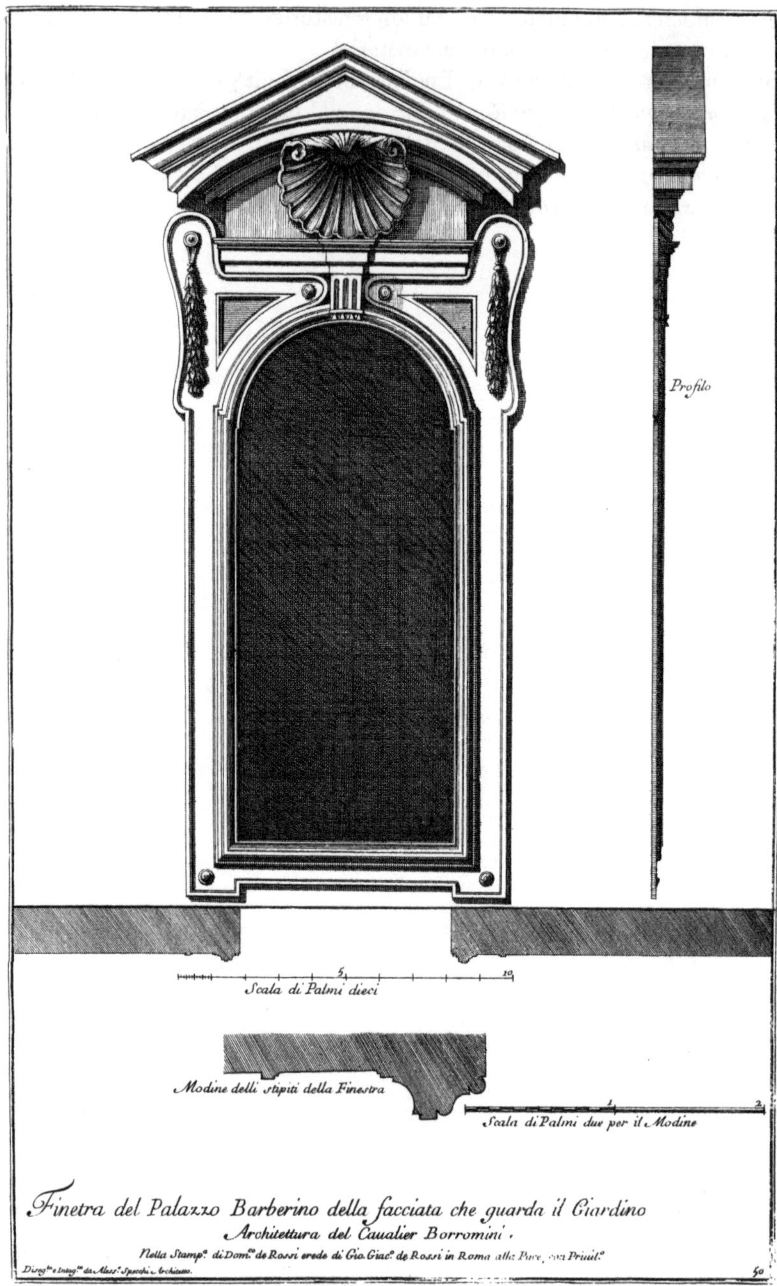
Profilo
5
10
Scala di Palmi dieci
Modine delli stipiti della Finestra
1
2
Scala di Palmi due per il Modine
Finetra del Palazzo Barberino della facciata che guarda il Giardino
Architettura del Caualier Borromini.
Nella Stamp.ª di Dom.co de Rossi erede di Gio. Giac.º de Rossi in Roma alla Pace, con Priuil.º
Diseg.to e Intag.to da Aless.º Specchi Architetto.
50

A few practical notes

Visiting the palaces

Most churches are open in principle, even if it does not always feel that way in Rome as one waits in hope at some strange hour. Indeed the whole point of a church is that it should be open. The presumption in the case of palaces is the exact opposite. Even if a detailed account of a palace has been published, that does not mean that any of the interior will be visitable.

The only palaces generally open to the public are those that are now museums. Visits are negotiable to some of the others, especially for people who have contacts with learned institutions. The banks that occupy many important palaces are usually quite cooperative, and many of them join in organising occasional open days, which tend to attract large crowds. Some other institutions occupying old buildings are extraordinarily unhelpful. Visits are also becoming increasingly difficult to buildings in private hands as more and more of them are split up into separate apartments. Furthermore, one effect of the devastating increase of tourism in Rome seems to be that concierges of private palaces are less relaxed about allowing people even to glance at the courtyards and entrance passages of the buildings that they guard, though there are many exceptions to this and it is always worth a try.

Visiting palaces that are not open to the public

Some of the institutions that occupy famous palaces are genuinely proud of them, and some banks have printed scholarly accounts that they give to enquirers without charge. Even these enthusiastic occupiers, however, are unlikely to show rooms that are normally closed to the public without a prior appointment, for which some kind of introduction is highly desirable, if not essential.

At any one time, however, it is quite possible that some palaces will have a special opening, and every year there are organised occasions when several buildings are opened to the public. The useful events guide, *Roma c'è*, is no longer published, so the only way to find out about such things is to look at the culture sections of the weekend newspapers.

There are a number of websites that advertise special guided tours of palaces.

Opposite: There are four windows of this unusual design on the garden front of Palazzo Barberini. This engraving is from De Rossi's Architettura Civile, *where they are attributed to Borromini, but Anthony Blunt preferred an attribution to Pietro da Cortona* *(see p. 64)*

Some special arrangements

The Galleria Colonna is open on Saturdays from 9 am to 1.15 pm. It is closed in August. For arranging visits to the Appartamento Principessa Isabelle at the Palazzo Colonna use the email address info@galleriacolonna.it or telephone 06 6784350.

For visiting the Palazzo Farnese use the website www.inventerrome.com and make your booking well in advance.

The Casino dell'Aurora at the Palazzo Pallavicini Rospigliosi is open on the first day of every month except January from 10 am to noon and from 3 pm to 5 pm.

As of 2015, arrangements for visiting the Palazzo del Quirinale (and, indeed the gardens) have been greatly expanded, so that visits are normally possible on every day except Mondays and Thursdays. Go to the website www.quirinale.it for the details. Bookings must be made at least 5 days in advance.

The essential things to see

While any selection is subjective, a visitor with an interest in the subject should certainly make a point of seeing the following palaces:

Palazzo Barberini: The most important of all palaces in the Baroque period, and now a national art gallery with long opening hours. Including the paintings, there is so much to see here that one should ideally allow several hours.

Palazzo Borghese: The interior is not accessible but it is possible to get a good idea of the hanging garden and Rainaldi's viewing gallery at the west (river) end, and one can usually glimpse the cortile behind the main entrance at the east end.

Palazzo Doria-Pamphili: Both Valvassori's astonishing façade on the Corso and Ameli's later one on via del Plebiscito are important Roman landmarks; visiting the Galleria also enables one to see the main cortile and the entrance vestibule on Piazza del Collegio Romano.

Palazzo Spada: It would be a shame to leave Rome without having seen Borromini's perspectival arcade, and the fascinating Galleria Spada has long opening hours.

Palazzo di Montecitorio: Together with the obelisk and piazza before it, Bernini's huge palace makes a stupendous theatrical statement.

If one's schedule can accommodate the weekend visiting arrangements (see above) the *Galleria Colonna* and the *Quirinale* should definitely be seen as well.

Some possible itineraries

Most of the important palaces of the period are grouped in the central area bounded to the north by Piazza Colonna, to the west by the Cancelleria, to the east by the Quattro Fontane and to the south by the Tiber. The following itineraries are no more than suggestions for linking several of the palaces in continuous walks, and there is certainly no need to follow them slavishly.

1 From Piazza Navona to the Palazzo Corsini

This walk takes you across the Tiber to the one important Baroque palace on the right bank.

Start in Piazza Navona, looking at the ensemble of the Palazzo Pamphili and S Agnese. Leave Piazza Navona by Corsia Agonale on the east side and walk through to Corso del Rinascimento. Stop and look at Maruscelli's façade of Palazzo Madama, turn right and walk down to S Andrea della Valle at the bottom of the street. Turn right on Corso Vittorio Emanuele, take via del Biscione (second left) and walk down to Piazza del Biscione to look at Arcucci's Palazzo Pio di Savoia da Carpi which has so much in common with Palazzo Madama.

Carry on, cross Campo de' Fiori and go down via Ballauri, with Specchi's first façade of Palazzo Pighini filling the block on your left. When you get to Piazza Farnese, stop and look at the Pighini's main façade, also by Specchi, which faces Palazzo Farnese across the square. (The workmanlike Palazzo Mandosi is on the left side of the square and Palazzo Sinibaldi is down via Mascherone on the left side of Palazzo Farnese.)

Here you have a choice. You could go down via Monserrato in the far corner of the square, stop in Piazza di S Caterina della Ruota to look at the stuccoes on Palazzo Mastrozzi, go down via in Caterina to via Giulia, where you will see Palazzo Falconieri facing you on your left, continue down the right side of the palace, and then walk back along Lungotevere dei Tebaldi, taking a good look at Borromini's work at the back of Palazzo Falconieri on the way. Or you could leave Piazza Farnese by via Capo di Ferro, between the Sinibaldi and Mandosi palaces, spend some time at Palazzo Spada, walk down to SS Trinità dei Pellegrini and turn right on via Pettinari. (Incidentally, SS Trinità seems to be open more than it used to be: if it is open when you pass, you should certainly go in to see the Guido Reni altarpiece.) Either way, you will end up at the pedestrianised Ponte Sisto.

Cross Ponte Sisto, with Borromini's belvedere on Palazzo Falconieri appearing as a prominent landmark as you look north, if it is not obscured by the leaves of the plane trees in the summer. Walk up to via della Scala by via Benedetta , or any other of the Trastevere lanes that appeals to you. Turn right on via della Scala and walk through to Fuga's Palazzo Corsini on the left hand side. It is well worth going to the Galleria Nazionale d'Arte Antica in the palace, but at the very least you should go up the stairs to see

Fuga's double-height vestibule. When you have finished at the palace you can have a pleasant walk in the Botanical Garden at the back.

2. From Piazza Navona to Piazza Venezia

Start from Piazza Navona as before, look at the façade of Palazzo Madama and then walk down the left side of the palace to Piazza di S Luigi dei Francesi, where you will see Palazzo Patrizi straight ahead and Palazzo Giustiniani to its right. Turn right down via della Dogana Vecchia and first left down Salita de' Crescenzi to Piazza della Rotonda. Just before you get to the piazza you will see all the original exterior work that remains of Palazzo Crescenzi on your right.

Leave Piazza della Rotonda by via degli Orfani and walk up to Piazza Capranica, where Casa Giannini fills the left end of the square. Then by way of via in Aquiro and via della Guglia go up to Piazza di Montecitorio. As you enter the square, Palazzo del Cinque (with its many points of similarity with Casa Giannini) is on your right, Palazzo Macchi di Cellere on your left and, of course, Bernini's great Montecitorio palace dominates the square in front of you.

Walk across the front of the Montecitorio palace into Piazza Colonna - leaving one great 17th century urban theatre for another. Palazzo Chigi (Aldobrandini) fills the north side of the square, with its altana challenging that of the Montecitorio palace alongside. Opposite is Palazzo del Bufalo Ferraioli.

Go down the Corso towards Piazza Venezia. The main palaces that you will pass on the left are Palazzo Sciarra, Palazzo Mellini, the 19th century faux-Tuscan back of Palazzo Chigi (Odescalchi) and Palazzo Mancini. On the right you will pass Palazzo de Carolis, the Valvassori façade of Palazzo Doria-Pamphili and Palazzo D'Aste.

3. From the Quirinale to the Campidoglio

Start from the splendidly theatrical Piazza del Quirinale, where you will want to look at both the Quirinale and Consulta palaces. Before you leave the square, you may want to go down via XXIV Maggio for a few paces to look at the gate into the Colonna gardens on the right. Leave the piazza by via della Dataria which will take you down to via dei Lucchesi; on the corner of these two streets is Palazzo Testa Piccolomini.

Carry on down via dei Lucchesi, passing Palazzo Lazzaroni on the right, turn right in Piazza Pilotta, and walk down via del Vaccaro, along the left flank of Palazzo Muti Papazzurri. This will bring you out at the façade of the adjoining Palazzo Muti Papazzurri (Balestra) at the head of Piazza dei SS Apostoli. As you look down the piazza, Palazzo Colonna is beyond SS Apostoli on your left, Palazzo Chigi (Odescalchi) is on your right and Palazzo Valentini is at the far end of the piazza on the other side of via Nazionale.

Walk down the piazza, turn right on via Nazionale, and carry straight on across the bottom of the Corso into via del Plebiscito, where four great palaces fill the right-hand side without a break. They are De Rossi's Palazzo D'Aste, the Ameli façade of Palazzo

Doria-Pamphili, Arcucci's Palazzo Grazioli and De Rossi's Palazzo Altieri on Piazza del Gesù. This is where the papal procession, coming from the Vatican in front of you, would have swung right (i.e. to your left) towards the Campidoglio, passing down via d'Aracoeli to the left of Fuga's façade of Palazzo Cenci-Bolognetti. Follow the processional route past Palazzo Muti Bussi on the left and finishing with Palazzo Massimo di Rignano on the corner with via del Teatro di Marcello.

Material on the internet

Following are three useful websites that might not be found in a casual trawl for information on the palaces.

'Falda publications' in the Princeton University Digital Library at pudl.princeton.edu/collections.php has images of all the plates in Falda's topographical books.

'Rome in the Footsteps of an XVIIIth Century Traveller' at www.romeartlover.it displays the whole of Vasi's *Magnificenze* together with the relevent parts of Nolli's 1748 map and various other supporting material, including many comparative pictures of the present-day city.

'Imago Urbis: Giuseppe Vasi's Grand Tour of Rome' at vasi.uoregon.edu also displays Vasi's plates together with the Nolli map, and has a highly developed interactive system for linking details of the plates with other material.

The best websites for individual palaces are probably those for Palazzo Barberini (http://galleriabarberini.beniculturali.it) and the Quirinale (http://www.quirinale.it) but all the official websites for historic State buildings are well worth looking at.

Porta che dà l'ingresso al Cortile del Palazzo del Sig.re Marchese Muti Papazuri, à SS.ti Apostoli.
Architettura del Caualier Mattia de Rossi.

Diseg.to da Carlo Quadri Architetto. Nella stamp.a di Dom.co de Rossi erede di Gio. Giac.o de Rossi in Roma alla Pace, con Priuilegio. Intag.to da Gio. Carlo Alet. 142

A note on the prints used to illustrate this book

Most of the illustrations in this book come from some famous sets of prints that were made in Rome between the 1660s and the 1770s. This note gives a very highly summarised account of the various series and the background to their production.

Probably no city has been the subject of so much painted and graphic depiction as Rome has been, and this is a fascinating and complex subject in its own right. While pictures and prints of the city certainly functioned like modern tourist publications, providing an alluring vision before the journey and a valued souvenir afterwards, there were other agendas too. Rulers have always wanted their capitals to look impressive as an implied statement of their political power, but in the case of Rome this theme had overwhelming importance because of the city's status as the seat of a church that claimed a universal authority going back in direct succession to the time of the ancient empire whose ruins still dominated the city.

Any project to illustrate the city inevitably had to operate against this political background, and interact with it. Furthermore, the images that were selected and disseminated through the art trade both reflected the current ideas of urbanism and in turn helped to shape the way in which those ideas developed. Whilst these issues go far beyond the scope of the present book, it is worth bearing in mind that the prints were made in a specific and changing historical context. It should also be remembered that the great prints discussed in this note did not suddenly emerge out of nowhere. Very accurate drawings of the city were being made in the 16th century, and there were several sets of – usually rather crude – prints by a variety of artists earlier in the 17th century. Nevertheless, the high-quality prints that emerged in the 1660s were a distinctly new development.

During the Middle Ages Rome had shrunk to a few small inhabited areas within the ancient walls, but from 1420, when Martin V brought the papacy back to the city after the Council of Constance, there was a more or less ongoing project to beautify and develop it, to match the splendour of the classical Roman remains, and to project the city as the centre of the civilized world. The high-point of the endeavour came after the Catholic Reformation, with the transformation of the city in the Baroque period – and particularly in the pontificate of the Barberini pope Urban VIII (reigned 1623-44) and even more markedly in that of the Chigi pope Alexander VII (reigned 1655-67). As has often been

Opposite: Mattia De Rossi's entrance (now destroyed) to the Palazzo Muti Papazzurri in Piazza della Pilotta. This engraving is from D. D. De Rossi's Architettura Civile. Alessandro Specchi's print of the palace is reproduced on p. 197

pointed out, these amazing achievements of art, architecture and town planning were effected during a time when the papacy's funding and its international political influence were rapidly declining. In his earlier career, Alexander VII, who spent so lavishly and imaginatively on the city's fabric, had been the papacy's representative at the negotiations leading to the Peace of Westphalia, where the Holy See's claims to be a major international player had been unceremoniously brushed aside for good.

During the age of the Grand Tour in the 18th century the papacy's external influence had sunk very low indeed, but some fine buildings and urban projects were still appearing and the papal administrations remained anxious to ensure that Rome retained its *réclame* as the supreme cultural and artistic centre. The perception that the architectural splendours of the city (including the palaces) had not died with the ancient Romans but had continued with Michelangelo and then with the 17th century masters was, in fact, as central to the papal city's opinion of itself as the constant flow of visitors was economically advantageous. All this was supported by the universally accepted belief throughout Europe that Rome was the one place that a painter, sculptor or architect had to visit before his studies could be said to be complete.

There were several printing presses and print shops in 17th century Rome but by far the most important was the printing/publishing/printselling business run from premises in via della Pace by the De Rossi family, which played a central role in establishing the image of the Baroque city. Many members of the family were involved in the trade, at several locations, but the main business was established in via della Pace around the beginning of the century by Giuseppe De Rossi, who set himself up as a printer and soon established a solid practice, publishing sets of topographical prints among other things. Giuseppe died in 1639 and the business was taken over by Giovanni Giacomo De Rossi, who was probably the son of Giovanni Battista De Rossi, who ran a printshop in Piazza Navona. Giovanni Giacomo was an imaginative and cultured businessman who enormously raised the status of the printshop in the via della Pace so that it became an essential component of Rome's intellectual life, and an institution with an international reputation. Although Giovanni Giacomo is now best remembered for the series of topographical prints that concern us here, he published a wide range of other material and handled the work of some of the most esteemed graphic artists of the time, such as Castiglione and Testa. On Giovanni Giacomo's death in 1691 the business passed to his adopted son Domenico De Rossi, also an ambitious publisher, who died in 1729. The final owner of the business was Domenico's son Lorenzo Filippo De Rossi, who soon began negotiating with English collectors for the sale of the business, including its huge and very valuable collection of original etched and engraved metal plates. This notion was vetoed by Cardinal Neri Corsini as soon as he heard about it, and after protracted negotiations the entire business, plates included, was bought by Pope Clement XII (Corsini) to form the Calcografia Camerale, of which the present Istituto Nazionale per la Grafica is the direct descendant.

The crucial point in the development of topographical prints of Rome came with

Giovanni Giacomo De Rossi's decision to make himself the de facto official visual chronicler of the wholesale changes being made to the city by Alexander VII. Of all the popes, Alexander was probably the most imaginative, cultured and energetic in the matter of urban development. He was responsible not just for some important and highly visible individual projects – the colonnaded piazza of St Peter's being obviously the most significant – but also for setting in train an enormous programme of widening and straightening streets, and clearing piazzas, so as to open up vistas and spaces and to present the city as a series of theatrical compositions. The word 'teatro' in fact came to be used not just in connection with individual projects, such as the development in front of S Maria della Pace (just outside Giovanni Giacomo's shop), but also for Alexander's urban development programme as a whole.

Giovanni Giacomo De Rossi began attracting Alexander's favour with a proposal to produce a set of portrait prints commemorating the existing College of Cardinals. He timed this proposal, which Alexander immediately accepted, to coincide with Alexander's first set of new nominations in 1657, and once he had established his credentials with the pope he moved on to propose what became the celebrated *Nuovo Teatro delle fabbriche, et edificii, in prospettiva di Roma moderna, sotto il felice pontificato di N S Papa Alessandro VII*, which appeared in two volumes in 1665, with a fulsome dedication to the pope's brother, adulating Alexander's programme to restore Rome to its former grandeur. A third volume, dealing only with churches, appeared in 1669 with a dedication to Alexander's successor Clement IX.

All the etchings in these first three volumes of the *Nuovo Teatro* were by Giovanni Battista Falda (1643-78), from Valduggia in Piedmont, whom Giovanni Giacomo De Rossi spotted as a talented teenager in Bernini's workshop. De Rossi must have quickly realized that Falda had just the skills for the project that he had in mind, and he took his education in hand, introduced him to the best artists in Rome and made sure that he was trained in all the disciplines necessary for accurate topographical printmaking. It is, indeed, the verisimilitude of his images of the piazzas, streets and prospects of Rome that makes Falda's work so extremely valuable. As can be seen from the several examples used in this book, Falda did not try to impose much drama or atmospheric feeling on the scenes he depicted, and his work generally gives a rather touching sense of self-effacing, transparent simplicity and candour. Although later printmakers were to attempt more ambitious artistic effects, many of the views selected by Falda became in effect the default images of the area in question, and were simply paraphrased by later artists. Another noteworthy aspect of the *Nuovo Teatro* is that many buildings are shown half-finished. This adds to the sense of verisimilitude and also provides a great deal of valuable information about the city's building history.

Falda died of cancer at the age of only 34 but in his short life he did a very great deal of work for De Rossi, including sets of etchings of the fountains of Rome (four volumes published from the mid-1670s to 1694, the third and fourth volumes with plates by Giovanni Francesco Venturini) and the gardens of Rome (published posthumously in 1680).

In 1676 he also made one of the most famous maps of Rome, on 12 printed sheets and using an unusual axonometric projection system, that was successively revised until well into the next century.

In 1699 Domenico De Rossi published a fourth volume of the *Nuovo Teatro* with etchings by the important Roman architect Alessandro Specchi (1668-1729). This volume was limited to palaces, and Specchi tends to present the buildings from a close view-point so that they bulk large and fill the picture space in a way that is different from Falda's more panoramic compositions. Specchi also comes across as a more forceful artistic character than Falda: the contrasts of light and shade are greater, the potentialities of the etching tones are exploited more fully, and the Roman people who inhabit the prints are rather more various and vigorous than Falda's endearing puppets. The concern with accuracy is not diminished but Specchi's prints make a greater demand to be considered as artworks in their own right.

The next great series of printed images of Rome was undoubtedly *Delle Magnificenze di Roma antica e moderna* by Giuseppe Vasi (1710-82) which came out in ten volumes between 1747 and 1761. Vasi came from Corleone in Sicily and established himself as a *veduta* specialist in Rome by around 1736, under the protection of the royal house of the Kingdom of Naples. He produced a famous panorama of Rome from the Janiculum (1765) and an up-dated version of Falda's map (1781) but it is the *Magnificenze* for which he is mainly remembered, and many of these images are used in this book.

With Vasi we are manifestly in the age of the Grand Tour. The *Magnificenze* consists of ten books of etchings, each book being devoted to a particular theme – Gates and Walls, Piazzas, Basilicas, Palaces, etc – so as to build up a total picture of the urban experience. As in the prints by Falda and Specchi, the main items in each view are numbered and named, but Vasi goes far beyond that by also providing quite a lengthy written commentary for each plate. In 1763 he also brought out a guidebook that aimed to enable the reader to find all the magnificenze of Rome in eight extremely strenuous one-day itineraries. This concern with the tourist visitor is reflected in the æsthetics of the plates themselves.These maintain quite a high level of accuracy (together with much juggling of perspective to enable buildings to be privileged by views that could not exist in reality) but Vasi aims to go beyond recording the precise appearance of the buildings and to evoke the experience of actually being in Rome and being part of the urban theatre. The *Magnificenze* thus span a great range of mood, from a sombre view up the Tiber on a stormy day to quiet streets on sun-drenched afternoons with few people about – and Vasi is skilful in handling the fall of light to achieve these effects. His subject matter also ranges from the great sights of Rome to unpretentious little corners that can never have had much reputation, and the people who populate his prints include every type from the pope taking the air in his garden to beggars outside churches, fast-food sellers, and women praying in the street before images of the Virgin. It all amounts to a remarkably vivid and convincing impression of the 18th century city.

The evocation of mood was taken to a completely new level by the Venetian printmaker and architect Giovanni Battista Piranesi (1720-1778) who briefly studied with Vasi in the early 1740s and who went on to become one of the most famous artists in Europe. Apart from his celebrated etched views of Rome (*Varie vedute di Roma* and *Vedute di Roma)* he produced a great deal of learned antiquarian work and a series of imaginary, fantastic prison scenes (*Carceri*) that became icons of the Romantic period. Although he did produce a number of conventional images of the modern city, he was mainly interested in the dramatically expressive possibilities of the decaying ancient ruins, and this book does not rely on him for illustrations.

In addition to the topographical work described above, there was a complementary way of describing Rome in the form of architectural prints. Many cultured gentlemen throughout Europe would have had these imposing books in their libraries, but these were specialist productions for the architectural profession, with illustrations that were carefully drawn to scale. While the very existence of such luxury books was an advertisement of the artistic pre-eminence of Rome, they were also professional tools that enabled architects anywhere to copy the plans and motifs of Roman architecture.

The two most famous publications of this kind were both published by the De Rossi firm, and this book contains many illustrations from each of them. All these architectural plates are, incidentally, engravings, as opposed to the topographical depictions described above, which are all etchings.

The first of these books was *Palazzi di Roma de' più celebri architetti*, which was published by Giovanni Giacomo De Rossi in 1655 and consists of elevations, together with a few plans, of Roman palaces from the time of Bramante onwards. The illustrations were drawn by the architect Pietro Ferrerio (active 1634 – died 1653), though we do not know the names of the engravers who made the plates. A few years later (both volumes are undated) De Rossi brought out a second volume under a slightly different title and with plates in the same form by Falda. The selection of palaces in the second volume is more weighted towards the Baroque period.

The second important book of architectural engravings was brought out in three volumes by Domenico De Rossi in 1702, 1711 and 1721. The generic title is *Studio d'architettura civile* though each title then goes on to describe the contents at length. The first volume, dedicated to Clement XI, is devoted to windows, doors and gates, porticos and porches, chimney pieces and stairs; the second shows chapels, tombs, and other items; the third illustrates the façades and plans of several Roman churches, and concludes with sections on the Farnese palace at Caprarola and the Royal Palace at Naples. The engravings were done by a team of artists including Specchi and the overall quality of this prestige publication is superb.

Last, a word about Paul-Marie Letarouilly (1795-1855), a French architect who spent many years in Rome after 1820 preparing the engravings that were published in 4 volumes between 1840 and 1855 under the title *Édifices de Rome moderne: ou recueil des palais, maisons, églises, couvents, et autres monuments publics et particuliers les plus remarquables de la ville de Rome*. He also published a separate volume on St Peter's and the Vatican. Letarouilly seems to have been a rather obsessive character who lived in penury during his time in Rome, dedicated to making carefully measured drawings of the major buildings as a resource for future students. In addition to the plans and elevations that make up most of the book there are several line drawings, delightfully peopled by men and women dressed as in the age of Stendhal.

One of the caryatid features that run around the cortile at Palazzo Lateranense. They provide an interesting comparison with the masks at Palazzo della Stamperia *(see p. 249)*

THE PALACES

23

Casa degli Agostiniani Scalzi

Via dei Crociferi, 23

A building of extraordinary invention and energy. It was picked out by Paolo Portoghesi forty years ago as being 'among the most interesting works of the Roman Settecento',[1] but it had to wait another three decades until its history was established and its architect identified. Portoghesi associated both it and the Convent of the Mercedari Scalzi of S Maria in Monterone with the name of Domenico Gregorini, but Bonaccorso showed that the architect of both buildings was the much less well-known Francesco Bianchi. S Maria in Monterone is not all that far away and is well worth visiting for comparison.

The building in via dei Crociferi was done between 1738 and 1740 for the Agostiniani Scalzi of the church of Gesù e Maria on the Corso. It was a purely commercial venture, offering two 'appartamenti nobili' and two 'mezzanini signorili' as well as shops and service rooms at street level and accommodation for servants and others in the lowest mezzanine and also in the low rooms under the roof. Although the project soon turned out to be a commercial failure, Bianchi had gone to great trouble with the internal arrangements, crafting a service staircase that would keep the servants completely out of the way of the great people, and providing a 'cortile ignobile' as well as a grander one that qualified to be called 'nobile'.[2]

The overall architectural scheme is a simple one of three storeys, each equipped with a mezzanine, plus a cornice containing the oval windows of the rooms crammed under the roof. All the detailing, such as the alternate bands of rough and smooth rustication in the ground floor and the multi-faceted corners and string-courses, is handled with ultra-careful finesse, but it is the quality, exuberance and sheer strangeness of the doors and window surrounds that make the building so exceptional. These stucco creations are just five years later than Valvassori's Doria-Pamphili façade and, like that masterpiece, they contain echoes of Borromini together with more bizarre forms for which it is virtually impossible to find a precedent. The central bay of the top mezzanine shows the clearest Borrominian influence, while Bianchi shows his more idiosyncratic quality in the weird undulating feature that combines three pediments over the central window of the first floor. But nothing else here can match the hyperplasticity of the entrance, where the architectural components are merged into each other as though they were formed by oozing lava. The entrance alone makes the building highly memorable.

Opposite: Francesco Bianchi's extraordinary entrance to the apartment building in via dei Crociferi that was owned by the Agostiniani Scalzi

Palazzo Albani (Mattei, Massimo, Nerli, del Drago)

Via delle Quattro Fontane, 20

The cross-roads where the palace stands was one of the important nodal points in Sixtus V's town-planning scheme, since it is where his new Strada Felice (via delle Quattro Fontane) crosses the Strada Pia (via XX settembre) leading to the Porta Pia. Sixtus decided to mark the spot with four fountains in 1588 and the palace was built at that time for Muzio Mattei. The striking thing about the exterior has always been the way in which the landmark corner is emphasised by the placing of the belvedere so that it provides the upper two storeys of the tall feature that rises above the fountain: Lieven Cruyl's 1665 drawing shows the general arrangement of the fountain and belvedere very much as it is today.[1] In the mid 18th century the belvedere was Winckelmann's home.

Muzio Mattei's palace, which was completed before Tempesta's map of 1593, was almost certainly designed by Sixtus's regular architect Domenico Fontana, who had planned the Strada Felice,[2] though Mascarino also made drawings for it. It consisted of a block of nine bays on the Strada Felice and five on the Strada Pia, with a five-bay loggia and a garden at the back.

From 1664 the palace belonged to Cardinal Camillo Massimo, the high priest of classicism and artistic adviser to the family of the Altieri pope, Clement X.[3] After his death in 1677 it was bought by Cardinal Francesco Nerli (d.1707) and was later acquired by Cardinal Alessandro Albani, together with the two other nephews of Clement XI. It was here that Albani established his first great collection of ancient sculpture (which was bought by Clement XII in 1733 to form the nucleus of the Capitoline Museum's sculpture collection) and the collection of drawings by 16th and 17th century artists (now in the Royal Library at Windsor Castle). The celebrated Albani library was under the direction of Winckelmann, and it was at this period that he had his quarters in the belvedere, writing enthusiastically about his airy and elevated lodging, which he decorated with casts taken from the classical sculpture in the cardinal's collection.[4]

Cardinal Albani greatly extended Muzio Mattei's L- shaped building. In the nucleus around the cross-roads he built a grand new staircase, converted the first-floor loggia into a gallery, and built two new wings to form a court with four uniform sides where the rather heavy form of the windows is set off against the papery handling of the surrounding walls. He also extended the main front on Strada Felice by building over an area where there had been a garden and external stairs, and incorporating a palace which had belonged to the Bonelli.[5]

Following Titi's attribution of 1763, the architect of Albani's alterations is usually said to be Alessandro Specchi, and this view has often been baldly stated as a matter of certainty. However, most of the early sources[6] say that the architect responsible was Filippo Barigioni. The point cannot be settled without the discovery of new documentation, but Delfini Filippi notes that of the two architects (who were both pupils of Carlo Fontana) it was Barigioni who was the closer to the Albani at the time. [7]

The three rooms on the piano nobile in the angle of the building below the belvedere are the Sala di Apollo, the Stanza dei Putti and the Sala di Efesto. They each contain a central ceiling painting amidst much decorative detail and it has been suggested that the central panels themselves are survivals of the work that Cherubino and Giovanni

Vasi's print of the Quattro Fontane, looking towards S Maria Maggiore in the distance with Palazzo Albani on the left and S Carlo alle Quattro Fontane on the right. On the extreme right is Palazzo Galloppi; the corner of the old Palazzo Barberini gardens is on the extreme left

Alberti carried out for Muzio Mattei.[8] The subjects are *A naked youth seated on clouds*, *A trio ofærial winged putti* and *The forge of Hephæstus*. The decorative work in the Stanza dei Putti is in the style of P. P.Bonzi (mid 1620s) while that of the other two rooms is 18th century.

Two nearby rooms have ceiling paintings by Giovanni Odazzi which, according to Pascoli, were done for Cardinal Annibale Albani around 1722.[9] The subjects are, in the first, *Peace and Justice* and, in the second, *Charity, Prudence, Faith and Hope*.

The major decorative ensemble done for Cardinal Alessandro Albani in the early 1720s, however, was the five-bay vault of the gallery, which was frescoed by Pannini on the theme of the *Phases of the Day* and the *Four Seasons*, with the *Gods of Olympus* appearing in monochrome tondi.[10] The composition strongly emphasizes the architectural forms of the vault in a rather old-fashioned manner and the overall effect is heavier and more conventional than, for example, that of Pannini's deliciously airy gallery in the Villa Patrizi at Frascati. No doubt, even in the 1720s the fantasy that was enjoyed in the setting of a villa was not thought appropriate for the more sober surroundings of a major palace.

In the mid 19th century the palace was bought by Maria Cristina, widow of Ferdinand VII of Spain and protagonist in the Carlist Wars. From her the palace passed to her son-in-law the Principe Filippo del Drago, whose descendants still own it. The piano nobile is now occupied by the British Council.

Falda's engraving of Palazzo Albertoni, without the disfiguring attic that was added in the 19th century

Palazzo Albertoni (Spinola)
Piazza Campitelli, 2

According to Baglione the palace was begun by Giacomo Della Porta in the early 1600s, and completed after Della Porta's death (1602) by Girolamo Rainaldi, who added the door incorporating the Albertoni lion and the balcony above. There are more heraldic symbols (lions and trestles) in the frieze. The bridge linking the palace to buildings on Piazza Margana was built in 1616-18.[1]

Della Porta's façade is a symmetrical, aristocratic design, with simple architraves supported by volute brackets above the windows on the ground floor and the piano nobile, and with more brackets supporting benches at ground level. The two tiers of windows below the cornice have stucco frames. Everything above the cornice was added in the 19th century and old prints show how much better balanced the façade was without that imposition.

The palace was the headquarters of the Albertoni clan and it was clearly intended to present them as the dominant power in the developing area around what is now Piazza Campitelli. The Albertoni intermarried extensively with the Roman nobility but the crucial event in their rise was in 1669 when Gaspare degli Albertoni married the heiress Laura Caterina Altieri, took her family name and was adopted by the bride's uncle Cardinal Emilio Altieri. In the following year the cardinal unexpectedly became

Pope Clement X and Gaspare and his relatives were catapulted to the pinnacle of Roman society. When Carlo Rainaldi's great church of S Maria in Campitelli was built in 1673-75 the first chapel on the left was owned by the Albertoni, but the rights to it were soon taken over by the ascendant Altieri, whose fine funerary monuments it now contains, together with a marble altarpiece celebrating the Blessed Ludovica Albertoni.

Palazzetto Alibrandi or Alivrandi (Cavalieri)

Piazza del Monte di Pietà, 22

A plain but dignified 18th century building of three storeys with a balconied entrance and a ground floor mezzanine, plus an additional storey added in the 1930 restoration commemorated in the new lintel that was then placed above the door. There is little to indicate the exact date, but one could hazard a guess of around 1730. Vasi's print of the Monte di Pietà (reproduced p. 147) shows this building with an enclosed glazed structure across the front at street level, which must have masked the entrance.

From the outside there is no hint of the extraordinary interior arrangement, with open balustraded stairs and landings running around the cortile in a rectilinear two-level grid that has all the functionality of a Peabody Trust building in Victorian London. Clearly the building was purpose-built for multiple occupation, with the two upper floors privileged quite equally. The Alibrandi themselves, who were a Roman merchant family, presumably also had an apartment in the building, since it was described as Palazzo Alibrandi in Nolli's map of 1748. It passed to the Cavalieri at the beginning of the 19th century.

Palazzo Altemps

Via S Apollinare, 8

The palace was originally built for Girolamo Riario in 1480 and passed to the Soderini in 1511. In 1568 it was bought by Cardinal Marcus Sitticus Altemps (Hohenems), nephew of Pius IV.

Between 1577 and 1589 Altemps had the palace splendidly refashioned by Martino Longhi the Elder, assisted by other architects including Giacomo Della Porta, Flaminio Ponzio and Tommaso Schiratti. The fine cortile, with its loggias at each end and high quality stucco decoration throughout, dates from this period, but all this work is firmly in the High Renaissance tradition of Roman palaces, and does not really look forward to the Baroque. A notable feature is the massive altana surmounted by the rearing goat emblem of the Altemps which emphatically blocks the view down via della Maschera d'Oro.

The palace now houses the Museo Nazionale Romano, where the celebrated antique Ludovisi Marbles are displayed. Many of the rooms retain decoration from Altemps's time (together with some earlier fragments) but, again, little of this has much bearing on the Baroque. The one exception is the north loggia, which was one of the last parts to be commissioned by Altemps before his death in 1595. It was painted betweeen 1592 and 1594 by Antonio Viviani, who created an elaborate feigned pergola, populated by birds and putti, that is well on the way to the superb pergola that Bril and Guido Reni were to make for Scipione Borghese in his palace on the Quirinale twenty years later.

The next significant addition to the palace was by Altemps's grandson, Giovanni Angelo Altemps, who had the chapel of St Anicetus constructed by Onorio Longhi

Vasi's print of Piazza di S Apollinare. Two wings of Palazzo Altemps, with its towering altana, fill the corner opposite the church

and Girolamo Rainaldi from 1603 to 1617. The occasion for this was the gift to him by Clement VIII (who had been his tutor) of some human remains that had been discovered in the catacomb of S Calisto and which were claimed to be those of Anicetus, a 2nd century pope and martyr. Giovanni Angelo used the chapel as part of a campaign to develop a cult in favour of his father (Marcus Sitticus's illegitimate son Roberto, Duke of Gallese) who in 1586 had been beheaded for adultery despite Marcus Sitticus's pleas for clemency to Sixtus V, who had various reasons for resenting the advancement that Roberto had been given. (This background is summarised in Scoppola and Vordemann and analysed more fully in Scoppola, 1992.)

The chapel is lavishly decorated, with much coloured marble, and its iconology is extremely odd. The paintings on the side walls, by Antonio Circignani (Pomarancio), emphasise a scene in which a woman is sponging up the blood that flows from the saint's headless trunk. (There was no historical authority for the idea that Anicetus had been executed by decapitation, but the whole point of the chapel was the assimilation of the decapitated Roberto with the saintly Anicetus, so that each absorbed the characteristics of the other.) In the confessio behind the altar — and not accessible for a visitor — there are murals in oil-paint of the life of St Anicetus, attributed to Ottavio Leoni. Pomarancio's frescoes on the vault depict processions of putti, with those on one side carrying martyrs' palms and crowns, while those on the other side bear weapons and instruments of torture. The atmosphere of the place is distinctly hysterical.

In the exhibition room known as the Sala della Duchessa is G. F. Romanelli's frieze of *The Stories of Europa, Acis and Galatea, Amphitrite* and *Aurora*. Baldinucci comments in the *Notizie* on the delicacy of this sweetly pretty classicising work, painted shortly before Romanelli left Italy for his second visit to France.[1]

When the State obtained the palace in the early 1980s the part to the east of the cortile was acquired by Confcooper, the federation of Italian co-operatives, who sold it to other commercial occupiers in 2006.

Palazzo Altieri

Piazza del Gesù, 49

The old Roman family of Altieri had long been the great landowners on the south side of this site and had, indeed, owned the land on which the Gesù was built. In 1650 Cardinal Giambattista Altieri began the grand rebuilding of the part of the family property that fronted on to the piazza before the great church. This was a prime site for a major palace because Piazza del Gesù — originally known as Piazza degli Altieri — was a turning point in the papal processional route between the Vatican and the Lateran, and a palace at this point offered a splendid opportunity for displays of family

Vasi's print of Palazzo Altieri with the Gesù on the right. Vasi widens via del Plebiscito so as to give an imaginary view of the entire palace. He also conceals the fact that De Rossi's original palace (three bays by ten on the corner nearest the viewer) is much lower than his later enormous extensions. On the distant skyline the Quirinale is to the left and Palazzo Pallavicini Rospigliosi to the right

grandeur on ceremonial occasions.

What G. A. De Rossi built for the cardinal between 1650 and 1654 was an exceptionally clean and well-proportioned façade, unecumbered with mezzanines save for small windows in the cornice, and with the five central bays set slightly in advance of the two-bay wings and marked off with plain pilaster strips running the full height of the building.* This palace was only three bays deep, as can easily be seen from the quoins after the third bay down via del Gesù.† At that stage there would not have been a proper courtyard behind the main entrance, but simply a service area surrounded by miscellaneous earlier buildings that did not all belong to the Altieri.

This first palace contained one very evident anomaly, flowing from the fact that the façade was desired to be centred on the piazza yet could not be allowed to challenge the dominance of the Gesù. In order to meet these demands, and still maximise the use of the available site, De Rossi simply tacked on an extra tenth bay at a slight receding angle outside the quoins that mark the right edge of the main unit. This typically pragmatic De Rossian solution is not as disconcerting as it sounds, since when one is looking at the palace head-on (as the centralised design almost forces one to do) the extra bay on via del Plebiscito is entirely hidden by the Gesù.

A smaller anomaly is created by the rounded windows inserted in the hoods of the ground floor windows of the eighth and ninth bays, and the starkly plain door and window in the tenth bay. These features must reflect the presence of a pre-existing building for which there are no reliable records.§

When Cardinal Giambattista's brother, Cardinal Emilio Altieri, became Pope Clement X in 1670 he soon decided to expand the palace to reflect the family's new status, and this work was pressed ahead by the all-powerful Cardinale Padrone, that is Cardinal Paluzzo Paluzzi degli Albertoni. He was the uncle of Gaspare degli Albertoni who had married the pope's niece Laura and been made his heir, both uncle and nephew being required by the pope to take the Altieri name. While the family bought up property on the north of the site, the young Carlo Fontana produced for them a typically

* Bernini's, far bolder, use of an advanced central unit at Palazzo di Montecitorio was virtually contemporaneous.

†That bay in via del Gesù was, however, heightened and modified in the 1670s campaign.

§ Needless to say, there is no evidence for the story that the door marks the entrance to the dwelling of an old woman named Berta who refused to leave her house, and that the merciful Altieri incorporated it in their palace rather than drive her out. Since this tour-leader's anecdote seems to have distorted the literature, however, some comments are in order. The usual version of the Berta legend ascribes the Altieri's benevolence to Clement X. But that is fatally undermined by the fact that the door and mezzanine windows are in the part of the building that was completed in 1654, while the pope did not start the second building campaign until 1670. Although Schiavo accepted that the story was but an oral tradition in the Altieri family, he had so much belief in it that he allowed it to dictate his view that the palace's tenth bay represented the first phase of the 1670s campaign and that work had been suspended while the Berta problem was resolved.[1] In fact, however, there is overwhelming evidence for the tenth bay's dating to the 1650s. The windows and door in the eighth to tenth bays are undeniably puzzling survivals in such an aristocratic piece of architecture, but the Berta story could well be a later narrative designed to counteract public resentment of the vast extension of the 1670s and to demonstrate that the pope was characterised by care for the needy and the clemency that his choice of papal name implied.

gigantesque proposal for the palace's enlargement that entirely ignored the fact that most of the site was surrounded by fairly narrow streets. This design would have retained the existing block simply as a corner pavilion of a vast symmetrical façade with three entrances leading into a single huge courtyard.[2]

Instead of adopting Fontana's wildly ambitious idea, the Cardinale Padrone re-employed De Rossi to produce a much simpler and more flexible plan, extending the general scheme of the existing palace for fifteen more bays alongside the flank of the Gesù and ending with an aggressive statement of Altieri presence in the form of a corner bay that is covered with reticulation on both of its faces and is equipped with heavy balconies at both first and second storey level.* A vast, but plain, service courtyard was built behind the new extension and at the same time De Rossi built a separate cortile d'onore behind the 1650s façade, with a terrace running above the north side, opposite the main entrance, and with a balustrade and statues marking the skyline above and beyond. This very effective piece of theatre — described by Elling[5] as 'a stroke of genius' — is an unusual device for Rome and is more reminiscent of Genoa, where palaces often had to be accommodated to sharply rising ground.† Surmounting the extended façade is what must be the largest altana of any Roman palace.

The Cardinal Padrone was in a desperate hurry because the gouty old pope was almost eighty when he was elected and, as a matter of practical politics, the project had to be completed during his reign. As it was, the building work was pressed ahead literally night and day, and the palace was substantially finished when the pope died in 1676. Thus, the Cardinale Padrone's enormous apartment running along the new façade and down via degli Astalli had been completely finished, together with the extension on the west side down via del Gesù. The north side of the site, however, was not finished until the 1730s; it is made up of two distinct units, both of which are more severe than De Rossi's work.§ The triangular single storey building with Altieri stars behind the palace, on via di S Stefano del Cacco, was added in 1734 to house the stables. It is currently used, very appropriately, as a garage.

* Connors noted the dominant way in which De Rossi's corner feature confronts and exploits the part of via del Plebiscito that had been widened under Alexander VII, and he also described how the new wing of the Altieri palace encroached into the street beyond the previous building-line.[3] It is not clear whether there had ever been a specific plan for the further widening of the street alongside the Gesù[4] but the Altieri certainly put an end to any such ideas for good and all, in the way that Connors described.

† Blunt was far from sharing Elling's admiration of the cortile. He always disliked De Rossi's smooth domestic style and in his comments on Palazzo Altieri he gave free rein to his feelings, as follows. 'The Palazzo Altieri is G. A. De Rossi's most important work, in which he demonstrates his opposition to the Baroque innovations of Bernini, Borromini and Cortona, and his determination to cling to principles established in the last decades of the 16th century. On the façade the windows are evenly spaced, and De Rossi does not even allow himself to use the alternation of straight and curved pediments which had been current practice in Rome for more than a century. The elevations of the courtyard — with the exception of some slightly Borrominesque windows in the upper storey — are equally austere, and the staircase, though grand in conception, is positively dry in its treatment of detail.'[6]

§ Of these units, the seven-bay extension that protrudes from the east end of the palace's north face is the so-called 'galleria imperfecta' that was originally planned as a gallery, was left unfinished for many years, and was turned into an apartment on two levels in the 1730s.

For the whole of his pontificate Clement X subsidised the building to the extent of 2,000 scudi a month, and in 1675 he had a medal struck to celebrate it. The construction of such a huge family palace during a time of recession caused a public scandal and the false story that the pope never set foot in the place[7] was presumably put about as a deliberate attempt to distance him from the project. In fact, the pope did visit the site on several occasions, and on one of these he took the opportunity to discuss with Bernini the progress of his commission for an equestrian statue of Prince Gaspare in emulation of Bernini's statue of Louis XIV.[8]

The weakest element of the enlarged palace is, quite obviously, that the new parts are considerably higher than the old, because of the need to accommodate vaults in the piano nobile rooms of the new part, whereas the rooms of the 1650s unit had flat wooden ceilings. This means not only that the elevation of the new part is much higher than that of the old, but that the separation between the windows of the first and second storeys is much greater. De Rossi made no attempt whatsoever to hide this dislocation (clearly visible after the tenth bay of the main façade and in the third bay on via del Gesù) and simply lifted the string-course of the second floor of the new part and gave the windows even greater height by placing them on pedestals similar to those on the piano nobile. The design of the façade windows themselves is identical in old and new parts, save that the second floor windows in the later part are given a touch of decoration on the brackets supporting the pediments.

Milizia's comment that the extended building looks like two separate palaces[9] is well founded, and the junction between the two parts looks extraordinarily brutal and untidy if examined from within the narrow via del Plebiscito. The fact is, however, that this is not the natural place from which to view the palace, and the dislocation is not evident from most of Piazza del Gesù. As with the anomalous tenth bay itself, in fact, De Rossi's approach was entirely pragmatic and he again showed that he had a cool eye for what he could get away with in the context of the site as a whole.

The palace's enlargement did, however, totally reverse its relationship with the Gesù. The 1650s façade, which remained untouched, looks quite modest alongside the great church, but the huge 1670s extension constitutes a challenge to it. The Jesuits were most upset at the prospect of their mother church having such an overbearing neighbour and they cast around for a sponsor who was prepared to air their worries with the pope. Unsurprisingly, nobody could be found to undertake such a hopeless mission.

INTERIOR

The piano nobile of the 1650s block, overlooking Piazza del Gesù was arranged as an apartment for Cardinal Giambattista Altieri, who died in 1654, a few months before it was finished. It consisted of five rooms in an enfilade along the main façade and one room at the back of the block, facing what is now the cortile. All six rooms were frescoed with friezes depicting religious themes, in the order in which they appear in the Old Testament. From east to west the subjects of the enfilade were the *Stories of Abraham, Isaac, Jacob, Joseph and Moses*, while the room at the back had as its subject the *Story of Gideon*. They are cheerful, rather naïve works, evidently by a number of hands, and including some landscape passages that look reminiscent of Giovanni Francesco Grimaldi. Their authorship will not be settled unless and until the Altieri archives are fully examined by schol-

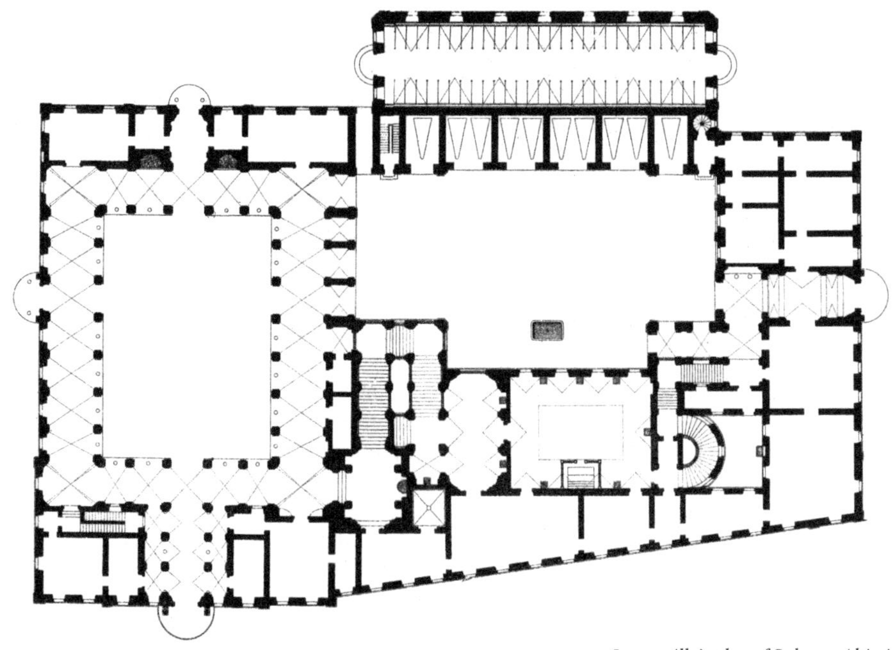

Letarouilly's plan of Palazzo Altieri

ars. Next to the room at the back with the *Story of Gideon* there is now a room with feigned curtains and landscapes of about 1675. The space now occupied by this room would doubtless have been taken up by the staircase of the 1650s building.

The main staircase for the enlarged building is an imposing feature, entered from the corner of the first cortile, at the junction between old and new work, and hugely projecting into the second cortile in order to obtain a light-well. It rises to a large landing which opens into two great rooms — the Sala di Romolo, which was the antecamera to the Cardinal Padrone's apartment at the front of the building, and the Sala della Clemenza, which was sometimes used as an audience chamber but seems normally to have been the reception area for both the Cardinal Padrone and Prince Gaspare, whose apartment ran towards the north part of the palace. That arrangement was reminiscent of Palazzo Barberini, where the Pietro da Cortona salone was a common entry point for the apartments of the ecclesiastical and lay members of the family.

The Sala di Romolo, with four windows on via del Plebiscito, was decorated in 1675-76 (immediately after their ceiling at SS Domenico e Sisto) by Canuti and Haffner with an exuberant *Apotheosis of Romulus*, featuring much quadratura and packed with Altieri symbols and arcane allusions celebrating the ancient Romans, with whom the Altieri sought to identify themselves.[10] The room marked the beginning of the Cardinal Padrone's apartment that ran eastwards along the new front opposite the Gesù. It was also connected to Cardinal Giambattista's old apartment on Piazza del Gesù by another new room decorated with a fine stucco frieze and ceiling that may have been designed by De Rossi himself.

The other large new room (the Sala della Clemenza) was built alongside the Sala di Romolo but further back, so that it was lit directly from the service courtyard. On the recommendation of Camillo Massimo, whom the Altieri had asked to supervise the palace's decoration, the commission for the ceiling was given to the rising star Carlo Maratta.[11] His fresco of the *Triumph of Clemency* has always been recognised as a highly important work, since it documents the arrival on centre-stage of the classicising style that came to dominate Roman art theory and practice, and which heavily influenced court art throughout Europe for many decades. Maratta worked out the scheme in collaboration with the great art theorist Gian Pietro Bellori and they intended to complete it by adding frescoes on the coves of the room according to a complex programme that Bellori had devised. The project was never carried out because of the death of the pope in 1676, but its scheme is known from the Maratta drawings analysed by Montagu. As Maratta himself acknowledged,[12] the empty coves look distinctly bare, and indeed the central painting looks far too small for the space it occupies.*

* An issue that perhaps deserves more critical attention than it has hitherto received is the stylistic difference between the major ceiling paintings that were done virtually contemporaneously here. Maratta's Sala della Clemenza is the epitome of the self-consciously correct classicising taste that is always associated with the Altieri under Massimo's tutelage, while the Canuti and Haffner ceiling is an energetic, sprawling piece. The contrast is something like that between Sacchi and Cortona earlier in the century and it hints that the Altieri patronage may not have been quite as monolithic and uniform in its æsthetic doctrine as is generally believed.

The most important rooms of Prince Gaspare's apartment are three that run northward, in the following order, along the east side of the entrance courtyard. All of these have ceilings in the flaccid classicising taste that the Altieri had adopted. The Sala Verde (1674-77 has a ceiling with *Allegories of Autumn and Winter* by Francesco Cozza, surrounded by quadratura and grisailles of the *Seasons* by Paolo Brozzi, and by large allegorical figures by Giovanni Andrea Carloni. The main ceiling subject (1675) of the Sala Rossa is an *Allegory of Love*,† and there are two rather livelier lunettes: all of this is by Nicolò Berrettoni, Maratta's leading pupil at the time. Marqués shows that the composition sketch for the astonishingly dix-huitième central scene was provided by Maratta himself. The two neoclassical overdoors are by Nicola Buonvicini (1790). The Sala degli Specchi has a ceiling (1675) by Fabrizio Chiari, another pupil of Maratta, with the *Chariot of the Sun with the Hours*, together with much surrounding feigned moulding, putti, etc.

Other parts of the palace have splendid late 17th century decoration. In particular, Angela Cipriani's essay 'A Programme Devised by Giovan Pietro Bellori'[14] makes it clear that there is a series of rooms with very fine stucco ceilings along via S Stefano del Cacco and via degli Astalli. As with other questions surrounding Altieri patronage, the full analysis of these programmes would require access to the family's archives.

All the rooms along the east side of the entrance courtyard, and especially the Sala degli Specchi, were much modified in the

† Marqués (1976) describes this room as the bedroom of Prince Gaspare and Princess Laura; she also speculates that the central scene could possibly be *Aurora*, which would link with the subject of the Chiari ceiling in the Sala degli Specchi.[13]

1790s when, under the oversight of the architect Giuseppe Barberi, a new apartment was formed along the north side. This includes a Pompeian Room decorated by Felice Giani and a Gabinetto Nobile of exceptionally high quality with a ceiling of the *Apotheosis of Romulus* by Stefano Tofanelli and a marble frieze of putti etc by Vincenzo Pacetti. The Gabinetto di Toeletta on the piano nobile of the north side of the second cortile is a fully rococo room of 1736.

Some of the shops at street level still have well-proportioned coved ceilings with plain stucco decoration (which in one case features Altieri stars) but the palace is not generally open to the public. On the piano nobile the Sala della Clemenza and the rooms to the east and north of the entrance courtyard are occupied by the Associazione Bancaria Italiana; the Sala di Romolo and the rooms running along the façade on Piazza del Gesù are occupied by the Banca Finnat Euramerica; much of the rest is occupied by the Banca Popolare di Novara. The half-length bust of Clement X by Bernini and assistants that used to be in the palace's famous library was acquired around 2000 by the Galleria Nazionale d'Arte Antica, and is now displayed in Palazzo Barberini.

In the 1950s and 60s the Altieri palace was known far and wide as the home of the great film actress Anna Magnani, whose top-floor apartment was an important meeting-place for the world of Italian literary and film culture. She lived here for some 20 years before her death in 1973 and her last moments on screen, in Fellini's *Roma*, were of her returning to the palace at night and firmly closing her front door in via degli Astalli both on Fellini's vain attempts to interview her and — symbolically — on her own glittering career.

Palazzetto Ansellini

Via dei Condotti, 55-57

A refined little building, and typical of the arrangements made by owner-residents in 18th century apartment buildings. The two main storeys have stucco decoration for their windows, while the mezzanine under the cornice is given a couple of ringhiere. The heavily rusticated ground-floor corner looks too assertive for the building's elegant presence. The storey above the cornice was added in 1866-72.

The Ansellini built it in its present form in 1732 and let out the parts they did not occupy in a variety of configurations. By 1793 there were two apartments on each floor, and the Ansellini had retreated to one of those in the third floor mezzanine.

Palazzo Antamoro (Strada)

Via della Panetteria, 15

The object of interest here is the vigorously designed (but coarsely executed) stucco wall fountain in the courtyard, with two entwined dolphins supporting a gaping clam-shell basin into which two juvenile tritons are poised to spout water. It was made for the palace's builder, Paolo Strada, who was cameriere segreto to Clement IX (Rospigliosi), and it originally bore the Rospigliosi arms as a token of Strada's gratitude for the pope's grant of the water rights in 1667.

The concept and energy of the fountain are clearly Berninian in nature, and Bernini himself may very well have had a hand in the design as he is documented as having certified the extraction of the water from the Acqua Felice.[1] Other than the caption to Venturini's print (reproduced overleaf), there is, however, no closer evidence for his

Venturini's depiction of the fountain in Palazzo Antamoro. It shows the fountain in a far more idyllic garden-like space than it currently enjoys, and with tiny figures to magnify its apparent size

participation, and the terracotta model for the fountain in the Accademia, Florence, seems too dryly executed to be from his own hand and is not generally accepted as autograph.

In the 18th century the palace was bought by the Antamoro family, who completely rebuilt it in various phases over the next two centuries.[2] They replaced the Rospigliosi arms on the fountain with their own, and left the fountain looking somewhat forlorn in a more crowded space than it had originally enjoyed. The fountain was restored in 1980, and again more recently; there is still water in the lower basin but the tritons and shell are now dry.

Palazzo Astalli

Via di S Marco, 8

The 16th century palace on this site was the subject of development plans by G. A. De Rossi from 1672. Letarouilly's plan shows that the result must have been an example of De Rossi's ingenuity in exploiting awkward sites and that — like its close neighbour Palazzo Muti Bussi — it used the device of doorways aligned opposite each other to open up a view beyond. In 1930-32 it was demolished and rebuilt in a smaller format to make room for the widening of via S Marco. Some of the 16th century fresco ceiling painting was taken to the Museo di Roma, though none of it is currently on

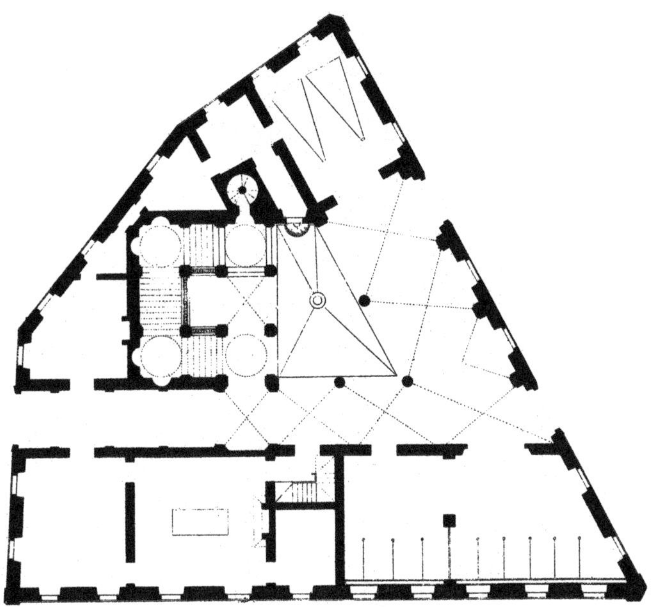

Letarouilly's plan of the (now largely demolished) Palazzo Astalli

display. The building is now a pastiche that gives virtually no idea of how De Rossi's building may have appeared. For another De Rossi palace that was destroyed and 'rebuilt' between the wars see Palazzo Carpegna (Baldinotti).

Palazzo D'Aste

Via di Ripetta, 142

The architecture of this palace is generally unremarkable, but the door and balcony make a splendid piece, with a panel invading the architrave (just like the door at Palazzo Lancellotti that Visentini so deplored) and displaying a fine female head emerging from strapwork set between a pair of rich swags.

The lion masks on the volute brackets supporting the balcony and the crowned lions rampant in the frieze under the cornice (where they appear together with rosettes) are emblems of the D'Aste family, who built three palaces in Rome in the 17th century. The date of this one would appear to be in the third quarter of the century, when G. A. De Rossi built the family's great palace in Piazza Venezia. As the decorative panel of the door here is of high quality and very much in De Rossi's style, it is tempting to suggest that he had a hand in this palace too, though there is no published documentary evidence for that.

Palazzo D'Aste (Bonaparte, Rinuccini, Misciattelli)

Piazza Venezia, 5

The palace at the junction of the Corso and Piazza Venezia was built by G. A. De Rossi between 1658 and 1667 for the Cavaliere Francesco Bonaventura D'Aste whose

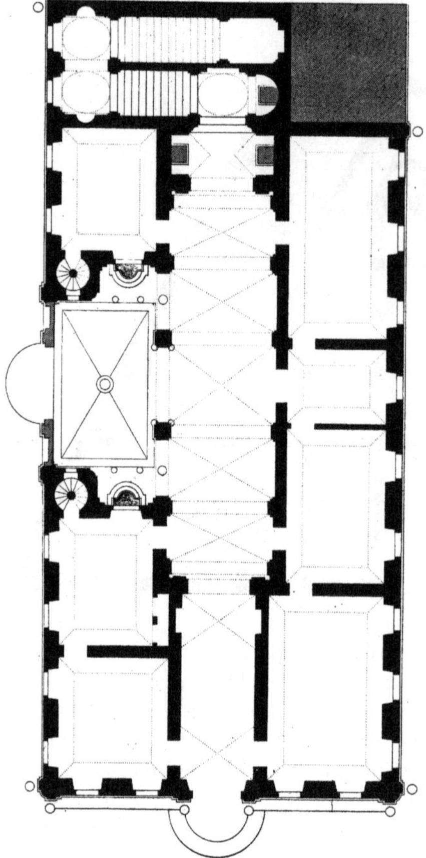

Letarouilly's plan of the ground floor of Palazzo D'Aste (Bonaparte) showing the central passage that runs through the building and the open entrance area on the west flank

family had amassed huge wealth since they settled in Rome at the beginning of the century, and already owned part of the site. Exploiting Alexander VII's wish to tidy the piazza and to widen via del Gesù (now via del Plebiscito), D'Aste bought out neighbouring property and conceived the idea of a long, narrow palace that would be worthy of the key position. Furthermore, as the importance of the site became yet clearer, D'Aste continued to elaborate his ideas even after De Rossi's first (and much more conventional) design had been given planning permission.[1] The lion emblem of the D'Aste appears in the form of lion masks in the pediments of the second storey windows and lions rampant in the cornice at the building's corners.

De Rossi's first design envisaged two entrances, a main one on Piazza Venezia and another, only slightly less grand, on the Corso. Presumably there would have been a central court for dealing with carriage traffic, though that would have been awkward in such a confined area. De Rossi's key change in plan was to do away with the Corso entrance altogether and to open a wide entrance area on the palace's subsidiary long flank on vicolo Doria. This must have helped to ease the traffic handling and, externally, it had the effect of privileging the prime Piazza Venezia façade that was no longer required to share attention with the long front on the Corso. Internally, De Rossi provided a uniquely long vestibule that occupies a full third of the area on the ground floor, bisecting the building through its entire length and connecting with the staircase at the northwest corner. Such an attenuated space risked becoming a monotonous tunnel, but De Rossi successfully dealt with that problem by opening out the central part of the vestibule into the side entrance area.

The essential elements of the palace's elevation are well within the Roman mainstream descended from Palazzo Farnese, though the nature of the site would always mean that the main front on Piazza Venezia had an unusually vertical emphasis. Where

Opposite: Falda's print of Palazzo D'Aste (Bonaparte) showing De Rossi's original ideas for the main door, and without the corner balcony

PALAZZO DE SIG.RI MARCHESI RINUCCINI SÙ LA PIAZZA DI S. MARCO È RIONE DELLA PIGNA
Architettura di Gio. Antonio de Rossi

Above: View by Falda across Piazza Venezia, with Palazzo D'Aste (Bonaparte) on the extreme right and Palazzo Grazioli further along via del Plebiscito. The huddle of buildings between the two palaces was destined to be replaced by the Ameli wing of Palazzo Doria-Pamphili in the following century

Below: in this print by Vasi the wing of Palazzo Doria-Pamphili built by Ameli fills the gap between Palazzo D'Aste (Bonaparte) and Palazzo Grazioli along via del Plebiscito. In the distance Palazzo Altieri stands massively across the line of the road

De Rossi broke new ground was in the detail of his decorative language and his suave packaging. Some of this was derived from Borromini (as in the 'pagoda' pediments on the second floor windows, borrowed from Borromini's Oratory) and some from Pietro da Cortona (as in the wrap-around composite corner elements) but it is all characterised by an elegant reserve that still remains firm and masculine. Amid this restraint, the naturalistic female heads looking down from the cornice above the mezzanine windows are something of a delightful surprise.

All in all, the palace is an extremely accomplished success. It was also destined to be very influential; the window shapes and plastic corner elements were to have a long life throughout the Roman barocchetto and were still alive and well when de Marchis built Palazzo Mellini eighty years later.

Changes had already been made to the main façade by the time that Vasi published his print and description in 1761.[2] These included the deepening of three of the mezzanine windows on the Piazza Venezia front, and their equipment with ringhiere, and the addition of the well-known covered balcony or 'busselotto' on the corner of the Corso. The most regrettable alteration, however, was the replacement of De Rossi's balcony and doorway with the present entrance that is so mean that it jars badly with the general treatment of the façade.*

From 1815 to 1838 the palace belonged to Letizia Bonaparte (Madame Mère), the mother of Napoleon, whose eagle appears in the centre of the façade in the place where there was originally a small window. She is known to have spent much time in the covered balcony, using the facility offered by these devices to maintain one's privacy while observing the street-life below. This particular spot commanded a view of the finish of the celebrated riderless horse race down the Corso, which was one of the major events of the Roman year.

The palace remained in the Bonaparte family until 1905. While the interior contains much neo-classical decoration, both Napoleonic and earlier, there is virtually nothing of the Baroque period.

*Although Falda's *Nuovo Teatro* plate (opposite) shows a significant decorative feature above the door, it does not include a balcony. Perhaps it was decided not to install the central balcony when the one on the corner (later to develop into the busselotto) was added.

Palazzo D'Aste (Pericoli, Sterbini)

Via Monserrato, 149

This is the latest of the three palaces that the D'Aste built in Rome. It is a substantial building with ten bays on Piazza Ricci and six on via Monserrato. The D'Aste lion-masks appear on the doors that stand in each façade between a series of uniform openings for shops. There are mezzanines with plain stucco window frames on the ground floor and immediately under the cornice; the two main floors have windows with straight pediments and brackets, with those on the first floor privileged by a slightly bolder design. The building's corner is emphasised by quite a strong composite wrap-around feature.

Spezzaferro noted that a document of 1718 recorded that the palace's hay-loft and stables had been begun in 1694 and he commented that this approximate date for the building would 'allow the hypothesis' that the design (especially that of the Piazza Ricci front and the stairs) could be by G. A. De Rossi, who stayed in touch with the D'Aste until his death in 1695.[1] This tentative suggestion has often since been quoted as though it were a certain fact, but that is to put far too much weight on what was apparently intended as no more than a conjecture. Whether or not De Rossi designed the building, it certainly does not aspire to the elegance of his major work, and is clearly well on the way to the utilitarian maximisation of usable space that became characteristic of 18th century Rome.

Palazzo Avila

Via di Monte Giordano, 2

A compact and seemingly hardly altered little palace, built by the Spanish family that commissioned the chapel by Antonio Gherardi in S Maria in Trastevere. It has plain windows firmly planted on solid stringcourses, and unadorned quoins at the corners. The semicirular arched doorway is surmounted by a heavy cornice supported by baluster brackets.

The noteworthy thing is the placing of the family's heraldic eagles clutching palms to make a centre-piece above the doorway. Crowned eagles with crossed palms preside at the sides of the S Maria in Trastevere chapel, while here each (uncrowned) eagle sits comfortably in a volute and holds a single palm that curves up in the reverse direction to form a further volute that embraces the central window. Other emblems on the palace are eagles, roses and fleurs-de-lys in the cornice, and roses in the spandrels of the entrance.

The palace apparently dates from the 17th century but — apart from the centre-piece — there is nothing in the design that would have looked out of place in, say, 1560. The centre-piece itself is a vigorous example of using a heraldic device to form a strong architectural motif, but the execution of the idea is rustic.

Palazzo del Banco di S Spirito (Spada, Bennicelli)

Piazza dell'Orologio, 7

What now exists is an overbearing piece in eclectic style that was created at the end of the 19th century for the Bennicelli family. Its architect, Gaetano Koch, was one of the designers of the Vittorio Emanuele monument and was responsible for many of the most grandiloquent Roman buildings of the time, including the esedra of Piazza della Repubblica, the Banca d'Italia building in via Nazionale and Palazzo Ludovisi, now the American embassy.

The idea of establishing the headquarters of the Banco di S Spirito in a new building alongside the Oratory was due to Virgilio Spada, Borromini's great champion, who was the elected leader (preposito) of the Oratorians and who had his quarters in the clock-tower at the other end of Piazza dell'Orologio. In 1660 Spada was nominated as commendatore of the Arciospedale di Santo Spirito, and the following year he obtained Alexander VII's approval both for the bank's transfer to the new building and for Borromini's employment as the architect. Visually, the plan would have echoed Borromini's clock-tower and stamped his vision across the piazza.[1] At the political and social level it would have created a new financial area in immediate proximity to the Oratory, which would have stood to benefit greatly from the association.

In the event, Spada died in December 1662, and the governors of the Banco di S Spirito, who had opposed his scheme from the start, quickly persuaded Alexander to rescind his earlier decision. The headquarters of the bank was established in the old Mint (which was closer to the traditional banking area), and Spada's nephew Orazio was instructed by the pope to buy the unfinished building

Falda's frontal view of Palazzo del Banco di S Spirito, with Borromini's clock-tower on the left. For another view of the palace by Falda see p. 75

and complete it at his own expense, which he did by 1669. Until it passed into other hands the palace was used by the family and known as Palazzo Spada.

The appearance of the palace is known from drawings and from the two prints by Falda that illustrate it from the side and the front.[2] It looks quite a festive building, articulated by four giant pilasters and surmounted by a balustrade over the centre section only. Koch destroyed all this and greatly heightened the structure. The vestibule and the court may still contain traces of the earlier building, however, in the superimposed arcaded loggias of the court and the arrangement of the vestibule leading to a fountain. (Blunt thought that both these features were reminiscent of Borromini's method of designing.)[3] The court has been greatly hacked about and is now in a very degraded state, so that only the faintest ghost of Borromini's presence remains.

Palazzo Barberini ai Giubbonari or Casa Grande ai Giubbonari

Via dei Giubbonari, 41

This unprepossessing, drab building had an important rôle as a seat of the Barberini. It is one of the clearest examples of the way in which a rather modest Roman dwelling could be progressively expanded to create a large palace equipped with several reception apartments.

The original nucleus on via dei Giubbonari was bought in 1581 by Monsignor Francesco Barberini, who began buying neighbouring properties in 1586 and by the time of his death in 1600 was able to leave his nephew Maffeo Barberini (the future Pope Urban VIII) a significantly expanded property. This was nevertheless too cramped for Maffeo's growing importance and for the accommodation of his brother Carlo's family, and the palace was therefore altered by Flaminio Ponzio between 1600 and 1603 and was more substantially remodelled in 1609-12 by Giovanni Maria Bonazzini, who was probably a kinsman of Ponzio. When Maffeo Barberini became pope in 1623 he gave the palace to Carlo who continued work on it until 1627 under the direction of Maderno. In 1624 Carlo (who died in 1630) bought the houses between the palace and the present Piazza del Monte di Pietà so as to occupy a long frontage on via dei Giubbonari but little was done at the time to exploit this, as the family were turning their thoughts to their major new palace at the Quattro Fontane.

In 1632 Prince Taddeo Barberini left for the Quattro Fontane, but he returned to the Casa Grande in 1634 and remained there until his flight from Rome in 1646. His major rebuilding of the palace in the early 1640s was greatly influenced by the decision of the Monte di Pietà in 1637 to clear the space between their foundation and the Casa Grande so as to create the present piazza. While Taddeo regularised the entire via dei Giubbonari façade, placing the Barberini bees on the corner, his main change was to switch the oriention of the palace so that the emphasis was on a new façade facing the piazza. Here his architect Francesco Contini constructed a grand entrance hall with three unequal bays articulated by double free-standing columns, to replace the alley by which the palace entrance had previously been reached. (The crude existing columns in the hall were inserted when the original polished oriental granite ones were taken to the Braccio Nuovo of the Vatican Museums in 1819.) The new façade could not be carried through to the left of the entrance hall before the Barberini fell from power on Urban's death in 1644.

From 1658 until his death in 1671 Taddeo's brother Cardinal Antonio Barberini kept the Casa Grande and used the ground floor to house his enormous art collection. In 1734 the property was bought by the Discalced Carmelites of S Teresa, who converted the entrance hall into a chapel dedicated to S Teresa and S Giovanni della Croce, and privileged its entrance with columns and a pediment, as seen in Vasi's print of the Monte di Pietà, shown on p. 184. In 1759 the palace was taken over by the Monte di Pietà who went on to complete the range facing the piazza, employing Nicola Giansimoni to construct a new entrance and oval vestibule around which a stairway climbs.[1]

The palace now belongs to the Comune of Rome and is occupied by a school and various other institutions including the Istituto Magistrale Statale Vittoria Colonna. Giansimoni's vestibule and stairs are behind the door in Piazza del Monte di Pietà at street no. 99, while no. 99A opens directly into a series of rooms with fine stucco ceilings featuring Barberini suns and bees together with monti and crowned eagles; they appear to be from the first quarter of the 17th century. Contini's entrance hall, now closed to the street, lies between these doors and access to it is via no. 99A. Having been successively used as a chapel, a theatre and a bar, the hall is now occupied by a printing works.

This palace was one of the case studies in Patricia Waddy's *Seventeenth Century Roman Palaces*, and its exceptionally interesting history has thus been established by meticulous archival research. Nevertheless, one may hope that the building's numerous occupants may one day co-operate in facilitating an inventory of what survives, since Prince Taddeo and Cardinal Antonio, in particular, must surely have had sumptuously decorated apartments and it is tempting to think that some remnants may still exist.

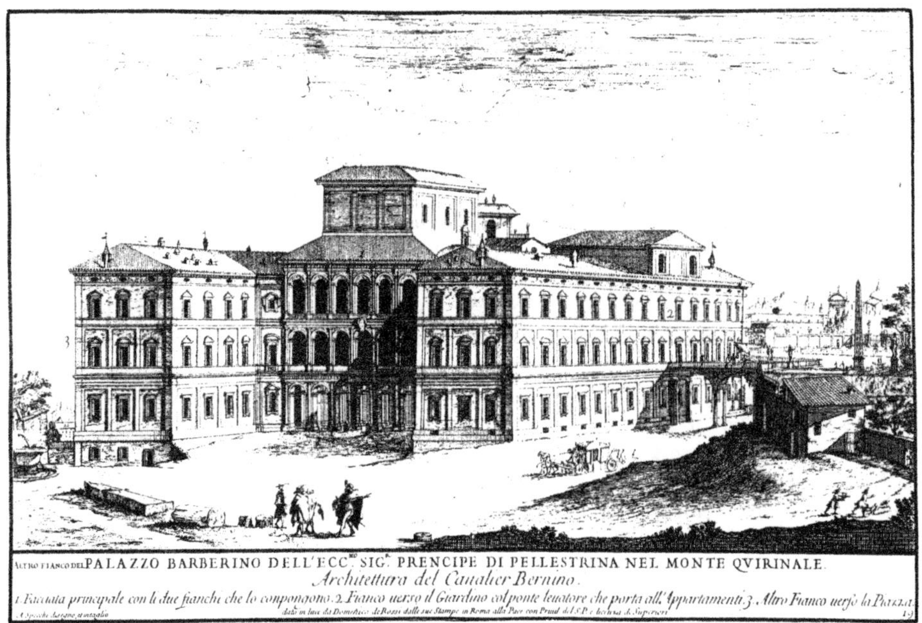

Specchi's print of Palazzo Barberini seen from the west, before the present grand approach was laid out in the 1860s. The 'ruined bridge' is on the right

Palazzo Barberini

Via delle Quattro Fontane, 13

The first and greatest truly Baroque palace in Rome, this place was central to the papal family's programme of aggrandisement during the reign of Maffeo Barberini as Urban VIII (reigned 1623-44), and several of the very greatest names of the Baroque were employed on it. The pope was himself a distinguished poet and the family promoted themselves as intellectuals and artistic innovators; the programme of publicity that they organised for the building represented it not only as a wonder of architecture and decoration but also as the site of a famous library and theatre. Against this background, it is not surprising that the building has generated an enormous literature.[1] However, the precise shares of the participants can never be settled, since the patrons encouraged the interplay of a wide range of opinions in the planning phase of the project, and during its execution there was a remarkable degree of collaboration between the architects.

THE CONCEPTION OF THE PALACE, ITS USE BY THE BARBERINI IN THE 17TH CENTURY, AND THE NEW ENTRANCE APPROACH MADE IN THE 19TH CENTURY

The new pope's brother Carlo had three sons to take forward the family's fortunes. Francesco and Antonio were destined for careers in the church, being made cardinals in 1623 and 1627 respectively. Taddeo was chosen to pursue a secular career and to transmit the family name; in 1630 he became

Prince of Palestrina on the death of his father, who had bought the title-carrying property only a few weeks before, and in 1631 he was made Prefect of Rome.

In 1625 Cardinal Francesco bought from Duke Alessandro Sforza a palace or villa, together with its vigna, that lay between the area that is now Piazza Barberini and via XX settembre, and he almost immediately transferred it to Taddeo. For the next three years the family held discussions about the form of the project with their architects and advisers, including the amateur architect Michelangelo Buonarotti the Younger. Taddeo seems to have been in the lead of all this, but Urban himself is recorded as making suggestions, and Cardinal Francesco and other family members surely did the same. There is no firm record of Bernini being involved at this stage but it is likely that he had some input, since he was already a prominent member of the Barberini circle.

When construction began under Maderno's direction in December 1628, it was on the basis of a central block over a west-facing atrium, with two projecting wings, the northern one of which incorporated the old Sforza palace. Blunt, reflecting the approach of his time, argued that a main reason for this unusual plan may have been that the siting in a large vigna on the edge of the inhabited area of Rome gave the building something of the character of a villa, so that it was logical to turn to the most famous of Roman villas, Peruzzi's Farnesina, as a model.[2] Wittkower had already pointed out that since the site could not be aligned with any major roads it was inherently unsuitable for a traditional palace design arranged around a courtyard. He, too, believed that the building should be regarded as a monumentalised 'villa suburbana'[3] and Hibbard saw it as 'a kind of gargantuan villa'.[4] The unique building clearly has both palatial and villa-like qualities, but ranking them in order of importance is, perhaps, a sterile pursuit. Patricia Waddy (who suggested that the Barberini may have been influenced in their design by the memory of noble town-houses in Paris) has said that 'simply to make the palace look like a villa would be meaningless'.[5] For the building's message, both Waddy and Scott[6] focus on the powerful way in which the design projected the idea of the secular and ecclesiastical branches of the Barberini family being united under the ægis of Urban's rule, symbolised by the massive papal arms over the balcony in the central loggia.*

It is important to remember that when the palace was built it would have looked both more isolated and more prominent than it does today, as there would have been no large buildings anywhere near it. Furthermore, the palace sat within a huge Barberini estate that has now been built over. Towards the north there was a large area called the Cortile della Cavallerizza that extended well beyond the spine of modern buildings into what is now Piazza Barberini and via Barberini. This space was enclosed by walls, and the main entrance from the north was by way of a gateway near Bernini's Tritone

*Both Waddy and Scott further draw attention to the broad resemblance between the palace's loggia and papal structures at the Vatican such as the Cortile di S Damaso, which at the time would have been directly visible on the far side of the Tiber.[6] One of the main aims of the programme of frescoes inside the palace was to project the whole family as an agent of the divine will that brought about Urban's election, and a deliberate visual echo between the new palace and the Vatican would certainly fit in with this, though it does not appear to be a point that was spelt out by any contemporary.

Opposite: Falda's map of 1676 with Palazzo Barberini in the centre. The Quirinale is in the lower right corner

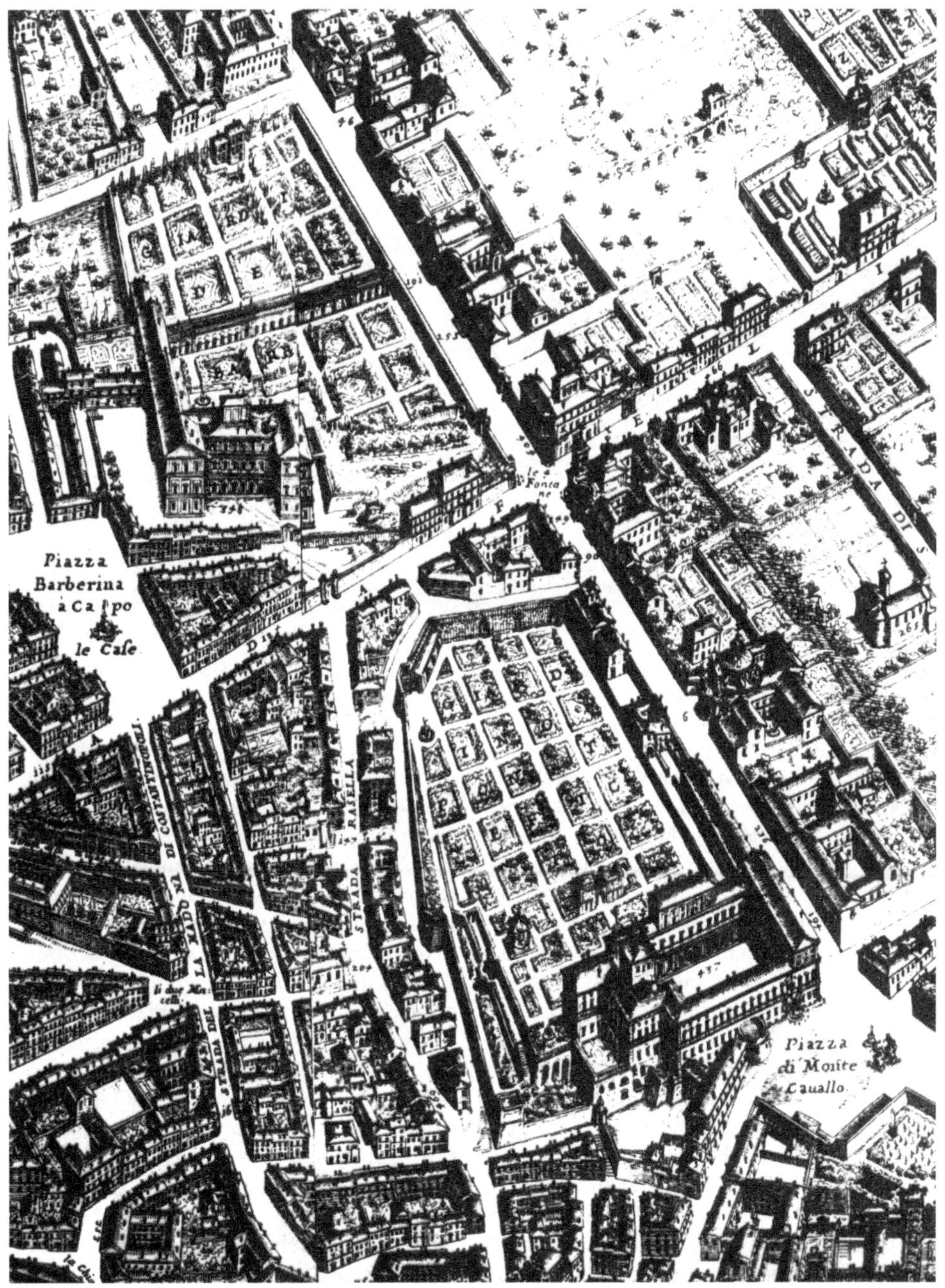
Piazza
Barberina
à Capo
le Case
STRADA RASELLA
Piazza
di Monte
Cauallo

Vasi's print of Piazza Barberini from the north, with Bernini's Tritone fountain on the right and Palazzo Barberini on the left. This shows clearly how dominant the palace was before the development of the area in the 19th century

fountain. As is shown in the Vasi print illustrated here, this gate would have stood more or less on the place of the present metro entrance in Piazza Barberini. The east end of the Cortile della Cavallerizza was screened off by a monumental wall behind which the stables stretched up towards what is now via XX settembre, while the palace's famous gardens filled the entire space up to the corner at the Quattro Fontane and extended as far as S Susanna. (For Pietro da Cortona's involvement in the ancillary structures, see the next section of this entry.)

Work on the north wing was paid for by Taddeo, while from 1632 Cardinal Francesco began paying for the construction of the south wing. What was anticipated was that Taddeo would occupy the ground floor of the north wing, with his apartment being reached from an entrance in the massive north façade, while his wife Anna Colonna (who had important ceremonial duties as the highest-ranking lady in Rome) would have her apartment one floor above in the piano nobile of the north wing. Under this scheme, the south wing would have been given over to the family's ecclesiastical representation, and Cardinal Francesco would have occupied an apartment in its piano nobile corresponding to Anna's set of rooms in the north wing. Visitors to Anna or Cardinal Francesco would go up one of the main staircases from the west front and would then go into the great central salone which served as the shared guardroom (sala dei palafrenieri) for the apartments that

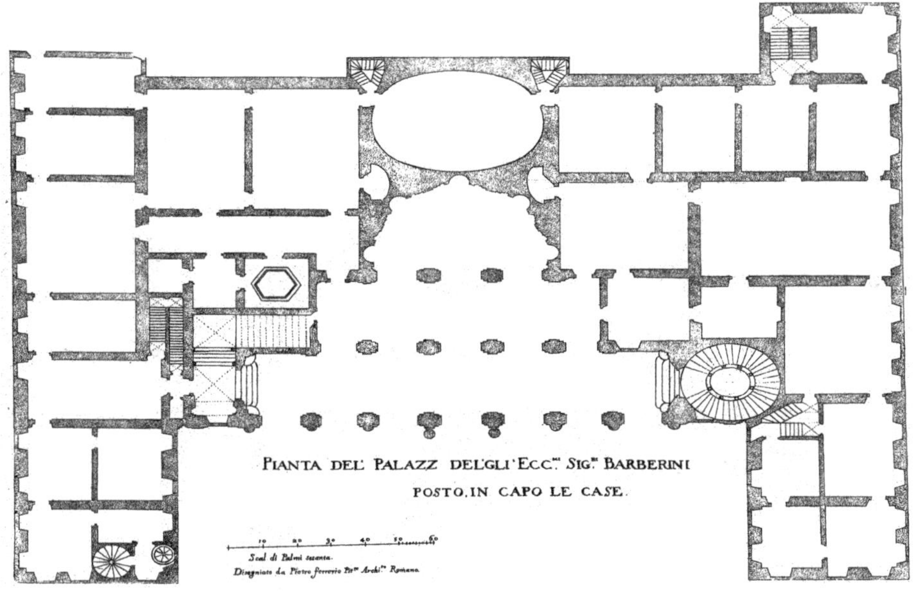

Ferrerio's plan of the ground floor of Palazzo Barberini, before the passage to the garden was cut through the centre of the building

branched off into either wing. Behind the great salone there was an oval room that was not part of either of the official reception areas.*

* This account of the ways of approaching the palace follows the analysis in Waddy 1990.[7] What it boils down to is that visitors normally entered either through the gate in the SE corner of Piazza Barberini (which was the closest entry point to Prince Taddeo's apartment), or else went round the outside of the compound to enter through the mean gate in the west wall, where the main entrance in via delle Quattro Fontane is now situated. In either case, visitors to the apartments on the piano nobile would use the staircases in the west atrium front. Both Blunt and Merz suggest that a main entrance route was via the Cortona gate by the Quattro Fontane, leading to the door into the oval room at piano nobile level.[8] The routine use of that route, however, would have involved constant coach traffic through the garden, and the use of the academically-associated oval room as a mere ante-chamber. Could it have been reserved for distinguished visitors coming from the direction of the Quirinale?

In practice, matters developed unexpectedly. Taddeo and Anna only used their part of the palace for two years before returning in 1634 to their earlier home in the Casa Grande ai Giubbonari, probably because Anna believed that she was more likely to have male children in the old palace. In 1632 Cardinal Francesco was made vice-chancellor and moved to his official residence in the Cancelleria. All this meant that Cardinal Antonio was able to move into the north wing in January 1635 and to

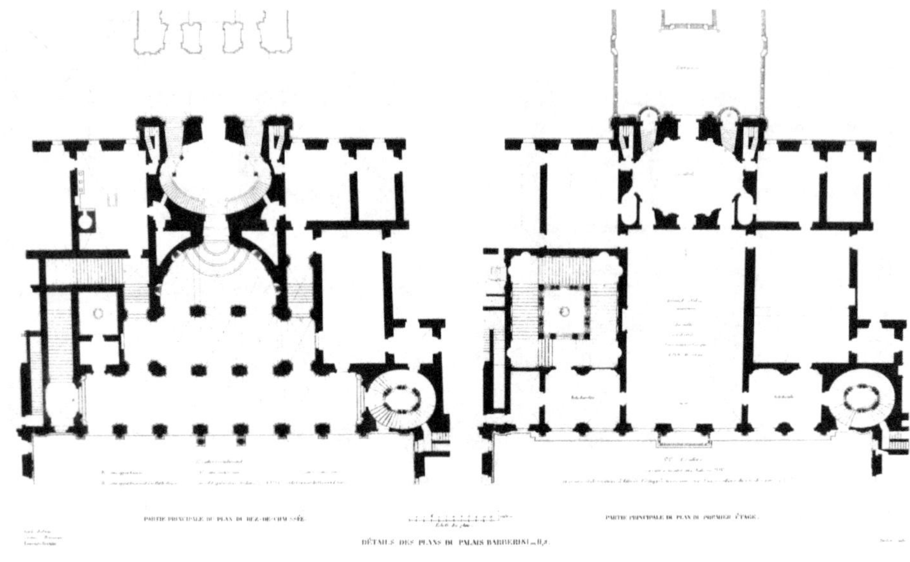

Letarouilly's plans of the ground floor and piano nobile of Palazzo Barberini in their final form

remain the palace's sole major occupant when the south wing was completed.

When Urban died in 1644 his family were very vulnerable. Their nepotistic greed had gone too far, even by the standards of the day, and the War of Castro, which Urban had launched against the Duke of Parma and Piacenza (with the hope of appropriating the Dukedom of Castro for Taddeo) had been a disastrous failure. The new pope Innocent X hated the Barberini and threatened a formal enquiry into the financing of the war. In October 1645 Cardinal Antonio fled Rome disguised as a charcoal seller, and sought the protection of Cardinal Mazarin in France. Prudently, he had assigned Palazzo Barberini to the King of France, and it became the residence of the French ambassador. In January 1646 Cardinal Francesco and Prince Taddeo followed their brother to Paris, allegedly disguised as a poor priest and a huntsman.[9] Taddeo died in France but Cardinal Francesco was able to return to Rome as early as February 1648. Cardinal Antonio, however, did not come back and repossess his palace from the French ambassador until July 1653, and even then he did not stay long before moving on to Palazzo Bonelli (Valentini).

Palazzo Barberini was left for the use of various younger members of the family until the 1670s when Cardinal Francesco paid for major modifications. Some of the changes in the interior were precipitated by his needing to find display space for Cardinal Antonio's enormous art collection that he had inherited, but the most obvious change was the cutting of a carriage-way through the atrium and up a ramp to the garden at the back. This destroyed the closed

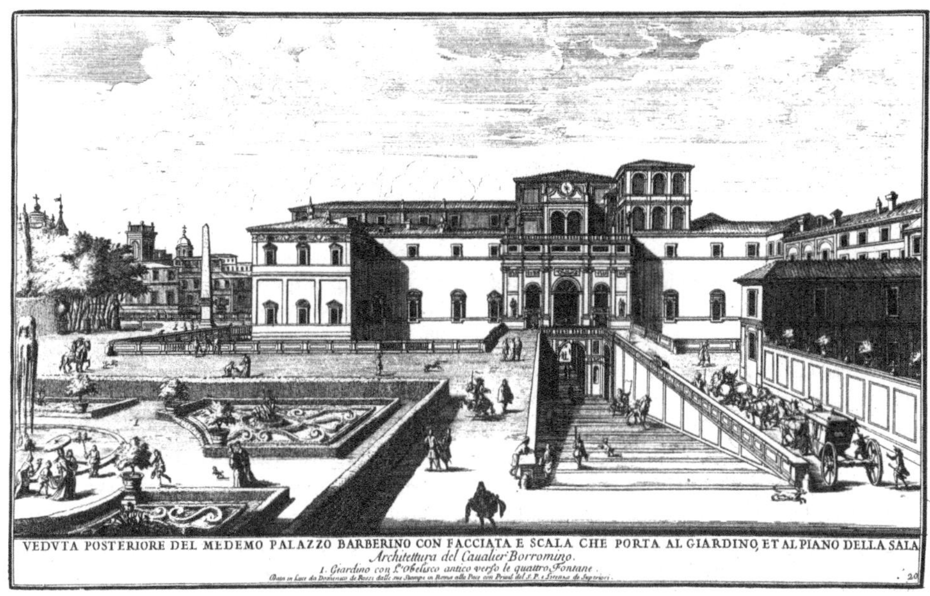

Specchi's print of the back of Palazzo Barberini, showing the passage beneath the palace and the ramp into the garden that were made in the 1670s

character of the atrium, enabled a visitor to drive straight through and ascend by a staircase below the oval salone, and overrode the balance between the approaches to the three official suites that had been implicit in Maderno's plan. In 1865-7 the approach was changed again. The wall which separated the palace from via delle Quattro Fontane was pulled down and replaced by the existing piers and railings. This effectively elevated the west-facing atrium and loggia to the status of a principal entrance front, which was something that the palace had avoided until that date.

THE INVOLVEMENT OF MADERNO, BORROMINI, BERNINI AND CORTONA

Many people contributed to the three years of discussion in which the palace was conceived, and it is misleading to think of a single designer. There is no doubt, however, that Maderno was the architect who was officially in charge, though most of the drawings are from the hand of his relative Borromini. When Maderno died in 1629 he was replaced by Bernini, who also succeeded him as architect to St Peter's. Borromini was disappointed at seeing the latter job go to Bernini, but he nevertheless agreed to work as Bernini's assistant on the palace, as he had done for Maderno. At this time Bernini had far less experience of building than did Borromini, who had previously worked for him on the St Peter's baldacchino. For four years the two men worked closely together on the palace, drawing inspiration from each other and often both putting their hands to the same drawings. Collaboration between such strong and disparate characters could hardly endure, however, and at around the end of 1632 Borromini left the project, feeling that he had been given insufficient recognition. His departure was also probably stimulated by his discovery that Bernini had been secretly taking a cut from building funds destined for St Peter's.[10]

Against that background, a search for rigidly compartmentalised attributions would be futile. Nevertheless, there are some attributions that have become so conventional that they have to be mentioned. Either side of the centrepiece of the entrance front, at the top mezzanine level, are the two famous windows that use the trademark Borrominian device of canting forward the side elements of the pediment, and also incorporate at the sides the 'ear' motif that would be widely taken up in the Roman barocchetto style. These extraordinary windows, often cited as being among the first manifestations of the Baroque, were traditionally attributed to Borromini alone but the modern view is that they represent a fusion of the inputs of Borromini and Bernini.[11] Borromini may also have had a hand in the final design of the false perspective windows in the top floor of the loggia, which are derived from Maderno's doorway to the staircase in Palazzo Mattei di Giove. For most of the details of doors, fireplaces etc., the final decisions seem fairly clearly to have been taken by Bernini, but he apparently left Borromini a substantially free hand with the doors in the corners of the great salone.[12] Like the famous mezzanine windows, these have characteristically Borrominian canted side elements. The central pavilion on the garden façade probably represents Bernini's modification of Maderno's composition (though the two balconies manifestly belong to the revisions of the 1670s — see below). It was always stated that the square staircase in the north wing was designed by Bernini, and all the early sources also say that the oval one in the south wing is by Borromini. The oval staircase is, however, basically just an adaptation of the one by Mascarino in the Quirinale palace, and it was built under Bernini's supervision after Borromini had left the project.[13] According to Sir Philip Skippon, who saw them in 1663, both staircases were then open to the sky.[14] The oval one, however, has long been topped with a cupola.

Pietro da Cortona's main contribution to the palace was to be the painting of the great salone, but he was also employed on the design of some of the ancillary structures (see below). According to his nephew Luca Berrettini he also made plans for the entire palace that were rejected on grounds of cost, and Cortona's surviving drawings for the west front indicate that he was already developing a distinctive architectural voice of his own.[15] Additionally, Blunt believed that two windows on each side of the central pavilion on the palace's garden front might be by Cortona as their unusual design reappears in his stucco decoration of the Sala di Venere in Palazzo Pitti, Florence.*

*The windows are illustrated at De Rossi, I, pl. 50, (reproduced p. 20) where they are attributed to Borromini. They have round pediments with triangular pediments immediately superimposed and resemble the pediments above Cortona's stucco cartouches on the short walls of the Sale di Venere. In noting the resemblance, Blunt commented that the 'very unusual combination of curved and straight pediments [is] not to be found in either Bernini or Borromini'.[16] It must be recorded that Blunt's suggestion of Cortona as the windows' author does not seem to have caught on: Merz, for example, ignores the suggested attribution.

Opposite: An engraving from De Rossi's Architettura Civile *showing one of the two celebrated windows designed by Borromini and Bernini on the west front of Palazzo Barberini*

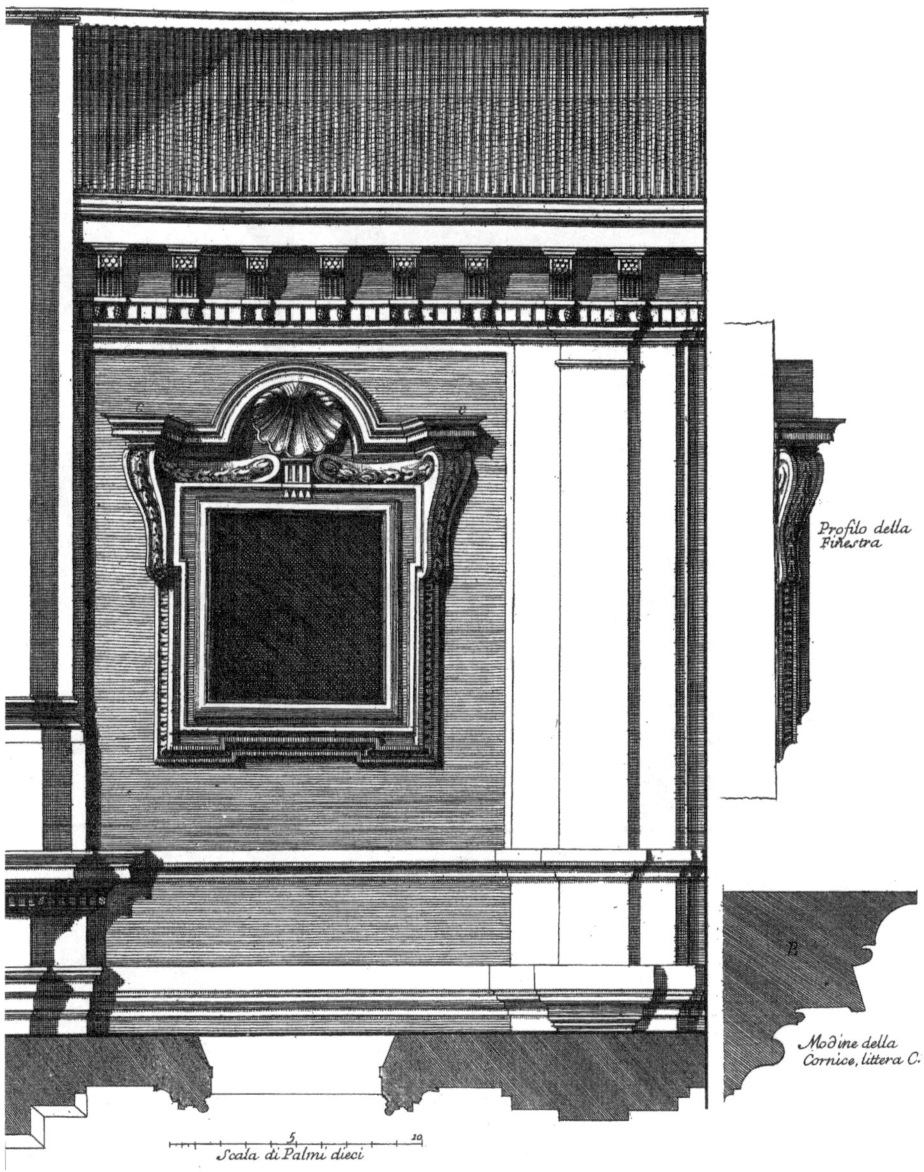

Profilo della Finestra
Modine della Cornice, littera C.
Scala di Palmi dieci

Profilo
Menzola
D
Scala di Palmi due per li Modini A. B. C. D.
C
Scala di Palmi dieci
Modine dello stipito della Porta
Modine della Base
A
B
Modine del Capitello
Porta del Teatro delle Commedie del Palazzo Barberino del Sig.re Prencipe di Pelestrina.
Architettura del Cavalier Pietro Berrettini da Cortona.
Nella Stamp.a di Dom.co de Rossi erede di Gio. Giac.o de Rossi in Roma alla Pace, con Priuil.o
52

Cortona was also responsible for the garden entrance gate in via XX settembre, immediately adjoining the Quattro Fontane,* and for the wall that sealed off the east end of the Cortile della Cavallerizza (see above). This had a fine doorway and four hanging mezzanine windows.† Cortona's five-bay composition did not remain for long as a freestanding wall, however, since it was soon used as one side of the Barberini theatre when this was built in 1637. The building one now sees in via Barberini is not the original theatre but one of the pastiches that were built in the 1930s to replace buildings lost in the road widening schemes of those years. It is, in fact, a compressed version of the theatre, built by Marcello Piacentini on part of the original site in 1932, and incorporating Cortona's doorway (at via Barberini 22) together with the mezzanine windows pressed together rather more closely.[19] Blunt also thought it safe to attribute to Cortona the large square doorway on the north face of the palace, immediately next to Piacentini's building, and he took the view that while 'the architrave round the door is without exact parallel in [Cortona's] work, [it] is in accordance with his method of designing in various layers, one superimosed on the other'. Merz, however, finds that 'the stylistic evidence is not convincing'.[20]

* Cortona designed both the frame for the fountain at the Barberini corner of the Quattro Fontane and the garden entrance gate which is the first doorway on the left along via XX settembre from the fountain. Both of these, and especially the gate, suffer horribly from being incorporated in a dispiriting 1930s office building.

† There is a similar arrangement of hanging windows in the short sides of the great central salone. As with so many features of Palazzo Barberini, some cross-current of influence between the two uses of the device appears quite possible. Although Pietro da Cortona is always credited with the design of the door and windows in the Cortile della Cavallerizza, the master drawing for the work is by the hand of Borromini.[18]

INTERIOR

The palace is occupied by the Galleria Nazionale d'Arte Antica, which includes highly important pictures of the Baroque period. For many years the Galleria was confined to the great central salone and the upper parts of the north wing, while the rest of the palace was occupied by an officers' club, the Circolo delle Forze Armate. In 2005 the Circolo began moving out and the Galleria started taking over the space made available. Turning the whole palace into a museum will be a major programme that will take many years.

The Galleria Nazionale has not only expanded its exhibition area and installed an inviting new hang of its paintings. It now does an exemplary job of providing visitors with information about both the building and the collections, with information panels in the main rooms and an interactive welcome display in the first room on the ground floor.[21] Although a visitor may wish to begin by looking at the welcome display, the following account deals with the piano nobile before the ground floor.

The door by Pietro da Cortona that was originally made for the screen wall of the Cortile della Cavallerizza at Palazzo Barberini, and was soon incorporated into the theatre that was established on the site. The door is now to be seen at Via Barberini, 22. This engraving comes from De Rossi's Architettura Civile

Hercules chasing away the Harpies to enable Justice and Plenty to come to the aid of the poor; *an episode from Pietro da Cortona's great ceiling in the salone of Palazzo Barberini. This engraving comes from a set by Bloemaert, Greuter and Cungio that was published by G. G. De Rossi around 1677, but which was originally made to accompany Girolamo Teti's* Ædes Barberinæ ad Quirinalem *of 1642*

PIANO NOBILE:
THE PIETRO DA CORTONA ROOM

The vault of the great central salone was decorated between 1632 and 1639 with a vast fresco by Pietro da Cortona of an iconographical programme, devised in consultation with the poet Francesco Bracciolini, celebrating Urban as the agent of divine providence, a theme that recurs throughout the decorations of the north wing. The action of the central scene may be summarised as Divine Providence instructing Immortality (with a diadem) to crown the emblems of Urban the Supreme Pontiff, while Rome simultaneously places the papal tiara over the Barberini bees, which are surrounded by Religion and the three Theological Virtues. On the cove are personifications and classical scenes indicating Urban's virtuous qualities.

This hugely important, exuberant fresco is one of the great triumphs of Roman Baroque painting and much has been written on its illusionism and its glowing Venetian colour. In fact, Cortona probably repainted substantial parts of the fresco after his visit to Venice in 1637.[22] In formal terms the illusionistic scheme is markedly different from earlier ceilings, such as Annibale Carracci's Farnese gallery, which rely on quadri riportati and on feigning a structure that seems to break through the real ceiling. Here the armature that divides the scenes appears to approximate to the line of the real ceiling, with some scenes apparently taking place in the space of the room itself, and with all the transitions blurred by the sheer elaboration of the imagined structure and the seductive depiction of the various materials of which it is made. The entire rhetorical outpouring of novel devices can be seen as the visual counterpart of the type of poetry that Urban VIII himself wrote, and which contributed much to the construction of his self-image.[23]

THE OVAL ROOM

The vaulted oval room between the great salone and the garden front was completed by 1639 and its niches were furnished with four classical statues and four busts, symmetrically arranged across the short axis. It was a private space and entering it after the exuberant public area of the great salone is still a strangely moving experience, since it renounces painted decoration and relies for its effect on the classical simplicity of its decoration and the clarity with which its volume is defined. The articulation is by pilasters with Ionic capitals and the plain vault is set back markedly behind the architrave. The overall effect is of calm, and grave serenity – entirely suitable for the literary discussions that Cardinal Antonio held here. In the 1930s the room provided the setting for something much more sinister – Mussolini's formal commitment to provide military assistance to Franco's rebels in Spain.*

The plan, with entrances on the short axis, was a remarkable innovation for a domestic building. Its origins here are somewhat mysterious. The idea first appears in an anonymous memorandum of sug-gestions of around 1627[24] where it is incorporated in the description of a conventional design around a courtyard. Although overall planning soon proceeded in much more novel directions, the feature of the oval room had evidently taken root, and it appears in preparatory drawings by Borromini before being incorporated in Maderno's final plans.[25] Although there is no documentation, it is perfectly possible that Bernini influenced the inclusion of the feature; indeed, it was the oval room more than any other item that led Howard Hibbard to argue that Bernini's 'exclusion from the game of designing Palazzo Barberini would have been extraordinary'.[26] Whoever may have conceived the basic idea, the detailing of the interior must certainly have been worked up while Bernini was in general charge after Maderno's death, and he must surely have been keenly interested in a room that was so unusual and in such an important position. Much later in his career Bernini was to revert to the oval layout at S Andrea al Quirinale, and the basic idea of an oval entered on the short axis is also, of course, fundamental to the colonnades before St Peter's.

Given the uncertainty about the room's

* Oral communication to the author by the administrator of the Circolo delle Forze Armate. While the Circolo was in residence the oval room continued to be furnished with the oval conference table and chairs with fascist emblems that Franco had sent Mussolini to mark his gratitude.

inception and the lack of early documentation, there is room for debate about the precise way in which the architecture was meant to convey philosophical messages. However, the room's coolly intellectual statement is in such striking contrast with the surrounding context that it is hard to believe that nothing of the kind was intended. In his *Ædes Barberinæ ad Quirinalem* of 1642 Gerolamo Teti — a learned publicist for the Barberini — wrote that the room's oval form, its whiteness and its reliance on sculpture rather than painting constituted an emulation of eternity itself.[27] The salone door into the oval room has a relief of the Medusa-bearing ægis of Minerva, goddess of wisdom, who can be seen quelling the barbarous giants in Cortona's ceiling immediately above.* The storks that also appear in the relief were birds sacred to Apollo.[28]

THE PIANO NOBILE ROOMS IN THE NORTH WING

The Barberini/Colonna arms over the doorway to the apartment in the north wing show that this was the boundary of Princess Anna's apartment, while the corresponding doorway to the south wing, on the far side of the Pietro da Cortona room, has the arms of Cardinal Antonio.† The normal entrance to Princess Anna's apartment was, however, via the door in the northwest corner of the great central salone,[29] so that the 17th century visitor would end, rather than start, with Princess Anna's audience chamber, which was the room that now has the 18th century ceiling painting by Pécheux (see below). For convenience, the following notes proceed in the reverse direction.

As soon as one enters the north wing it is apparent that, in the haste to enable Taddeo and Anna to move in, the Barberini retained many of the ceiling paintings that had been done under the Sforza. The four rooms to one's left as one enters are, in fact, part of an extension completed by the Sforza to provide accommodation for Mario Sforza and Renée de Lorraine-Mayenne who married in 1612. The ceilings depicting the *Flood* and *Noah and his Sons* are by Antonio Viviani, while those depicting *Abraham and God* and *Abraham and the Three Angels* are probably by assistants working under Viviani's oversight. The lilies and dolphins in the frame of *Abraham and the Three Angels* refer to the families of Sforza and Lorraine.[30]

The larger room at which one entered was also part of the Sforza extension, and was also frescoed by Viviani. His ceiling representing the *Creation of the World* was, however, first repainted in the early 18th century and then replaced around 1770 by the present oil painting by Laurent Pécheux,

* The relief was designed by Bernini. One small point in its interpretion is that the storks are biting Medusa's snaky locks, rather than just supporting the ægis. Traditionally, a stork killing a snake was an emblem of virtue overcoming vice, and perhaps that meaning is alluded to here, in addition to the dominant Apollonian association discussed by Scott.[29]

† It is worth noting that the entrances to both apartments are surrounded by feigned perspective framing and that this device is carried round all the walls of the lobbies that lie between the central salone and the apartments. This is surely a deliberate echo of the famous feigned perspective loggia windows on the exterior of the second floor, immediately above. The device also occurs at the ends of the open atrium at ground level.

Opposite: Another engraving from De Rossi's Architettura Civile *showing the door leading from the great salone of Palazzo Barberini into the oval room at the back of the building, with Bernini's relief of storks supporting Minerva's shield*

after lightning had struck the room above. (The elaborate surround by Michelangelo Ricciolini is a survival from the early 18th century work.) The Viviani ceiling may nevertheless have influenced the Barberini in their choice of themes for the rest of Princess Anna's apartment.

This is especially obvious in the next room, to the right, with a ceiling by Andrea Camassei (a protégé of Taddeo Barberini) depicting the *Creation of the Angels*. This follows naturally from the *Creation of the World* but also provides a further variation on the theme of the Barberini family's predestined greatness, since several other Barberini commissions support the cult of angels and Urban VIII chose the feast of S Michael and All Angels for the day of his coronation.[31]

Camassei's effort to support the family's self-promotion was formally quite conservative. Not so the next room, Princess Anna's salotto, which is decorated with Andrea Sacchi's strange *Divina Sapienza* (1629-31), showing the terrestrial globe floating in an open sky peopled with delicately painted personifications and featuring arcane astrological references and symbols of the Barberini. Both the abstract subject of divine wisdom and the austere treatment of it by Sacchi (who was to be championed by Cardinal Antonio) are most unusual; a contemporary note makes it clear that the purpose was to show that, since the Barberini family were elected to rule the church as God's vicar on earth, they governed with divine wisdom. The stucco frieze is packed with family symbols including strange mutating Daphne-like figures that Scott believes could only have been devised by Bernini.[32] Leading off the salotto is a small chapel (recently restored) that was frescoed (1631-32) by Cortona and assistants. It was Cortona's success here that gained him the commission for the great salone, which was to be as different from Sacchi's conceptual rigour as it is possible to imagine.

The ceiling of the next room depicts *Scenes from the Story of Joseph* amidst typical late 16th century decoration. This is manifestly work that was done for the Sforza, as proclaimed by their heraldic devices in the corners.[33] The figure of Clemency holds an open book bearing the name of the painter Baldassare Croce, but Scott, who dates the ceiling to about 1585, considers that only the eight personified *Virtues* in the corners are by Croce and that the rest was done by a team of painters including N. Circignani (Pomarancio).[34]

Princess Anna's main apartment ended at this point, and the next group of rooms along the north wing comprised a small garden apartment for her use in the summer. The first of these rooms was later given a classicising ceiling of the *Chariot of the Sun* by G. B. Chiari on the occasion of a Pignatelli/Barberini marriage of 1693, with a stucco frieze displaying the emblems of both families. Beyond this room there is a little gallery decorated by Cortona and assistants before 1632. This includes a fresco by Romanelli of the *Founding of Praeneste*, that is to say Palestrina, the principality that had recently been acquired by Taddeo. At the opposite end of the gallery is a *Sacrifice to Juno* by Gimignani.[35] Next to the gallery are two rooms with very dilapidated ceilings by Croce.

THE GROUND FLOOR

The part of the ground floor that is now open as part of the Galleria Nazionale is the set of rooms occupying the whole of the north wing that formed Prince Taddeo's apartment. After the splendid architecture and painting on the piano nobile, it all looks rather subdued.

One enters the apartment in a large salotto in the middle of the wing, immediately under the room of Sacchi's *Divina Sapienza* on the floor above. The ceilings of both rooms show an airy view of the open sky, but the resemblance stops there, as the ceiling of Taddeo's room (by Simone Lagi and Agostino Tassi) has no deep intentions but is a routine piece enlivened with birds and surrounded by a quadratura balustrade on which monkeys and peacocks are playing. Most of the remaining rooms in the apartment have ceilings with elaborate stucco frames bearing Sforza emblems; the paintings within them are interesting iconographically but not of very high quality.

The sequence of rooms running west (left) from the salotto, towards via delle Quattro Fontane, was frescoed by Giovanni Domenico Marziani and Andrea Camassei with ceilings depicting stories from classical mythology. Jennifer Montagu has shown that these were drawn from an exhortatory ode to virtue that Urban had written in 1613-14 and dedicated to the future Cardinal Francesco.[36] None of them survives in its original form, since Camassei's Parnassus has been lost and in 1678 Cardinal Francesco had the rest of the series replaced and extended (still on the theme of Urban's ode). The existing paintings are *Ulysses and the Sirens* by Giacinto Camassei; *Bellerophon slaying the Chimera* and *Jason and the Argonauts* by Giuseppe Passeri; and *Theseus and Ariadne* by Urbano Romanelli.

At the opposite (east) end of the ground floor, Taddeo retained three ceiling frescoes that had been executed for the Sforza at around the turn of the 16th century. These are *Minerva, Apollo and the Muses on Mount Helicon* from the circle of the Cavaliere d'Arpino, and *Orpheus Charming Wild Beasts* and *Orpheus and Eurydice* both probably by Camillo Spallucci. The last room that is open to the public is the Sala delle Colonne, with a large wall-fountain (1653) with a figure of *Bacchus* on the garden side, and four polished antique grey granite columns introduced at the time of Cardinal Francesco's alterations.

THE SOUTH WING

Cardinal Antonio's side of the palace is entered through the enormous Sala dei Marmi, alongside the great central salone. As the name implies, the Barberini used this to display their statuary, and it was also used for theatricals and other events. It is a bleak room with virtally no decoration.

As explained above, the Galleria Nazionale is engaged in a rolling programme of expansion into the South wing, and this account will not try to keep up to date with it. From an architectural point of view, the interior of the South wing cannot compare with the riches in the rest of the palace. The top floor was radically changed in the third quarter of the 18th century for the accommodation of Cornelia Costanza Colonna. The lower floors still contain some 17th century features, but were heavily altered in the 19th century. By far the most interesting feature is Borromini's spiral staircase, described above.

GARDENS

The remaining fragment of the once-famous gardens has recently been refurbished. It is well worth walking through the central passage, to see the pavilion at the back of the palace and to understand the changes made by Cardinal Francesco in the 1670s. The passage incorporates a space under the oval room, with two secondary stairways on either side.

Immediately facing you as you emerge into the garden is an ungainly fountain incorporating a huge classical torso that was transformed into an *Apollo* by Gioseppe Giorgetti and Lorenzo Ottoni in 1677. This originally stood on the very edge of the estate, and the view that one had of it from vicolo S Nicola da Tolentino (then vicolo Sterrato) became one of the famous 19th century images of Romantic Rome.[37] It was moved to its present site against the wall of Palazzina Savorgnan di Brazzà when that building was erected in 1936. Cardinal Francesco's intention in so privileging a representation of Apollo was presumably to make a statement about the palace's rôle as a home of learning and the arts, in the same way that Carlo Cardelli had placed a statue of Apollo in his palace in 1654.[38]

Finally, there is the 'ruined bridge' that was built in 1678 to connect the south flank of the palace to the garden, across the dry moat that was then being widened as part of Cardinal Francesco's improvements. It can easily be seen to the right of the palace as one enters from via delle Quattro Fontane (and in the print by Specchi on p. 57). This famously witty conceit purports to be a ruined structure made out of classical *spoglie*, with the arch nearer to the palace being left incomplete so that the walkway was carried on a wooden drawbridge. Virtually all writers on the palace have followed the early sources in attributing the bridge to Bernini but Patricia Waddy points out[39] that Bernini's name does not appear in any of the records of Cardinal Francesco's building work of the 1670s (which was executed under the supervision of the 'house' architect Angelo Torrone) and she suggests that once the idea of the conceit had been formed in the circle around the cardinal no great architectural expertise would have been required to turn it into stone.

Palazzi Bernini

Via della Mercede, 11 and 12A

Bernini came to Rome in 1606, and lived for many years with his parents at via Liberiana 24. After his father's death in 1629 he moved to S Marta, near St Peter's. He married in 1639, bought these two buildings from the marchesa Fulvia Naro in 1641, and moved in during 1642. (Via Liberiana was, incidentally, lowered by several metres in the late 19th century, so that the original entrance to the Bernini building is now high above street level.[1])

Bernini lived, worked and died in the building at via della Mercede, 11, which is an authentic 17th century building, albeit heavily restored. It has a reticulated door-case, three windows and three rimesse on the ground floor, and two tiers of plain windows set on string-courses above. The storey above the cornice is modern. Within there are two 17th century murals honouring Bernini, and a fresco of *Jupiter and Vulcan*. Altogether, the palace is a sober affair, in great contrast with Borromini's nearby Propaganda Fide and S Andrea della Fratte.*

The neighbouring building at 12A was let out by Bernini and was never his residence. It was totally rebuilt in the 19th century and a monument erroneously stating that Bernini had lived and worked there was placed on it in 1898. The hotel that now occupies the third floor is named the 'Historic Bernini House Hotel' which seems calculated to give a fillip to the confusion.

* Blunt speculated 'it must have been galling for Bernini when in the 1650s his rival Borromini, whose architecture he hated, erected immediately facing his palace two of his most eccentric buildings, the dome and tower of S Andrea della Fratte and the Collegio di Propaganda Fide, the latter of which involved pulling down Bernini's chapel.' (Blunt *Guide*, p. 166)

Falda's print of Piazza dell'Orologio, facing Borromini's clock-tower with Palazzo Boncompagni Corcos on the left and Palazzo del Banco di S Spirito on the right. Palazzo Capponi now stands on the site of the building on the extreme left. For another view by Falda see p. 55

Palazzo Boncompagni Corcos (Scarinci)

Via del Governo Vecchio, 3

The rich Jewish banking family of Corcos added Boncompagni — the family name of Gregory XIII — when Lazzaro Corcos was baptised in 1581. They moved in high circles, with eminent cardinals acting as godparents at their christenings, and they were devoted to the Oratorians of the Chiesa Nuova, where most of them were buried. Pietro Boncompagni Corcos fully shared this devotion. He commissioned from Algardi the statue of S Filippo Neri that is now in the sacristry of the Chiesa Nuova and when he decided to build himself a fine palace he naturally chose to use the site very close to the Oratory where his family already owned some property. The building must have taken place between 1645, when a licence was issued for the main door, and 1658, when a final licence was issued to authorise the façade.

Pietro employed the young G. A. De Rossi to unify the existing buildings and erect new façades on Piazza dell'Orologio and via degli Orsini, and he produced an extremely elegant building. The doorway (with Boncompagni dragons sitting on top of Doric columns) is a fine piece, and a few further dragons decorate the cornice. The windows of the piano nobile have silenus heads under heavy semicircular hood-moulds, while those of the second floor are a notably effective design that features female heads within complex shapes that are an elegant derivation from Borromini. (For the energy of the genuine article one has only to glance immediately opposite at Borromini's Torre dell'Orologio which, incidentally, caused Pietro Boncompagni to attempt a legal action against the Oratorians for blocking his view.[1]) The long side on via degli Orsini has exactly the same system but without a main entrance to interrupt the shops at street level. The cortile is an elegantly managed space that features coupled columns of coloured marble with Ionic capitals. Its effect owes a good deal to its unexpectedly small scale.

The restoration of the early 2000s[2] revealed a comprehensive scheme of interior decoration in mostly good condition. In addition to a *Triumph of Bacchus and Ariadne* in the vault of the main salone there is a series of rooms along via degli Orsini with ceilings and friezes of personifications and classical stories, and also a chapel. All of this was carried out by Carlo Cesi, presumably in the years immediately following 1658. Cesi had worked with Pietro da Cortona and he was completely au fait with all the decorative cycles in Rome as he made his living from doing engraved reproductions of them. The salone ceiling is the most finished performance here, but the friezes of classical stories have a genuine charm. It is touching to see the supreme elegance of Guido Reni's *Atalanta and Hippomenes*, for example, translated into this homely idiom.

Palazzo Boncompagni Ludovisi (Cerasi)

Via del Babuino, 49-52

Fontana del Babuino

This palace, arranged round a courtyard and incorporating various earlier buildings, was built in 1738 by the enormously rich Princess Maria Eleonora Boncompagni Ludovisi, who was heiress to both the papal families whose names she bore. With its even distribution of windows and stucco ornamant over the façade and the elegant little ringhiere at the upper mezzanine, it has much in common with the speculative bourgeois residential property of the time, but Varagnoli shows that none of it was actually let out, that the first and second floors were arranged as traditional piani nobili and the mezzanine was for the 'famiglia bassa' or servant corps. In fact the Princess built it to fulfil her 'capriccio' of wanting a Roman dower-house of her own, despite owning the Ludovisi family's famous property at Porta Pinciana. Elling guessed that the architect may have been Domenico Gregorini,[1] but it could have been any one of the architects whom the Princess employed, including Ameli, who built the via del Plebiscito façade of Palazzo Doria-Pamphili, which also reflects a fusion of noble and bourgeois architectural traditions.

The seven, very slightly projecting, central bays of the thirteen-bay façade are accentuated with rustication and barocchetto windows but the memorable feature is the pair of openings with heavily rusticated surrounds and pediments that feature, on the right, the Boncompagni dragon and, on the left, a pair of fine twisting dolphins. (The dragon is in stucco, while the dolphins are in travertine.) The imitation of natural rock in these doorways is reminiscent of Bernini's use of this motif in Palazzo Montecitorio and Elling speculates that this may be a deliberate reference, since that palace was originally built for the Ludovisi.

In the cortile, lined up with the central entrance, there is a niche fountain including a stucco statue of *Diana as Huntress* by Bernardino Cametti. This is an almost full-size modello for Cametti's highly-finished marble in the Bode Museum, Berlin.[2]

The rusticated opening with dolphins originally functioned as the surround of a niche that contained a piece that was both coarser and more famous than Cametti's suave figure. This was the Fontana del Babuino, which consisted of a satyr reclining on a rock beneath which water flowed into an antique granite rectangular basin. It had been made in the 1570s as part of the deal whereby the then owner of the site, Alessandro Grandi, obtained a concession of water from the Acqua Vergine. The grotesquely maladroit carving of the satyr immediately earned it the sobriquet of 'babuino' (ie baboon), and this became the usual name for the whole street as early as the 1580s. The figure also became one of Rome's *statue parlanti*, and the satirical verses attached to it were given their own name of 'babuinate' corresponding to the 'pasquinate' associated with the more famous Pasquino statue.

In 1887 the fountain was dismantled because of sewerage works in the area; the granite basin was taken to the fountain of Julius III on via Flaminia, while the 'baboon' was set up in the cortile of the palace. In 1957, following a campaign by local historians, the pieces were reunited and erected as a functioning fountain on the other side of the street between the Studio Tadolini and S Atanasio dei Greci.

Palazzo Borghese

Largo Fontanella di Borghese, 19

Palazzo Borghese is by far the most important private palace built in Rome in the period between Palazzo Farnese and Palazzo Barberini. Its harpsichord-shaped groundplan has inspired the nickname 'il cembalo' at least since the time of Milizia, and it has always been reckoned a major landmark. While most of the exterior architecture is a rather awkward reflection of the building's 16th century origins and of the exigencies of the site, the interior includes exceptional

Palazzo Borghese: Two bays of the main court as seen in Tempesta's map of 1593

features of the Baroque period. However, the palace, still owned by the Borghese family, is divided up between several private occupants and is difficult of access. As a result it is still perhaps not as well known as it deserves, although it has been given significant scholarly attention following Hibbard's ground-breaking work in the archives.[1]

EARLY HISTORY

In 1560 Monsignor Tommaso del Giglio bought a building plot on what is now the south east end of the palace, facing the Largo Fontanella di Borghese, and in 1566 it was recorded that building was in progress on the site. Del Giglio's activities were interrupted by absences from Rome but at the time of his death in 1578 the entrance block of the palace was mainly built (though still unroofed) and the court had been begun. In 1586 the palace was bought by the Spanish Cardinal Pedro Deza, who set about completing the building under the direction of Martino Longhi the Elder. At Deza's death in 1600 Flaminio Ponzio was in charge,[2] the right wing had been built along

Specchi's view of Palazzo Borghese from the east, with the Palazzo della Famiglia Borghese facing it across the piazza

via di Monte d'Oro and the court was still unfinished. The Deza arms on the keystones show that five bays of the court arcades had been completed by then on both the entrance side and the via di Monte d'Oro side, but that only one bay was standing on the western side.

There has been much dispute about the architects involved in the del Giglio phase, and the extent to which the present court design was established in that period. Hibbard proposed in 1962 that Vignola could have been the architect of both the entrance façade and the court. While more recent opinion (see Fumagalli) seems solidly behind Longhi as the architect of the court, the authorship of the façade — which was later to dictate the elevation of the entire palace — remains uncertain.

The façade is in fact a rather tentative piece of mid-16th century design with mezzanine windows above the main windows on all three floors and articulation by means of modest pilaster strips, with shallow rustication (bugnato liscio) on the ground floor and the upper two floors of the outermost bays. The piano nobile windows have alternate triangular pediments and semicircular tympana, while the portal is a simple but grand structure of two detached columns and a square balcony above a metope and triglyph frieze. The court, on the other hand, is a highly original yet completely confident design with two storeys of arcades carried on coupled columns, Doric below and Ionic above. Such a use of double columns in line with the arcade seems to have been unprecedented in Rome, though Longhi had already employed it in the upper arcade of a cloister at S Croce, Bosco Marengo (Piedmont).

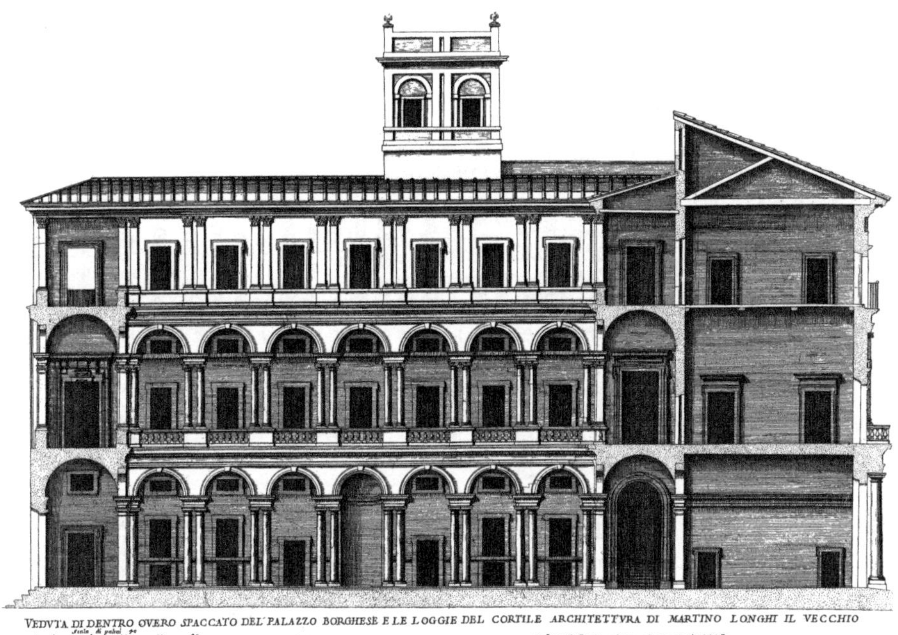

Palazzo Borghese: cross-section by Falda, showing the twin-column system that Martino Longhi the Elder used for the court

THE BORGHESE; 1605-1631

In February 1605 the palace was bought by Cardinal Camillo Borghese, to whose family it has belonged ever since, save for the years 1891-1911. Cardinal Camillo was elected Pope Paul V three months after the purchase and in December of the same year he gave the palace to his two brothers, Giovan Battista and Francesco, though he would continue to take a close personal interest and to contribute hugely to the expenditure.[3] From this point on we are on firmer historical ground and it is certain that Flaminio Ponzio (who had been appointed papal architect) was the superintending architect for the project's next phase.

Francesco and his family were squeezed into the existing entrance block straightaway but the favoured brother Giovan Battista and his household had to wait until the palace could be substantially expanded for them in a building campaign that went on until mid 1608, followed by two years of internal decoration, all of which the pope financed by raising the tax on pork.[4] In the event, Giovan Battista died in 1609, lamenting that his life was ending just as his palace was being finished.

For this rapid expansion Ponzio ran up thirteen bays along Piazza Borghese leading to the Tiber, using a simplified version of the original façade design, without the contrast provided by the rustication, and with a portal copied from the one in the del Giglio façade, albeit without the heraldic emblems that decorate the metopes in the original.

Specchi's print of the western aspect of Palazzo Borghese. Nearest the spectator is Rainaldi's viewing gallery, with the hanging garden immediately behind it. Between the first and second windows to the left of the viewing gallery is the opening for the prospettiva which gave a view across the Ripetta on the bank of the Tiber

Initially there seems to have been some idea of extending the via Monte d'Oro façade to make the palace roughly symmetrical around the original entrance, but this was dropped before the end of 1607 when it was decided to extend the new wing yet further towards the Tiber by incorporating the neighbouring Palazzo Farnese-Poggio, owned by one Enea Orlandini. That modest building now formed the core of a further nine-bay extension, with the break between the two sections still clearly marked by quoins running the full height of the building. At this point in the process, it would have been very difficult indeed to re-cast the entire façade in a unified form and Ponzio simply unrolled more of the existing elevation, which was quite inadequate to control the great length that the façade now attained. Furthermore, nothing could disguise the fact that the latest addition was angled slightly away from the line of the rest of the new wing on Piazza Borghese. This distortion of the façade was reflected in many rooms within and an avviso of July 1608[5] records the pope's dissatisfaction.

Ponzio was more successful elsewhere and especially in the court, where he made two significant innovations. First, he lengthened by two bays the east and west sides of what had been envisaged as a five-bay square, to create a rectangle that on its long axis linked the original main entrance with the garden at the back. Second, and in pursuit of the same dynamic idea, the upper floor of the side of the court opposite the entrance was left as an open arcade on both sides so as to form a 'bridge-loggia' that individuated this side of the court, let in the light, and provided a splendid approach to the garden beyond. All in all, the combination of Longhi's original design and Ponzio's modifications produced a tremendous success, which has always been greatly celebrated. There have, however, been two significant changes that pull in contrary directions. First, the upper arcades on the three sides of the court that are now closed and glazed were originally left open. Second, there was originally just one door in the centre bay of the ground floor of the bridge-loggia, with the outer bays closed on the garden side by sham windows; it was only in the second half of the 19th century that the arcade was made entirely open. Amongst other things, that change privileged the visual impact of two of the three colossal antique statues that Paul V obtained from the Canons of S Salvatore in Lauro and gave to Giovan Battista in 1608.

Ponzio's other notable contribution in this phase was the oval staircase at the back of the new wing, near the north-west corner of the court and approximately in line with the quoins that mark the end of the initial 13-bay unit. This was directly modelled on Mascarino's famous staircase in the Quirinale and the way in which this pedigree is emphasised in an avviso[6] suggests that the feature may have been included, at least in part, as a deliberate allusion to the palace's papal status.

Between 1612 and 1614 the new extension was completed at ground-floor level by a three-bay trapezoid addition overlooking the river-port at the Ripetta. This was aligned at a yet steeper angle from the original façade on the piazza and included a

Palazzo Borghese: Letarouilly's print of the cortile, seen from the main entrance

hanging garden bounded by a balustrade with energetically carved Borghese dragons and eagles. At the river end the balustrade protrudes to form a balcony supported by three fine brackets; below the balcony there was originally a grand entrance, but that was obliterated by the closed loggia that was added in the 1670s. Ponzio was joined for the Ripetta extension by two other regular Borghese architects, Maderno and Vasanzio, and their shares of the work have not been disentangled, though the intricate planning of the interior may well be mainly due to Maderno.[7] However the idea of the Ripetta extension took shape, its violent contrast in scale and feeling with the palace's monotonous bulk, and the daring way in which the hanging garden is thrust forward into an external space, are quite remarkable. The spirit of the feature seems very much in keeping with that of the garden of the palace on the Quirinale (now Palazzo Pallavicini Rospigliosi) on which Cardinal

Scipione Borghese was using the same group of architects at exactly the same time.*

Following Giovan Battista's death, the new work was paid for by his son Marcantonio (born 1601) for whom the pope had bought the title of Prince of Sulmona, and who lived with his uncle Cardinal Scipione at the papal court. Although Marcantonio must have been too young to have been involved in the planning, the large court for ball-games built at the back of the new addition was presumably intended for his use when he took up possession.

In 1614-18 the piano nobile was refurbished in preparation for Marcantonio and his bride Camilla Orsini to take up residence in 1619. From this period there remain two rooms with friezes by Giovan Francesco Guerrieri and two more with friezes by Paolo Piazza. One of the Guerrieri friezes is a decorative grisaille with putti, trophies etc, while the other is a much more ambitious affair depicting *Parnassus* and the *Triumphs of Religion, Science and Virtue*. The Piazza rooms have friezes of the *Rape of the Sabines* and the *Meeting of Solomon and the Queen of Sheba*. Although this work seems to have pleased the Borghese, it all looks very old-fashioned and uninspired in comparison with the exceptional work by Guido Reni, Cigoli, Paul Bril and others that Cardinal Scipione had very recently been commissioning for the garden buildings of his own palace. Guerrieri, who came from the Marches, painted in a manner resembling early Orazio Gentileschi while Piazza, a pupil of Palma Giovine, used rich Venetian colouring to depict scenes full of exotic fancy-dress figures in a style that was firmly rooted in the conventions of the 16th century. Piazza, in particular, seems to have completed a large number of rooms and the disappearance of most of his work may well be connected with his technique of painting in oil on prepared plaster. His most important lost scheme here was for the great salone which stands for the height of two storeys in the four bays to the right of the quoins in the Piazza Borghese façade. The subject was *Mark Antony and Cleopatra* which, playing on Marcantonio Borghese's name, implied a consonance between him and the heroic figures of ancient Rome. In the 1670s Marcantonio's grandson would develop that kind of allusive enhancement of family pretensions by making the early Roman emperors the theme of his new gallery.

On Paul V's death in 1621 Cardinal Scipione moved into the palace. He displaced Marcantonio from the Ripetta wing, established a gallery on the ground floor for his famous collection of paintings, and continued to make adjustments to improve his apartments until his death in 1633. In 1631 he commissioned Agostino Tassi and Marco Tullio Montagna to decorate seven rooms on the piano nobile with landscape friezes, and three of these survive.

THE BAROQUE TRANSFORMATION OF THE 1670s

Nothing noteworthy happened to the palace until 1671 when Marcantonio's grandson Prince Giovan Battista Borghese began a programme to transform much of the palace under the direction of Carlo Rainaldi. Giovan Battista was immensely rich as he was heir not only to the Borghese fortune but also (through his mother,

* To imagine the Ripetta extension in its original form one must not only envisage a fine entrance feature by Ponzio below the balcony, but also bear in mind that the great windows of the loggia that opens on to the hanging garden from the piano nobile were heavily modified in the 18th century, notably by the incorporation of Madernesque false perspective inserts.[8]

Olimpia Aldobrandini, Princess of Rossano) to half of the enormous Aldobrandini inheritance. His wealth was yet further increased by his marriage to Eleonora Boncompagni.

The palace that Giovan Battista inherited had always looked old-fashioned — Hibbard calls it 'the great private palace of the Roman Counter-Reformation'[9] — and the half century since it was built had seen the inception and flowering of the Roman Baroque. After the Borghese, the papal families of Barberini, Pamphili and Chigi had all employed the most celebrated architects and painters to contribute to their great palaces and in the first half of the 1670s there were, in particular, two ongoing projects against which Giovan Battista must have measured his efforts. First was the vast but sober palace being hastily erected alongside the Gesù by the current papal family, the Altieri. Second, and in a totally different mood of unbridled High Baroque splendour, Lorenzo Onofrio Colonna was completing his palace's sensational gallery on a truly regal scale. The innovations that Prince Giovan Battista and Rainaldi worked into the old Borghese palace were, in fact, extremely imaginative, and they reflected diverse current trends.

At the east and west ends of the existing palace there were already means of opening the building to the outside world through, respectively, the garden complex and the loggia overlooking the Tiber, and both these features were to be substantially re-worked. Between the new emphases that were thus created Rainaldi systematised the interior of the ground floor of the entire long wing from the Piazza Borghese entrance to the Ripetta, ripping out the mezzanine, smoothing the irregularities stemming from Orlandini's house, adjusting floor levels and aligning doorways so as to create a splendid summer apartment, with the Prince's rooms facing out towards the piazza and those of the Princess looking on to the garden at the back. The outstanding feature in all this was the extension of the enfilades of aligned doorways that run through the two apartments. The one in the Princess's apartment is extended only slightly beyond the apartment itself but the one that runs diagonally through the Prince's rooms is developed into an immense prospettiva that begins in the room to the right of the piazza entrance, runs virtually the full length of the palace, is transformed into a closed-in corridor, and emerges under the hanging garden at the obliquely cut opening in the north face of the palace in via dell'Arancio. Prince Giovan Battista could not wait to show off this invention, and he delayed its completion several times by mounting demonstrations that involved the temporary removal of all the scaffolding.[10]

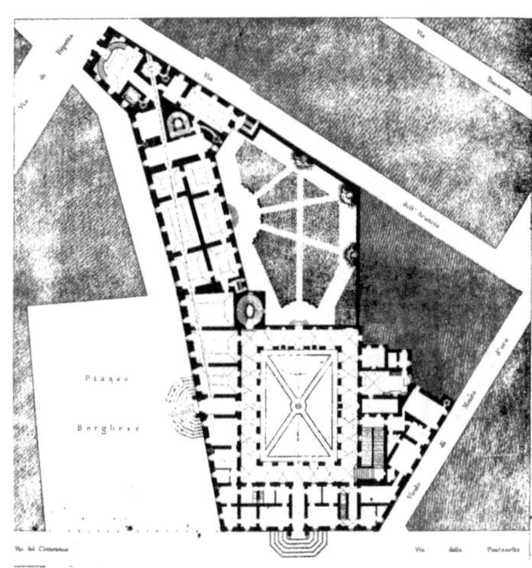

Palazzo Borghese: the harpsichord shape of the building's plan, as shown by Letarouilly

The onward and outward view from the prospettiva was blocked by the nearby

Letarouilly's illustration of Palazzetto Baschenis, showing the fountain and the opening above the door by which the view from the Palazzo Borghese's prospettiva was prolonged to the river

Palazzetto Baschenis (ie the building filling the corner of via di Ripetta and via dell'Arancio) that the Borghese had acquired in 1658. Rainaldi turned this obstacle into a positive enhancement, however, by cutting an enfilade diagonally through it to extend the view yet further. This passage (completed in 1671) was equipped with five small fountains, eight sculptured dolphins, four sculptures of female heads with garlands and other decorative elements. It ended with a pedestal fountain suspended within the Palazzetto Baschenis's portal overlooking the Ripetta port so that, when viewed from inside the main palace, the view of the river and the distant hills beyond must have presented a shimmering and baffling mirage. This marvel of High Baroque architectural theatre appears in any number of old prints of the Ripetta and it lasted well into the age of photography. It was only in 1899 (when, incidentally, the main palace did not belong to the Borghese) that it was obliterated by the architect Giulio de Angelis, who assured the Borghese of the time that he was doing his best to remove every trace of Rainaldi's work and to restore Palazzetto Baschenis to the form in which it had been acquired by their ancestors. Since then, Palazzetto Baschenis has been yet further modified in 1939, 1945 and 1953, so that its 17th century appearance is now quite irrecoverable. It has also been painted an alarming shade of mustard.

Rainaldi's only significant modification to the exterior architecture of the main palace was the addition in 1676 of an enclosed balcony to the short Ripetta façade immediately under the open balcony of the hanging garden. This is, in reality, quite a small structure, but the robust modelling of its Tuscan columns and attached pilasters gives it a genuinely imposing presence. From within, the new balcony is reached by a room, the Stanza della Ringhiera, that was carved out of the existing chambers; it takes its name from the elaborate railing that guards the actual viewing platform and the stairs that curve up to it from both sides.

The purpose of Rainaldi's addition was to provide a comfortable and private place from which to look outward; it is, in fact, a kind of permanent version of the temporary palchi that were often erected for watching public festivals. The very simple (and currently dilapidated) glazed enclosing structure itself is made of wood rather than any grander material and, against the surrounding palatial architecture, it makes an almost comical statement of its modesty and quiet domestic function. In contributing that distinctive tone, it provides the palace's third option for enjoying the river view, in addition to the open-air ambience of the loggia and hanging-garden, and the rigidly controlled aesthetic experience of the prospettiva.

Venturini's print of the central fountain in the garden of Palazzo Borghese. Much of the elaborate wall decoration shown in the print has since been lost

The changes that Prince Giovan Battista made to the main garden at the other end of the complex reflect a similar care for managing the relation between the palace's internal and external aspects. Ever since Ponzio's building campaign there had been a garden covering approximately the same area and containing two fountains, but Prince Giovan Battista vastly increased the scale of the ornament and the complexity of its planning. This work was first entrusted to Giovanni Paolo Schor (who continued to be engaged on the ceiling of the gallery in Palazzo Colonna) but he was dismissed for extravagance and replaced by Rainaldi in August 1672. What we now see does generally represent Schor's conception, albeit with the deletion of some further decoration that he had planned and with a more rigorous sense of design imposed on it by Rainaldi.

The two main elements of the garden are the three elaborate wall fountains originally designed by Schor, and the two semicircular 'theatres' (marked out by paving, flights of steps and statues on plinths) that were finalised by Rainaldi. The fountains (made in 1672-3) share the same broad design, with a profusion of life-size stucco statuary in the most exuberant High Baroque fancy style, but the central one is privileged by an extra range of figures around the pediment. The iconography is unclear, since the documentary sources do not agree and some of the stucco figures have lost their distinguishing attributes, but some theme to do with water and fertility seems to have been intended. Reading from the left, the possible subjects and the responsible sculptors are as follows: *The Three Graces* (Francesco Cavallini and Michel Maille (ie Michele Maglia); *Diana and the Nymphs* (Leonardo Retti); *Flora* or *Primavera* (Filippo Carcani and Maille).

The 'theatres' are arranged to mark out a main axis and a secondary one. The main one is focused on the privileged central fountain from a viewpoint at the door/window of Princess Eleonora's audience chamber, which was the middle room of the summer apartment newly created for her by Rainaldi. The secondary one is on a line from the palace's main entrance on Largo Fontanella di Borghese, through the central arch of the bridge-loggia and ending at the left-hand fountain. The ambiguity of this cumulative focus on a subsidiary, lateral feature, and the sense of mystery about the parts of the garden that lay out of sight, must have been far greater when the side arches of the bridge-loggia were still filled with sham windows.

Like Schor, many of the artists who were called in for the completion and decoration of the new spaces in the Borghese palace had worked under Pietro da Cortona on the gallery of Alexander VII at the Quirinale in 1656-57. They include Giovanni Francesco Grimaldi, Ciro Ferri, Gaspard Dughet and Filippo Lauri. The work was concentrated at the extreme ends of the palace — near the Ripetta extension at one end, and at the angle of Piazza Borghese and Largo Fontanella di Borghese at the other — and the two projects could not have been more different. The main work at the Ripetta end was a new gallery that was plainly intended as a massive statement of Borghese status, while the rooms at the corner of Piazza Borghese were an intimate little winter apartment.

The new gallery was placed transversely across the prospettiva which carries on to bisect an adjacent tiny oval chapel before exiting through the oblique opening described above. It is a high, narrow, barrel-vaulted room with seven bays on each long side and one at the short ends, with the upper part of the walls and the entire vault area thickly encrusted with stucco decoration that includes numerous relief panels imitating ancient Roman models. Notwithstanding Piazza's *Mark Anthony and Cleopatra* frieze in the salone, the main way in which the Borghese had previously implied a connection with ancient Rome had been through their renowned collection of antique sculpture. Now the weighty magnificence and the overtly classical revival quality of the new gallery would have constituted a much more explicit statement of the family's self-image. There is an additional point, too. When the gallery was made the prospettiva would have been fully functioning, so that one would have stood in the overwhelming classical ambience of the gallery while simultaneously experiencing the prospettiva's astonishing presentation of the view across the Tiber. The total control imposed by the prospettiva and its ancillary devices must have conveyed a strong sense of cultural domination and possesssion of the observed external scene, complementing the galleria's implied appropriation of the classical legacy. All in all, Prince Giovan Battista marshalled a wide range of both simple and subtle means to convey the unwavering message of his culture, status and authority.

Each of the sixteen bays of the gallery contains a niche holding a bust of a Roman emperor,* flanked by allegorical personages

* Or, to be more exact, a Roman ruler, since some of these personages (such as Julius Cæsar himself)

and surmounted by a relief depicting a scene from his reign; along the centre line are further reliefs of allegorical scenes, with *Invicta Roma Æterna* in pride of place. Hibbard, in his 1962 article on the gallery, showed how all this was a development of the common practice of using representations of Suetonius's canonical Twelve Cæsars to assist family pretensions, and he also published the documents showing that, although both Rainaldi and Grimaldi had made projects for the gallery, it was Grimaldi who was in charge from the end of 1674 to its completion in 1676, and who was named as the 'architetto' of the vault and as being responsible for its 'disegno'.[12] Hibbard also suggested that the gallery was important in the emergence of what he called a Late Baroque Classicism. Although he viewed the gallery decoration as a generally Cortonesque performance, he noted the knowledge of antiquity that had gone into creating the classical look of the individual reliefs and he suggested that this might imply some connection with Grimaldi's son-in-law Pietro Santi Bartoli. That speculation has since been verified by Batorska, who showed that a large number of drawings for the Borghese gallery in the Leipzig Museum are apparently by Bartoli rather than Grimaldi.[13]

Bartoli was one of the most eminent contemporary antiquarians and a close friend of Bellori, whom he eventually succeeded in several positions, including that of antiquarian to the pope. At the very time that the Borghese gallery was made, Bellori was in fact advising the Altieri family on the decoration of their palace, and he was closely involved in the iconography of Maratta's ceiling there which became an icon of the new classicism. In formal terms, the highly refined Maratta ceiling is very different from Grimaldi's combination of imitation antique reliefs and powerful decorative forms derived from Pietro da Cortona, and it was the Maratta style that was destined to sweep the board. Despite the formal difference, however, it seems clear that the ideas for both the Borghese gallery and the Altieri ceiling came from the ambit of the same group of antiquaries and theorists, and that both works should be understood as projecting the very latest cultural preoccupations of the time.

The actual execution of the stuccoes both in the gallery and the neighbouring chapel[14] was entrusted to Cosimo Fancelli and, as so often in work organised by Grimaldi, the fineness of detailing is not equal to the richness of the overall effect. Grimaldi also organised the decoration of the neighbouring rooms, notably the Stanza della Ringhiera which he and a team of assistants covered with decorative motifs and landscapes in his typical workshop style. An addition to the gallery in 1675-76, but apparently not included in the original design, was the set of eight Venetian mirrors painted with flowers by André Bosman and Niccolò Stanchi and with putti by Ciro Ferri. These were presumably by way of riposte to the famous mirrors painted for the Colonna gallery by Maratta and Mario Nuzzi (Mario de' Fiori) in the previous decade and, however unhistorical they may be in such overtly classical surroundings, their glitter and colour is highly effective.

Although the ground floor mezzanines had been ripped out of most of the Ripetta

were technically no more than consuls. The busts now in the palace gallery are replacements for the original porphyry and alabaster set, probably dating from the time of Paul V, that were removed to the Galleria Borghese on the Pincio between 1830 and 1832, and are now to be seen on red granite pedestals there in the Stanza degli Imperatori, the large ground-floor room at the back of the building.[11]

wing in order to create the new summer apartment and prospettiva, they had been left in place at the other end of the building, and it was in the south east corner of this mezzanine that around 1672-74 Rainaldi created for the Prince's use[15] a small winter apartment, with very low ceilings (and hence easy to keep warm). The decoration of these rooms was carried out by a team including Dughet, Lauri, Ferri and Luigi Garzi; the first three of whom had worked with Cortona at the Quirinale. The first two rooms, looking on to the piazza, are particularly successful schemes in an excellent state of preservation. The first has a ceiling with a central scene of *Venus and Mars* by Garzi and coves featuring fine Dughet landscapes, while the second has a central scene of the *Marriage of Bacchus and Ariadne* by Lauri and enchantingly attractive coves by Lauri and Dughet filled with scenes from Ovid. Lauri's roundels here are unmistakably developed from the ovals that he, Grimaldi and Dughet had executed in the gallery of Alexander VII at the Quirinale some fifteen years before.[16]

OTHER WORK

Rainaldi's work was not confined to the ground floor, though none of the refurbishing that he carried out in the higher storeys was as important and innovative as the work that has been described here. After the 1670s campaign the interior arrangements were often modified to provide different combinations of apartments, and there is a great deal of later painting, some of it inserted into the original 17th century stucco frames. The only rooms to be noted here, however, are the second floor gabinetto with a Corrado Giaquinto ceiling of around 1746, and the ground floor audience chamber, completed by the Roman painter Ermenegildo Costantini in 1775. The latter is an astonishingly confident reprise of the Roman High Baroque of a hundred years earlier. It must be the last example of its kind in the city, and it is not an unworthy one.[17]

ENVOI

Although it is hard to get to see the interior of the Borghese palace, it is usually possible to glimpse the court from the entrance passage, even if one is not allowed to enter. The court is indeed one of the great sights of 17th century Rome and is not to be missed. Hibbard perfectly caught the overall effect as follows, 'the progression from the palace's sombre exterior through the festive court to the little baroque garden has never ceased to surprise and delight.'[18]

Palazzo della Famiglia Borghese

Piazza Borghese, 3

From 1609 the Borghese bought adjoining properties in order to demolish them and create a large piazza which they soon surrounded with walls and chains between bollards (some of which are still in place).[1] On the far side of this stands the Palazzo della Famiglia Borghese, built in 1624-7 by Antonio de Battisti or Baptistis. Hibbard notes that other Borghese architects involved were Sergio Venturi, an architect recorded only as 'Bolini', and the much better-known G. B. Soria.[2] This palace, with stables at ground level and four floors of small apartments above, was built to provide for Scipione Borghese's retinue after he moved in to the main palace. By echoing the presence of the major building across the piazza it makes a strong political statement, emphasising yet further that the Borghese viewed the whole area as their autonomous enclave. (This is made clear in Specchi's print, which shows the

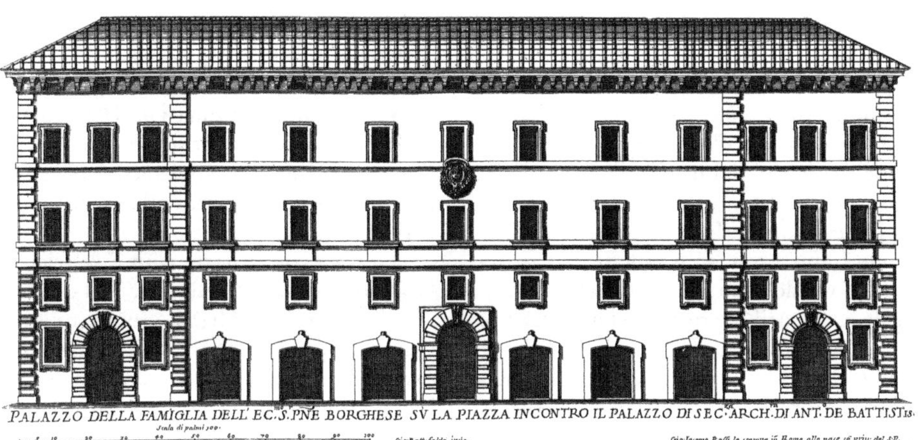

Falda's elevation of the Palazzo della Famiglia Borghese

piazza being used for horse-training.) The dignified restraint and efficiency of the subsidiary palace led to its being taken as a model by Maruscelli for his unrealised design for the Oratory of S. Filippo Neri.[3] Palazzo del Bufalo Ferraioli in Piazza Colonna must also reflect its influence, and Palazzo Mandosi in Piazza Farnese is another palace in the same functional tradition.

Palazzo Bossi

Via Monserrato, 154

The previous palace on this site was entirely rebuilt in the early 18th century, while the place was occupied by a community of religious women belonging to the Congregazione dei Filippini. The architect is unknown, but the ensemble of entrance passage, vestibule and stairs shows that he knew how to generate tension and surprise in a confined area.[1] The most notable single item is doubtless the small vestibule which conveys a feeling of intense plasticity with its curved walls and boldly sculpted ceiling

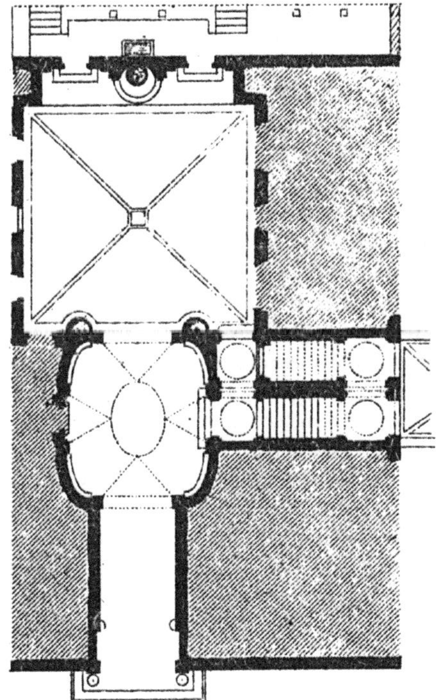

Letarouilly's plan of Palazzo Bossi

that together contain virtually no flat surface whatsoever.[2]

The fountain niches (with eight-pointed Filippini stars) and the double bridge on the side of the cortile facing the entrance all appear original and have a distinctly individual character.

The exterior of the palace makes a handsome impression with much bold rustication, windows in a vaguely 16th century style, and a striking rusticated door feature which is continued into the window above and ends in a finial bearing a Filippini star. One can only guess how much of this is due to the 1900s restoration. There are further Filippini stars in the cornice.

Palazzo Braschi

Piazza S Pantaleo, 10

The Museo di Roma, housed in this palace, contains Cigoli's frescoes from the destroyed Casino di Psiche in the garden of Palazzo Pallavicini Rospigliosi, and Michetti's model (around 1712) of a preliminary design for the celebrated chapel of that family in S Francesco a Ripa. There is also a great deal of material to do with Baroque Rome, including depictions of elaborate entertainments and state events, and some splendid portraits and busts. The view of Piazza Navona from the windows of room 10 is an additional bonus.

The palace itself (by Cosimo Morelli) is not, of course, a Baroque building but it provides some kind of epilogue to the era, since it was the last palace to be built in Rome by a nepotistic papal family. The site was bought by the family of Pius VI (Braschi) in 1790 in order to provide a grand abode for the pope's nephew Luigi Braschi Onesti, who financed its construction with the revenue from the many sinecures that he had been given, despite storms of criticism. The work was interrupted when the pope was exiled and imprisoned by Napoleon in 1798. Construction resumed in 1802, and the building was still not entirely finished when Onesti — who had reinvented himself as an enthusiastic supporter of the Napoleonic regime — died in 1816.

The trapezoid palace, with a restricted façade on Piazza S Pantaleo, would be better described as eclectic High Renaissance rather than Baroque, though the staircase and the oval atrium clearly have strong echoes of Baroque buildings.[1] (The atrium provides an appropriately unsympathetic home for Mochi's rebarbative group of the Baptism of Christ – with additional figures of St Peter and St Paul – originally made for the high altar of S Giovanni dei Fiorentini but supplanted by Raggi's much more successful group of the same subject and never installed in the church.) The staircase with its 1st century pink granite columns taken from a cloister at the Ospedale di S Spirito is indeed overwhelming, and Terry Kirk drew a shrewd comparison between its eclectic effects and Onesti's calculated construction of his public and political persona.[2] It is a soulless piece that fully merits Elling's gibe that it was destined to be repeated in 'bank buildings (and in some national museums too)'.[3]

Palazzo del Bufalo

Via del Bufalo, 8

The history of this huge palace has not been clearly established, but it is mentioned in the literature on the Baroque period because Borromini designed a door for the casino in the garden which was destroyed in the 19th century.[1] The casino was originally famous for its frescoes by Polidoro da Caravaggio,

Borromini's celebrated door (now destroyed) for the casino of Palazzo del Bufalo, as shown in an engraving from De Rossi's Architettura Civile

Falda's elevation of the highly functional Palazzo del Bufalo Ferraioli in Piazza Colonna

some of which are said to have been transferred to canvas and preserved by the Museo di Roma.

There are two heavily-reticulated round-headed portals beneath windows with broken pediments and flanking colonettes. The main entrance on the right has a del Bufalo ox's head emblem in the keystone and a balcony supported on massively emphasised brackets. The subsidiary entrance, at no. 3, bears the motto CUM FERIS FERUS and has a later stemma inserted in the pediment of the window. Whatever may be the building dates for all this — and Lombardi states that Peparelli worked on the building after it was acquired by the del Bufalo in 1612 — the design appears to be of the 16th century, and nothing that is clearly of the Baroque period is to be seen. There is apparently no evidence to support the much repeated attribution to Del Duca.[2]

The attic above the cornice is modern and the whole building is much restored.

Palazzo del Bufalo Ferraioli (Niccolini)

Piazza Colonna, 355

Begun in 1626 by the del Bufalo family, incorporating earlier buildings. In 1627 Francesco Peparelli took over the design. It was substantially finished by 1635, though the last two bays were not completed until 1645. As Metzger Habel has shown, at the turn of the 1650s it may have been briefly considered by the Chigi as a possible development site in the Piazza Colonna area. In the 18th century it passed to the Niccolini and then to the Ferraioli. The corner balcony is not original; it was apparently added in the 19th century.

The palace shares the function of defining Piazza Colonna with Palazzo Chigi opposite (though the piazza was still cluttered with minor buildings when the palace was built). It was planned from the start to incorporate shops at street level along the whole of the front (something that the grandest aristocratic families might not have contemplated in the 17th century in such a prestigious site). Its barracks-like functionality, and the way in which the side bays are delineated with rusticated quoins, are similar to the Palazzo della Famiglia Borghese, which was going up at exactly the time that the del Bufalo started building.

Palazzo della Cancelleria

Piazza della Cancelleria, 1

Built from 1485 (together with the rebuilding of the church of S Lorenzo in Damaso which it incorporates) for Cardinal Raffaele Riario, great-nephew of Sixtus IV. The architect is unknown, but may have been Antonio Montecavallo, brother of Andrea Bregno. In 1517 Riario was involved in a plot against Leo X who forced him to agree to surrender the palace. Under Clement VII it became the seat of the papal Chancery and the residence of the Vice-Chancellor.

As Vice-Chancellor Cardinal Alessandro Farnese was responsible in 1546 for Vasari decorating a great hall with scenes from the life of Paul III, which are in the same vein as the rooms celebrating Farnese achievements at Palazzo Farnese itself, and at Caprarola. The hall is named Sala dei Cento Giorni because Vasari is supposed to have completed it in a hundred days. The same cardinal had a small private chapel decorated by Salviati (1548-50). Under Sixtus V the palace was restored by Domenico Fontana, who designed the door (1589). An earlier design for the door had been made by Vignola, who was Cardinal Alessandro Farnese's favoured architect.

The only work of the Baroque period is the Gran Sala, which was organised in its present form for Clement XI (Albani) in 1718, and which was intended as a celebration of his reign. The job was manifestly done on the cheap, with the main decorative elements being the cartoons (in tempera on paper, mounted on canvas) that Marcantonio Franceschini had made in 1711-1712 for the mosaic decoration of the vestibule to the Cappella del Coro in St Peter's. The large scenes represent a *Heavenly Host of musician-angels* and *Old Testament Patriarchs*; the smaller ones are *Scenes from the Old Testament* and some miscellaneous figures. Running round the room is a frieze with ten vedute of Clement XI's public works and church restorations by the otherwise unrecorded Tyrolese artist Andreas Spägl; these are interspersed with six feigned bronze medallions of Clement engaged in various pastoral activities, probably by Giuseppe Nicola Nasini, who also contributed half a dozen feigned statues of *Personifications* in niches.

On the end wall there is a clock incorporated in a tondo with *Chronos, Apollo and the Horses of the Sun* by Gaulli, which Enggass dates to around 1670 (ie two years before Gaulli started work at the Gesù, and at a time when Francesco Barberini was Vice-Chancellor).[1] The supporting figures that Nasini added around the tondo are maladroit in comparison with Gaulli's work.

After 1870 the palace was given extraterritorial rights and it still houses some administrative units of the Holy See.

Palazzo Capizucchi (Troili, Massimo, Gasparri)

Piazza Campitelli, 3

The Capizucchi clan had lived in the Campitelli area since at least the fourteenth century and from the mid-sixteenth century they were systematically expanding their

View of Piazza Campitelli by Falda. Palazzo Capizucchi, on the corner to the right, is seen before its remodelling in 1672-4. Beyond it is Palazzo Albertoni

property holdings on this site. The present palace is documented as being built in 1588 for Mario Capizucchi, though some of the finance for the project may well have been provided by his illegitimate brother Biagio Capizucchi, who was a highly successful mercenary soldier (and exiled murderer).[1] At least part of it is shown in Tempesta's map of 1593, and it was certainly finished by 1601, when it was described as 'new'.

There is no direct documentary evidence to identify the architect, but Baglione's attribution of the design to Giacomo Della Porta has usually been accepted. A later seventeenth century historian of the family, however, states that Vignola had made a design for the new building, and the 1588 documents show that Gregorio Caronica was at that time doing surveys for the Capizucchi.[2] Caronica had been a pupil of Vignola, and then of Della Porta, and Cantatore suggests that the building may well represent Della Porta's reworking of a design by Vignola, with Caronica acting as on-site supervisor.[3] Be that as it may, the design is extremely sober and restrained, with detailing that looks much less confident than the work on Della Porta's later Albertoni palace next door. The meagre portal and balcony are placed asymmetrically because of the need to adapt to pre-existing buildings; the lilies on the brackets under the balcony were probably intended to indicate the family's adherence to the Farnese faction.

In 1669, the year in which a scion of the neighbouring Albertoni family was adopted by an Altieri prelate, the Capizucchi took the inverse route to mending their fortunes by adopting a Marescotti cousin. Soon after this, in 1672, the property on the corner of via Capizucchi and Piazza Capizucchi was bought up, and between then and 1674 this corner was incorporated in the palace and some striking Baroque ornament was added. All this development doubtless reflected a mood of optimism and renewed assertivenes following the alliance that had saved the family from extinction.

The main item of the new decoration is the privileging of the piano nobile windows with the motif of a broken round pediment embracing a vertical blind oval panel. This Borrominesque device* is applied to all the palace's exterior (ie to both the main façade facing S Maria in Campitelli and the subsidiary one on Piazza Capizucchi, and also down the flank on via Capizucchi). Additionally, the courtyard was completed with a decorative scheme of coupled pilasters and with the east and west sides incorporating blind arches with illusionist perspective surrounds. The names of Girolamo and Carlo Rainaldi have been suggested for all this work but the former cannot have done it and there seems no good reason to choose the latter either. Cantatore suggests[4] that the likeliest candidate is Mattia De Rossi, whose name appears on a document relating to the property that was bought in 1672, and who in 1685 was to make the austerely splendid Capizucchi chapel in the nearby S Maria in Campitelli, with its green and yellow marble revetments and funerary pyramids.

The extra storey above the cornice was partly added in 1889 when the palace was owned by the Troili; it was modified and expanded from 1925 by Pio Piacentini for the Gasparri.

The palace is now occupied by the Irish Embassy.

* The right-hand door of the Roman Oratory seems to be the closest parallel to be found in Borromini's work. For a later version of the same idea, see the door of Ferroni's Casa dei Chierici Minori in via del Lavatore.

Palazzo Capponi (Orsini, Stampa, Pediconi)

Via degli Orsini, 34

The palace originally belonged to the Orsini, whose Monte Giordano stronghold is close nearby. In 1622 it passed to the Florentine family of Capponi, who kept it until the 18th century when it was owned by the Stampa family from Milan. In the 19th century it passed to the Pediconi, and then to the Cavelletti. The extra storey above the cornice is a 19th century addition.

The elevation (which is consistent on the three façades) gives virtually equal emphasis to all three storeys. Reading from the top down, the windows feature female heads under 'bowler hat' tympana, mensole under plain architraves, and buckle motifs under triangular pediments. At all corners of the building are reticulated quoins with Stampa emblems of turrets and eagles immediately under the cornice (and with extra buckle motifs artlessly added beneath the turrets for good measure). Presumably, the entire restoration of the building and the addition of the Stampa emblems was done by that family in the early 18th century. No documentation on this point has been published, however, and the window designs are of a type that could have been produced at any time after De Rossi's Palazzo D'Aste, which was being built in the 1660s.

The most notable things at the palace are undoubtedly the two exceptionally elegant doors in via degli Orsini and the fountain in the cortile behind the door at no. 34. These feature fanciful, delicate stucco work that is of a totally different character from that of the windows, and they must all have been made for the Stampa half a century later. The doors are of the type that has a continuous semicircular inner roll moulding, with an outer moulding that diverges and then ends in inward-turning volutes to create a 'breaking wave' effect. The space below the volutes is occupied by a nervously intense 'green man' mascherone appearing through sprays of oak leaves. Both the design of the doors and the execution of the foliage are so close to Alessandro Dori's entrance of Palazzo Rondinini that the resemblance may be more than coincidental. At all events, the Capponi doors must be of around the same date as the work at Palazzo Rondinini, which was carried out in the 1760s. There are more oak leaves on the fountain, where they surround the Stampa eagle under the pediment and also the mascherone from whose mouth the water flowed.

This is the appropriate place to note that the north side of Piazza dell'Orologio and via dei Banchi Nuovi provides a splendid display of architectural motifs and stuccoes from the mid-17th century onwards, since Palazzo Capponi faces G. A. De Rossi's Palazzo Boncompagni Corcos across via degli Orsini, and is adjoined by the excellent unnamed palazzetto at via dei Banchi Nuovi, 22-26.[1] Furthermore, the echoing quoins of the Capponi and Boncompagni Corcos palaces provide a marked sense of entrance into the wide via degli Orsini leading up to Monte Giordano.

Palazzo Capponi ('della Palma')

Via di Ripetta, 246

An eight-bay palace on the corner of via di Ripetta and via Angelo Brunetti (formerly via delle Scalette), with a huge and massively rusticated door, above which are niches containing statues of two naked youths (ephebes) holding shields bearing the Borghese emblems of the eagle and the dragon.

The nucleus of the palace was built in the second half of the 16th century by the Serroberti family, who sold it in 1615 to Amerigo Capponi, a member of the well-known Florentine family who had settled in Rome and had been Vice-Castellan of the Castel S Angelo since 1591. The building that he bought lacked the two left hand bays of the present palace, but the layout of the elevation was otherwise broadly similar to what we now see, and in particular the door was already in place. Before his death in 1619 Amerigo had extended the façade to its present length and regularised the fenestration. The ephebes with the Borghese emblems — intended to signal Amerigo's close ties with the family of the reigning pope, Paul V — were carved in peperino at this time by Francesco Caporale, a Lombard sculptor in the circle of Stefano Maderno. Originally two further such figures with the Capponi arms stood at the ends of the balustrade that then surmounted the façade.

In the first half of the 18th century the palace housed the famous library and collections of the marchese Alessandro Gregorio Capponi. In 1818 the Capponi sold it, and it passed through various hands before being acquired by the Jesuits in 1887, for use as the headquarters of the periodical *La Civiltà Cattolica*. Since 1951 it has belonged to the Istituto Nazionale Assistenza Infortunati sul Lavoro. The building has clearly been much restored and there have been a number of enlargements and changes, including the insertion of a new staircase in 1858 and work in the 1950s to stabilise the foundations. Nevertheless, the main façade is still close to the print of 1638 opposite.

The palm tree with the legend VINCENTI DABITUR ('it shall be given to the victor') in the keystone of the entrance is something of a puzzle. Papini rejects the idea that it could be a stemma placed there by the Serafini family (for whose residence in the palace there is no evidence), and suggests that it

A print of Palazzo Capponi (della Palma) published by G. B. De Rossi in 1638

may simply be a generic device counselling improvement, without any specific family connotations.[1] It apparently dates from the second half of the 19th century.

Two rooms on the piano nobile contain parts of routine landscape friezes surviving from the Serroberti palace. Papini illustrates them in her comprehensive account of the building.

Palazzo Cardelli

Piazza Cardelli, 4

The façade, with its elaborate cornice featuring the Cardelli emblem of the thistle (cardo), was begun in 1592 for Alessandro Cardelli by Francesco da Volterra and the interior was continued from 1601 by Gaspare Guerra. After a pause of some thirty years, work was resumed for Asdrubale Cardelli by Francesco Peparelli in 1633. The grand staircase, with grey marble doorcases dates from this time.

In 1651 Carlo Cardelli became head of the family and he soon set about a programme that included a fine loggia on the piano nobile at the back of the palace, with tondi containing busts of Roman emperors and a large niche fountain with a statue of Apollo by Pietro Paolo Naldini, while the main room on the ground floor was given a ceiling fresco by Giovanni Battista Magno (Modanino) depicting *The Sciences and the*

Arts with Time and Fortune, surrounded by a complex setting of feigned stucco. All this must have been completed by 1654 when Modanino was paid for the ceiling and Dughet painted the niche containing the Apollo with an imitation sky background that has long since disappeared.

The general message of Carlo Cardelli's programme must have been to present his palace as the home of learning and the arts, implying that his own presence as the presiding genius of the place was in some sense an Apollonian rôle. He was, in fact, a prominent member of the circle of intellectuals and antiquarians around Camillo Astalli and Camillo Massimo, for whom such Apollonian references would have been entirely in character.[1]

In 1663-64 (ie shortly after Carlo Cardelli's death in 1662) the staircase was decorated with a number of miscellaneous fragments of antique mythological sculpture, freely restored and expanded by Orfeo Boselli and placed within lavish stucco frames.[2]

In the window embrasures of a small room near the loggia there are 17th century landscapes that appear to incorporate scenes from Ovid's *Metamorphoses*, including *Apollo and Daphne*. There are further landscapes in the windows of an adjoining corridor. It is not clear when any of this was painted, or whether the figurative scenes have any iconological connection with Carlo Cardelli's programme. Although these landscapes have traditionally been ascribed to Dughet, that definitely seems incorrect.[3]

The palace has suffered several drastic enlargements. The curiously rustic trapezoid extension at the right (south) end of the façade was added in the 18th century. The new wing (architect, Mariano Raffaelli) comprising seven bays in via Clementino (Piazza Nicosia), three bays in via della Scrofa and five bays in via Pallacordia was added in 1889 by Alessandro Cardelli, as a long inscription in via Clementino records. (All this extension follows the elevation of the original façade, but is easily distinguishable as it is painted in a different shade.) Finally, the heavy balustraded attic (architect, Carlo Grazioli) was added in 1925.

From via Pallacordia one can get a tantalising glimpse of the loggia with its tondi of Roman emperors.

Palazzo de Carolis (Simonetti, Banco di Roma)

Via del Corso, 307

This is in a prime position on the Corso, opposite the little Piazza di S Marcello. In 1714 the hugely rich banker and grain merchant Livio de Carolis began buying the buildings on the site and commissioned Alessandro Specchi to build him a great palace. The final piece of land was bought in 1726 and Specchi's building, covering the whole isolato, was finished in 1728. The façade is a massive affair of nineteen bays, with composite attached pilasters to mark the central mass, and a big, simple balcony on four widely-spaced Doric columns. Although some features (the handling of the corners, the second floor windows with buckle motif, the stucco female head over the door) are derived from De Rossi, the building has none of that architect's suavity, and it is much more crowded and old-fashioned than Specchi's own Palazzo Pighini, which was going up at much the same time. The back of the palace was not built up to match the other three sides, since the Jesuits of the Collegio Romano were anxious about the size of the project and in 1719 obtained a papal chirograph forbidding the heightening of any buildings around the Collegio.[1]

The expense of the building, including its lavish furnishing and decoration, was the talk of Rome and, although de Carolis was granted the lucrative monopoly of the papal postal service, it still bankrupted the family. On the death of de Carolis's last close relative, it was bought by the Jesuits of the Collegio Romano in 1750. It was then let to a succession of famous occupants including Monsignor de Canillac and Count Kaunitz. The architect Ferdinando Fuga was also grand enough to have an apartment here. Two famous periods when it was one of the main centres of intellectual, political and artistic life in Rome were when it was the French Embassy under Cardinal de Bernis (who occupied the palace in one capacity and another from 1769 to 1794) and Chateaubriand (1828-1830).[2]

In 1833 the palace was bought by Prince Luigi Boncompagni Ludovisi, who added the heavy frieze containing the Boncompagni dragons and Ludovisi bends. His son Baldassare (died 1894) added the attic in 1846 and established a famous scientific library in the palace. In 1908 it was bought by the Banco (now Banca) di Roma, who employed the architect Pio Piacentini to convert the palace for their use. Amongst other changes, he established a new wing at the back of the building, installed a new marble staircase, and built a splendid public hall in the Liberty style in what had been the cortile. The side and back wings were raised and further major alterations were made in the 1920s and 1940s. These changes destroyed much of Specchi's interior, but retained a gallery and an oval spiral staircase on the via Lata side and a grand apartment on the piano nobile along the main front on the Corso. All these features are of considerable interest.

The oval staircase opens from the vestibule behind the via Lata entrance, so that on its way to the top of the building it runs up immediately behind the gallery on the piano nobile. In its essentials it is not very different from earlier Roman examples deriving from Mascarino's original at the Quirinale, but it is an impressive piece, packaged so compactly that it has an eerie sense of extreme height. It must have seemed a very strange throwback when it was built in the 1720s.

The gallery occupies eight bays along via Lata and two on the Corso. It has a depressed barrel vault and is divided into three sections by pillars veneered in giallo antico. The frieze and the surrounds for the ceiling paintings are sumptuous stucco pieces that feature the de Carolis emblems of stars, doves and ears of corn. In the ceiling are *The Sun* by Luigi Garzi; *The Moon* by Benedetto Luti and *Ceres, Bacchus and Venus* by Giuseppe Chiari.

In the piano nobile rooms along the main façade there is a series of ceilings that comprise one of the more notable groups of Roman secular painting of the period. They are unidentified *Allegories* by Sebastiano Conca and Domenico Maria Muratori; *Minerva taking Youth from Venus and sending him to Hercules* and *Venus in the Forge of Vulcan* (the latter signed and dated 1725) by Francesco Trevisani; *Aurora* by Andrea Procaccini; and *Primavera and the Zephyrs driving away Winter* by Giovanni Odazzi.

One of the houses bought by de Carolis had belonged to the painter Jacopino del Conte and incorporated in its façade on the Corso the 16th-century fountain called 'Il Facchino', representing a Roman water-carrier from whose keg the real water flows into a basin. This was famous as one of the *statue parlanti*, to which ironical verses were affixed, and Specchi incorporated it in his grand façade, still in its original position. In 1872 it was moved to the side of the palace on via Lata as part of an operation to clear obstructions from the pavement of the Corso.

Palazzo Carpegna (Baldinotti)

Corso del Rinascimento, 44

This palace, occupying the awkward triangular site between the Sapienza and Palazzo Madama, was a late work of G. A. De Rossi. In the period 1926-39 it was demolished, reconstructed for use as offices of the Senate, and linked by a bridge to the adjacent Palazzo Madama. It is now of virtually no interest but is said to retain a couple of original ceilings.

Palazzo Carpegna (Accademia di S Luca)

Piazza dell'Accademia di S Luca, 77

In 1638 Count Ambrogio Carpegna bought from Louis XIII's agent Pierre Eschinard (or Pietro Eschinardi, as he was called in Italy) a 16th century palace which occupied the northern end of this site and fronted on the present Piazza dell'Accademia di S Luca. (It has been customary to refer to this palace as Palazzo Vaino, but Salvagni's researches show that this is not correct.) In 1639 he was granted a licence to acquire the whole block, and he succeeded in doing this the following year. From around that time Borromini produced for him a series of astonishing plans for the development of the palace. The most remarkable of them envisaged an extension across the road to the east, with prodigious semi-elliptical courts echoing each other across the road, and with the two parts of the palace linked by bridges.

As Connors has shown,[1] these ambitious ideas were but one part of a Barberini scheme to stamp their image and authority on the area surrounding the Fontana di Trevi, which was itself projected to be refashioned by Bernini. In the event the scheme never took shape. The Barberini lost their authority in the disastrous War of Castro and Urban VIII was a disgraced figure when he died in 1644. Ambrogio Carpegna (who was a protégé of the Barberini and their ardent supporter) had already died in 1643, leaving the palace building project to be taken forward by his brother Cardinal Ulderico Carpegna, a more prudent figure who was sceptical about the Barberini. Within the year the cardinal gave the building commission to Borromini (who came to know and trust him so well that he eventually made him the executor of his will); but the project that he authorised — which was completed by 1649 — was limited to remodelling the modest Eschinardi building at the northern end of the site, well away from the projected Barberini showcase area around the Trevi fountain.*

Although Ulderico's building has been considerably adapted at various times, it is still very easy to appreciate the main features that were inserted by Borromini and his faithful assistant Righi. These are the passage from the north door into an open-sided three-bay portico, which in turn opens directly into an extraordinary oval helical ramp that climbed to the piano nobile and has since been extended to the upper floors of the building. The entrance into the ramp is through an arch that is festooned with a truly astonishing display of Borrominian ornamental stucco, loaded with emblematic significance. Minerva's shield with Medusa's head indicates that Ulderico's abode was a

* There was no major building on the east side of Piazza di Trevi until Palazzo Castellani was built in 1868-9.

Borromini's stucco decoration of the arch leading to the helical ramp in Palazzo Carpegna

seat of learning. The inverted cornocopias pour out, on the right, flowers and fruits implying fecundity and, on the left, chains of office, mitres, crowns, a sword and a child, which together indicate earthly success handed on to heirs.[2]

The Accademia di S Luca took over the palace in 1933, when their longstanding quarters adjacent to SS Martina e Luca near the Roman Forum were destroyed. The Galleria of the Accademia (open to the public on weekday mornings) contains several works of the Baroque period, and the visitor to it can see all the Borromini features of the palace.

Palazzo Cavallerini Lazzaroni

Via dei Barbieri, 6

A dour 13-bay palace with little architectural attraction. It was built for Cardinal Giangiacomo Cavallerini and first appeared in maps of Rome in 1676, when Falda showed it as no. 363. The four oculi in the piano nobile are probably a later modification. After 1870 the interior was modified to accommodate the Banca d'Italia until it moved to its present home in via Nazionale.

On the piano nobile there are rooms with ceiling frescoes by Giacinto and Ludovico Gimignani. They are the *Chariot of Venus*; *Aurora*; and *Time Discovering Truth* by Giacinto; and *Justice* by Ludovico.

Palazzo Celani

Piazza Scanderbeg, 85

Bonaccorso's research demonstrates that this was originally an apartment block, built as a purely commercial venture for the Chierici Minori of SS Vincenzo ed Anastasio by the architect Giuseppe Ferroni, who also built the better-known building in via del Lavatore for the same patrons. Both buildings abutted the community's convent, which filled the block between them, and were built when the Chierici Minori were reorganising the entire isolato in the period following the completion of the Fontana di Trevi in 1762. The Piazza Scanderbeg building itself can be precisely dated to 1763-1766. It was designed to offer self-contained 10-room 'appartamenti nobili' on each of the upper three floors, with five small apartments in the mezzanine, and stables and storerooms at street level.

The part of the building that attracts attention is the three-bay entrance façade that dominates the little Piazza Scanderbeg, though this is in fact simply the end of the short arm of a substantial L-shaped structure that has three other similar faces to the street. Apart from the addition of an extra storey in 1905, which badly spoiled the proportions, it appears unaltered.

In the via del Lavatore building Ferroni was allowed a lavish outpouring of invention. The Piazza Scanderbeg building is far more discreet and relies on the simplicity of its proportioning and elegant handling of detail. Note, for example, the crispness and variety in the treatment of the corner features and the elegant curved framing lines immediately under the cornice. The one proudly Borrominian feature here is the

Palazzo Celani — the Borrominian door

door, which combines tapering edge-set jambs derived from the Propaganda Fide with a tympanum (containing a large shell) that is a descendant of the famous windows between the loggia and the wings of Palazzo Barberini. Here, however, Ferroni springs a surprise by bending the horizontal part of the tympanum backward rather than forward, as in the jambs of Specchi's door at Palazzo Pighini.

The building was acquired by the Celani family in the late 19th century.

Palazzo Celsi (Viscardi)

Corso Vittorio Emanuele 18

The elegant door is attributed to G. A. De Rossi in Domenico De Rossi's *Architettura Civile*, (I, 139, shown opposite). Both door and staircase are attributed to De Rossi by Pascoli.[1] The door, androne and staircase (which is illuminated at each landing by an opening into a light-well) are sited at the very end of a façade that shows no other sign of De Rossi's involvement. The likeliest explanation, therefore, is that De Rossi was

Opposite: G. A. De Rossi's door at Palazzo Celsi. Engraving from D. D. De Rossi's Archittetura Civile

B
C
Profilo
A
Modine delli stipiti della Porta
Scala di Palmi due per il Modine A. Capitello, e Basa B. C.
Scala di Palmi Venti 10 20
Porta del Palazzo de Signori Celsi, al Giesu.
Architettura di Gio. Antonio de Rossi.
Nella Stampa di Dom.co de Rossi erede di Gio. Giacomo de Rossi in Roma alla Pace, con Privilegio.
Intag.to da Antonio Barbey. 139

called in to add these features to an existing building, and Spagnesi dates his modest but refined contribution to about 1678.[2]

In the early 18th century the Viscardi family acquired the palace and incorporated their heraldic eagles and swords in the cornice (together with eagles in the first floor window pediments). They may have made more substantial changes to the upper parts of the building, though that seems to be uncertain. At all events the façade is now strangely dislocated and top-heavy, since there is a huge blank space above the lower piano nobile* and the second floor windows are awkwardly amalgamated with the over-elaborate cornice. All the superstructure above the cornice is modern.

Palazzo Cenci-Bolognetti (Petroni)

Piazza del Gesù, 16

The 16th century palace on this site was enlarged in the 1730s for Conte Alessandro Petroni by Ferdinando Fuga, the dominant architect in Rome at the time. Manfredi has shown that the work was done in two phases between 1734 and 1737, the first phase comprising the façade giving on to Piazza del Gesù, and the second devoted to reorganising the courtyard. The flanks of the big building are very bare; all the effort went into the front part of the palace, and especially the show-piece façade.

As noted in the entry for Palazzo Altieri, the Piazza del Gesù's position on the papal processional route made it a prime spot for displays of family pretension, and Petroni's project was clearly intended to echo and rival the Altieri palace opposite. In addition, the scale and exact placing of Fuga's design plays very effectively against the Gesù and the adjoining Casa Professa, albeit at the cost of the ungainly two bays tacked on to the left side. These are exposed quite baldly and therefore are far more disfiguring than the analogous extra bay of De Rossi's Altieri façade, which is masked by the Gesù.

Fuga was building this façade at the same time as his great administrative Palazzo della Consulta and, although the site of the Petroni palace enforces a vertical emphasis in contrast to the Consulta's horizontality, the two buildings have many elements in common. These include the two-tier distribution, the weighting of the lower tier with rustication, the use of giant Ionic pilasters (derived from Bernini's Palazzo Chigi) to mark out the central bays and outer ends of the upper tier, the balustraded roofline above a frieze incorporating small mezzanine windows between mensole, and the use of elaborate composite windows derived from the regional tradition of Fuga's native Tuscany.

Despite those similarities, the two buildings have a very different feel to them. In the Petroni palace there is a chilly hardness in the decoration, a touch of perversity in the way that the windows play against the hardly discernable setting-forward of the central three bays, and a pervading sensation that the massive window designs are on the edge of being too assertive for the space they occupy. This distinctive tone of controlled unease is increased by the inverted tapering jambs of the massive main entrance, which Fuga borrowed from Michelangelo's Palazzo dei Conservatori.[1] The device is echoed in the lower piano nobile windows, the brackets under the

*The usual explanation for this kind of excessive gap between floors is the need to accommodate rooms with vaulted ceilings but it has not been possible to check whether this holds true of Palazzo Celsi.

Vasi's view of Piazza del Gesù, with the Gesù and the Casa Professa on the left and Palazzo Cenci-Bolognetti on the right. Between them runs the papal processional route leading up to the Campidoglio

windows of the piano terreno, and in the mensole under the cornice.

The palace has not had an altogether enthusiastic press. Wittkower — who dated it too late at c.1745 — cited it as an example of Fuga's slide into 'a somewhat monotonous form of classicism'.[2] Nevertheless, it does articulate a very distinctive and personal architectural language and represents Fuga's only opportunity in his Roman period to develop his ideas of palace design on an occasion when he was free from the sober Corsini aesthetic creed.

The stucco foliage that plays over the entrance and across the capitals of the giant pilasters, and also appears in the windows of the lower piano nobile and the mezzanine, is made up of the sprays of roses that were the heraldic emblem of the Petroni.

The lamp-holders in the form of dragons are virtually the same as those at Palazzo Lazzaroni. They do not appear in Vasi's print of 1756.

The palace was long the headquarters of the Christian Democrats, so that 'Piazza del Gesù' became Italian journalistic shorthand to denote that party.

Palazzo Centini (Toni, 'dei Pupazzi')

Via Capo le Case, 3

A modest-sized five-bay palazzetto that is famous for the herm-caryatids (the 'pupazzi' or dolls) on the piano nobile windows. The pediments of these windows (with shells and alternating outward and inward turning volutes) and the ground floor mezzanine are also very exuberant, so that the building is encrusted with decoration up to the second floor, where it becomes much more staid. These extraordinarily lavish stuccoes are well set off by the pinkish wash currently on the walls and, together with Borromini's amazing campanile at the nearby S Andrea delle Fratte, they give this corner of Rome a marked atmosphere of over-the-top fantasy.

The plan was devised by Francesco Rosa after 1722 for Felice Centini who died in 1727. His heir, Annibale Centini, continued the project with Tommaso Morelli as his architect and by 1731 Francesco de Sanctis was superintending the work. The relative share of these three architects is not known, but a 1728 drawing by Morelli (the architect of the original Teatro Valle) shows the building much as it is now.

Already by 1731 the building comprised five separate apartments which were occupied by a large number of people from Umbria, the Romagna and the Marches (the Centini themselves coming from Ascoli).[1]

Palazzo Cerri (Gaucci)

Via Larga, 12

Built for the Cerri family by Francesco Peparelli, probably in the late 1620s. After passing through several hands it was used after 1870 as the seat of the Council of State, which explains the arms of the House of Savoy over the entrance on Corso Vittorio Emanuele II. In 1888, when that street was cut through the area, the north end of the building was sliced off and, according to Lombardi, the original façade was re-erected further back. That looks very possible; at all events, the unadventurous elevation is virtually identical with that of the original Peparelli façade on via Larga. The building now houses part of the medical faculty of the University of Rome.

The most interesting features are in the entrance bay on via Larga. The entrance itself (which must be by Peparelli) features a heavily balustraded balcony above a bewilderingly confused assembly of motifs including a lion mask on a central bracket within a broken pediment beneath which is a panel with a swag. The highly decorated lateral brackets support pedestals with the Cerri emblem of an uprooted tree, and this appears again on the building's cornice along with other devices (stars and bees).

Above the main entrance, on the second floor, there is a small subsidiary balcony supported by a female bust surrounded by spreading oak foliage in stucco. This, rather striking, composition appears to be several decades later than the Peparelli entrance below. It must have been added to privilege the second floor in deference to some forgotten occupant.

Casa dei Chierici Minori

Via del Lavatore, 38

Together with its near neighbour, Francesco Bianchi's apartment building for the Agostiniani Scalzi in via dei Crociferi, this remarkable building was picked out for special mention by Portoghesi in 'Roma Barocca', though its date remained a mystery. The door, vestibule and steps are strikingly Borrominian in spirit[1] but the building was traditionally attributed to Bizzacheri and was not associated with the new choir of SS Valentino ed Anastasio which Giuseppe Ferroni had constructed in the 1760s. It was not until Bonaccorso's research that Ferroni was established as the architect and the true date — much later than previously imagined — was established.

In fact the building was just one part of the reorganisation of the isolato by the Chierici Minori of SS Vincenzo ed Anastasio following the completion of the Fontana di Trevi in 1762. At the opposite side of the convent site Ferroni built in 1763-1766 the apartment building in Piazza Scanderbeg that is now called Palazzo Celani, while the present building in via del Lavatore was built between 1764/5 and 1768. It provided a monumental entrance and vestibule leading through to the convent's cloister, but everything else that one sees from the street appertained to an apartment block, containing three 'appartamenti nobili' and entered from the simple subsidiary side doors. The Chierici Minori built this solely to raise revenue but, just like the apartment building of the Agostiniani Scalzi, the project incurred an uncontrolled cost overrun and turned out to be a commercial disaster.

Ferroni's career, reconstructed by Bonaccorso, began with Filippo Barigioni, who was himself closely associated with Alessandro Specchi. Later he became the pupil and assistant of Francesco Bianchi, the architect of the apartments in via dei Crociferi. All this heritage is indeed apparent in the via del Lavatore building.

The overall layout of the façade, which is articulated with shallow giant pilasters, is somewhat akin to Specchi's suave and much more seigneurial Palazzo Pighini, with a simple flat surface, a very large area of windows, ringhiere distributed at low and high levels, and decorative features carried the whole way up the central bay above the entrance. The remarkable thing here is the sheer inventiveness of all the motifs that climb up the centre of the façade from the street to the cornice, with a marked difference in character between the splendidly severe central entrance that was dedicated to

The door-head of Ferroni's Casa dei Chierici Minori

the religious complex and the much more fanciful style of the stuccoes ornamenting the three luxury apartment windows above. The use of these different styles — both executed in a masterly way — must surely have been intended to signal the ecclesiastical and worldly natures of the two premises that lay behind.

The sombre machine over the very slightly curved entrance is made up of just two lateral volutes and a baluster-shaped central element under a pagoda pediment, and it makes its effect simply by the contrast between the solids and voids thereby created. The complexity of the vestibule spaces behind comes as a surprise, and is astonishingly close to Borromini's style for such a late date. Above the entrance the stuccoes get more and more elaborate, with a remarkable ensemble on the second floor consisting of an inclined three-dimensional wreath under an ogival form that bursts through the architrave like an arrowhead. Altogether, this highly individual, maverick masterpiece can be seen as marking the very end of the Borrominian tradition in Rome.

Part of the building is occupied by the State elementary school 'Luigi Settembrini'. There are still apartments above.

Palazzo Chigi (Aldobrandini)

Piazza Colonna, 370

In 1587 the lawyer Pietro Aldobradini sold a palace that he had built on part of this site over the previous few years. The family became vastly more important and powerful when Pietro's brother Ippolito became pope Clement VIII (reigned 1592-1605) and in 1615 the builder's son Cardinal Pietro Aldobrandini re-acquired the palace and began buying up nearby property. When he died in 1621 he left the palace to his sister Olimpia, who ceded it to Cardinal Deti on condition that he continue the building work that was then in progress. On Deti's death in 1630 the palace returned to Olimpia and eventually descended to the celebrated Olimpia (junior), the Princess of Rossano, who married first Don Paolo Borghese and second Camillo Pamphili. The palace was occupied by various tenants before Olimpia sold it in 1659 to Alexander VII's brother Don Mario Chigi and his nephew Don Agostino, who had married her daughter Virginia Borghese the previous year.

The palace that the Chigi acquired was an L shaped building with ten bays on the Corso and nine on what is now Piazza Colonna. (This is clearly marked on the Piazza Colonna front, where the cornice of the nine bays from the Corso displays the Aldobrandini star, eagle and 'rastrello', while the remaining six bays are marked with the Chigi star.) Of this structure, the bays immediately embracing the corner had been built by Cardinal Deti. Baglione and Totti both stated that Giacomo Della Porta was the architect, but Borromini wrote in very definite terms[1] to contradict this and to say that the palace was built by Maderno after Della Porta's death (which ocurred in 1602). In fact there is no definite reference to either architect in the primary documents, which refer only to Matteo da Città di Castello in the 1580s and to the journeyman practitioner Antonio De Pomis in the post-1616 period. Lefèvre speculated that both Della Porta and Maderno could have provided designs, while never having been superintending architects on the project.[2] Hibbard accepted that both of the two main façades of the building acquired by the Chigi were substantially by Maderno, and he was clear that the portal of the Corso façade was attributable to Maderno on stylistic grounds.[3] The portal is, indeed, an impressive piece in typical Maderno style, with the engaging feature of vivid little mascheroni in the brackets that support the balcony (cf the keystone in the arch of Maderno's entrance to the Quirinale).

As explained in the following entry, Mario and Agostino Chigi had been living in the palace in Piazza SS Apostoli, which they rented from the Colonna, and which Bernini was soon to transform for the Cardinale Nepote, Cardinal Flavio Chigi. Among the possibilities that were considered for this secular branch of the family were Palazzo del Bufalo in Piazza Colonna and Palazzo Bonelli (now Valentini) in Piazza SS Apostoli, which would have enabled the family to rival the Colonna on that piazza with two great palaces. Furthermore, only a matter of months before the Chigi bought the Aldobrandini palace in 1659, Pietro da Cortona had been providing the family with drawings for a new palace of truly imperial grandeur on the west side of Piazza Colonna.[4] Whether or not the Chigi were fully committed to the Aldobrandini palace at the time they bought it, they began buying up neighbouring property in 1661 and set Felice della Greca to work on preparing plans for occupying the whole of the isolato on the north side of Piazza Colonna, as the palace does today.[5]

Piazza Colonna, with Palazzo Chigi (Aldobrandini) beyond the fountain to the right of the Column of Marcus Aurelius. To the left of Palazzo Chigi is the unfinished Palazzo di Montecitorio. Palazzo del Bufalo Ferraioli is on the extreme left, and the Corso on the extreme right. This print was made by Lieven Cruyl in 1666, though most of the figures were not added until 1693

Work on the ground under the Chigi started in 1661 and proceeded steadily, with the early addition of an assertive extra altana on the west edge, as an obvious visual put-down directed at the neighbouring unfinished Ludovisi palace of Montecitorio.[6] In 1677 della Greca was succeeded by G. B. Contini. In 1693 Cardinal Flavio Chigi died and his collections and library came to be housed in the palace. In order to accommodate them Contini replaced della Greca's balustraded roof-line with the present heavy attic and he fitted up the library, which still exists (albeit without the Chigi books).

The main motif of della Greca's design was the creation of a uniform cortile, with a fine frieze and elaborate stucco decoration over the upper storeys. The double apartments on the piano nobile were probably arranged with Don Mario occupying the Piazza Colonna side and Don Agostino the north side, together with part of the side facing Palazzo di Montecitorio, which was also used for a long narrow gallery that has

Engraving by Falda of the elevation of the Corso façade of Palazzo Chigi (Aldobrandini). Note the very uneven window spacing

since disappeared.[7] From the beginning, the main entrance had been the one on the Corso, and della Greca emphasised this by adding an impressive atrium, leading to a princely staircase on the right to serve the piano nobile.

In 1739 the palace passed to Don Augusto Chigi, who immediately put in hand work to regularise and complete the Piazza Colonna front. This work included a new portal, replicating the fine one on the Corso,[8] and an attractive internal fountain with a splendid mascherone was completed in the following year. The balcony on the corner of the Corso for many years supported a closed 'bussoletto' like the one that still exists on Palazzo D'Aste.

After having served as the Austro-Hungarian embassy, the palace was acquired by the Italian State in 1916. It was used first as the Ministry for the Colonies and then as the Foreign Affairs Ministry before becoming the Prime Minister's office (Presidenza del Consiglio dei Ministri) after heavy restoration in 1959-61. The main external change in the 20th century was the tidying-up of the Piazza Colonna façade, including especially the creation of windows on the ground floor to the right of the portal in replacement of the stabling for coaches that had been there hitherto. Finally, the palace was given a fairly relentless cleaning in 1999.

Internally, the palace has been greatly reorganised. The main surviving 17th century item is the series of piano nobile rooms on the corner with the Corso that were decorated in 1625-26 under Cardinal Deti. They consist of a studio and anteroom with scenes of Aldobrandini achievements, and a gallery with Old Testament scenes, all by Flaminio Allegrini and assistants.[9] Another room on the piano nobile has mythological figures and landscapes by Schor.

As it is now, the palace suffers from the monotony of the long façade on Piazza Colonna. The total regularity of the fifteen bays — with nothing even to mark the central window — is distinctly tedious, and Contini's substitution of an attic for della Greca's balustrade increases the plainness of the overall effect. The façade on the Corso, on the other hand, groups the bays in a way that more than merits Hibbard's judicious description of it as 'exaggeratedly rhythmic'.[10] The irregular spacing of the windows must be largely due to della Greca rather than Maderno, and Hibbard speculates in particular that the wider spaces either side of the central portal were introduced by della Greca in order to align with his new atrium.[11] The staccato spacing of the bays nearest Piazza Colonna (which della Greca symmetrically repeated when he extended the Corso façade to the north) is far harder to explain, however, since it appears to go back to the building carried out under Cardinal Deti in the 1620s. The strong central focus of della Greca's façade would originally have been emphasised yet more markedly by the display of the papal arms above the broken pediment of the central window. (The papal stemma is now kept in the atrium.)

Palazzo Chigi (Odescalchi)

Piazza SS. Apostoli, 80

The original palace on this site was owned by the Colonna, forming an enclave with their huge palace opposite. In 1622 Cardinal Ludovico Ludovisi, the all-powerful nephew of Gregory XV, bought it from Pierfrancesco Colonna, but he sold it back to him the following year when he became vice-chancellor and had official lodgings at the Cancelleria. During his short ownership Cardinal Ludovisi made many changes, and in particular he employed Maderno to work on the court. Although the court that we now see was mainly built at a later period, its 'Palladian' unit of a columnar arcade between piers is apparently due to Maderno and represents a considerable innovation for him, since most of his palace architecture was notably conservative.[1] In early 1623 Agostino Tassi painted a vaulted room on the piano nobile with four marine lunettes that are amongst his best work in this genre.[2]

In 1657 the palace was rented by Don Mario and Don Agostino Chigi, Alexander VII's brother and nephew whom the pope had brought to Rome the previous year when he dropped his original intention of abjuring nepotism. For the next few years, while remaining Colonna property, it was a large factor in the complicated schemes and permutations that the Chigi pursued in working out sufficiently impressive accommodation for the church and secular branches of the family. During this period, probably around January 1660, Felice della Greca, the Chigi family architect, prepared two sets of plans for a major redevelopment incorporating Palazzo Mancini and thus enabling a long façade on the Corso.

Nothing came of that, however, and in 1662 the palace was bought by the Cardinale Nepote, Cardinal Flavio Chigi, who obtained the services of Bernini to adapt the palace within its existing limits in a building programme that lasted from 1664 to 1669. While the heterogeneous collection of buildings that comprised the interior was only lightly remodelled, Bernini designed a novel kind of intensely focused composition for the façade on Piazza SS Apostoli.[3] Bernini had several discussions with the pope about the work on the palace and at least one of his drawings bears the pope's annotations.[4]

The new façade consisted of seven bays articulated by giant pilasters over a plain ground floor, surmounted by a balustrade

Vasi's print of Piazza SS Apostoli, looking south towards Palazzo Valentini, with Trajan's column beyond. Palazzo Chigi (Odescalchi) fills most of the far side of the piazza, facing Palazzo Colonna on the extreme left of the image

with statues, and flanked on each side by a wing of three rusticated bays without an order. The strength of this composition runs through all the detailing, especially in the piano nobile windows which are fine tabernacles with alternating triangular and round pediments. From the moment of its completion the façade was greatly celebrated, and it soon became a prime model for princely residences throughout Europe.

Bernini's design was totally different from the traditional Roman palace formula which still followed the model of Palazzo Farnese. Michelangelo's Palazzo dei Conservatori on the Campidoglio has often been mentioned as the source of Bernini's inspiration to use giant pilasters, though an obvious difference is that Michelangelo's pilasters spring from the ground. In point of fact, a more direct, albeit less glorious, precedent for Bernini's scheme was provided by Palazzo Senatorio on the Campidoglio, where the pilasters above the ground floor had been added by Giacomo Della Porta. But the real point is the extent to which Bernini's concentrated design eclipsed all such precedents as existed, and established a new form.[5]

Despite the palace's fame, Prince Odescalchi, who bought it in 1746, employed Nicola Salvi and Luigi Vanvitelli greatly to increase the length of the central pilastered section to fifteen bays and to add a second entrance, thus completely wreck-

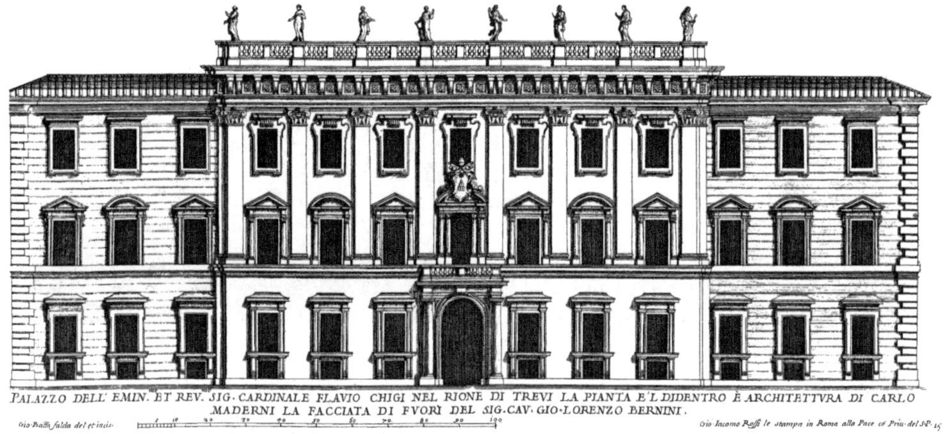

Print by Falda of Bernini's powerful façade of Palazzo Chigi (Odescalchi), before it was extended

ing Bernini's design. Furthermore, the northern wing was soon extended from three bays to six, thereby rendering the façade asymmetrical.[6]

In 1887, following a fire that damaged the top storey of the palace's rear façade on the Corso, the then owner Prince Baldassare Odescalchi built a replacement in Tuscan quattrocento style in honour of his wife, who was a Rucellai. The architect, Raffaele Ojetti, jibbed at this, but he eventually knuckled under and produced the massive Tuscan pastiche that jars so pitilessly with all its neighbours on the Corso.

Palazzo Cimarra

Via Panisperna, 200

A large palace built for Prospero Cimarra in the 1680s on a prominent site opposite the church of S Lorenzo in Panisperna.

Blunt, who did not question the then commonly ascribed building date of 1736, thought it an 'undistinguished building'.[1] Connors, on the other hand, thought it a 'magnificent palace' and it was he who published the document that makes it clear that the palace was being built on 4 December, 1682, probably by the otherwise unknown architect Giacomo Moraldo.[2] The site is on the south side of a piazza in front of S Lorenzo that had been cut in half by the construction of via Panisperna in 1588, and the architect used a good deal of ingenuity in responding to this. The way in which the main façade is wrapped around the outside of the corner of the old piazza is the memorable feature, but the palace's vehement prow-like corner in the direction of S Maria Maggiore is also highly effective.

The palace is now occupied by the Dipartimento della Pubblica Sicurezza of the Ministero dell' Interno, and the interior has been completely reorganised.

Palazzo del Cinque

Via Colonna Antonina, 52

A splendidly cheerful barocchetto palace that moulds the ante-piazza before the Piazza Montecitorio itself, and which manages to avoid being overwhelmed by the mass of Palazzo di Montecitorio that dominates the area.

The palace was built by the architect Francesco Ferrari between 1741 and 1744 for the del Cinque family, who claimed descent from the ancient Roman Quintili. The del Cinque were themselves a family of lawyers and this was a period when there was heavy pressure on accommodation in the area from lawyers and associated professional people who were keen to establish themselves near the law courts that had been set up in the Montecitorio in 1697. Bevilacqua's article identifies Ferrari as the architect, while Curcio describes how the del Cinque patiently negotiated for permission to build but until the reign of Benedict XIV were frustrated by planning blight that lasted until the redevelopment of Piazza di Montecitorio was finally settled.[1]

The tiers of windows – grouped 1-2-1-2-1 on the main façade and with a very different design for each storey – are an exuberant display of energy and fancy. The ones on the piano nobile contain lions modelled on those of Palazzo Pio di Savoia da Carpi, with the corners of the main façade being marked by busts of Hercules that probably refer to the del Cinque's pretensions of ancient Roman ancestry. Above that, the next storey shows the del Cinque emblem of stars, and then there are successive dis-plays of mensole, swags and female heads set in shells. Both the main entrance and (especially) the balcony on the subsidiary west face are fine, swaggering compositions.

An energetic bust of Hercules occupies this window pediment of Palazzo del Cinque

A comparison with the nearby Casa Giannini in Piazza Capranica is instructive. Both buildings were obviously designed to produce income from shops on the ground floor and from the greatest possible number of self-contained one-storey apartments above the piano nobile. Unlike the Giannini, however, the del Cinque were nobles and their amour propre is reflected in the grandeur of the entrance, the balconies and the profusion of their heraldic symbols in the first and second floors. They seem to have been successful in attracting up-market tenants. A document of 1762 shows them living in the piano nobile and part of the second floor, while the higher floors were all inhabited by prominent lawyers, whose importance was in inverse ratio to their altitude above the street. But the rooms under the roof were occupied by two families of tailors, a locksmith and a couple living in sin.

Apart from the shops on the ground floor, the palace is now given over to offices for the Montecitorio parliament building.

Vasi's etching of the gardens of Palazzo Colonna, connected to the palace (at extreme left) by bridges over via della Pilotta. The casino at the far end of the garden was destroyed in 1927 to make way for the Pontificia Università Gregoriana

Palazzo Colonna

Piazza SS Apostoli, 66

The Colonna have always been one of the greatest noble Roman families; they were politically and militarily prominent throughout the middle ages, and this area was their stronghold long before the Colonna pope Martin V (reigned 1417-31) built a palace here. The present building occupies the entire site running south from SS Apostoli to via IV Novembre, and from Piazza SS Apostoli east to via della Pilotta, over which four bridges connect the palace to the gardens of the Giardino Colonna on the slopes of the Quirinal. It is a striking example of the way in which Roman palaces absorbed and engulfed pre-existing buildings, the most important of which in this case were the quattrocento palace alongside SS Apostoli that was used by Cardinal Bessarion and the 'palazzina' (about 1484) in the second courtyard that was built by Cardinal Giuliano della Rovere (later Pope Julius II). The palace still contains important earlier features (eg the ground-floor Sala della Fontana in the 'palazzina' with a vault splendidly decorated by Pinturicchio) but most of it now dates from the 17th and 18th centuries.

The main 17th century extensions were begun by Cardinal Girolamo Colonna in the 1650s and were continued and elaborated by Lorenzo Onofrio Colonna, Gran Connestabile (ie High Constable and honorary military supremo) of the Kingdom of Naples. Until his death in 1671 their house architect was Antonio del Grande who was responsible for the façade with blocked arches in the main court.[1]

The finest 17th century part of the palace is manifestly the famous galleria, which occupies the piano nobile on the palace's south flank alongside via IV Novembre (though the external front here is a 19th century composition by Andrea Busiri Vici, made necessary by the widening of the street). With its marble revetments and outstanding late Baroque ceiling, and with its huge length extended yet further into two subsidiary chambers, the galleria is a truly splendid space. Many sovereign rulers have had to make do with less regal accommodation than this, and the self-esteem of the Colonna was, indeed, almost boundless.

The galleria was among the works attributed to del Grande by Pollack in 1911, when he rediscovered the long-forgotten architect, and until recently that attribution was not seriously questioned, though it was always surprising to think that such a journeyman figure could have been responsible for so confident and imaginative a display. Thanks to Christina Strunck's essay of 2002 we now know that the true story is much more complicated, and that some of the most striking features of the design are due to the involvement of Bernini himself, as follows.

Del Grande did indeed carry out the first work, carving out the galleria's central space from a number of existing rooms. This was done for Lorenzo Onofrio Colonna very soon after his marriage to Maria Mancini in 1661 (when, incidentally, Cardinal Girolamo still had five years to live). The central space was vaulted by 1665 and from that time Giovanni Paolo Schor was engaged in designing and executing stucco work (probably the frieze) and the astounding painted confection of feigned stucco quadratura, banners and vividly foreshortened exotic figures that frame the narrative panels of the ceiling. Schor died in 1674 and the direction of the stucco-work was entrusted to Bernini's close associate Mattia De Rossi who clearly also had some wider responsibility for the project since he soon organised a mock-up display of the proposed elevation, featuring coupled Corinthian pilasters. By this time Bernini himself was also involved, making the crucial decision to extend the gallery by incorporating the square rooms at each end. The addition of these spaces, partially screened with columns, transformed a pedestrian rectangular unit into something much more various and dynamic. Furthermore, in a display of ingenuity in extracting positive benefits from awkward features, Bernini retained the floor level of the eastern annex (now the Sala della Colonna Bellica) so as to provide Lorenzo Onofrio Colonna with a throne room that was elevated above the main gallery and thus calculated to assist the aura of authority and distance surrounding his public appearances.

Work on the creation of the two end-rooms was put in hand immediately following Bernini's intervention, and in the following year (1675) the elevation of the long sides of the gallery took shape, with pilasters of a composite order. The trophies between the pilasters were inserted in 1686 while Carlo Fontana was the superintending architect; the Colonna traditionally saw themselves as exemplifying the military virtues, and the clear function of the trophies and ceiling paintings (see below) is to declare that self-image as proudly as possible. In 1689 (the year of Lorenzo Onofrio's death) Fontana's nephew Gerolamo Fontana took over, continuing the long programme of installing the marble revetments and making the final significant architectural change by walling up two bays of windows on each side so as to create a much stronger sense of rhythmic progression.

Vasi's view of Piazza SS Apostoli with Palazzo Colonna occupying most of the east (right) side. The two pavilions are by Michetti but most of the wall between them was remodelled in the 19th century. At the far end of the piazza is Palazzo Muti Papazzurri

The main fresco of the great ceiling had been completed by 1678 by Giovanni Coli and Filippo Gherardi. The subject — a hectic confusion of ships' prows, rigging and bodies — is the *Battle of Lepanto*, the Holy League's naval victory against the Turks in 1571, where the papal contingent of galleys had been commanded by the family hero Marcantonio Colonna. (The pope had, in fact, only contributed a dozen galleys to an allied fleet of over 200 vessels under the supreme command of Don John of Austria, but in this epic confrontation between Christendom and the Infidel the command of the pope's own battle squadron had special symbolic force and was a most tremendous honour.) Coli and Gherardi's four other narrative panels in the ceiling are altogether more pedestrian.

Lorenzo Onofrio intended to continue the Lepanto theme in the ceilings of the subsidiary rooms and in 1682 he commissioned this work from Luca Giordano who, however, did no more than make a start in the eastern room before he transferred to Spain in 1692. With Giordano's departure, Lorenzo Onofrio's successors had to look elsewhere, and the documents published by Strunck indicate that the Venetian painter Sebastiano Ricci had completed both ceilings by 1695. Very soon, however, the Colonna had second thoughts and brought in the Roman painter Giuseppe Bartolomeo Chiari to replace the ceiling in the eastern room, which he finished by 1700. The end result of all this was that Chiari's *Apotheosis of Marcantonio Colonna* in the Sala della Colonna Bellica is in a dialogue with Ricci's

Allegory of the Victory of Lepanto in the western room (Sala dei Paesaggi). Since Chiari, a pupil of Maratta, was an exemplar of the Roman classical tendency of the time, and Ricci could be taken as representative of Venetian colourism, it is likely that the painters were chosen in a spirit of *paragone* to illustrate the opposing trends.

Lorenzo Onofrio was a great enthusiast for landscape painting, as the private Colonna collection still attests. In 1667-68 he had very impressive landscape frescoes carried out in a summer apartment on the ground floor at the back of the 'palazzina'. In the Sala della Fontana, beneath the Pinturicchio ceiling, the short walls were given landscapes that are sometimes attributed to Dughet but look far too elegant for him.

The adjoining two rooms both have elaborate decorative settings by Giovanni Battista Magno (Modanino), within which the landscapes cover the entire walls. The first, the Sala del Tempesta, has a set of marines by Pieter Mulier, known as Tempesta for his speciality of storm scenes. The second room has a set of landscapes by Dughet and is named after him. Both of these cycles begin with scenes of tempests and rocky crags, of the kind that in the 18th century would be called 'sublime', and gradually evolve into prospects of peace and calm. They therefore lend themselves to speculation about the philosophical ideas that the patrons or painters may have harboured, and there has been some critical writing of that kind about them. Be that as it may, the one thing that does seem inherently likely is that the rooms' users enjoyed the pleasing variety that was presented to them and that the painters were glad of a chance to demonstrate their ability to produce fine landscapes of many different kinds.

Beyond the Dughet room there is a further room that served as Maria Mancini's bedroom; it has a small alcove covered with landscapes that Bandes speculates might be by Dughet's only pupil Crescenzio Onofri.[2]

The Colonna family continued to display an outstanding level of artistic discrimination and intelligence in their improvement of the palace, and in the 18th century they demonstrated their independence from Roman norms by commissioning two superb decorative schemes in Rococo taste. The first of these was an airy coffee-house in the pavilion on the corner of Piazza SS Apostoli and via IV Novembre, which was part of the new screening wing (since much altered) that Niccolò Michetti added in 1731-1733. The painting in the ceiling and in the grisailles around the walls is by Francesco Mancini and depicts the *Story of Psyche*. Until the 1930s the coffee-house operated as a public café, and one can only wish that the opportunity of enjoying such a delightful space were still available.

The second Rococo scheme is the Salone Turco on the opposite side of the main cortile from the great gallery. The walls here are filled with landscapes seen through architectural features, and these theatrical spaces are inhabited by a most engaging cast of idling characters in Turkish, Russian and generic exotic fancy dress. Some of the figures in this early piece of orientalism seem to have strayed in from the world of Tiepolo, others look forward to that of *Così fan tutte*. They were created by Stefano Pozzi and his brother Giovanni, and one of the scenes displays the legend 'Fecit anno 1758'.[3] The ceiling of the room was originally a 1650 allegory in the style of Lanfranco but this was heavily repainted by Stefano Pozzi.[4]

The Galleria Colonna contains an extremely important collection of paintings, including many of the Baroque period. Entering from via della Pilotta, the visitor ascends directly to the Sala della Colonna Bellica, at the east end of the gallery under the Chiari ceiling. From here it is worth looking out over the bridge across via della Pilotta to get a view of the gardens of the Villa Colonna opposite. (The fine 17th century gate to the gardens is still in its original position in via XXIV Maggio but it was left marooned at the top of a flight of steps when the road was lowered after 1870.)

Proceeding through the main gallery, the visitor arrives at the Sala dei Paesaggi, under the Ricci ceiling, before turning right down the suite of rooms along the principal façade. From here, one looks out on to the main court, with Cardinal Bessarion's palace on the right and Michetti's coffee-house pavilion on the far left.

The palace is still owned by the Colonna family. The Galleria Colonna is open on Saturday mornings. The short itinerary includes the galleria itself, but the reader is strongly advised to get the full itinerary which also takes in the Appartamento Principessa Isabelle, thus including the private picture collection and the rooms by Pinturicchio, Tempesta and Dughet. For all details go to the website https://galleria colonna.it.

Palazzo della Consulta

Piazza del Quirinale

When Lorenzo Corsini became pope Clement XII in 1730 he soon appointed his fellow-Florentine Ferdinando Fuga as architect of the Sacri Palazzi Apostolici. Fuga was immediately set to work on projects around the Quirinale, which had assumed greater importance as an administrative headquarters since the time of Alexander VII. The financial underpinning for this and for the rest of the public building programme under the Corsini pontificate was largely provided by Clement's restoration of the lottery that had been suppressed by his predecessor. Fuga was first employed (1730-1731) on the completion of the Scuderie (which had been begun by Alessandro Specchi, but had been left untouched for a decade) and on the extension (1731-1732) of the Quirinale palace's Manica Lunga along via del Quirinale. Even discounting the Consulta, therefore, today's appearance of the whole area owes a lot to Fuga, though the only part of these first two projects where he had a completely free hand was the Palazzina del Segretario delle Cifre which ends the Manica Lunga next to Palazzo Galloppi at the Quattro Fontane.

In functional terms the building of the Palazzo della Consulta to house a new bureaucratic complex on Piazza del Quirinale belongs squarely within the movement to provide Rome with an efficient government infrastructure appropriate to the capital of a modern state, which can be seen as starting with Fontana's law courts at the Montecitorio at the turn of the century. With the new building the pope not only brought under one roof various government units that he wanted to have close by him at the Quirinale, but he also saved the rent that had previously been spent on housing them. The commission was given to Fuga in 1731; construction began the following year, and in 1737 Fuga wrote to the pope to declare the building finished and to seek extra recompense for his efforts.[1]

The architect's brief was exceptionally difficult, as it entailed accommodating four different self-contained units within an irregular trapezoid plan on uneven ground, originally occupied by the Baths of Constantine, where the soil conditions demanded exceptionally strong foundations. The units were as follows.

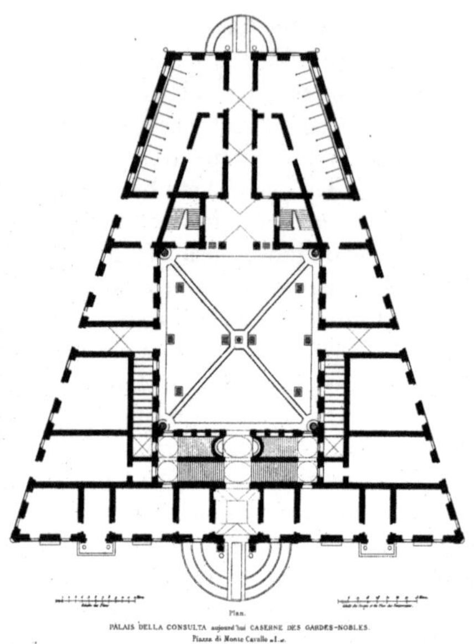

Letarouilly's plan of the Palazzo della Consulta

The Segretaria della Congregazione della Sacra Consulta. This department of the papal administration was the main organ for the temporal government of the Papal States, acting as something like a combined Ministry of the Interior and Ministry of Justice. It was in general charge of the administration of law and order issues, and also furnished the supreme court for both civil and criminal cases, though in practice it concentrated on criminal work. The ultimate head of the Congregazione was the Secretary of State, but the daily work of the department was supervised on-site by the Segretario, who was himself a high-ranking prelate.

The Segretaria dei Brevi Pontefici. This department was in charge of the preparation, dissemination and archiving of the briefs which were a common way of transmitting papal decisions. It was headed by the Segretario dei Brevi, who was always a cardinal.

Two squadrons of Cavalleggeri, or light cavalry, who provided the pope's honour guard and were also sworn to act as his personal bodyguard.

A squadron of Corazze, or cuirassiers, whose duties were much the same as those of the Cavaleggeri. In fact the honour guard and security details involved both units, though they were not under a unified chain of command.

In addition to the prestigious apartments for the two Secretaries themselves, Fuga thus had to provide barracks, stables, kitchens, offices, archive space and every other ancillary for four organisations that required separate facilities, and which had very different logistical and ceremonial needs. All this required numerous entrances and a complex system of subsidiary staircases and corridors, and there was general agreement at the time that Fuga had been extraordinarily successful in resolving all the technical and operational problems.[2]

While the side elevations of the palace are extremely plain, something much more imposing was needed for the main façade, both as a contribution to the grandeur of Piazza del Quirinale and as reflecting the eminence of the two high officials who had their quarters in the building. Fuga rose to the challenge by producing the first large-scale masterpiece of his career — an austere yet splendid design that projects the grandeur asserted by the papal government, but is nevertheless imbued with the same Corsini aesthetic of restraint and clarity that is exemplified in the huge palace that Fuga was to build for the papal family in Trastevere.

The basis of Fuga's design was a rigorously controlled rectilinear grid, bisected horizontally into two equal tiers, with light rustication on the lower tier and with the bays on both tiers clearly defined by plain, pale pilaster strips; in the central bays and at the extreme ends of the elevation these strips

Print by Sgrilli of the double staircase in the cortile of the Palazzo della Consulta

are replaced by giant Ionic pilasters above and heavy rustication below. Within this stern matrix, a carefully controlled element of richness and contrast is provided by the elaborate composite windows (which clearly derive from the specifically Florentine tradition with which Fuga would have been very familiar from his youthful training under Foggini[3]) and by the groups of sculpture (although these are not now as Fuga envisaged them). Fuga's first complete drawing of the elevation shows all the main elements of the design already in place, but with a strong movement forward from the plane of the wall, a marked privileging of the central pavilion, and heavy rustication throughout the ground floor. All this was scaled down and flattened out in the definitive final drawing, which corresponds closely to the actual building, and this quieter tone of voice can be assumed to reflect the instructions of Cardinal Neri Corsini, the Secretary of State.[4]

The groups of sculpture are highly important to the overall effect of the building, but Fuga's own intentions would have been more restrained and more consistent in style. The groups are as follows.

Over each of the side entrances an uncannily live-looking military trophy, supported by a bracket consisting of a weird, old-fashioned mascherone with wings. These groups, installed in 1735, are by the Florentine sculptor Filippo Della Valle. They mark the entrances to the quarters of the Corazze (on the right) and the Cavalleggeri (on the left), and they must have contributed significantly to the ceremonial atmosphere as the guards turned out for duty and returned to their quarters. Of all the sculpture on the façade, these groups are the most unusual, and they must also be the closest to Fuga's intentions, as they clearly appear in his drawings.

In the centre of the roofline, and high over the balustrade, two figures of Fame supporting the Corsini papal arms. These are by the Neapolitan sculptor Paolo Benaglia and are manifestly in a far more full-blooded Baroque style than anything else at the Consulta. Although they were also installed in 1735, they appear in Fuga's drawings only by way of a slip of paper that could be folded back to show the effect without them. Benaglia's actual group is, in fact, much larger and more prominent than what is indicated in this alternative sketch of Fuga's, and it imposes a far stronger central emphasis than Fuga would have been likely to welcome.

Above the central entrance, solid, classicising figures of *Justice* and *Religion* (referring to the Segretarie of the Consulta and the Brevi, respectively) by Filippo Della Valle[5] and installed as an afterthought in 1739. Fuga had never planned anything more than a reticent Corsini stemma here, and the reason for adding the two figures is not known. One can speculate that the two Secretaries may have thought that they were at least as much entitled to sculptured signs of their presence as were the military units alongside them. At all events, the heavy mass of the Della Valle figures is another addition to the central emphasis, and this was yet further accentuated in the early 1870s when the arms of Savoy were added to fill the empty space between Della Valle's figures.

The most extraordinary single feature of the Consulta, however, is the double staircase that occupies the entire entrance side of the cortile. It is a functional, virtually unadorned and flat structure, with open flights rising towards the centre and with landings at the centre and at each side. Its brutally transparent statement that the building was there to give impartial service to two departments of the papal government would have been yet more powerful before it was closed in with glass screens. It is astonishing that such a radical, austere design could have been developed at the same time that Valvassori's Doria-Pamphili façade was going up on the Corso.

Fuga would certainly have seen Sanfelice's courtyard staircase (1724-1726) at the Sanfelice palace in Naples, but that aims at an airy gracefulness that is very different from Fuga's stern statement of purpose at the Consulta. The staircase in Palazzo Pighini in Rome is much closer, as it is a flat structure of parallel flights, similar to one half of Fuga's invention. The Pighini staircase was still incomplete in 1732 when the Consulta stairs were begun, but it must have been designed before Specchi's death in 1729 and Fuga could well have been aware of its nature before he began the Consulta design.

After the unification of Italy the Consulta was used for various government departments. Since 1955 it has been the seat of the Constitutional Court. In these security-conscious days it is hard for private individuals even to get into the cortile to see the great staircase, let alone visit the interior where some of Antonio Bicchierai's decoration remains in place.

Houses at Piazza delle Coppelle, 64 and 66

An astonishing pair of barocchetto buildings.

The larger, no. 64, is a compendium of many characteristic barocchetto devices. The door — flanked by a rimessa and a pagoda-pedimented window — is a wild composition with a shell sunk between volutes that fly out centrifugally. Above, the door merges into a ringhiera below the elongated central window, while the windows of the upper two floors are similarly 'stacked' together. All the stucco decoration is of high quality. The attic is a recent addition.

No. 66 adjoins the larger building at right angles around the corner of the piazza. Lombardi states that this is the building shown as no. 824 in Nolli's map of 1748 where it is identified as 'Casa Rita', but in fact the placing of the number in Nolli's map is ambiguous. The building's impact is due to its tiny size, set against the massive statements made by its architectural components. The ground floor is entirely taken up by a vast rimessa with a wayward composite opening. Above this, the central window is even more extended than that of its neighbour, while the upper floor consists of nothing more than two blind oval niches and the strangely moulded form of the top of the central window. Above, and set back, there is a curtain wall with an elaborate cartouche that is now empty.

It is not clear whether these two buildings were conceived together, as the differences between them are just as strong as the similarities. However, no. 66 seems too small to have been an independent unit and it does have the appearance of an exceptionally decorative coach-house.

Palazzo Corsini (Riario)

Via della Lungara, 10

Palazzo Corsini was the last significant palace built in Rome by a papal family in the Baroque era (and only one more papal palace, Palazzo Braschi, was ever built). It was sited right on the edge of the inhabited area, directly across via della Lungara from the Farnesina. The best way to approach its long and low main façade is by foot across the Ponte Sisto and then through the lanes of Trastevere, as this brings home the building's essential nature. Although it would be facile to classify it as nothing more than a monster villa, in competition with the Farnesina, its strong relationship with the gardens at the back, and its open structure in that direction, are undisguisedly villa-like characteristics. Some other Roman palaces (notably the Barberini and Falconieri) do make references to the villa type, but despite its huge size only the Corsini is so manifestly suffused by a suburban character.

The first palace on the site was built in 1511 by Cardinal Raffaele Riario.[1] It included the present south (left) wing and part of the southern main front, all now occupied on the piano nobile by the Galleria Nazionale d'Arte Antica. In the 17th century it was lived in by Queen Christina of Sweden.

After the Florentine Cardinal Lorenzo Corsini became Pope Clement XII in 1730 his family moved their residence to Rome, acquiring the Riario palace in 1735, and setting the official papal architect Ferdinando Fuga to work on extending and rebuilding it in 1736. Cardinal Neri Corsini, the pope's nephew and Secretary of State, was the leading spirit of this enterprise. Like the pope (who was totally blind by 1732) he was a serious-minded man with a principled preference for austere classicism in architecture, and this is clearly reflected in the rectilinear emphasis of Fuga's design, and its restrained decoration. Fuga's first addition was the north (right) wing, and the work proceeded in phases, with the pavilion containing the central staircase not being completed until 1753. The Corsini were great patrons of learning and when Cardinal Neri finally transferred their famous library to the palace on via della Lungara in 1754 he made it freely open to the public. That tradition is still maintained.

Vasi's view of Palazzo Corsini, emphasising its attenuated proportions

The stairway ensemble is certainly the most remarkable part of the design, and in its sheer bulk it comes as an astonishing piece of scenography after the long, low façade. It consists of a three-aisled vestibule leading to a passage which goes right through to the back and is flanked by two flights of stairs. These unite at the half-landing to form a single reversed flight which takes the visitor up to the piano nobile. This is the opposite of the normal 18th century arrangement with a single flight dividing into two,[2] but it has the advantage of allowing a carriage-way to be laid out on the main axis of the palace through to the garden and stables. At piano nobile level in the centre of the palace is a double-height room giving access to the apartments on either side; its undulating gallery makes it a memorable space but the detailing is dry.

Apart from the practical advantage of making a clear run for carriages, the arrangement of the stairway was a carefully calculated preamble to the elaborate gardens that Fuga superimposed on an earlier garden behind the palace. Fuga's design consisted of an area of parterres and fountains, and then a steep landscaped tract furnished with a stairway and cascade, the Scalinetta delle Undici Fontane. The terminus of the vista, almost at the ridge of the Janiculum, was a nicchione housing a colossal statue, supposedly of *Cornelius Cornutus*. The whole area is now occupied by the botanical garden

Opposite: Letarouilly's plan shows how the organization of Palazzo Corsini is integrated with the terrace and parterres at the back

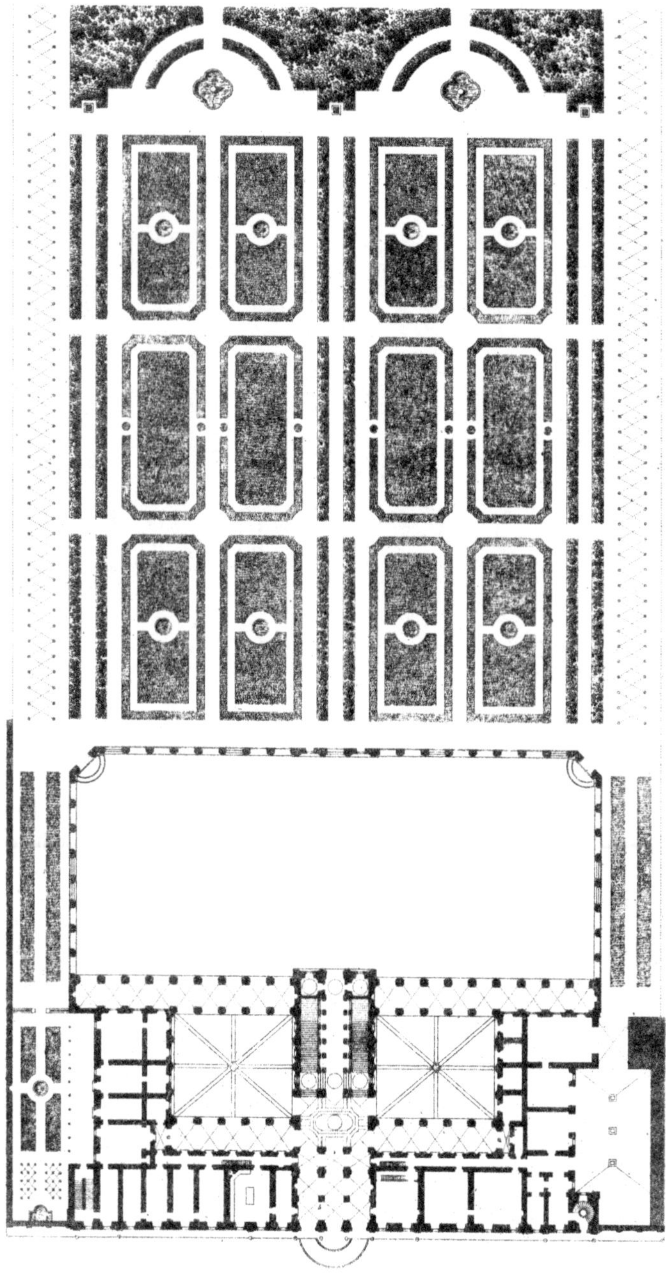

Letarouilly's view of the stairs of Palazzo Corsini, showing the central passage running through the palace to the garden with the stairs rising on either side

run by La Sapienza, and at the time of writing the cascade is being restored.

The garden area had been used by Queen Christina of Sweden for meetings of the circle of intellectuals and artists who formed themselves into the Accademia degli Arcadi in 1690, the year after her death.* The room in which she died, the Sala dell'Alcova, was deliberately preserved in Fuga's rebuilding, and it is the only part of the Riario palace to retain its original 16th century decoration. The Sala dell'Alcova was, in fact, formed by Fuga out of two rooms that were originally separate, and their ceiling frescoes are clearly by different hands. Acidini Luchinat ascribes the *Scenes from the Life of Moses* and the *Virtues* in the second ceiling to a collaborator of Federico Zuccari (possibly Domenico Passignano) and suggests a date between 1567 and 1583; the *Scenes from the Life of Solomon* in the first ceiling are of lower quality and their author has not been identified.[3] Both ceilings feature elaborate grotesques.[4] The Sala dell'Alcova is open to the public as Room V of the Galleria Nazionale, which includes much of the original Corsini collection, acquired by the State in 1883 along with the palace. Anyone inter-

*The open-air complex at the Bosco Parrasio that was built for the Accademia degli Arcadi in the 18th century lies immediately outside the Aurelian Walls that line the southern side of the Corsini gardens. Queen Christina's circle, and indeed the Accademia in its early years, may not have had such a single designated meeting place but to have met at various garden spots.

ested in the Baroque will certainly want to see the collection, which contains many fine paintings of the period.

The north (right) part of the palace is now administered by the Accademia dei Lincei. This section includes the Corsini library (Biblioteca Corsiniana), still kept in the rooms that were designed for it in the north wing, and still functioning as a scholarly library in the way its founders intended. It also includes the area of the the slightly later reception suite running from the central vestibule to the north wing on the piano nobile. This area was converted to library use in the 1920s, partly in order to accommodate a bequest by a scion of the Caetani family.

The whole of the piano nobile on the north side of the palace is decorated in somewhat different styles by many hands whose identity remained a mystery until the commissioning programme was established from the documents by Borsellino in the 1980s. The main items are the four frescoed ceilings in the Biblioteca Corsiniana and the three further ones along the old reception suite. The library ceilings (1746-48) are by Gregorio Guglielmi, Stefano Parrocel, Sebastiano Conca and Vincenzo Meucci.[5] They are all classicising representations of the various subjects to which the books below them are devoted; Meucci's is the largest, coolest and most classicising, while in this company Conca's ceiling appears quite robust and painterly. The three painted rooms along the reception suite (1750-58) are by Liborio Mormorelli;[6] each ceiling consists of a central scene and four thematically linked coves. The subjects are *Aurora*, the *Fall of Phæthon* and the *Chariot of Apollo*. Of these, the (rather coarsely executed) *Fall of Phæthon* is clearly derived from Albani's celebrated ceiling at Palazzo Giustiniani (Odescalchi) at Bassano di Sutri, and indeed the Corsini paid for Mormorelli to go to Bassano to study the Albani ceiling at first hand.[7] Although Mormorelli's work here is of uneven quality, much of it reinterprets 17th century motifs with real vigour, displaying a 'Baroque revival' character that is quite distinct from the earlier work in the library.

The Galleria Nazionale has conventional opening hours. The Accademia dei Lincei is also open to the public, but it is very advisable to make a prior arrangement for a visit.

Palazzo Costaguti (Patrizi)

Piazza Mattei, 10

The palace is celebrated not for its rather indifferent architecture but for the ceilings by notable painters in the rooms of the piano nobile. The most important of these were done in the 1620s while the palace was owned by the Patrizi family.[1]

In 1598 Solderio Patrizi bought a palace on this site from the Quattrocchi family, and he proceeded to have it improved by the architect Carlo Lambardi.[2] The hopes of this branch of the Patrizi were pinned on Solderio's son Costanzo (b.1590) who expected a glittering career in the Curia under the protection of Cardinal Scipione Borghese. In 1615 — the year after his father's death — Costanzo bought the important and lucrative post of Treasurer General, became a Monsignore, and began spending lavishly on equipping himself with all the trappings of a powerful prelate. He appears to have been a respected administrator, keeping his post under Gregory XV and being privately selected as a future cardinal by Urban VIII. The family's dreams were suddenly ended, however, when Costanzo unexpectedly died in January 1624, leaving a mountain of debt. These debts included large sums owing to the Costaguti, who were a Genoese banking family, and in September 1624 the palace was sold to the Marchese Prospero Costaguti and his brother Ascanio. The new owners took possession in 1626 and soon began a new programme of modification and expansion. At some point in the 17th century they incorporated part of the Boccapaduli palace on via dei Falegnami.

The earliest part of the present building is the wing along via della Reginella, which is a survival from the original Quattrocchi palace. This is made clear by the Quattrocchi arms (a crowned eagle above a chevron bearing four eyes) which appears in the cornice along the entire length of the wing, and also in the fine door (now blocked) at Piazza Mattei end of the street. At the back of the palace, on what is now Piazza Costaguti, the Patrizi had the church of S Leonardo in Albis destroyed to provide room for their stabling and carriages, and Passeri attributed their later misfortunes to this action.[3] The current façade in this area, however, displays the Costaguti arms of three chevrons and three stars in the windows, and must date from some time not long after 1626. The door on Piazza Mattei proudly bears the name COSTAGUTI and the façades on the piazza and along via dei Falegnami show the Costaguti emblems in the cornice. They were all presumably made in the same period. According to Mola, the parts on Piazza Costaguti were done by Antonio De Battisti and the sections around Piazza Mattei by Ascanio De Rossi.[4]

In the 1990s there was talk of turning the palace into some kind of publicly accessible museum in exchange for State assistance with long-overdue restoration work,[5] but that idea came to nothing. The Costaguti family still occupy part of the palace, which also houses the headquarters of ACRI (Associazione fra le Casse di Risparmio Italiane), together with several private apartments.

A room along via della Reginella has a frieze of the Months and Virtues in landscapes that is traditionally attributed to Federico Zuccari and his brother Taddeo (who died as early as 1566). Acidini Luchinat, however, believes that if Federico Zuccari had any involvement, it could only have been with the figures of *Virtues*; and that *The Months* are in the northern landscape style introduced by Bril. Röttgen, on the other hand, attributes the frieze to Bernardino Cesari, the brother of the Cavaliere d'Arpino.[6]

Whatever may be the authorship and dating of the *Months* and *Virtues*, when Costanzo Patrizi began his programme of improvements, probably not long after he became Treasurer General in 1615, he seems to have first turned to the Cavaliere d'Arpino, who painted in the gallery a *Venus and Cupid* that Titi described as being in the painter's 'buona maniera'.[7] That painting has disappeared and what remains from the d'Arpino workshop are two traditional quadri riportati in rich stucco frames, representing *Venus Arming Æneas* and *The Hours*. The first of these may be by the Cavaliere himself, while the second is probably by Flaminio Allegrini; Bernardino Cesari may have been involved in both.[8]

Around the time that the Ludovisi pope Gregory XV was elected in 1621 Costanzo Patrizi employed Agostino Tassi to paint quadratura surrounds in a group of rooms that were to be completed by Guercino, Domenichino and Lanfranco. The choice of these Emilian painters was, in effect, a statement of Patrizi's standing with the new Bolognese pope, who was the protector of Guercino in particular. Furthermore, the open sky compositions of Guercino and Lanfranco marked a decisive move away from quadri riportati and showed Costanzo

Palazzo Costaguti: Guercino's revolutionary ceiling fresco of The Sleeping Rinaldo Abducted by Armida

as a patron who was just as up-to-the-minute in his artistic tastes as he was politically.

Tassi, who may have provided the quadratura for only two of the rooms,[9] was probably in overall charge of organising the work, and was given accommodation on site. In 1622 he was charged with assaulting a courtesan but his sentence was commuted to one of house-arrest in the palace under Costanzo Patrizi's guarantee; true to form, he was soon thrown out when it was discovered that he had managed to hide the woman in the quarters he had been assigned.[10]

The Lanfranco ceiling, probably painted in 1623, depicts *Justice and Peace* sailing across an open sky on a cloud supported by putti, with numerous further putti waving foliage and cavorting on the quadratura balustrade.[11] Guercino's ceiling depicting the *Sleeping Rinaldo carried off by Armida* is a more full-blooded Baroque piece, with Armida's chariot drawn by dragons careering wildly across the ceiling. It must have looked startlingly painterly, vigorous and original when it was executed, and it clearly has close connections with the superb *Aurora* ceiling that Guercino painted for the pope's family in the Casino Ludovisi.[12]

Domenichino's ceiling of the main audience chamber was probably done in 1622, immediately after the Guercino ceiling in the adjoining room. It is a very curious, disjointed composition set in a cross-shaped area that is created by massive quadratura in the four corners. In the centre is a *Chariot of Apollo* surrounded by a cloudy oval; three of the arms created by the quadratura are occupied by putti bearing emblems, and the fourth is filled by a group of *Truth Disclosed by Time* in which the figures are on a much larger scale than either the putti or the central image. While the figures in the four arms are all painted dal di sotto in sù, as though they were floating in an open sky, the central group is depicted frontally, as in a traditional quadro riportato. The reasons for so many incoherent features have never been fully resolved, but Pedrocchi plausibly speculates that Domenichino may have planned his painting without knowing that the space was to be restricted and defined by the quadratura, and also that there may previously have been a stucco frame in the ceiling.[13] Despite all its oddities, the painting clearly has a place in the sequence of major paintings in Rome, and Spear points out that it must have been painted not only in competition with the Guercino ceiling in the adjoining room but also in a spirit of dialogue with the Ludovisi and Pallavacini Rospigliosi *Auroras* by Guercino and Guido Reni.[14]

None of the ceilings done for the Costaguti after 1624 is as ambitious as Costanzo Patrizi's programme, and they are all conventional quadri riportati in stucco frames. The first was a *Hercules, Nessus and Dejanira* by Lanfranco, probably commissioned around 1630.[15] Despite the powerfully drawn figures it has often been attributed to Albani and also to Sisto Badalocchio. Lanfranco also completed a ceiling of *Polyphemus and Galatea* in the palace, but this was destroyed in the 19th century.

The next two ceilings were probably commissioned by Cardinal Vincenzo Costaguti in the 1640s, before he left Rome as Papal Legate to Urbino in 1649. Mola's *Bacchus and Ariadne* must have been done not long after the painter's return to Rome in 1647. It is a charming, romantic piece, with the main figures still much under the influence of Albani, and with several small Titianesque Bacchanalian groups scattered over a very Venetian landscape.[16] Romanelli's *Arion* was probably similarly done after his first visit to Paris in 1646-47.[17] It shows the youth Arion riding on a dolphin while being crowned by a putto, observed from one side by three mariners on a ship and from the other by two sportive Raphaelesque nereids. It is essentially a reprise of the same subject in the Galleria Farnese, with some extra personages thrown in for good measure, and is typical of the fluent, if rather vapid, classical formula that Romanelli had developed by mid-career. Titi (1763) thought it very elegant ('molto vaga').

Last, and quite distinct from anything else in the palace, there are the Sala della Storia Romana and the Sala Cartagina, with (very crowded) *Scenes from Roman and Carthagininian History* respectively. These rooms originally formed part of the adjoining Palazzo Boccapaduli. They are often said, in accordance with a Costaguti family tradition, to be wholly or partly by Dughet, but Boisclair firmly rejects the idea that Dughet could have had any involvement and suggests that they are entirely by Francesco Allegrini.[18]

Palazzo Crescenzi (Bonelli, De Dominicis)

Piazza della Rotonda 23

In the Baroque period the palace was thought of sufficiently well to merit two plates in Ferrerio's *Palazzi di Roma* and

Falda's print of the façade of Palazzo Crescenzi, once quite celebrated but now sadly mutilated by street-widening

three more in De Rossi's *Architettura Civile*. Most of what one now sees from the outside, however, is a 19th- and 20th-century pastiche.[1]

The Crescenzi were established in the S Eustachio area from around the 10th century. When Virgilio Crescenzi was expanding his palace into neighbouring buildings in the 1580s he employed Giacomo Della Porta, who was the unquestioned leading architect in Rome.[2] Precisely what Della Porta built is not known, but it may well have extended to the limits of the isolato, on via della Rotonda and via di S Eustachio. These façades, however, were not given any architectural significance, and remained untidy, meagre items until well into the 19th century.[3] The side facing the Pantheon was built so close to the ancient building that it reflected its curvature.

The showcase façade was built to the north, along Salita de' Crescenzi, and it is this that is illustrated in Ferrerio. It was a handsome seven-bay design, with three storeys and a mezzanine, a central door, heavily reticulated quoins at the corners, and elaborate windows with female heads and swags beneath a cornice supported by volute brackets with mascheroni. The part between the top of the ground floor and the cornice is now all that remains of this 17th century work.

Falda's plate in Ferrerio attributes the design of the new façade to Giovanni Battista Crescenzi and Niccolò Sebregondi, but the recent work in the archives has established that the main architect was Carlo Lambardi and that the work was proceeding in 1602.[4] The involvement of G. B. Crescenzi and Sebregondi came a few years later, around 1607, and Sebregondi's part was limited to designing the windows, door and interior stuccoes.[5]

Mensola della Porta
B
Scala di palmi due per il Modine
A. e Mensola B.
A.
Scala di Pasmi dieci
Porta del Palazzo del Sig.re Marchese Crescentij. Architettura del Sig.re Gio. Batta Crescentij.
Diseg.to da Carlo Quadri Architetto
Nella Stamp.a di Dom.co de Rossi erede di Gio. Giac.o de Rossi in Roma alla Pace.
Intag.ta da Fran.co Bartoli. 128

Count G. B. Crescenzi was an intriguing character, to whom Baglione devoted one of the *Vite*, but exactly what part he played in the design of his own palace is an open question. He was taught drawing and painting by Cristoforo Roncalli (Pomarancio), and he became a skilled architect and painter who used the palace as the site of an informal academy of disegno for young people. Since he acted as supervisor for some important Borghese projects, he may well have played that role here.

The palace remained essentially unchanged until 1871, when the then owner Filippo De Dominicis accepted the municipal authorities' decision to widen the space alongside the Pantheon, and he seems immediately to have reorganised the side on via di S Eustachio, creating shops and a mezzanine on the ground floor, imitating the upper floors from the Salita de' Crescenzi side, and providing a new entrance within a large reticulated feature rising the full height of the building. The more substantial modifications followed in 1873-74, when the entire east side was cut back by the depth of two to three bays, the door on the north face was removed, and a new façade was constructed to face the Pantheon over the wide new gap.[6] The piano nobile and upper floors were now, for the first time, substantially uniform around the building.[7]

In 1905-07 the attic was added, with its decorative heads set in tondi.[8] Last of all, in 1910, the assertive new door was created in via della Rotonda.[9] The crowned eagle that dominates this confection is a Mattei emblem, reflecting the palace's ownership at the time by the Antici Mattei family.

The Sala dell'Accademia on the piano nobile contained frescoes of allegorical figures (*Fame*, *Abundance*, *Peace*, *Charity*, *Inspiration*) by Pomarancio that were detached from the wall before 1961. Next to it is a small room with ceiling panels by the school of Pomarancio and a frieze including seven landscapes. Although Toesca disputed the attribution, Roethlisberger maintained that these were the paintings that Baldinucci says Claude executed in this palace after his return to Rome in 1627. In that event, they have a special importance not only for their early date (c. 1630) but as being Claude's only known surviving work in fresco.

Palazzo Donarelli (Ricci)

Via Giulia, 97

A 17th century nine-bay palace with plain windows haphazardly disposed, due to the need to accommodate at least two earlier buildings. The upper windows of the first four bays have volutes and lion masks, and they clearly belong to a part that was added later — perhaps in the early 18th century.

To the left of the entrance passage there is an ingeniously contrived oval staircase that is lit by windows with balconies looking on to the cortile. This staircase is already shown in a survey signed by Carlo Rainaldi and Camillo Arcucci in April 1663, and Tafuri suggests that it was probably Rainaldi who was responsible for the feature.[1] It is not known what involvement Rainaldi — or any other architect — had in the rest of the palace.

Opposite: The door of Palazzo Crescenzi from De Rossi's Architettura Civile *. De Rossi attributes the design to Count Giovanni Battista Crescenzi, who was an amateur architect among other accomplishments, but this is open to question. The door was destroyed in the 19th century*

This print of 1665 by Falda shows what an insignificant appearance Palazzo Doria-Pamphili presented on the Corso next to S Maria in via Lata until the Valvassori front was built in the 18th century. On the right is the Jacopino del Conte building with the 'Il Facchino' fountain; at the bottom of the Corso on the left of the image is Palazzo D'Aste

Palazzo Doria-Pamphili (Santorio, della Rovere, Aldobrandini)

Via del Corso, 304

The first palace on this site, of which nothing much is known, was begun by Cardinal Niccolò d'Appiacci in the 1440s and extended before 1469 by Cardinal Dionysius Zech. After a gap of twenty years or more it was obtained by Giovanni Fazio Santorio, who became an important figure at the court of Julius II. As soon as Santorio was made a cardinal in 1505 he set about improving his palace in the latest style, beginning the construction of a Bramantesque two-storey arcaded cortile in the angle between S Maria in via Lata and the Corso. This is still one of the main features of the building, though it is much altered by later modifications. In 1507 Julius II was so impressed by Santorio's splendid new scheme that he forced him to cede the palace to his nephew, Francesco Maria della Rovere, whom he made Duke of Urbino in 1508. The disconsolate Santorio died in 1510. The della Rovere continued to build the cortile in accordance with Santorio's intentions, and sporadically bought neighbouring buildings in order to expand the palace, but they never gave their full attention to developing the site in a concerted way. Falda's print of 1665 on this page shows that even at that late date it was still incomplete, lacking at least the piano nobile on the flank along the Corso.

In 1601 the Duke of Urbino sold the palace

This view by Vasi shows the wings built at the back of Palazzo Doria-Pamphili by Antonio del Grande. The altana behind the long wing is a survivor from the time when the Aldobrandini owned the palace and it still bears their emblems. The Collegio Romano is on the extreme left

to Cardinal Pietro Aldobrandini, the Cardinale Nepote of Clement VIII. His most memorable action in connection with the place was to commission, around 1603, six lunettes to decorate the pre-existing chapel. These 'Aldobrandini lunettes' are now on public display in the palace's gallery, close to the (inaccessible) room for which they were painted. By far the most impressive of the series is the *Flight into Egypt*, conventionally ascribed to Annibale Carracci, and a very early example of the intellectually regulated ideal landscape of the Baroque period. The other five lunettes appear to be substantially from the Albani workshop and there is endless scholarly dispute about the degree of involvement of various Bolognese masters who were associated with that enterprise.

For the next half-century the Aldobrandini continued to buy property and expand the palace both west and south towards Piazza Venezia. The largest of these projects was the construction of new wings to enclose the huge quadrangle of the Giardino dei Melangoli at the back. They are by Giovan Pietro Moraldi, a regular Aldobrandini architect, albeit one of modest talent.*

In 1647 the palace passed to the Pamphili family when the sole Aldobrandini heiress Donna Olimpia Aldobrandini, Princess of

*The altana above the Giardino dei Melangoli does, however, have a remarkably jaunty frieze made up of the Aldobrandini emblems of the rastrello and the star.[1]

Vasi's view shows the Valvassori façade of Palazzo Doria-Pamphili in place and, on the extreme right, Palazzo de Carolis incorporating the 'Il Facchino' fountain

Rossano, married Innocent X's nephew Camillo Pamphili, who resigned his position as cardinal in order to make the marriage. In 1659-61 Antonio del Grande was employed to build new wings along the east and south sides of the space in front of the Collegio Romano that had been freed by the demolition of Palazzo Salviati. The creation of this new piazza was the result of much negotiation between Alexander VII, the Jesuits of the Collegio Romano and Camillo Pamphili, and the pope continued to take a close interest in the details of Camillo's new building.[2]

Del Grande's fifteen-bay façade on the south side of the piazza is externally a fairly unexciting piece of work that follows the general arrangement of Girolamo Rainaldi's Palazzo Pamphili in Piazza Navona, with the added device of unequally spaced windows à la Giacomo Della Porta. The short five-bay façade on the east side follows the same elevation but with equally spaced windows. Metzger Habel shows that the uncomfortable proportions of the top storey immediately under the cornice of the main wing (and especially the area where the centre feature collides with this space) are due to the top storey being an addition for which Camillo only secured the pope's approval late in the day.[3] She also draws attention to the way in which the staircase preserved from Palazzo Salviati is linked to the Corso by an oval vestibule and an extraordinarily long passage.[4] This meant that the vestibule was arranged transversely to its immediate entrance from Piazza del Collegio Romano, and this arrangement is certainly the most striking feature of the new wing. The staircase leads to the double-height Salone del Pussino (so named because of the paintings by Gaspard Dughet that hang in it). This room was presumably the sala dei palafrenieri or guardroom that marked the beginning of the reception suite running down the new wing towards the north-west corner of Santorio's cortile.

Between 1731 and 1735 Gabriele Valvassori radically changed the parts of the palace towards the Corso. The upper loggias of Santorio's cortile were closed and turned into galleries for the display of painting and sculpture, and a completely new façade was built on the Corso itself. This masterpiece sets a range of close-set piano nobile windows of extraordinarily complex, vaguely Borrominian, shape above balconies that form a virtually continuous motif, curving out over three great entrances and continuing as a screen to link the palace with S Maria in Via Lata. The windows of the second storey are less licentious. The great length of the seventeen bays is broken up into a complex system of sub-units, so that the rhythmical massing of the elements can be read in various ways.[5] Altogether, the façade makes an effect of light-hearted magnificence that is very characteristic of one strand of 18th century sensibility. More sober tastes were already massing, however, and Valvassori's great design was not generally liked at the time. Valvassori himself was never allowed another chance to pursue a major project in such adventurous style.

Many of the rooms of the palace were redecorated at this time by a team including Pompeo Aldrovandini, Pietro Angeletti, Genesio del Barba, Filippo Catapani, Tommaso Maria Conca, Liborio Mormorelli and Stefano Pozzi. By far the best known is the celebrated Galleria degli Specchi, which forms the east side of the new gallery around the Santorio court; the ceiling fresco is by Aureliano Milani (illustration overleaf).

In 1739 Valvassori was succeeded as Pamphili architect by Paolo Antonio Ameli who was commissioned by Cardinal Camillo Pamphili in 1740 to build a new wing along what is now via del Plebiscito.[6] This was different in kind from anything else on the site, as it was conceived to meet the dual function of providing accommodation for the family's horde of servants and dependants, and also to generate rental income, especially from the fine apartments on the main floors. It proved to be financially successful and was one of the most favoured addresses for high church dignitaries up until the Napoleonic invasion. As might be expected against that background, Ameli's façade shows all the features of contemporary bourgeois speculative building, but on a truly palatial scale. Thus, there is a profusion of upper floor windows, many ringhiere, and several lower floors of broadly similar status. In contrast with the aristocratic swagger and confidence of Valvassori's wing on the Corso, the rhythms of Ameli's extension are far more quiet and unassertive. This neighbourly spirit is, indeed, exemplified by the care that Ameli clearly took to ensure that his corner mouldings should echo those of De Rossi's Palazzo D'Aste next door.

On the death of Girolamo Pamphili, brother of Camillo, the palace became the property of the Genoese Prince Giovanni Andrea Doria, who was descended from a daughter of the elder Camillo Pamphili. Prince Giovanni Andrea moved his residence to the palace in 1760, and in 1763 his family formally took the name Doria-Pamphili. In the second half of the 19th century many of the rooms were remodelled by the architect Andrea Busiri Vici.

The palace is still owned by the Doria-

Pamphili family but the art gallery, with its fine collection of mainly 17th century pictures, has generous opening hours to the public. (The throne room, containing several paintings by Dughet, is in the private apartments and is not accessible.) The Santorio cortile, as modified by Valvassori, can easily be seen from the gallery windows and also at street level from the entrance on the Corso. The Giardino dei Melangoli (as well as the contemporary altana with its frieze of Aldobrandini emblems) can be seen from the subsidiary space at the back of the entrance vestibule on the Collegio Romano side.

The strikingly severe architecture of the doorway of Palazzo del Drago in via Arcione

Palazzo del Drago (Gentili)

Via Arcione, 70

Apparently built by Monsignor Antonio Gentile or Gentili, who was made a cardinal in 1731. It passed to the del Drago family and in the later 18th century was well-known for its theatrical and literary gatherings. What now exists is the five bay central section together with a six bay wing to the right. The left wing was demolished when the Traforo running under the Quirinale was constructed in 1902.

The building presumably dates from the first third of the 18th century, and the second floor windows are decorated in conventional barocchetto style. The monumental austerity of the door and piano nobile windows, however, is highly original. The door has jambs that taper down and are set edge foremost. Heavy horizontal mouldings are carried across the lintel, with a powerful V at each side above the capitals; the same general scheme is echoed in the uniform windows of the piano nobile.

It is hard to find any close parallels for the unidentified architect's language of restraint and authority. While the tapering door jambs and sharp angle above are clearly derived from Borromini's door at the Propaganda Fide, the overall effect is totally different here because of the static, rectilinear massing of the elements and the very sparse decoration.* The architect of the Palazzo Galloppi doors, which were presumably roughly contemporary with Palazzo del Drago, incorporated similar motifs within a far more energetic, Borrominian framework. For a later door with analogous side elements, but combined with a Borrominian tympanum, see Palazzo Celani.

*Blunt noted the 'nervously carved capitals' of the door and the 'unusually vigorous barocchetto hoods over the [second floor] windows'.[1]

Opposite, a detail of Aureliano Milani's ceiling of the Galleria degli Specchi in Palazzo Doria-Pamphili. The central scene depicts Hercules and Achelous

Casa del Falco (Casa di Biagio Puccini)

Via del Falco, 18

A sizeable (two bays by six) apartment building rather than a palace, but unmissable because of its congested profusion of strange architectural motifs.

The general conception of the building is clearly indicated in the background of a pen and ink self portrait of 1700 by Biagio Puccini, a fairly successful minor Roman painter of the time but otherwise unknown as an architect.[1] His unadventurous paintings give no hint whatsoever of the exuberant fancy that he brought to this design. Construction of the building lasted from 1709 to 1735, though Puccini himself died in 1721, seemingly having bankrupted himself with the project. It is not clear how far his widow obtained professional architectural assistance in completing the work, though Francesco Ferruzzi was involved in the dealings over Puccini's estate and Zanella suggests that a colleague of his could have participated in the work.[2]

The building is equipped with giant attached pilasters that bear pseudo-aristocratic stars on their flaccidly moulded capitals. These giant pilasters are one of the building's most attention-seeking features, as they are a motif that is normally associated with only the most high-ranking palaces. Otherwise, the lower two storeys are quite restrained, except for the Valvassorian pagoda-pedimented entrance at via del Falco, 18 which features another pseudo-aristocratic star.

In the upper levels (disregarding the recently added topmost storey) the weight and power of the decoration builds up incrementally, with the strangest compositions reserved for the windows of the storey above the main cornice. These are equipped with ringhiere and feature semicircular window heads under an inverted buckle motif within a broken pediment, with a strip with two guttae at each side. The whole ensemble has an almost manic energy.

The building and, indeed, the street take their name from a long-gone tavern in the place. There is still a trattoria there today.

Palazzo Falconieri

Via Giulia, 1

The 16th century palace on via Giulia originally belonged to the Odescalchi, elements of whose arms (leopards, eagles and incense containers) can still be seen in the cornice. In 1606 they sold the building, which then had a frontage of eight bays on via Giulia running north from the church of S. Maria dell'Orazione e della Morte, to Pietro Farnese, Duke of Latera. In 1633 he granted an option to purchase the palace to Orazio Falconieri, a member of the wealthy Florentine family who were among the main financiers of the church of S Giovanni dei Fiorentini at the north end of the street. (In particular, the Falconieri endowed the presbytery of S Giovanni as a family chapel, and employed Borromini on that work as well as on their palace. The tombs of Orazio Falconieri (effigy by Domenico Guidi) and of Cardinal Lelio Falconierei (effigy by Ercole Ferrata) are either side of the high altar.) Orazio did not formally exercise the purchase option until 1638, though by then he had probably already been living in the palace for some time.

Orazio Falconieri must have consulted Borromini about remodelling the palace before he formally took possession of it, as three drawings by Borromini are earlier than 1638.[1] There was then some minor work around 1640 in which Borromini may

Elevation of Palazzo Falconieri by Falda, showing the falcon-headed herms at the outer edges (though the one on the left was not put in place until the 1730s) and the belvedere with its Janus heads

have been involved, but work did not really get under way until Falconieri had acquired an adjacent building at the north (right) end of the palace in 1645. Borromini's rebuilding then went ahead between 1646 and 1651.

Borromini added three bays to the north end of the via Giulia front to provide accommodation for Orazio's brother Cardinal Lelio Falconieri, and he also added an attic above the cornice along the entire façade. The new work was basically just a continuation of the 16th century design, but Borromini balanced the elevation with a second (sham) doorway in the eighth bay, and he conceived the idea of marking the ends of the façade with giant pilasters bearing herms with falcons' heads. The employment of herms to delimit an area is a scholarly reference to ancient practice, while the falcons' heads obviously refer to the Falconieri family name. All is not quite so simple, however, since the birds' heads emerge from human female busts, giving the herms a distinctly unsettling, vaguely Egyptian, appearance of which the significance has not yet been satisfactorily decoded. Only the north (right) herm was installed during Borromini's lifetime, though his drawings make it clear that he intended both. The southern herm had to wait until the 1730s when it was probably put in place by Michetti and Fuga during the construction of S Maria dell'Orazione e della Morte.[2]

The second (sham) doorway is a copy of the original except that Borromini inserted a falcon in its keystone and added luscious rosettes and palmettes under the balcony. The thin stucco rustication of the upper storeys of the façade may be a 19th century addition.[3]

Vasi's view privileges Palazzo Falconieri's belvedere in the centre, and shows how it visually challenges the loggia of Palazzo Farnese on the right

Borromini's work at the back of the palace was not constrained by pre-existing buildings and it is far more personal and exciting than the regular façade on via Giulia. When it was built the new work ran right down to the river bank, from which it is now separated by the Lungotevere. In essence, the new work consisted of a wing for the secular members of the family, with an open U-shaped court and a shorter wing on its south side. The main wing, which extended to the river and then turned north along the river bank for four bays, was mutilated when the Lungotevere was made in the 19th century, but the court remains packed with powerful architectural concepts and fine detailing.

The complex is dominated by an extraordinary tall belvedere that Borromini placed on the west-facing rear of the via Giulia block, and the entire composition has a notably forceful vertical emphasis. As Wittkower pointed out, a main reason for this is Borromini's reversal of expectations, so that the storeys increase in weight and plasticity as they ascend, rather then diminishing in the conventional manner.[4] The three bays of the belvedere itself are separated by detached columns and are treated as Serliane with extremely narrow side elements, while the structure is crowned by a balustrade of which the bays are marked by double-facing Janus heads mounted on curiously rustic moulded pedestals. As a final surprise, the short sides of the belvedere are markedly concave, though the wall, together with the cornice and balustrade, begins by being sharply canted outwards to produce a typically energetic Borrominian reversal of direction.

Seen from across the Tiber, the belvedere forms a clear challenge to Giacomo Della

Porta's loggia on the adjacent Palazzo Farnese. The affirmation of Falconieri status was emphasised by the large stemma* carried high on the belvedere so that it could be clearly seen from as far away as the Janiculum. The implied claim to rival the esteem of the Farnese was, however, not confined to competition with Palazzo Farnese itself. In contrast to the closed via Giulia front facing the city, the open planning of the back of the palace recalls the traditional relaxed design of a suburban villa, and the height of the belvedere resonates with the most famous of all such villas — the Farnesina, which is directly across the Tiber.†[5]

The windows in the north and east faces of the second floor of the wing that runs along the Lungotevere are extremely unusual.[6] They can be seen from the junction of the Lungotevere and via dell' Armata and also from the gate by the side of the palace in via Giulia. The windows are surrounded by very shallow and crisp naturalistic stucco foliage that covers the space in an undifferentiated way that makes a telling contrast with the strong articulation of the surrounding wall.

Borromini's most striking work in the palace is, however, in the interior where he constructed splendid vaulted ceilings in a dozen, mostly quite small, rooms in the new parts that he had built. Four of these ceilings are in the northern addition along via Giulia, which had been designated for Cardinal Lelio Falconieri, who died in 1648, shortly before work on the ceilings began. These are among Borromini's most remarkable inventions, both for their architectonic power and for the quality and subject matter of their stucco decoration. Two of them carry large abstruse emblems that manifestly represent philosophical themes[7] and it may well be that a system of hidden meaning also extended to the other two rooms of the group, where stucco decoration of almost neo-classic detailing is restricted to the periphery of shallow saucer domes. All four ceilings should doubtless be read as conveying messages about Cardinal Lelio's high qualities and virtuous character. The ceilings in Borromini's new wing for secular members of the family are far more conventional, and they have not been improved by the addition of painted decoration in the 19th century.

When the palace was sold in the late 19th century, the original block along via Giulia was ruthlessly modernised, with the addition of a grandiose staircase. This involved the destruction of Borromini's stuccoes in the vestibule, together with the chapel he had inserted in the piano nobile. However, the chapel's appearance is known from an old photograph and some of Borromini's drawings for it survive. One Borrominian doorway in mottled purple marble was also saved (probably from the chapel) and is now in a corridor on the piano nobile.

The palace is now the seat of the Hungarian Academy.

Palazzo Farnese

Piazza Farnese, 67

None of the architecture of this illustrious building can sensibly be called Baroque, though Sangallo's false perspective motif in the main vestibule may have some bearing on developments in the Baroque period. It

*Now appearing not to bear the Falconieri arms, although avian supporters are retained.

†The resonance between the three buildings can best be appreciated in the winter since they are all masked when the leaves are on the plane trees along the river bank.

Annib. Carracci dip.
Gio. Volpato fece all' Acqua forte

has, however, become a commonplace to cite Annibale Carracci's superb frescoes in the Galleria as ushering in that period — with Caravaggio's very different work acting as some kind of honorary joint sponsor.

The palace was begun in 1516 for Cardinal Alessandro Farnese (later Pope Paul III) by Antonio da Sangallo the Younger, and was continued after his death in 1546 by Michelangelo. After Michelangelo's death Giacomo Della Porta closed the open, three-bay loggia on the first floor of the rear block and built on the second floor, facing the river, the new loggia mentioned above in connection with Palazzo Falconieri.

The Sala Grande or Sala delle Guardie on the piano nobile contains the sculptures of Abundance and Peace by Guglielmo Della Porta, originally on Paul III's tomb in St Peter's. The neighbouring Sala dei Fasti Farnesiani was frescoed by Salviati and Taddeo Zuccari with scenes of Farnese achievements.

In 1595 the young Cardinal Odoardo Farnese commissioned Annibale Carracci to fresco the small Camerino on the piano nobile and in 1597 the commission was extended to the larger Galleria, the vault of which was completed by 1601 and may have been intended to mark the marriage of Cardinal Odoardo's brother Duke Ranuccio in 1600. After an interval the walls of the Galleria were finished in 1604 and these show much involvement by the group of Emilian painters, including Domenichino, Lanfranco and Sisto Badalocchio who had followed Annibale to Rome.

The vault was a ground-breaking work, and its conception and execution by Annibale within some three years was a phenomenal achievement. (Apart from two episodes painted by his brother Agostino, the entire vault seems to be essentially by Annibale himself.) Its theme is the *Dominion of Love* with a central *Triumph of Bacchus and Ariadne* and various subsidiary *Scenes of Love* drawn from classical mythology. Both this erotic subject-matter and the witty, urbane mockery with which it was treated must have been quite startling in the Counter-Reformation atmosphere of 1590s Rome, and at the level of formal language the unprecedented variety and power of Annibale's revived classical aesthetic must have been equally astonishing.

On the far side of via Giulia there is a nondescript building that is linked to the palace by a bridge over the road. This is Palazzetto Farnese, which was originally a casino and garden complex overlooking the river. Between the Palazzetto and the church of S Maria dell'Orazione e della Morte Cardinal Odoardo fitted up a room for his private devotions. This romitorio — the Camerino degli Eremiti — had windows that opened both into the church itself and also into the oratory that lay behind the church at that time. Lanfranco decorated it in 1616[1] with frescoes of hermit saints and ceiling paintings on themes of humility and asceticism, but the room disappeared when the church was rebuilt by Fuga and Michetti in the 1730s. Three of Lanfranco's frescoes are, however, preserved in the church, and two of the ceiling paintings are in the Museo di Capodimonte at Naples.* Although the

*Two of the frescoes – *St Paul the Hermit with St Anthony Abbot*, and *St Simeon Stylites* – are prominently displayed in the church. The third – *St Bruno discovered in his Hermitage by Count Roger* – is behind the organ and not readily visible. The paintings now at Capodimonte are *Mary Magdalene raised to Heaven by Angels* and *Christ in the Desert, succoured by Angels.*

Opposite: the Galleria in Palazzo Farnese. Engraving by Giovanni Volpato

romitorio was clearly a much more personal space than the public rooms of the palace,[2] it is not altogether easy from a modern perspective to discern the mindset of the cardinal who commissioned both these lugubrious aids to meditation and the display of sensuality and worldly irony in the Galleria.[3]

The Lanfranco paintings from the romitorio and the Annibale Carracci *Choice of Hercules* from the ceiling of the Camerino represent only a tiny fraction of the works of art that were transferred to Naples from the palace and from other Farnese possessions after the Farnese heir Carlos became the first Bourbon king of Naples in 1735. When the last of the dynasty, Francesco II, was expelled from his kingdom by Garibaldi's forces in 1861 he was welcomed by Pope Pius IX, who still ruled Rome, and he used the palace as the site of his court-in-exile. That arrangement lasted only until 1870 when the French withdrew their garrison from Rome, the new government of united Italy occupied the city and Francesco had to flee. The palace was then leased to France by the new government and it has remained the French Embassy ever since.

Guided tours on Monday, Wednesday and Friday afternoons can be booked online at https://visite-palazzofarnese.it. The Camerino is part of the Ambassador's private suite, however, and is not normally opened to the public.

Palazzo Ferrini (Cini)

Piazza di Pietra, 26

Demofonte Ferrini, from Calvi dell'Umbria, bought up the property on this site at the beginning of the 17th century and in 1605 he commissioned Onorio Longhi to build a palace here. One of the houses Longhi incorporated at the back of the palace (at what is now via della Guglia, 59-61A) had a famous façade painting of the *Theological Virtues* by Polidoro da Caravaggio and Maturino; traces of this were visible until a few decades ago, but there is now no hint that anything of interest ever lay beneath the pristine 21st century plaster.

The palace was still unfinished at the time of Ferrini's death in 1628 when he left his property both in Calvi and Rome for the foundation of convents. The palace was transferred to a community of Augustinian nuns from Calvi who were still there in 1748[1] and it must have been modified internally both for their use and that of subsequent owners such as Conte Giuseppe Cini who owned it in the 19th century and left his name, IOSEPH CINI, over the door.

The main façade has an ungainly gap between the first and second bays which must reflect the existence of earlier structures. The best exterior feature is the door, which features on the pedestals supporting the balcony the emblems of Ferrini and his wife Aurelia Grana (a sword-bearing angel with a star, and a dove with an ear of grain, respectively). The same emblems alternate along the length of the cornice all round the palace.

The other notable original feature is an enormous altana which would not look out of place on a much larger and grander building. It bears the legend FERRINA between stars, and there are more stars in the spandrels of the altana's open arches.

The doors of Palazzo Galloppi: left, the door in via dei Giardini; right the main entrance in via del Quirinale

Palazzo Galloppi (Santovetti, Volpi di Misurato)

Via del Quirinale 21

The palace is on the corner of the Quattro Fontane, diagonally across from Palazzo Albani. Thus, its corner incorporates one of the fountains and is set in opposition to Palazzo Albani's notable corner composition, and its long side along via del Quirinale is immediately across the road from S Carlino, so that the palace's entrance is virtually opposite Borromini's beautiful door into the cloister. The building was described as 'casino Galloppi' in Nolli's map of 1748, and the cock (gallo) which appears in the cornice below the third storey was a Galloppi family emblem. The emblems of eight-pointed stars and monti (usually associated with the Chigi) figure profusely over the main façade and in the railing of the corner balcony. The arms that are now on the portal on via del Quirinale are those of the Volpi di Misurato family, who bought the palace in 1939.

The nucleus of the palace, including the fountain at the crossroads, is shown in a drawing by Lieven Cruyl of 1665.[1] There must then have been a major intervention in the early 1700s when the long façade was remodelled to its present length up to the height of the cornice, and the two doorways were constructed. The extra storey above the cornice (which must have included heightening the corner feature) is a 19th century addition that may have been done when an additional building was erected on via delle Quattro Fontane in 1893. That building was incorporated in the course of a comprehensive and very free restoration by Armando Brasini in 1926-28.

The features that immediatly attract attention are the well-known, and very fine, 18th century doorways on via del Quirinale and via dei Giardini. Both of them have angled side elements that are confidently absorbed into the overall composition, and the one on via dei Giardini has a continuous inner roll moulding with a wave motif unfurling over the top. Both doors have an unmistakable Borrominian air, and the one on via del Quirinale openly echoes the form of Borromini's door into the cloister opposite. At the same time, however, the doors also show some important differences from Borromini's own work; although they are splendidly inventive, their forms are more flaccid than the master would have approved and they do not aim at the nervous tension and precision that characterises his work.[2] Nevertheless, to attain such success in the immediate proximity of a great masterpiece by Borromini was no mean achievement.

Portoghesi included the doors in a group of works that he suggested might be attributed to Alessandro Specchi, and that attribution has often been repeated as a fact. There is, however, no documentary support for Specchi's involvement.[3]

The other part of the palace that appears to retain early 18th century work is the north wall of the small cortile (ie opposite the via dei Giardini entrance), where the stucco tympana over the windows on all floors are richer than those on the exterior and, like the doorways, echo Borrominian forms. The whole cortile does, in fact, make a definite success of its bewildering accumulation of motifs, but much of it (including the terrace with a basin on the via del Quirinale side and the wall with blank perspective doorways and niches that faces it) must owe its present form to the restoration of 1926-28.

The palace is now occupied by an insurance regulatory organisation.

Palazzo Gambirasi

Via della Pace, 8

The palace's history is interwoven with that of Alexander VII's urban teatro, focused on Pietro da Cortona's celebrated façade for S Maria della Pace and the immediately surrounding piazza.[1]

Alexander VII began thinking about the scheme in 1656 and Donato Gambirasi (a rich Bergamesque businessman) bought the site on the west side of via della Pace, extending along the left flank of the church as far as Arco della Pace, on 7 July the following year. Since the plan attached to his purchase document shows the site with all the changes necessitated by Cortona's final design, it is a reasonable deduction that Gambirasi must have appeared on the scene quite early on, and been involved in the scheme's elaboration. The site had previously been partly occupied by the Confraternity of S Giacomo degli Spagnoli and, at the point where it was cut back to create the new piazza, by the Casa Santa for poor widows and the Canons of S Maria della Pace themselves. The pope resorted to a complex financial process that involved the Camera Apostolica first acquiring the site and then almost immediately selling it to Gambirasi for 10,000 scudi, while the chirograph authorising the sale notes that the money was earmarked for extending the Manica Lunga of the Quirinale palace.[2]

Gambirasi employed as his architect G. A. De Rossi, who had acted as surveyor for the Confraternity of S Giacomo degli Spagnoli when they had been bought out, and the work on the new palace went ahead quite quickly; by March 1659 the windows were being put in place, and the final touches were completed in 1660. Although Gambirasi's purchase extended along the left side of the church, the main element of his palace was the ten-bay façade on via della Pace

Falda's print of Palazzo Gambirasi, with S Maria della Pace to the right. Gambirasi's palace occupied a smaller area than did the previous buildings on the site, mainly to allow room for the manouvring of the coaches that were expected to throng to the remodelled church when it became more fashionable. The change also enabled a transverse sight-line to the church of S Biagio della Fossa, shown at the extreme left of Falda's print. S Biagio was deconsecrated under the Napoleonic occupation in 1812, and demolished before 1820

which is set back behind the line of earlier buildings on the site, in order to enable the widening of the street. It is of three storeys with mezzanines on the ground and second floors, and there are several features where compromises were evidently made to adapt the design to the demands of the neighbouring piazza buildings by Cortona. First, the triangular structure immediately to the right of the palace created manifest problems. This building is visually an integral part of Cortona's piazza, but internally it was an extension of the Gambirasi palace and contained one of its staircases. Its connection with the — much higher — palace façade is extremely awkward, and the inclusion of this bay in Cortona's piazza unit also meant that the main portal of the palace could not be placed in the centre of the façade. Furthermore, the ground-floor of Cortona's piazza buildings is very high, and the ground foor and mezzanine of the palace façade is higher still; this leaves the portal looking stranded beneath the high string-course. Spagnesi particularly noted the lack of an adequate cornice and one cannot but agree with his general conclusion that the building fails to reflect De Rossi's customary 'ordine rigoroso'.[3]

The ground-floor of the palace was given over to shops, reflecting Virgilio Spada's original suggestion that the inclusion of shops would assist the economics of the development. Although the same arrangement can be seen at Peparelli's Palazzo del Bufalo in Piazza Colonna, using a main palace façade for shops was not usual at the time, and it marks Gambirasi as a rich bourgeois rather

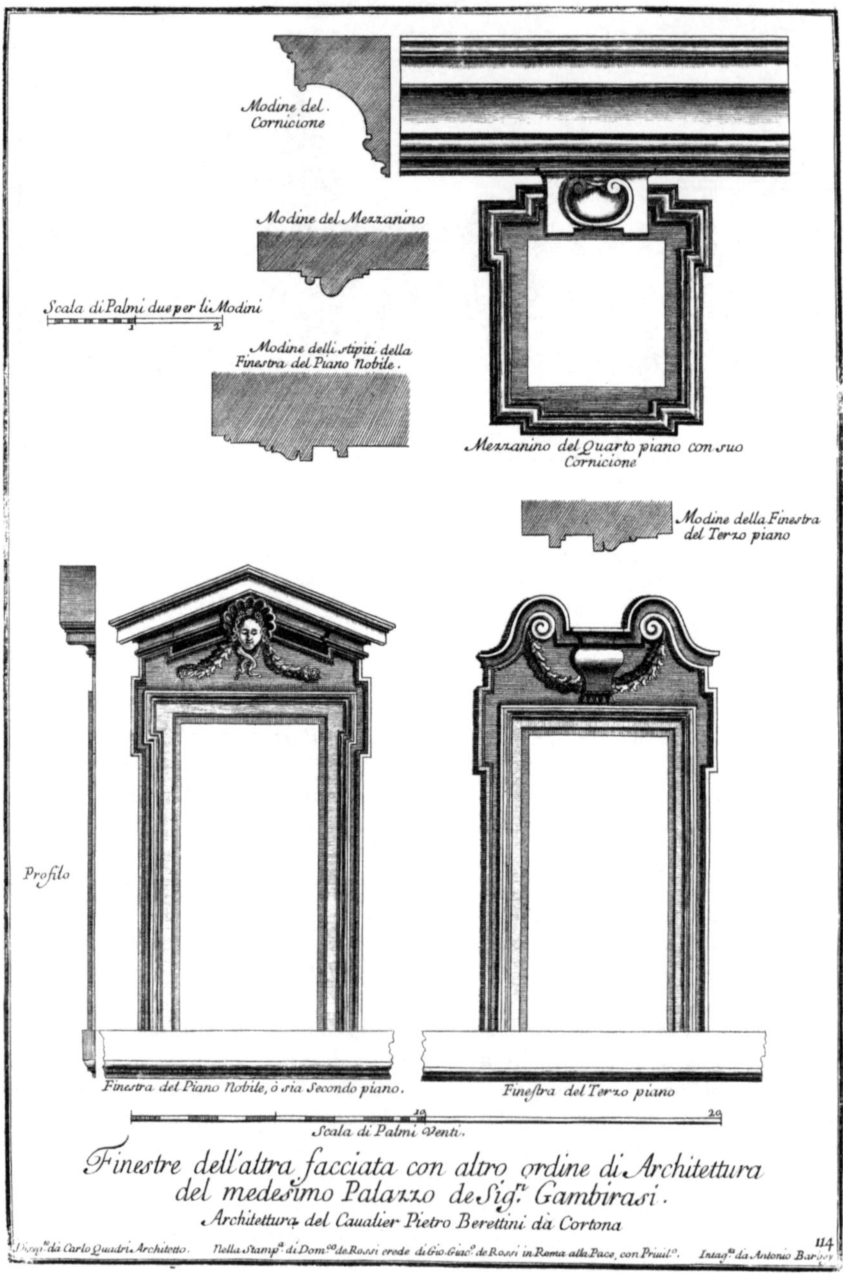
Modine del Cornicione
Modine del Mezzanino
Scala di Palmi due per li Modini
1
2
Modine delli stipiti della Finestra del Piano Nobile.
Mezzanino del Quarto piano con suo Cornicione
Modine della Finestra del Terzo piano
Profilo
Finestra del Piano Nobile, ò sia Secondo piano.
Finestra del Terzo piano
10
20
Scala di Palmi Venti.
Finestre dell'altra facciata con altro ordine di Architettura del medesimo Palazzo de Sig.ri Gambirasi.
Architettura del Caualier Pietro Berettini da Cortona
Disegn.to da Carlo Quadri Architetto.
Nella Stamp.a di Dom.co de Rossi erede di Gio. Giac.o de Rossi in Roma alla Pace, con Priuil.o.
Intag.to da Antonio Barbey
114

than an aristocrat. The rather characterless door has excellent volute brackets containing miniature mascheroni: in the centre a cartouche displays the Gambirasi emblem of a crayfish (gambero) clutching a cross in its claws. The piano nobile windows have triangular pediments with alternating male and female stucco heads, several of which are equipped with a swag that oddly runs over the head without a break. The second floor windows have pediments consisting of opposed volutes with a mensola and swag between them, while the upper mezzanine has windows in stucco frames with a 'buckle' motif above.[4] On all four faces of the altana there is the legend 'GAMBIRASIA'.

By 1659 the piazza was finished and Alexander issued a chirograph forbidding any heightening of the buildings or other modifications that might spoil the effect of the teatro. An inscription recording these prohibitions was placed at what is now via della Pace, 13.

Whatever financial benefit there was in the development, it clearly did not flow in the direction of the Chapter of S Maria della Pace, since they were selling off property by 1664. In June 1665 Gambirasi bought from them two houses beyond Arco della Pace, thus establishing a bridgehead beyond the Cortona buildings and completing his ownership of the whole isolato. Some ambitious plans were considered for building along the left flank of the church but in the event the Cortona buildings were left untouched and Gambirasi's new building (ie the bays in via Arco della Pace north of the bridge over the street, and the corresponding section at the back of the palace in vicolo dei Osti) was run up in a journeyman fashion with a high ground floor without a mezzanine, and with the second floor mezzanine substantially enlarged. A separate altana, of rustic crudity, was built for this part of the palace, and the north face takes the form of a two-bay balconied feature with the first and second floor windows equipped with the same decoration as on the main façade. This is clearly meant to echo De Rossi's two bays with a corner balcony at the south end of the site, but De Rossi's name does not appear in the documents for the northern extension, and it is difficult to imagine that this famously suave architect could have been personally involved in it.

In 1671, soon after the completion of the new wing, Gambirasi died. His estate was heavily encumbered, partly because he and his son had been forced to pay 6,000 scudi as out-of-court settlement of an action taken against them for malpractices during their management of the Treasuries of Campania and Marittima. The heirs soon began to sell off the property in stages to the nearby German church of S Maria dell'Anima. By 1710 the Germans had obtained virtually the whole of the Gambirasi isolato — thus encircling S Maria della Pace — and were anxious to maximise the rental income from their new property. In that year they sought authority to increase the height of the attic of the Cortona building to the left of S Maria della Pace, arguing that it was too restricted to provide an adequate passage between the main Gambirasi palace property and the later wing to the north. Notwithstanding Alexander VII's specific prohibition recorded in stone, some heightening was authorised and a simple additional attic was erected above the cornice of the Cortona buildings. This addition, which was carried

Opposite: The façade windows of Palazzo Gambirasi: an engraving from De Rossi's Architettura Civile. *De Rossi unconvincingly ascribes all these windows to Pietro da Cortona*

round both sides of the piazza, raised the roofline to the full height of the church façade, and it must have diluted the privilege that the original design gave to the church itself.[5] Nothing in the area has been significantly changed since, though the whole Gambirasi side of the complex has become extremely dilapidated.

Palazzo Ghetti

Largo dei Librari, 89

This simple palace dates from the second half of the 17th century; Falda's map of 1676 does not yet seem to show the structure in its present form, and the panel with a ribbon and swag over the piano nobile window in the entrance bay must surely be later still. The ground floor mezzanine is placed unusually high and its windows are equipped with stucco framing similar to that of the two floors above; all three levels of windows being almost equally privileged. At street level the building is much disfigured by recent openings for shops.

The noteworthy feature is the entrance bay, which is marked out with shallow rustication up to the roof. The high mezzanine here forces the piano nobile balcony almost half-way up the height of the building, with its huge supporting brackets astride a substantial mezzanine window. However uncomfortable the design may be, this is a very good example of the way in which a balcony could be used to dominate an enclave and convey a message of authority.

Declarations of status are also made by the display of heraldic emblems in the elaborate cornice. The double-headed eagles and crowns belong to the Goggi family which originally owned commercial property on the site, while the grasshopper on a heraldic bend is the emblem of the well-known Grillo family. It was Agostino Goggi's marriage with a Grillo heiress at some date before 1643 that made the family fortune and provided the money for building the palace. Their daughter married a Ghetti in 1684.[1]

Palazzo Giangiacomo

Via Monserrato, 105

and

House at via Monserrato, 102

An extraordinarily eccentric pre-Baroque building that crams a bewildering assortment of motifs into its tall three bays on a narrow frontage. It is dominated by its entrance feature which rises two-thirds of the height of the building. Above a curious tripartite balcony over a door set within heavy rustication between Doric columns, there rise two ponderously rusticated pilasters surmounted by women's heads. The whole machine is topped off with a great broken pediment, and below that there is a smaller one that contains a cartouche with the inscription:

GEORGIUS BRE/
CHUS EQUES S. TOR./
MAURITII ET LAZARI ANNO D.NI M.C.LXXXII

(Giorgio Brechi, knight of the order of Saints Maurice and Lazzaro, in the year 1582).

It is hard to think of any Italian pedigree for this extravaganza. The architect is unknown, but the whole thing has an engaging amateur air.

Next door, at via Monserrato, 102, there is an elegant late 17th century house of four narrow bays, with three storeys of almost equal height above the ground floor. The simple stuccoes over the windows of the two main floors feature stars and shells. The extra storey above the cornice is 19th century.

Casa Giannini

Piazza Capranica, 95

This seven bay building that occupies virtually the entire west side of Piazza Capranica was built by Alessandro Dori for the Cavaliere Carlo Giannini in 1744-46. Giannini, who was a rich Neapolitan with an honorary position in the Papal Guard, must have been a keen businessman as he operated as a bookseller, printer and grain-merchant. The building is one of the purest examples of an 18th century Roman house designed not just to accommodate the owners in some style, but also to be let to several other occupants and thus maximise the revenue from the site.

The building consists of a ground floor that was given over to shops, a mezzanine, two floors with elegant fancy windows and two further floors of similar height but with simpler windows. The attic above the cornice is original.[1] All the upper floors were designed identically as self-contained apartments with their own reception rooms and service accommodation, so that each tenant could see himself as having a 'piano nobile' of his own, and be charged accordingly. Surprisingly, there was no service stairway, so workers in the ground-floor shops had to use the grand staircase to get to the mezzanine.[2]

As with the nearby Palazzo del Cinque, the owners intended to live on the piano nobile, which has the most elaborate window cornices and is privileged with a large central balcony. Giannini, who subsequently moved up to the fourth floor, apparently felt less need than the del Cinque to advertise pretensions to ancient lineage, and all the decoration here is much more chaste than the frenetic display of emblems on the del Cinque palace. Both buildings catered for a clientele of lawyers and clerics (often noble) who needed to be near the Curia established in Palazzo di Montecitorio, but the Casa Giannini also attracted a significant number of prosperous bourgeois families.

Alessandro Dori's best known domestic architecture is Palazzo Rondinini on the Corso, which is some twenty years later than the Casa Giannini and very different in nature. The only obvious point of similarity between the two buildings is that both have double entrances.

Palazzo Giustiniani

Via della Dogana Vecchia, 29

The palace — apparently newly built for the Vento family — was bought in 1590 by the Giustiniani, a branch of the Genoese family who had settled in Rome. It is attributed in the early sources to Giovanni Fontana. In the early 17th century it housed the great collection formed by the marchese Vincenzo Giustiniani (d. 1638), of which the ancient sculpture is recorded in engravings in the two volumes of the *Galleria Giustiniana.* The collections were sold immediately after the Napoleonic Wars, 171 of the paintings being acquired by Frederick William III of Prussia as part of his project to found a public art museum in Berlin.[1]

The building is a typical example of a Roman palace that was extended by incorporating many neighbouring buildings over the course of a century. It was slightly modified or extended by Maderno (c.1590-1) and between 1650 and 1655 Borromini acted as master-builder supervising alterations and enlargements for Prince Andrea Giustiniani, Vincenzo's adopted son and heir. While he adjusted the enfilades in the several reception suites contained in the palace, Borromini's main work was concentrated

B
C
Modine delli Stipiti
A
Profilo
Scala di Palmi due, qual serue per il Mod.° A. Capitello B. Basse C.
Scala di Palmi Vinti
Porta del Palazzo del Sig.r Prencipe Giustiniani
Architettura del Caualier Francesco Boromini.
Dissej.to da Carlo Quadri.
Nella Stamperia di Dom.co de Rossi erede di Gio. Giac.° de Rossi.
Intagl.to da Ant.° Barbey. 102

in the north-west corner, where Vincenzo Giustiniani had his renowned *pinacotheca* — two great rooms crammed with nearly 250 of his best paintings. Although Borromini made plans for an extended north wing along via Giustiniani and for a vast new gallery along the east face of the palace, these were baulked by a lawsuit initiated by the neighbouring Patrizi and came to nothing during Borromini's lifetime. They did, however, provide a starting-point for the completion of the palace by Domenico Legendre during the 1670s and probably later.[2] As it stands, the palace is something of a massive, unrelieved block and Borromini's most evident contribution is the rather tame doorway facing the piazza. Ferrerio and De Rossi show this with the eagles and tower of the Giustiniani arms over the door and similar motifs appear in a drawing for the door in the Albertina, but as it exists today the area over the door is plain. Within the palace the Sala delle Colonne still contains two columns with Borrominian composite capitals with cherubs' heads and swags, but in the various modern restorations the room has lost all other traces of Borromini's original conception.[3]

The great galleria and three other rooms on the piano nobile were sumptuously frescoed in the three years from 1587, with the Vento arms appearing in the galleria and the Giustiniani arms in the small rooms. The vault of the galleria has five quadri riportati of *Scenes from the Story of Solomon* in a style close to Salimbeni. They are set in a lavish surround of grotesques, incorporating figures of *Virtues* and several landscape medallions by Tempesta and P. P. Bonzi. The 1970s restoration of the galleria, which the Carabinieri had been using as a dormitory for many years, revealed that the walls too were covered with painting (including a fine Tempesta marine) between feigned bronze Solomonic columns.[4] Vincenzo Giustiniani used the galleria for the display of sculpture, together with a mere sixteen religious paintings.[5]

The palace is now a dependency of the Senate (Palazzo Madama), with which it is connected by an underground passage.

Palazzo Gomez (Lepri, Gallo di Roccagiovine, Silj)

Via della Croce, 78A

Ascribed by Pascoli to G. A. De Rossi and universally accepted as being by him; the work must have been begun around 1678 as the doorway was licensed in 1679.[1]

The door is elegantly fluted, with a mask in the lintel beneath a rectangular balcony supported by brackets. On the second floor, above the main doorway, there is yet another balcony on brackets. The two subsidiary entrances, now used for shops, appear to be essentially original.

From the doorway a vaulted passage leads straight through to the back of the building, with the stairs leading off modestly half way along. The picturesque courtyard at the end has been turned into a sort of informal sculpture garden, full of miscellaneous antique fragments. It is not known exactly when it was laid out, but Blunt's opinion that it was done in the 19th century seems right. At all events, the courtyard has been so much modified that it is impossible to discern what De Rossi's intentions may have been.

Opposite: Borromini's door at Palazzo Giustiniani. This has since been stripped of the Giustiniani eagles and tower, and now presents a much more utilitarian appearance. Engraving from De Rossi's Architettura Civile

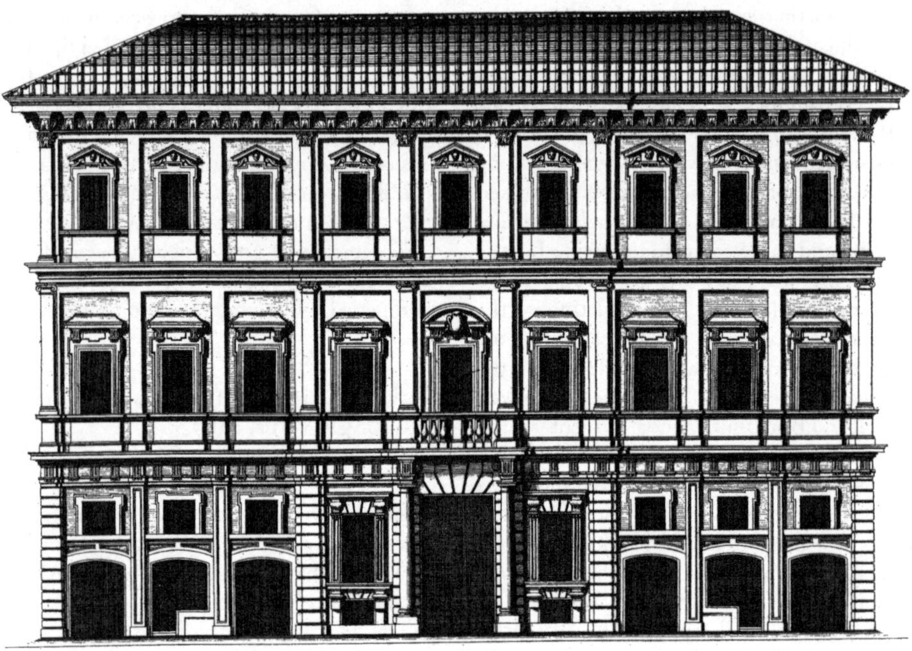

Falda's print of Palazzo Grazioli. The elevation of the ground floor was considerably changed by Sarti in the 19th century

Palazzo Grazioli (Gottifredi)

Via del Plebiscito, 102

The Gottifredi owned property in this area for a long time, and they had a palace built here by Giacomo Della Porta in the 16th century. The present palace was built in 1659/60 by Camillo Arcucci for Francesco Gottifredi, who had become chairman of the planning authority (Maestri di Strade) in 1658 and who was later to be official antiquarian to Queen Christina.[1] He obtained planning permission by setting back the alignment of the new building in accordance with Alexander VII's road-widening plans, and relinquishing various acquired and inherited property of his that stood in their way.[2] Falda's print on p. 52 gives a good idea of how this part of Rome looked at the time. As the print's original caption makes clear, this is a good example of Falda celebrating one of Alexander's road-widening schemes, which were an important part of his *teatro* of urban planning.

In 1824 the palace was bought by Vincenzo Grazioli who had it very substantially rebuilt by Antonio Sarti during the period 1838-74. While Sarti retained most of the façade, the rest of the building was effectively replaced.

The façade is still an effective, carefully proportioned composition but in order to appreciate Arcucci's original design (recorded by De Rossi and Falda) one must ignore the relentless tread of four heavily barred windows either side of the entrance, and envisage the three outer bays on each side as being occupied by elegant open arched shop fronts with mezzanine windows over them. These open spaces would have set up a rhythm with the heavier central pavilion which would have been echoed in a lighter way in the upper zone by the pilasters of the central bays being given capitals and bases while the outer ones were left plain. There would thus have been a light/heavy contrast both between the centre and the outer panels, and also between the ground floor and the upper parts. Although Arcucci's palace can hardly match G. A. De Rossi's exceptionally elegant and innovative Palazzo D'Aste that was going up at the same time on the key corner site just down the road, it is a competent design that fits its location well.

There are Gottifredi lion heads in the pediments of the upper floor windows, and rampant lions in the cornice.

The palace is owned by Silvio Berlusconi.

Palazzo del Grillo (de Robilant)

Piazza del Grillo, 5

This decorative palace, built for the Conti family in the last quarter of the 17th century, is in an intensely evocative corner of Rome, close to the Forum of Nerva and the palace of the Knights of Rhodes. It incorporates a medieval arch — the Arco dei Conti — and a tower, the Tor de' Conti of 1223, which is

The left side of this view by Vasi is taken up by the church of S Maria Annunziata and the remains of the Forum of Augustus. The right side shows Piazza del Grillo, with Palazzo del Grillo filling the entire far side of the piazza, either side of the medieval Tor de' Conti. In the distance is the Torre delle Milizie. One of the palace's remarkable doors can be seen to the right of the arch (the Arco dei Conti) that leads through into the Salita del Grillo

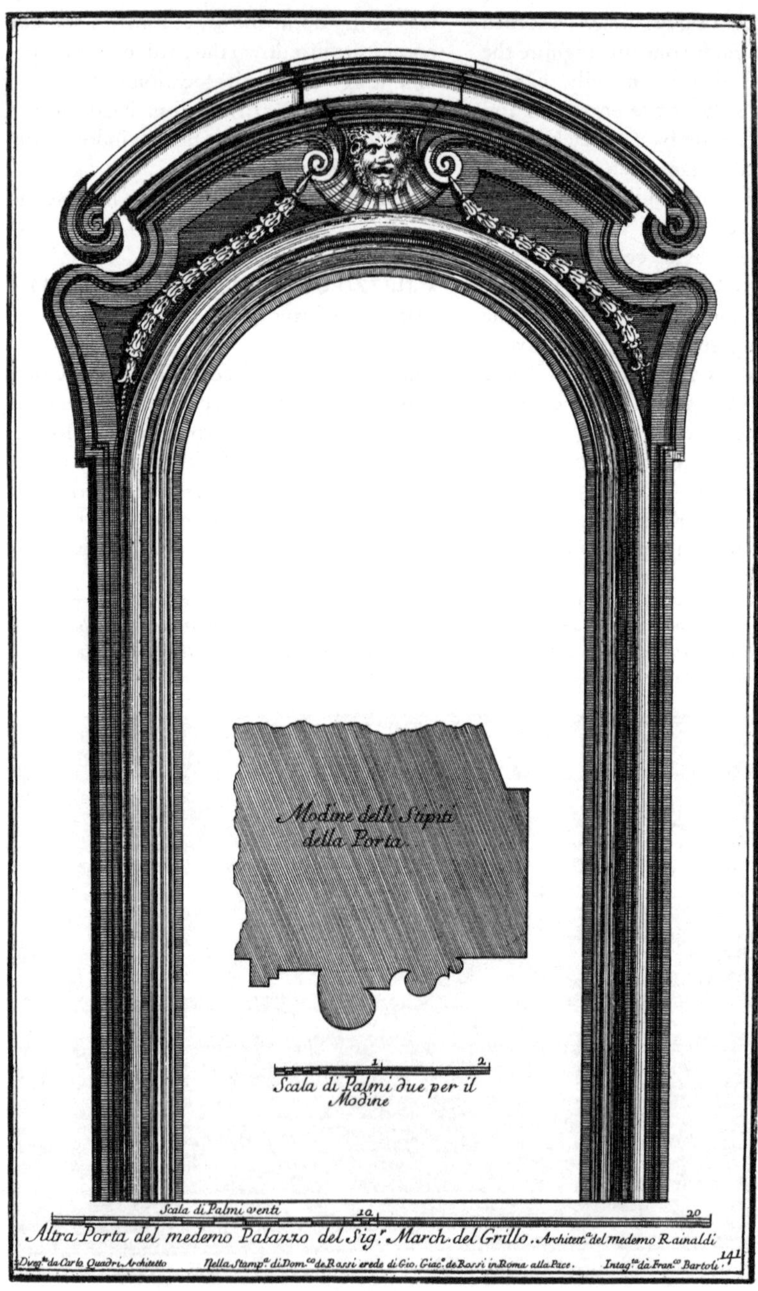
Modine delli Stipiti
della Porta
1
2
Scala di Palmi due per il
Modine
Scala di Palmi venti
10
20
Altra Porta del medemo Palazzo del Sig.r March. del Grillo. Architett.a del medemo Rainaldi
Dieg.ta da Carlo Quadri Architetto
Nella Stamp.a di Dom.co de Rossi erede di Gio. Giac.o de Rossi in Roma alla Pace.
Intag.ta da Fran.co Bartoli.
141

also called the Torre della Miliziola in contrast with the great Torre delle Milizie nearby. The building is wrapped around the sides of Piazza del Grillo to the south of the arch and has another main façade of similar elevation in the Salita del Grillo to the north. The prominent inscription EX MARCHIONE DE GRILLIS was added to the tower by the del Grillo family when they acquired the palace in the 18th century. The top storey of the palace, above the original roof-line, was added in the second half of the nineteenth century when the palace was owned by the de Robilant.

Although many adjustments had to be made for the exigencies of the site, and to absorb several previously existing buildings, the overall design is a pure and delightful example of Roman barocchetto. Thus, there are no less than four storeys of closely-spaced windows that are privileged with stucco decoration that ranges from curvilinear framing on the ground floor to splendid lion masks under semicircular pediments on the upper piano nobile. The two doors, one in Piazza del Grillo and the other in Salita del Grillo, are notable for the wayward fashion in which the main motifs are squashed into one another and the mouldings run around the opening without a break. They typify, in short, exactly the kind of thing that infuriated Visentini and he picked out these doors (or, to be strictly accurate, the one on Piazza del Grillo) for especially abusive criticism.[1]

De Rossi illustrated both doors and ascribed them to Carlo Rainaldi, but nothing about the building looks remotely like any other known work by that architect. Fasolo believed that the doors show Rainaldi suddenly becoming one of the founding fathers of the barocchetto in his old age, but a more sober conclusion would be that the architect is unknown.[2]

The most celebrated feature of the palace is the steep, small garden.[3] It is reached by stairs that curve up from the courtyard, which is itself at a higher level than the entrance passage, and contains a stucco fountain of two nude youths supporting a basin, in a style similar to that of the side figures of the fountains in the garden of Palazzo Borghese.[4] Attached to the boundary wall are two stucco herms of satyrs bearing baskets of fruit that Asche identified as being works of 1675-76 by Balthasar Permoser.[5] Leading into the palace from the courtyard itself is an astonishingly elaborate door within coupled pillars encrusted with vine leaves and flanked by figures of *Minerva* and *Mercury*. Above, set in a broken pediment within a concave cornice, there are a nude figure and a putto supporting an oval cartouche, and the whole thing is surmounted by a relief and more foliage. It is hard to think of any close parallel for this showpiece, which draws at least as much from church monuments as from any garden designs, but it looks appreciably later than the fountain and the Permoser work.[6] Within the palace there are several rooms with stucco decoration of the very highest quality, and probably of different dates, but no proper account of this has ever been published.[7]

The painter Renato Guttuso had a studio in the palace from 1965 until his death in 1987; it is now the seat of the Archivi Guttuso, devoted to his work. The building is otherwise given over to exclusive private apartments, whose occupants' privacy is carefully protected.

Opposite: the door of Palazzo del Grillo in the Salita del Grillo. Engraving from De Rossi's Architettura Civile

Palazzo Guelfi Camajani (Montauto, Rovarella, Polidori, Pericoli)

Via del Corso, 337

Built by the Guelfi Camajani in the 17th century on the site of buildings that had been owned by the Del Bufalo, whose emblems appear on an earlier doorway in the cortile. The building was completely refashioned by the Pericoli in the 19th century; the print of 1835 reproduced by Carpaneto shows that at that date the façade had very little of its present symmetry and order.[1]

The reason for noting this essentially 19th century façade is the fine decorative work around the entrance and on some of the brackets supporting the balconies. This looks to be a survival from the original building and appears to date from around the very end of the 17th century.

Palazzo Lancellotti

via Lancellotti, 18

The Lancellotti came to Rome in the 15th century, dogged by rumours that they were descended from converted Spanish Jews, but determined to establish themselves in the high Roman nobility.[1] The family reached its apogee in 1726 when the head of the house, Orazio, was granted the title of Prince of Marzano. Around 1750 Orazio carved out the piazza on the Tiber side of the palace and built a subsidiary palace for his retainers on the far side, creating a family enclave, albeit on a smaller scale, exactly as the Borghese had done in the previous century. (The retainers' building, designed by Egidio Malescotti, incorporates the conventional innovations of up-market 18th century apartment blocks, with large windows on all floors, the uppermost now, but perhaps not originally, equipped with elegant ringhiere.) The piazza fronting the palace's main façade was made only in 1939.

The palace is a severe building that was begun by Francesco da Volterra around 1591 for Cardinal Scipione Lancellotti (d 1598) and continued under the supervision of Maderno for Cardinal Orazio (d 1620). The notable feature of the main façade is Domenichino's doorway, probably designed in the later 1620s.[2] It is the only work in architecture that Domenichino is known to have executed and it was sharply criticized by Visentini.[3] The doorway's plain rectilinear main structure is in a clear Roman tradition running from Palazzo Valentini to Palazzo Santacroce and beyond, but the feature that attracted Visentini's dislike was the way in which the lintel is invaded by a decorative panel that incorporates a mascherone and cornucopias and is supported by volutes. This must have looked incorrect and wilful when it was made, though only someone of Visentini's extreme purist views would have found it offensive by 1771.

The cortile is lavishly decorated with classical statuary and with sarcophagi set in the walls. While this was the common fashion at the time, the Lancellotti may have had a particularly strong motive to make the implication of descent from ancient Roman forebears, at which all such displays hinted. It is possible that something similar lay behind the decoration of the Sala dei Palafrenieri (see below) with its general evocation of views from a well-sited villa as described by Pliny.

The frescoed decoration of the interior is exceptionally interesting. It consists of five rooms on the piano terreno and five more on the piano nobile, in all of which Agostino Tassi or his followers had a hand. It is likely, in fact, that Tassi supervised the whole

Etching from Visentini's Osservazioni *illustrating Domenichino's door at Palazzo Lancellotti which Visentini severely criticized*

project. The most interesting rooms on the ground floor are the three in which Tassi collaborated with Guercino and Lanfranco. The two Guercino rooms consist of one featuring a large figure of *Nobiltà* and another with a group of putti gesturing towards Tassi's ovals depicting *Scenes from the story of Rinaldo and Armida*. Cavazzini dates all these to 1621, immediately before the same partners painted the great *Aurora* of the Casino Ludovisi. The Lanfranco room, dated by Cavazzini to 1625, features a grand figure of *Generosità*.

On the piano nobile the outstanding rooms are the Sala dei Palafrenieri, which serves both the reception suites on that floor, and the Sala da Ballo. Both of these show Tassi's interior decorating business working at its highest level of quality, though there is a marked difference in scale and feeling between the ovewhelming quadratura arcades framing landscape vistas in the Sala dei Palafrenieri (1620 or very shortly before) and the delicate frieze in the Sala da Ballo (1625 or a little later). Several of the vistas in the Sala dei Palafrenieri are painted with a poetic Claudian naturalism that is markedly beyond Tassi's more formulaic approach to landscape. The frieze in the Sala da Ballo also has distinct overtones of Claude, though here the resemblance lies less in the subtle atmosphere and description of light effects than in the use of strongly Claudian compositional motifs, especially in the grouping of classical buildings with landscapes and marines.[4]

We know that Claude himself was employed in Tassi's workshop between 1620 and 1625, and the Sala dei Palafrenieri landscapes (which remained virtually unknown before Cavazzini's exemplary study) do appear to come closer to the Claudian aesthetic than anything else in Tassi's large output. The obvious inference is that these may be among the earliest surviving paintings to reflect Claude's direct involvement.

That would, however, presuppose that he was much more precocious at the outset of his career than has hitherto seemed likely.[5]

Palazzo Lante (Medici, Lante Della Rovere, Grazioli, Aldobrandini)

Piazza dei Caprettari, 70

This is one of the most important early 16th century palaces in Rome. It was begun in 1513 by Leo X for his brother Giuliano de' Medici, and was built over property belonging to Alfonsina Orsini, the wife of Pietro de' Medici. As Frommel has shown, the palace could have formed part of a new Medici urban nucleus including the nearby Palazzo Madama, but any hopes for such a project fell with the death of Giuliano in 1516. The palace's dynastic origins are displayed by the Orsini roses and Medici lion-masks under the ground floor windows, and by the roses and Medici ostrich plumes on the capitals in the cortile.

The original architect was Giuliano da Sangallo (d. 1516) who was probably followed by Jacopo Sansovino before the work under the Medici was finished by another of their house architects, Nanni di Baccio Bigio. The Sangallo design (which still provides the core of the palace) was a straightforward affair of a symmetrical seven-bay façade of three storeys separated by heavy string-courses, and an airy cortile of three bays by five, with two superimposed open arcades using antique columns, some of which may have come from the Colosseum. This structure was still incomplete when it was given to Marcantonio Palosi in 1533 and then passed, in 1558, to Ludovico Lante, of a rich and distinguished Pisan family, who placed his name LUDOVICUS LANTES over the elegant Sansovinesque portal. Lante soon completed the building, incorporating two neighbouring houses in the process.

Baglione records that Onorio Longhi adjusted some things ('ha raggiustato alcune cose') in the cortile at the behest of Cardinal Marcello Lante, and this must refer to the closing up of most of the arcades on both levels, while leaving the columns and the balustrades of the upper arcade still visible. This massive change was presumably done in the early 17th century, and it was soon followed by work to incorporate the adjacent building of five bays to the left of the main façade, with an entrance at via Monterone, 84.[1] That had been a Della Rovere palace, and it came to the Lante as a result of the marriage between Lucrezia Della Rovere and Ludovico Lante's son, Marcantonio. The final significant change to the exterior was the addition of the upper mezzanine and cornice as part of a general restoration by Carlo Murena for Cardinal Federico Marcello Lante in the mid-18th century.

The painted rooms on the piano nobile are the palace's only real Baroque items. Most of them are fairly routine mythological ceilings and friezes, some apparently by Romanelli and Calandrucci, but Romanelli's decoration of the main salone was a much more significant effort, ranking with the major schemes of the period.

The painting of the salone was commissioned from Romanelli in 1653 by Duke Ippolito Lante Della Rovere, Ludovico Lante's grandson. The ceiling has a complex shape, with a four-lobed central area supported on each of the long sides by a single pendentive, and on each of the short sides by three vaulting bays that end in lunettes and are separated by two roughly rectangular panels. The central panel shows *Mars, Venus and Mercury*; the pendentives

Romanelli's ceiling of the salone in Palazzo Lante

depict *Italy* and *Rome*; the panels (one of which includes the Della Rovere oakleaves) are filled with a variety of personifications; and the six lunettes have *Venus Displaying Arms to Æneas* and *Stories of the Foundation and Early History of Rome*. As Mecolli shows in her detailed analysis (from which these identifications are taken), the message of the programme was clearly to celebrate the Lante family's ascent to a central position in Roman society. Such buttressing of family pretensions by appropriating the Aeneid and the heroic classical past was becoming, in fact, a virtually routine procedure not only for successful newcomers like the Lante but also for well-established Roman families like the Pamphili and Altieri. In formal terms, the cycle shows Romanelli moving away from his earlier, painterly, style to a less ingratiating, linear, hard-edged mode that owed a good deal to Domenichino.

Much of the palace, including the part containing the painted rooms, is now occupied by the Istituto di Fisica Nucleare.

Palazzo Lateranense

Piazza di S Giovanni in Laterano, 6.

The huge, charmless, palace was one of Sixtus V's major projects and was mainly built for him by Domenico Fontana between 1585 and 1590, but the east wing was finished by Galilei for Clement XII (whose arms appear over that wing's door). The ten rooms of the papal apartment — together with the staircases, loggias etc — were very rapidly frescoed in 1588-89 by a team of painters led by Guerra and including Paul Bril, Croce, G. and C. Alberti, Viviani, Nebbia, Laureti, Muziano and Baglione. The numerous allegorical and religious scenes comprise one of the largest and most complex programmes of Counter-Reformation imagery and are a virtual compendium of the late Mannerist devices that characterised the official art of the period.[1] As with other Sistine commissions, there are many landscapes and marines, of which the best is probably Bril's *Naval Battle* in the Sala di Costantino. Most of the 16th century decoration can be seen during a visit (guided tours only) to the Museo Storico Vaticano, which is entered from the atrium at the cathedral's west end.

The only piece of Baroque work in the palace is Borromini's double door (1650) leading to the cathedral, which is very well worth seeing as the stucco decoration over the door is one of Borromini's most delightfully ambiguous conceits. To see this, enter

Palazzo Lateranense: the palace side of Borromini's double door leading into the basilica

the palace at Piazza di S Giovanni in Laterano, 6 (between the Benediction Loggia and the obelisk) and turn right when one reaches the courtyard. The decoration comprises a cherub supporting an orb bearing the arms of Innocent X. Two of the cherub's wings suppport the orb while the other two are curved over the doors to perform the function of architectural pediments. A final touch of ambiguity is provided by a glimpse of the cherub's hand over the moulding between the doors since, on close inspection, the 'hand' is seen to be made up of feathers.

A much simpler forerunner of the composition is the door into the cloister at S Carlo alle Quattro Fontane.

Palazzo Lazzaroni (Grimaldi)

Largo dei Lucchesi, 26

A long, low 19-bay palace with two courtyards within and a rusticated ground floor on the façade. Most of the windows are arranged in a staccato pattern of uneven spaces, though the first four bays are placed at a regular and close interval. On the right there are two rusticated doors in quattrocento style. Several earlier buildings must have been incorporated in the unified new structure. The attic was added in 1853, when the façade was tidied up in various ways, including the removal of two rimesse at the left end and the closing of windows into the basement at street level.[1]

There does not appear to be any direct documentary evidence about the building of the palace, but the census register of 1710 shows Cardinal Niccolò Grimaldi living here with a retinue of 17 attendants and domestics. He was made cardinal in 1706 and died in 1717.

The door consists of panelled jambs with volute brackets decorated with a floral band down the centre and with a buckle motif beneath. The same brackets re-appear in the building's lavish cornice, where they make a fine display together with the lozenge emblem of the Grimaldi family, which is repeated both between the brackets and in a frieze beneath.

The door is now surmounted by a bare shaped slab above an empty panelled lintel, but the drawings made at the time of the 1853 modifications show that both before and after those restorations there was an iron railing in place to make a balcony.[2] Furthermore, the drawings show that the lintel was then filled with a central object (doubtless a mask or heraldic device) flanked by swags. If the door was indeed made in Cardinal Grimaldi's lifetime, it was a very precocious design, since the sides are uncannily like those of the piano nobile windows of Fuga's Consulta of the 1730s.

The dragon-shaped lamp-holders are virtually the same as those at Palazzo Cenci-Bolognetti. They were probably added by the wealthy, art-collecting Lazzaroni who lived here after the unification of Italy, and who made various changes to the interior. The date and provenance of the lamp-holders are unclear.

Palazzetto Lupardi ('Casa dei ritratti')

Via del Governo Vecchio, 104

Bartolomeo Lupardi, a wealthy printer, bought the two houses that occupied this site in 1685 and 1692, and he amalgamated them into the present palazzetto in 1698, giving precise instructions that the lavish decoration of the windows — featuring stucco swags and heads of old men, women and smiling putti — should be copied from that on the (since destroyed) Palazzo Ceva on the Corso.[1] This is an engagingly transparent example of a successful bourgeois appropriating features of the public face of an aristocrat's residence in the hope that they would carry with them something of their original statement of status.

Lupardi was not content with appropriation, however, and he invented his own somewhat weird ways of demonstrating his learning and taste. No documents have been found about the commissioning of the 19 stuccoes of oval portrait medallions hanging from ribbons that are unevenly distributed over the façade, but they must have been part of Lupardi's original project as they were in place by 1699. The medallions bear the abbreviated names of the subjects, who were all medieval and later lawyers whose books were owned by Lupardi and his son.[2] The strange illusionistic paintings in the two blocked windows on the third and second floors are also undocumented, but they too must have been part of Lupardi's scheme as the upper one incorporates a feigned ringhiera that matches the real ones that are known to have been licensed in 1698.[3] That upper painting appears to show a man (Lupardi?) and his secretary; the lower one depicts a parrot.[4]

The two left-hand windows on the first floor lack stucco decoration because Lupardi never resolved a dispute with his neighbour about the ownership of that part of the building. Apart from two shops at street level, the whole building appears to have been intended for the use of Lupardi and his family.[5]

The door has a large aperture in the tympanum, which gives it a jaunty Borrominian air.

Palazzo Maccarani Odescalchi

Piazza Margana, 19

Apparently an early 17th century palace, originally built for the Maccarini but already shown in De Rossi's plan of 1668 as belonging to the Odescalchi. It presents an extremely reserved face to the piazza, with double string-courses below the windows and not a trace of decoration anywhere except for reticulation around the door. The upper storey is a 19th century addition.

Letarouilly's plan[1] clearly shows how the building appears to combine two structures that intersect confusingly. The small polygonal cortile in line with the main entrance has a nymphaeum in an ædicule surmounted by a stemma with the Odescalchi arms. The larger cortile is aligned with the façade on via Margana, from where it would originally have been entered via an ingenious atrium that also leads to a second staircase.

The quoins after the third bay down via Margana must mark the original limit of the main building on Piazza Margana. It would be interesting to know more of the patrons and architects responsible for the expansion down via Margana and around the corner into vicolo Margana, and what structures originally existed in the new area. Although the internal arrangement does not appear well integrated, the details seem quite skilful.

Palazzo Maccarani Savorgnan di Brazzà

Largo Pietro di Brazzà, 86

A palace originally built in the 16th century for the Maccarani; in the 19th century it belonged to the sculptor Ascanio Savorgnan di Brazzà. Between those dates it was modified on various occasions.

The thing to note here is the door — a good Baroque piece with a curvy balcony supported by two polished grey granite columns — which is perfectly adjusted in scale to the space in which it stands. It must date from the second half of the 17th century.

The windows were evidently refurbished and brought up to date at some point, or points, in the 17th and 18th centuries. The shells above the top-floor windows look later than the 'ears' that have been added to those on the ground floor.

The palace is now occupied by the Ministero delle Poste e Telecomunicazioni.

Palazzo Macchi di Cellere (Capranica)

Piazza di Montecitorio, 115

The energetic, reforming pope Innocent XII and his architect Carlo Fontana were successful in converting the uncompleted Ludovisi palace at Montecitorio into new law courts in a remarkably short time in the mid-1690s. Managing the untidy area in front of the palace, however, proved to be much more complicated, and hung fire for more than 30 years. The pope sought a redevelopment that would provide accommodation for the army of officials required by the law courts and would also add to Rome's visual presence as an efficient modern capital, but Fontana's proposal to turn the entire piazza into a huge semicircular exedra was manifestly too ambitious and was not pursued. By the time of the pope's death in 1700 a number of private properties had been bought up and put under the management of an institution under the control of the papal administration, but there were unresolved disputes about the compensation for demolished property, and the amount of new building was quite limited.[1]

The old Roman family of Capranica owned virtually all the property that bounded the south-west sector of the area. It was made up of several rambling old buildings and a garden, within which the Capranica had wished to build a theatre for which they were denied permission. In 1695 G. B. Contini, the architect retained by the Capranica, put forward a design for the replacement of the Capranica buildings by a large L-shaped four storey building for multi-occupation; the design was aligned with the new boundaries that were being proposed at the time (more or less in their present position). Contini's proposal was absolutely uniform and ruthlessly functional, with round-headed openings for shops, and plain windows on each floor. In 1701 the alignment of the boundary was finally approved, but there matters rested until the accession of Clement XII (Corsini) in 1730.[2]

Clement insisted on the planning system being used to exercise a tight control of new building, to ensure coherent development and to protect the public interest. Within that framework he appears to have encouraged pragmatic administrative solutions to the manifold problems of private interests and compensation in the Montecitorio area. Most importantly, he provided a great deal of public money.

In the case of the Capranica, the family and the Tribunale delle Strade agreed in 1732 to develop the site in partnership, and to split the costs. The architect for the whole building was Sebastiano Cipriani (not Tommaso Mattei as is often said) who was retained by the Tribunale. Cipriani's design was clearly based on the one prepared by Contini nearly forty years before. The, very plain, elevation runs uniformly around the south-west corner of the piazza and then heads due south, where the line of the old Capranica houses had been pulled back to enable the construction of a new road to run into what is now via della Guglia.[3]

The one striking feature is the central entrance bay of this south wing, which is marked out for the full height of the building with shallow rustication between pilaster strips. It contains a doorcase with a curvy broken pediment awkwardly combined with a heavy composite feature surrounding the first floor window and culminating in volutes that proudly support a tablet put in place on 4 May, 1733. The inscription on the tablet reads

CLEMENS XII P.M.
LATIOREM VIAM
ROMANIQUE FORI PROSPECTUM
DISIECTIS DOMIBUS IGNOBILEM
VICUM INSIDENTIBUS
LIBERALI SUMPTU APERUIT
ANNO DOMINI MDCCXXXIII
PONT III

(In the year of Our Lord 1733 and the third year of his pontificate Pope Clement XII with generous funding opened a wider road and a prospect towards the Roman Forum, having demolished the houses that stood in a mean alley.)

Matters did not rest there for long, however, since on 3 July 1734 a papal chirograph was issued to require the Pia Casa degli Orfani who occupied the site opposite the Capranica palace (i.e. what is now the Colonna Palace Hotel) to demolish their building and rebuild it further back, so as to create a subsidiary space or antepiazza. Another chirograph soon required them to ensure that the antepiazza was centred on the entrance of Palazzo Montecitorio, and further instructions ensured that the Pia Casa took the Capranica palace as a model. The result of all this was that a great deal of the piazza ended up in conformity with Contini's design of 1695.[4]

The Capranica palace was acquired by the Macchi di Cellere family in the early 19th century. In 1990 it was restored and adapted for use as office accommodation for the Chamber of Deputies.[5]

Palazzo Madama

Piazza Madama, 11

The palace incorporates what must have been a rather undistinguished 15th century building that the Medici used as their family palace in Rome during the pontificate of Leo X.[1] It takes its name – like the Villa Madama – from Madama Margherita of Austria, natural daughter of Charles V, who married Alessandro de' Medici and then Ottavio Farnese.

In the early 16th century Giuliano da Sangallo prepared a project for the enlargement of the palace, as did Cigoli a century later. Neither of these came to anything, however, and it was left to Paolo Maruscelli to carry out a comprehensive redevelopment of the palace for Grand Duke Ferdinando II. The work (finished in 1642) included reorganisation of the cortile and the provision of a grand new staircase as well as the splendid main façade, which is the building's main feature.

In its overall arrangement the façade basically conforms to the Roman palace formula established by Sangallo, and it shows no interest in the dynamic articulation of the Baroque. Its splendid effect is achieved by the weight and variety of decoration, especially the mouldings of the windows and the frieze of putti, lions and trophies which is incorporated with the mezzanine under the heavy cornice. The windows of the piano nobile are flanked alternately by caryatids and telamons, and the other decoration includes many lions and a stretched-out lion skin over the door, all intended to memorialise Leo X and to invoke Herculean associations.

Maruscelli seems to have been something of a passive jack-of-all-trades, willing to turn his hand to anything from this display of princely magnificence to some notably austere work for religious patrons such as the Oratorians and the Dominicans of S Maria Sopra Minerva.[2] Here, the repetitive accumulation of decoration on a simple architectural armature clearly lacks the intellect and creativity of the great architectural minds of the time. The palace was, however, a prestige project for the Grand Duchy of Tuscany and this unsubtle, rather provincial, mode of magnificence must have represented what the patrons wanted from the architect they had chosen. The building's first occupant was Cardinal Carlo de' Medici and his personal wishes may have been a major factor. Soon after the building's completion the Medici were acquiring some great, up-to-the-minute art with Cortona's planetary rooms in the Palazzo Pitti, Florence.

The critical fortunes of the palace have not been happy, and its profusion of deco-

Vasi's view of Palazzo Madama with, behind and to the right, the cupola and spire of S Ivo della Sapienza

ration and excessively heavy cornice and mezzanine have attracted criticism from Milizia to Wittkower.[3] Nevertheless, the quality of the detailing is high, and only the most austere observer would fail to get a good deal of pleasure from all this Medicean show in the midst of Baroque Rome.

The palace was bought by Benedict XIV to house the law-courts, and it was also used as the police headquarters and as a prison. Since 1871 it has been the seat of the Senate, which has necessitated a good deal of internal remodelling and, in the 1930s, linkage with the adjacent Palazzo Carpegna.

In 1925 the State acquired the building at the rear of Palazzo Madama, on the corner of via della Dogana Vecchia and Piazza S Eustachio. During the 1930s it was incorporated in the Palazzo Madama complex, with much remodelling of the previous plain façades. The bombastic five bay façade on Piazza S Eustachio, with four pairs of coupled inanellate columns and three windows with heavy masks, is entirely of that period. It is the work of an architect named Nori.

The lion skin over the door of Palazzo Madama refers to the Medici pope Leo X

Casa di Carlo Maderno

Via dei Banchi Nuovi, 3

The Compagnia della Pietà dei Fiorentini gave Maderno the life-time use of a house in 1601 and in 1607 he obtained the next-door property. He then united the two buildings, creating a sequence of windows with alternate triangular and semicircular pediments on the upper floor, and adding stuccoes of his heraldic emblems (eagle, turret, chequers, obelisk) to the windows and the cornice. The date of this work is not known, and it might not all have been done at the same time.

The obelisk in Maderno's arms was to commemorate his role in the transportation of the Vatican obelisk; Domenico Fontana similarly included the device in his arms.

The photograph in Hibbard shows the stucco-work terribly dilapidated, but it was restored around 1997 and now looks brand-new.

Palazzo Maffei (Peretti, Sannesi, Ludovisi, d'Este, Acciaioli, Marescotti, del Vicariato)

Via della Pigna, 13A

While not documented to him, this has always been attributed to Giacomo Della Porta, and it ranks as one of his very finest Roman palaces. The main façade on the narrow via della Pigna combines quite lavish decoration in the windows of the two main floors with the perfectly calculated proportion that characterises Della Porta at his best.

The palace involved rebuilding separate

Vasi's print of Palazzo Maffei on via della Pigna, in reality a very narrow street

palaces that existed on via della Pigna and via Cestari. The façade on via della Pigna was incomplete at the death of Cardinal Marcantonio Maffei in 1583, but was finished by 1593, two years after it had passed to the Peretti. At that time the via Cestari front consisted of only four bays, replicating the design of the main façade. By 1676, when the palace was owned by the d'Este, the via Cestari front had grown to seven bays.

The palace was bought by the Acciaioli in 1714 and passed to the Marescotti in 1746, around which time Fuga was employed to make improvements. The extra floor over the loggia on the west and entrance sides of the cortile, complete with strange little windows equipped with ringhiere, is presumably Fuga's work.

In 1864 the palace was bought by the Holy See and the architect Antonio Sarti was employed to complete the via Cestari front and add a portal to it. The constraints of pre-existing buildings forced him to space his four new bays more closely than the seven that had already been built, and this creates a distinctly uncomfortable effect.

Under the name 'Palazzo del Vicariato' the palace remains a possession of the Holy See, enjoying extraterritorial privileges.

Palazzo Magnani

Via Campo Marzio, 46

The Magnani family were settled in Rome from the early 17th century and this palace looks as though it was built for them in the early 1700s. The imposing door has massive volute brackets supporting an architrave with a square balcony above.

In comparison with the assertiveness of the door, the restrained stucco decoration of the windows looks slightly tentative. The third floor windows have characteristically 18th century ringhiere with curved iron railings.

After having been quite dilapidated in the 1990s, the palace has now been heavily restored.

Palazzo Malta (del Sovrano Ordine Militare Gerosolomitano di Malta etc)

Via dei Condotti, 68

The exterior is now entirely the result of the rebuilding of 1889-94, but (if one mentally eliminates the attic) it may give a reasonably good idea of the palace that was built by Carlo Aldobrandini in the 1630s as the embassy of the Knights of Malta. At all events, it is worth a moment's attention in view of its illustrious history. The commemorative tablet on the corner tells the story and may be roughly translated as follows, 'The Military Order of the Hospital of St John of Jerusalem, inheriting the estate of Giacomo Bosio, the Order's historian, and of his nephew Antonio, their agent in the city, [ensure that] their names shall never be forgotten in the houses where they dwelt in their lifetime. Carlo Aldobrandini, brother superior and the aforesaid Order's representative at the court of Urban VIII in the year 1631.'

The Knights were expelled from Malta by Napoleon in 1798 and after various wanderings they established their headquarters here in 1834. The palace is still the seat of the Grand Master and the administrative headquarters of the Order, and (together with the Villa of the Order's Priory on the Aventine) it is given extraterritorial sovereign privileges by the Italian State.

The fountain in the courtyard is 18th century, as are some fine rooms in the palace.

Vasi's view up the Corso from Piazza Venezia, with Palazzo Mancini on the right and Palazzo D'Aste on the extreme left. Looking up the Corso, the first gap on the right marks the piazza in front of S Marcello; immediately beyond this is Palazzo Mellini and opposite Palazzo de Carolis

Palazzo Mancini (Salviati)

Via del Corso, 271

The site belonged to the Mancini family since at least the 16th century and was one of the meeting-places of the celebrated Accademia degli Umoristi, the prestigious and influential literary society founded by Paolo Mancini in 1603. In 1634 Lorenzo Mancini married Geronima Mazzarino, sister of Cardinal Giulio Mazzarino (Mazarin) and the fortunes of the Mancini family were transformed as they were swept into Mazarin's european diplomacy. The residence on the Corso was the childhood home of Mazarin's four celebrated and spirited nieces Ortensia, Maria, Vittoria and Olimpia – the so-called 'mazzarinette' – before they were called upon to perform their duty and contract politically advantageous marriages.

In 1660 Mazarin bought a house at the north end of the Corso frontage and commissioned Carlo Rainaldi to build a palace on the extended site, but although Rainaldi wrote to make various suggestions nothing came of this before Mazarin's death in 1661. His nephew and heir, Filippo Mancini, duke of Nevers, went to live from 1674 in Scipione Borghese's old palace on the Quirinal (the present Palazzo Pallavicini Rospigliosi) but then in the 1680s he commissioned Rainaldi to return to the project on the Corso. The present palace, which incorporates parts of the earlier building, was built between 1687 and 1689. It was let to various tenants until, in 1725, it was leased to the duc d'Antin, on behalf of the French Crown, for use as the French Academy in Rome, which had moved between various Roman sites since its foundation in 1666. In 1737 Louis XV bought the palace outright and the French Academy had its seat here until the end of the century, with the twelve pensionnaires occupying austere cell-like rooms on the third floor that were in perfect accord with the rigid artistic disciplines to which they were subjected. From 1792 the Academy went through a turbulent decade and then in 1804 the Napoleonic king of Etruria was required by Cardinal Fesch (Napoleon's uncle and ambassador at Rome) to take Palazzo Mancini in exchange for the Villa Medici, which has been the home of the French Academy ever since.

Palazzo Mancini passed through the hands of many royal and noble owners including, in 1853, those of duke Scipione Salviati. In 1919 it was acquired by the Banco di Sicilia, who covered over the central cortile in the normal bank manner, added a staircase and made various other substantial changes to the interior.

The thirteen bay façade has attached pilasters at the corners and to mark the central mass, and a large central balcony on four Doric columns. It is certainly a very static composition for Rainaldi, though it presents a varied surface with its overall rustication, balustrades at the deeply modelled piano nobile windows, subsidiary lateral balconies, and very heavy cornice ornamented with putti carrying Mancini and Mazzarino emblems (lictoral fasces for the Mazzarino family and pike (ie the fish) for the Mancini). It has often been asserted[1] that it is a mixture of French and Italian styles, reflecting the character of the Duke of Nevers, who was equally at home in either country. While that line of thought is entirely speculative, and it is hard to identify specifically French features, the palace does present a somewhat un-Roman type of frosty grandeur. It was destined to be totally outgunned by Valvassori's astonishing Palazzo Doria-Pamphili opposite.

The frescoed ceiling over the main staircase is by some early 18th century follower of Maratta.[2] Within a quadratura surround it depicts the Mancini emblem (two fine wriggling fish) being crowned by a putto at the behest of Fame. Some rooms retain landscape friezes that may be of around 1633, when the original building was enlarged. The one (now detached from the wall) depicting the *Story of Jacob* has recently been attributed to Herman van Swanevelt.[3]

Palazzo Mandosi (Castelli-Mignanelli)

Piazza Farnese, 51

A sober palace of around 1630, with the outer bays demarcated by reticulated quoins in the manner of the Palazzo della Famiglia Borghese and Palazzo del Bufalo Ferraioli. The door-case is also reticulated and all the windows (ground-floor and top-storey mezzanines, with two equal storeys between them) are firmly planted on string-courses, to create a totally rectilinear grid. There is a degraded stemma over the door with traces of the eagle that was a component of the Mandosi arms.

The palace has a real function in the city's scenography as it largely forms the side of the famous piazza and acts as a moderator between Palazzo Farnese and Palazzo Pighini. Until 2006 its faded Roman ochre

Vasi's view of Piazza Farnese shows Palazzo Mandosi on the left and, next to it, Palazzo Sinibaldi

also made a contribution, but the building has now been drastically cleaned and restored.

Palazzo Manfroni

Via del Corso, 146-154

Bernini owned a building on this site. In 1812 the Manfroni sold it back to Bernini's descendants. It was rebuilt in the later 19th century and now has no architectural interest whatsoever.

Palazzo Marescotti

Via Campo Marzio, 69

The Marescotti were a powerful family in Rome, but this uniform nine-bay 17th century palace is rather a nondescript building. The one intriguing feature is the feline heads hidden away in the brackets supporting the balcony over the entrance, with the animals' paws uneasily resting on awkwardly contrived triglyphs. They probably represent the panthers that were part of the Marescotti arms.

Palazzo Maruscelli (Lepri)

Via dei Condotti, 11

This substantial palace fills the whole stretch of via Mario de' Fiori between via Condotti and via Borgognona. The Maruscelli (or Marucelli) family owned houses here before the earthquake of 1703 led them to commission Sebastiano Cipriani to rebuild their damaged properties into a single palace, which was completed in 1742. Cipriani's building had an unusual open cortile along the flank on via Mario de' Fiori, reminiscent of the arrangement at G. A. De Rossi's Palazzo D'Aste, which was similarly confined within a long, narrow site. Judging from the plans and drawings published by Bentivoglio, the part fronting onto via Borgognona was not much more than a low pavilion at this stage. In 1776 the palace was bought by the Lepri (see the stemma of eagle and hare – *lepre*– above the sarcophagus fountain in the cortile).

In 1869 the palace was largely rebuilt by the architect Virginio Vespignani, and the present exterior of the main block on via dei Condotti and via Mario de'Fiori must belong to that time. Apart from the ground floor of the main façade, however, the Cipriani drawings published by Bentivoglio agree quite closely with the present building, so Vespignani must have followed the original building fairly faithfully. The most striking feature of the main façade is the grouping of the three central windows of the two main floors under shared compound pediments, and this comes straight from Cipriani's drawing. The long, complex androne also coincides with Cipriani's plan and must be much as he envisaged it.

In 1892 Vespignani was employed again to build the wall with an entrance that now screens the cortile off from via Mario de'Fiori. In either the first or second of Vespignani's involvements the block on via Borgognona was enlarged into its present mass.

Although much of what one now sees belongs to the 19th century rebuilding, the ground plan is interesting in itself, the rebuilding did preserve the original forms, and a substantial amount of Cipriani's work survives around the cortile.

Palazzo Massimo di Rignano (Colonna)

Piazza d'Aracoeli, 1

The basis of this building was a 15th century palace of the old Roman Boccabella family. In the 17th century it passed to the Massimo di Rignano, who had it rebuilt in its present form. In the flank down via del Teatro di Marcello there are many irregularities, and the existence of the Boccabella palace is forcefully proclaimed by the survival of two (apparently restored) rusticated doorways of the quattrocento or earlier. Next to one of them are traces of a yet earlier medieval entrance. In 1916 the palace was inherited by the distinguished politician Don Prospero Colonna, whose family still own much of it. When via del Teatro di Marcello was made in 1938-39 the corner facing the Aracoeli was cut back diagonally, with the loss of two bays from each of the palace's façades.

Above the cornice there is a complex superstructure of different styles (and very possibly of different dates). It culminates in a little 19th century pseudo-medieval tower, bearing the legend MAXIMA on each side. Here the astronomer, mathematician and politician Mario Massimo di Rignano (1808-1873) had his observatory.[1]

Pascoli tells us that Carlo Fontana completed the embellishment and modernisation of the palace at around the end of Innocent XII's pontificate (1700), after the work had been laid aside for some time while Fontana concentrated on papal projects.[2] The bulk of the visible architecture is run-of-the-mill, however, and shows little sign of Fontana's active involvement. The items for which Fontana must certainly have been responsible are the doorway and the fountain, which are both highly individual pieces.

Originally the street in front of the palace was narrower than it is now, and the planning authorities would probably not have allowed Fontana's entrance to protrude very far; it has a single column each side and a very shallow concave cornice below a plain window that is dignified with a round tympanum. The use of such a concave form in a doorway is itself unusual, but the memorable feature is the way in which the laurel swags flanking the window are swept forward and outward to make an architectural statement. (For another example of Fontana's use of decorative vegetable motifs to emphasise a concave architectural structure, see the palms flanking the upper aedicule of the façade of S Marcello on the Corso.) The fountain in the cortile is also concave and flanked by columns, but here Fontana had more room at his disposal and the recess is much deeper than that of the entrance, while the columns are doubled. There are two main basins — one, at ground level, containing a triton that is a crude derivative from Bernini, and another, set very high, filled by the spouting of two lions that crouch on the pediment. Between the lions, at the summit of this grand (and altogether too busy) machine, there is a stemma and ducal coronet.

Venturini's print of Carlo Fontana's fountain in Palazzo Massimo di Rignano. In fact the engraving gives an almost absurdly exaggerated idea of the scale and grandeur of this palace. It does, however, succeed in capturing the bombastic quality of Fontana's fountain, with its triton motif barefacedly appropriated from Bernini's famous original in Piazza Barberini

Vasi's view of Piazza di S Caterina della Rota, which is practically unchanged today. To the right is Palazzo Mastrozzi with its doorway incorporating decorated antique columns. In the centre is the church of S Caterina della Ruota and to the left is S Girolamo della Carità

Palazzo Mastrozzi (Graziosi)

Piazza S Caterina della Rota, 91

A palace of around the turn of the 17th and 18th centuries, said to incorporate remains of the Corte Savella, the prison that was operated by the Savelli family until the establishment of the Carceri Nuove in 1657.

It has some of the most sumptuous barocchetto stucco windows in Rome. Those of the piano nobile have deeply-moulded, calm but sensuous female heads under gently curving pediments; the second floor has shells containing masks, all set in a fantastically swirling framework, and a simplified version of that motif is used to decorate the mezzanine. Presumably this effort to give weight to every storey reflects an intention by the original builders to make money from letting apartments on the upper floors.

The central two bays of six on the piazza are slightly privileged by enlarged mezzanine windows and, more noticeably, by the inclusion of an apparently 16th century door that incorporates two bluish marble columns decorated with bands of leaves. These are very similar to a pair in S Prassede, and both sets are apparently ancient work of the first or second century AD.[1]

One of the sumptuous stucco windows at the Palazzo Mastrozzi

AS D·MATTHAEIVS·

Specchi's view of Palazzo Mattei di Giove with S Caterina dei Funari on the right and the dome of S Carlo ai Catinari on the far left. The coach is entering the main entrance on via dei Funari: the subsidiary entrance is in via Gaetani on the right-hand side. Further up via Gaetani is the addition containing the gallery

Palazzo Mattei di Giove
Via Michelangelo Gaetani, 32

The powerful and wealthy Mattei were long settled in this part of Rome, on the edge of the area where the Jewish ghetto was formally established in 1555. The family eventually acquired the whole site between via delle Botteghe Oscure and via dei Funari, which became known as the 'insula Mattei' and was filled with their palaces, of which this building was the fifth and last to be built. It was commissioned by the great art patron Asdrubale Mattei, who had acquired the fiefdom of Giove which entitled him to the rank of marchese, later elevated to a dukedom.

The palace was designed by Maderno, and building took place in two phases. The main block, including six bays down via Gaetani, was built between 1598 and c. 1611. Almost immediately – between 1613 and 1617 – the via Gaetani wing was extended to include a galleria. As Hibbard points out,[1] Maderno did not revisit the design of the via Gaetani façade when the galleria was built, but simply tacked on an extension that looks from the street like a further small palace with its own

Opposite: Letarouilly's print of the cortile of Palazzo Mattei di Giove, looking out through the main entrance

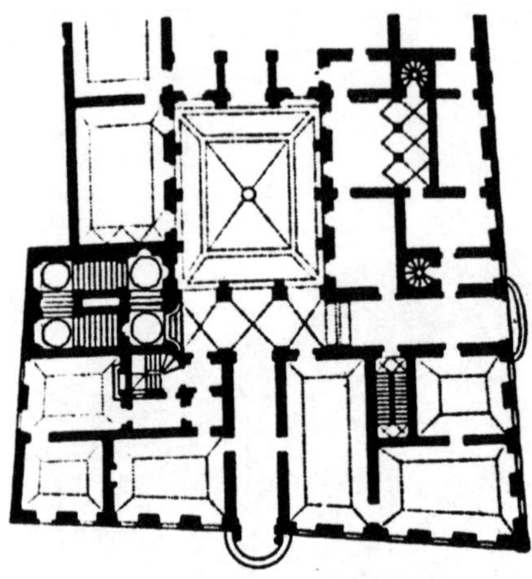

Plan of Palazzo Mattei di Giove, from Letarouilly

portal and balcony. Originally the view into the garden was blocked by a fountain-niche that closed the vista from the via dei Funari entrance. This was removed in the late seventeenth century and there was substituted an arched opening leading to the garden, which joined on to that of the neighbouring Mattei palace to the north.

The palace has always been noted for the planning of its entrances and for the overpowering effect of its courtyard. The entrance planning depends on the fact that Maderno exploited the corner site to include a subsidiary entrance on via Gaetani, lined up with the loggia on the south side of the cortile. This sets up a transverse movement across the line of the main doorway and focuses attention on the entrance to the stairs in the cortile's south-west corner. That entrance has canted sides to create a false perspective effect, as Maderno was later to use in the upper windows, ground-level loggia and piano nobile lobbies of Palazzo Barberini. The stairs themselves go round three sides of a square so that the visitor emerges with a view back along the upper loggia.

The massive architectural forms of the cortile's superimposed loggias themselves make a strong statement in what is a fairly confined space, and this is greatly increased by the large amount of applied classical sculpture from Asdrubale's collection. These pieces (placed within stucco frames presumably designed by Maderno since an inscription dates the decoration to 1616) are individually not as fine as, for example, those used by Scipione Borghese in the Casino dell'Aurora at Palazzo Pallavicini Rospigliosi. Nevertheless, the cortile makes an overwhelming impact of severe yet profuse decoration that contrasts with the restrained façades that the palace presents to the streets.

A very peculiar later addition is the series of bas-reliefs of emperors from Heraclius to the reigning emperor Ferdinand II, mostly based on engravings after Goltzius. These were installed by Asdrubale in 1634-36 to proclaim that he was related to Ferdinand II by marriage – both he and the emperor having married women of the House of Gonzaga.[2]

INTERIOR

Asdrubale Mattei began to commision frescoes for his palace in 1600, using Cristofero Roncalli (Pomarancio) as his adviser. The work proceeded in several phases over the next 25 years, beginning with retardataire work by Antonio Circignani (also given the sobriquet Pomarancio), Prospero Orsi and Gaspare Celio, but later involving much more modern and forward-looking painters. The Mattei family were, in fact, important figures in the Roman art world in the early Baroque period, supporting and patronising young painters including, in particular, Caravaggio.

One room on the ground floor, to the right of the main entrance, has a ceiling fresco of *Jupiter Fulminating the Giants* by Gaspare Celio.

On the piano nobile, in the sala dei palafrenieri is Celio's fresco (1607) of *Moses Giving Thanks after the Crossing of the Red Sea* within an elaborate stucco frame of the period.

East of the sala dei palafrenieri is a room with compartmentalised *Scenes from the Life of Joseph* by Antonio Pomarancio set amidst grotesques by Prospero Orsi. This scheme, in particular, must have looked very old-fashioned even when it was produced.

West of the sala dei palafrenieri are three rooms, each with a single fresco on the ceiling: first *Isaac Blessing Jacob*; second *Jacob's Dream*; third *Jacob and Rachel*. The composition of all three is much influenced by the corresponding scenes of Raphael's Vatican loggias. *Jacob and Rachel* has an elaborate surround of feigned stucco that covers the entire vault, while the other two have much more meagre feigned stucco framing. They were painted in 1606-7 by Albani and a group of Emilian assistants, and the scholarly arguments about their respective shares have been partly influenced by an ambiguous reference in Bellori that could be read as giving the *Jacob and Rachel* to Domenichino. The best assessment appears to be that all three central paintings are substantially by Albani, but that the decorative surround to *Jacob and Rachel* is mainly by Lanfranco and Domenichino.[3]

The first rooms to the north along the via Gaetani side once had ceilings by Sisto Badalocchio, and then there are two rooms with fine, fully mature, ceiling frescoes (both 1615) by Lanfranco. The subjects are *Joseph and Potiphar's Wife* and *Joseph Interpreting Dreams*.

These rooms lead to the galleria which has a vault frescoed with six subjects from the *Life of Solomon*, surrounded by complex decorations including work in grisaille and feigned stucco, bronze and terracotta. Pietro Paolo Bonzi was contracted to do this work in May 1622 but the young Pietro Cortona's performance on two of the feigned bronze medallions so impressed Asdrubale Mattei that he gave him four of the main narrative scenes (ie the two central scenes and *The Death of Joab* and *Solomon's Thanksgiving*), leaving Bonzi to do the other two narratives and the rest of the decorative surround. This splendidly confident work, which was Cortona's first significant fresco commission in Rome, was finished in December 1623.

The palace was sold to the Italian state in 1938. The piano nobile is now occupied by the Centro dei Studi Americani. The rest of the palace is occupied by the Istituto Storico Italiano and, on the top floor, the Discoteca di Stato.

Palazzo Mellini (Cesi, Salviati, Michiel)

Via dell'Umiltà, 43

A palace on the site belonged to Cardinal Giovanni Michiel, who was poisoned on the orders of Cesare Borgia in 1503. His tomb by Sansovino is in the neighbouring church of S Marcello.

By the early 17th century the Cesi owned the palace and they probably employed Maderno to work on the via dell'Umiltà wing during the period 1617-24. In the 1740s and 50s Cardinal Mario Mellini employed the Roman architect Tommaso De Marchis (a rather minor figure who for forty years acted as architect for the Presidenza delle Strade)[1] to produce a palace to occupy the whole site. De Marchis was successful in incorporating a heterogeneous collection of structures into a coherent design with a

Vasi's view of S Marcello on the Corso, with Palazzo Mellini on the left. On the extreme right is a corner of Palazzo de Carolis

lavish façade on the Corso featuring a composite band of decoration below the cornice, a long balustraded balcony, very elaborate decoration of the windows and the use of pilasters and mouldings at the building's corners.

Several writers have stressed the similarities with De Rossi's Palazzo D'Aste further down the Corso.[2] (It is, in fact, just possible to get an instructive view of the corners of both palaces simultaneously if one positions oneself carefully in Piazza Venezia, though Vasi's print – reproduced on p. 172 – exaggerates this.) The use of pagoda window pediments is one clear point that the two palaces have in common, but Palazzo Mellini is generally much more ponderously decorated than De Rossi's polished building, and makes a less suave overall impact. There is nothing here of the grace and fancy of much Roman barocchetto. Instead, an accumulation of massy, vaguely Borrominian, decorative motifs is applied to what is essentially a conventional, old-fashioned Roman palace elevation. For example, no fewer than six different window designs are employed in the nine windows that fill the palace's short side on Piazza S Marcello.

In 1910 the palace came into the possession of the Società Generale Immobiliare who, having been denied planning permission to change the façades, employed Cesare Bazzani to remodel the interior completely and to build the structure that now links the palace to the church of S Marcello. During this phase the quattrocento doorway of Cardinal Michiel's palace was moved to the opposite side of Piazza S Marcello.

The building is now occupied by the Banca di Roma.

Casa dei Merolli (Partini)

Via S Giovanni in Laterano, 122

This elegant building, with the name 'Partini' over the door, faces the flank of the courtyard before S Clemente, in an enclave that has changed very little since the 18th century. It was built for the rich merchant family of the Merolli, probably by the architect Francesco Dalmazzoni, and was finished by 1747. At the outset various units of the Merolli family lived in different parts of the building, and the remainder was rented out.[1]

It is a competent, polished design with several features of crisp detailing. See, in particular, the moulding of the string-courses and the treatment of the corners, which emerge very simply between pilaster strips. The bowler-hat pediment of the main window contains a star within a buckle motif, and is virtually the only area of decoration; there are more stars in the balcony's ironwork. The elegant tripartite balcony is a reprise of De Rossi's successful formula at Palazzo Nari in Campo Marzio. All the windows have simple stucco framing; the outermost ones on the upper storey are deepened and equipped with ringhiere.

What is really interesting about this building is the extent to which, in its simplified architectural language, it apes the type of the noble palace of the previous century. Although it is attached to other buildings on its north face, it is much higher than them and gives the impression of being free-standing. Very unusually at this late date, the roofline is not flat but features a prominent altana equipped with volutes at the sides — an echo of Palazzo D'Aste.

Palazzo del Monte di Pietà

Piazza del Monte di Pietà, 32

The Monte di Pietà was founded by Paul III in 1539 as an official pawnshop, intended to combat the loansharks of the day. It developed into one of Rome's most important banks, while maintaining the pawnshop operations, and it moved to its present site in 1604 when it occupied a building that roughly corresponded to the middle six bays of the existing palace. This had originally belonged to Cardinal Prospero Santacroce but by the time the Monte di Pietà moved in it was owned by the Petrignani and was being altered and extended by Mascarino. The (largely undocumented) first phase of work by the Monte di Pietà consisted of miscellaneous adaptations under the supervision of Carlo Maderno and extended to around 1618 when his plans for a chapel were approved. The (distinctly clumsy) ædicola containing a relief of the *Man of Sorrows* is dated 1604 and is surrounded by four stemmi of Clement VIII's reign. Both the external fountain and the one in the cortile probably date from around 1613 when the palace was connected to water from the Acqua Paola, and both bear the Borghese emblems of dragon and eagle.

Between 1625 and 1631 there was a further campaign that was directed by Maderno until his death in 1629, and was thereafter supervised by his colleague Bartolomeo Breccioli. In this campaign a new wing was added to the left of the old central block, which was itself comprehensively overhauled. The door and the original piano nobile windows were retained, but all the other windows on the façade were replaced, and all this is what we see today. A drawing by Borromini for the clock and campanile is in the Albertina, Vienna.[1]

Vasi's print of the Monte di Pietà. At the far end of the piazza is Palazzo Barberini ai Giubbonari with its entrance hall transformed into the church of S Teresa e S Giovanni della Croce. At the extreme left is Palazzo Alibrandi, apparently equipped with a glazed structure across the front at street level

Breccioli died in 1637 and was succeeded by Francesco Peparelli, who himself died in 1641 and was succeeded, both here and at the nearby Palazzo Santacroce, by his pupil Giovanni Antonio De Rossi. The building campaign of 1638-42 was surely planned by Peparelli, as Baglione asserts, though Breccioli may have left some preliminary suggestions, and the project was left for De Rossi to complete. In this stage a wing containing a new chapel was added to the right of the original block. In 1735 Salvi and others extended the building towards the river, with a neat façade on via S Paolo alla Regola; the arch connecting with the Casa Grande dei Barberini was made in 1759, and in 1859 an upper storey was added. The interior of most of the palace has been very heavily modified.

The important thing in the Monte di Pietà is the new chapel in the corner of the cortile to the right of the main entrance. This was consacrated in May 1641, six months before Peparelli's death in November of that year. Peparelli's responsibility for the original design has nevertheless excited a good deal of speculation on purely stylistic grounds. For example, Hibbard accepted that it was initially the work of Peparelli but added that he was 'not even sure that its present shape (oval, with the main axis the shorter) is actually Peparelli's'. Blunt ignored Peparelli and believed that the chapel was almost certainly designed by De Rossi.[2] The simplest explanation is the one that Marina Carta reached after extensive work on the building records, that is, that the original plan and decorative scheme were established by Peparelli and that De Rossi's rôle at this time was limited to supervising the execution of the final work.[3] Be that as it may, the programme of embellishment over the next 85 years left the chapel fully meriting Blunt's comment that 'with its rich marbles on the walls, elaborate gilt and white stuccoes on the dome, and white marble high reliefs and life-size statues, the chapel is one of the most splendid late Roman Baroque ensembles'.[4] Most of the sculpture is of notable quality, and such high-level patronage by a public institution – rather than by the papacy, religious orders, prelates or noble families — was perhaps unique in Baroque Rome. The project went forward in distinct phases, as follows.[5]

In 1659 Domenico Guidi was commissioned to provide the relief of the Pietà over the altar and he prepared a bozzetto for it. This was Guidi's first major commission after the death of his master Algardi. For some unknown reason it was blocked by Alexander VII and the commission languished until Clement IX was elected in 1667. Within three weeks of the election the Ministers of the Monte di Pietà sought the new pope's approval and the project was given the go-ahead. Even then, Guidi did not produce the work until 1676, when he delivered a far more elaborate piece than that envisaged in the bozzetto and was paid an extra 1200 scudi for his pains.

Immediately Guidi's relief had been delivered, the Ministers turned their attention to obtaining marble for the revetment of the entire chapel up to the level of the architrave. De Rossi was in charge of this work, which was still going on in 1686, and his hand is evident in the four fine giallo antico niches with the pagoda pediments that were one of his favourite motifs (cf. Palazzo D'Aste). The grey-green, honey-coloured and yellow marbles create a most magnificent effect, reflecting the importance of the Monte di Pietà and the confidence of the Ministers.

The next phase of improvement was the covering of the dome with sumptuous gilt stuccoes incorporating five white stucco reliefs that record main events in the Monte di Pietà's history. This work was carried out from 1696 to 1708 under Carlo Francesco Bizzacheri. The reliefs are as follows.

In the centre, and thus presiding over the historical reliefs below:

The Holy Spirit in Glory amidst Seraphim by Michele Maglia.

In the four ovals on the chapel's main and transverse axes:

Sixtus V pointing the needy towards the Monte di Pietà at the Coronari (where it had moved in 1586) by Lorenzo Ottoni;

Clement VIII handing down to Cardinal Pietro Aldobrandini the chirograph in favour of the Monte di Pietà also by Ottoni;

Paul III confirming the Monte di Pietà's privileges in the presence of Cardinal Santacroce and Fra Giovanni da Calvi by Maglia;

Pius IV confirming the institution of the Monte di Pietà by Simone Giorgini.

In 1702, while the work was still proceeding on the dome, the Ministers decided to commission reliefs from Théodon and Le Gros to be placed above the doors at the left and right ends of the chapel. Fine surrounds of black and green marble were made for them (and for Guidi's altarpiece) in 1704 and the two reliefs were put in place the following year. Both illustrate arcane episodes from the Old Testament that give biblical authority for the act of lending. To the left is Théodon's *Joseph lending grain to the Egyptians*[6] and to the right Le Gros's *Tobit lending money to Gabael.*[7] In the immediate aftermath of their work on the altar of St Ignatius in the Gesù, these two sculptors were probably the most celebrated in Rome. Their work here is of very high quality and breathes the spirit of the early 18th century. It must have made Guidi's sub-Algardian altarpiece look distinctly old-fashioned.

The last addition to the chapel was the series of marble statues that were commissioned in 1721 and were placed in De Rossi's yellow marble niches in 1724. They are of the three theological virtues plus *Alms-giving* (*'L'Elemosina'*) and each life-size figure is accompanied by two putti (with a third for *Charity*). They are:

Faith by Francesco Moderati;[8]
Hope by Augusto Cornacchini;[9]
Charity by Giuseppe Mazzuoli;
Alms-giving by Bernardino Cametti.[10]

The last piece is typical of Cametti's elegant refinement, and is generally the most successful of the four.

In 1725 an inscription was placed over the entrance to the chapel recording that the entire decorative scheme had been completed.

In the vestibule there is more of Bizzacheri's stucco decoration, including *God the Father Surrounded by Angels* by Maglia. In an oval niche there is a half-length marble bust by Guidi of *St Charles Borromeo* who was Protector of the Monte di Pietà in the previous century. Guidi was paid 50 scudi for it in 1657.[11] Judging from a reference in Titi it may have been commissioned as one of a pair of saints originally intended to occupy the lateral positions now taken by the Théodon and Le Gros reliefs.[12]

Palazzo di Montecitorio

Piazza di Montecitorio, 33

In 1644 Prince Niccolò Ludovisi (the nephew of Gregory XV and brother of Cardinal Ludovico Ludovisi) married Innocent X's niece Costanza Pamphili. In 1653 Innocent gave him a late dowry of 100,000 scudi with which to build himself a palace in the place of a Capponi building on the Montecitorio site that he had just bought. Within months Bernini produced a design, and work on the ground began quickly. However, the costly project soon ran into problems, and these were not helped when the capricious old pope quarrelled with Prince Niccolò over policy towards Spain and began diverting stone earmarked for the palace to the building work at S Agnese in Piazza Navona.[1] The pope died in 1655; Princess Costanza got tired of waiting for her home and bought the nearby Palazzo Peretti al Corso; and work on the palace came to a halt, with the extremities built to virtually full height but the whole middle section barely started.

The Chigi pope Alexander VII toyed with the idea of buying the Ludovisi palace as well as the neighbouring Aldobrandini palace (now Palazzo Chigi); Pietro da Cortona proposed a gigantic new palace on the north/south axis; Bernini suggested transplanting Trajan's Column to join the Column of Marcus Aurelius in Piazza Colonna. All these ideas for developing the area came to nothing. The Chigi contented themselves with extending Palazzo Aldobrandini and erecting on it a strikingly assertive new altana to confront the half-built Ludovisi building, which was left to languish for forty years.[2]

In 1694 Innocent XII bought the palace for conversion to his new civil and criminal

Details of Palazzo di Montecitorio, showing Bernini's use of natural rock forms in the windows and quoins. Engraving from De Rossi's Architettura Civile

Vasi's view of Piazza di Montecitorio before the obelisk was set up by Pius VI. To the immediate right of Palazzo di Montecitorio the corner of Palazzo Chigi in Piazza Colonna is just visible

courts (Curia Innocenziana) and police headquarters, and Carlo Fontana completed this work by 1697. It incorporated a semicircular cortile at the back, which Fontana hoped would be echoed in a vast semicircular rearrangement of the piazza in front of the palace, though that plan never made progress.[3]

In 1871 the palace was chosen as the seat of the Camera dei Deputati of the new Italian State and a temporary chamber was created in the semicircular cortile. This was replaced in 1888, but the permanent rebuilding to accommodate the Camera had to wait until 1908-1918 when Ernesto Basile's Liberty-style development was built, with a huge pink and white façade on Piazza del Parlamento.

The main façade is still as Fontana left it, but the painting of Bernini's original project, reproduced opposite, shows two important differences. First, instead of Fontana's exceptionally austere portal, Bernini would have had a splendid entrance feature with twisting Herculean telamons supporting a balcony below a fine Serliana surmounted by the papal arms supported by angels. Second, instead of Fontana's belfry, which now provides such a strong centralising and vertical accent, there would have been a far calmer Palladian balustraded roof-line with statues. In other words, Bernini would have had an

A painting of Palazzo di Montecitorio as it was originally conceived by Bermini

upward-thrusting central feature countered by a flat roof-line, while Fontana's design reverses these polarities and creates a simple upward movement. These changes were not just the result of Fontana's personal design preferences; the dominant clock and belfry proclaimed the building's new function as a court, and the pope took a personal interest in their inclusion.[4]

Whatever one may think of Fontana's changes, however, Bernini's façade is incontestably one of the great theatrical compositions of Baroque Rome. Its single most striking feature is the way in which it is split up into a triptych form, with the side wings sloping backwards. Each of the side wings is, in fact, further split at an increasing angle, so that there is a total of five facets. The other notable feature is Bernini's stupendous use on the façade of blocks of travertine cut to look like natural rock. There is no entirely convincing explanation for this motif, though the Four Rivers Fountain in Piazza Navona must surely have some relevance. At Montecitorio the natural rock forms are confined to the sills and some other parts of the lower three outermost windows on each side and the quoins that define the outer facets. As many writers have pointed out, however, Bernini was to return to the motif on a larger scale in his designs for the Louvre. For what may be a subtle 18th century reference to the motif by the Ludovisi family, see the entry for Palazzo Boncompagni Ludovisi in via del Babuino.

Palazzo Montoro (Chigi Montoro, Patrizi, Naro, Lepri)
Via di Montoro, 8

A sprawling building of no fewer than nineteen bays incorporating a Montoro palace of the 16th century, as attested by the survival of the original heavily-rusticated round-headed entrance. Through marriage, the family became the Chigi Montoro and, after 1736, the Chigi Montoro Patrizi.

Few palaces make a more hectic show of heraldic devices. The piano nobile windows display monti with six mounts; the livelier second floor windows have eight-pointed stars; those of the upper mezzanine have oak leaves and ribbons. The monti and star are well known Chigi emblems that were also used by the Chigi Montoro, and an uprooted oak tree was a Patrizi device. The heraldry probably indicates, therefore, that the palace was given its new façade soon after the Patrizi connection in 1736, and the building's general appearance would match such a date.*

Irregularly arranged along the front are seven subsidiary doors of two types – two doors have a star supported between volutes above a square opening, while five doors have monti and stars on a panel above an opening of complex form. The different designs may denote different purposes to which these entrances were originally devoted. Their architect is not known.

There is a crenellated altana which appears more likely to be an unusual survival from the 16th century palace than a piece of medievalising 19th century whimsy such as the turret above Palazzo Massimo di Rignano.

*Apart from being used by the Patrizi, the oak tree was yet another well-known Chigi emblem, and it therefore may have been used by the Chigi Montoro regardless of the Patrizi connection. The oak leaves on the Montoro palace mezzanine are, however, privileged in such an unusually pronounced way for this position that it is reasonable to infer that they were intended to convey a special message.

Palazzo Muti Bussi

Via d'Aracoeli, 2

The Muti were a great Roman family who claimed descent from Mutius Scævola, the mythical hero who, when his attempt to assassinate the Etruscan king Porsenna had failed, calmly thrust his right hand into a flaming brazier to show his enemy the fortitude and resolution of the Romans. Their palace is sited in the area immediately beneath the Campidoglio that had huge symbolic importance for the old Roman nobility, and it had the added kudos of being directly on the papal processional route along what is now via d'Aracoeli. The balcony on the south-west corner of the building would have been used for demonstrations of family grandeur on ceremonial occasions, in just the same way as the balconies of the Altieri and Cenci-Bolognetti palaces at the nearby Piazza del Gesù where the route turned up to the Campidoglio. The balcony, which originally had a stone balustrade that would have done much to privilege its representational and assertive function, is supported on brackets that still show defaced traces of the Muti emblem of two crossed maces linked by a chain. Originally — as Vasi's plate shows — the entire building nestled amid a network of medieval streets, and the east side directly faced the church of SS Venanzio e Anzovino dei Camerinesi.[1] That church, together with all the neighbouring buildings, was demolished in 1928 to make way for wider roads and for the gardens in front of the Vittorio Emanuele monument. All this left the, somewhat reticent, east flank of the palace cruelly exposed.

The palace's plan is an irregular hexagon, with a long side on the east (on via S Venanzio), a very short side containing a

Vasi's print of Palazzo Muti Bussi, on the left. In the centre is the now vanished church of SS Venanzio e Anzovino dei Camerinesi on which the passage that runs through the palace was focused

doorway on the corner of vicolo degli Astalli and via d'Aracoeli, and four other sides arranged more or less symmetrically. In 1578 the Maestri di Strade granted Orazio Muti a licence to build on the site, where he already owned two houses. The identity of Orazio's architect is not recorded in the source documents, but there is no reason to doubt Baglione's statement that it was Giacomo Della Porta, who at the time was unchallenged as the leading architect in Rome. The precise form of Della Porta's building is not known, but it probably did not extend to vicolo degli Astalli since that part was incorporated much later; Claudia Conforti suggests that it had a cortile arranged as a semicircular exedra, and that the entrance and exit routes were by way of two vestibules intersecting at right angles.[2]

The work that established the character of the present palace was done between 1636 and 1642, with Francesco Peparelli acting as supervising architect at least until 1639, and his assistant and successor G. A. De Rossi taking over for the last two years of the project, after Peparelli's death in 1641. During this phase the palace was considerably enlarged to provide separate apartments for the several Muti brothers who occupied it. A particular reason to hurry the work along may well have been to provide an acceptably attractive home for Cleria, the sister of Cardinal Mazarin, who married Pietro Antonio Muti in 1643. In view of the considerable work done on the foundations at the south end of the palace at this time, another reason for the building campaign may have been structural instability that

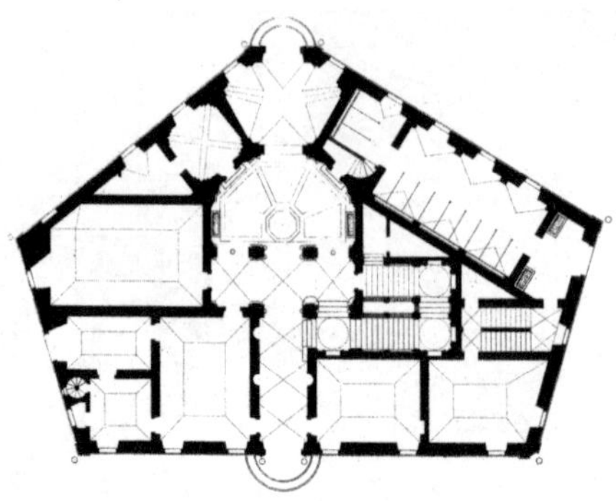

Letarouilly's plan of Palazzo Muti Bussi

could have been caused in 1589-90, when the Acqua Felice was extended to the area to feed Della Porta's fountain in Piazza d'Aracoeli.[3] It is not known how far Peparelli made an individual contribution to the subtle and elegant planning that emerged; the overall conception is accepted as being De Rossi's but it must have taken shape while Peparelli was still active.

So prestigious a palace would have attracted a weight of coach traffic that would have been hard to handle on such an irregular and constricted site, and it was De Rossi's solution to this problem that provides the essential core of the 1636-42 phase. Basically, De Rossi constructed a route straight through the palace, with coaches entering at the centre of the long façade on via S Venanzio and leaving by the door at the angle of via d'Aracoeli and vicolo degli Astalli. De Rossi made this into a kind of scenographic progress by opening out the entrance vestibule into an open loggia that preceded a small hexagonal cortile at the centre of the palace.[4] The main staircase (ornamented with many antique statues in niches) was placed at the side of the vestibule where it joined the loggia, with entrances from both directions.

Although the mandated direction of physical transit was from east to west, there is a strong visual pull in the reverse direction. Looking into the palace from the old exit door at via d'Aracoeli, 2, one is faced across the little cortile by the entrance to the stairs and the loggia, above which are three great windows (now glazed but presumably meant to be open). And that is not all. As Joseph Connors pointed out, the vista through the palace from via d'Aracoeli was lined up on the church of SS Venanzio e Anzovino dei Camerinesi so that one would have looked right through the palace to see the distant church façade framed in the palace doorway.[5] Apart from the sheer visual surprise, this would have acted to appropriate the outside space as a counter to the unavoidable density of the palace's planning, and it was also doubtless intended to convey a diffuse sense of Muti dominance over the surrounding area.

The first new parts to be completed in 1636 were the summer apartments on the ground floor, one to the south of the vestibule and cortile and one to the north. The apartment to the south, with an entrance from Piazza d'Aracoeli, consists of four rooms with elaborate stucco ceilings. That of the entrance room features the emblem of a sword-bearing arm above a brazier, in reference to Mutius Scævola. In the ceiling of the largest room, to the west of the entrance, the heraldic braziers have transmuted into flambeaux and they are joined by the Muti crossed maces and depictions of the *Four Seasons* as reclining figures.[6]

Also in 1636 the main room on the piano nobile was heightened, and before work ended in 1642 the entire top floor of the building (which must previously have been a mezzanine) was increased in height by some two metres. At some point between those two dates — quite possibly soon after the heightening of 1636 — Dughet painted the landscape frieze in the main room. Although this ensemble of fourteen landscape scenes in alternating rectangular and oval format was mentioned by Baldinucci and Pascoli, it dropped out of scholarly sight until it was noted by Ilaria Toesca in 1960[7] and its importance was later appreciated by Boisclair. It has now been more comprehensively described and placed in the wider context of Roman landscape painting by Ilaria Miarelli Mariani and the excellent illustrations that accompany her analysis make it clear that Dughet was already at a high level of achievement in what was probably his first independent commission.[8] The familiar Dughet repertoire of motifs is well on the way to being formed but there is nothing formulaic about them here, and the whole frieze is characterised by an engaging freshness of vision.

It has sometimes been asserted that the palace also contains a galleria decorated by Calandrucci, but this is incorrect.[9]

Pietro Antonio Muti and his wife Cleria both died in 1649 without leaving heirs and the family pinned their hopes to a new marriage alliance with the Vecchiarelli family in the same year. At this time De Rossi was again engaged to incorporate the houses standing on vicolo degli Astalli into the main body of the palace, and to regularise the building's occupation of its full hexagonal site.[10]

In 1664 (perhaps to mark the birth of a Muti heir, Giovanni Andrea Giuseppe, in the previous year) Carlo Fontana was employed to decorate the door at via d'Aracoeli, 2. It was one of his first independent undertakings, and he contrived a splendid confection of emblematic motifs. Above two cornucopia the Muti crossed maces are displayed on a cartouche held in the beaks of two eagles, while on either side a shield bearing the emblem of Mutius Scævola's hand and sword is held in the teeth of the mask of a Nemean lion-skin. The lion heads were, in fact, moulded from the renowned antique Farnese Hercules, and the payment records for this still survive.[11]

Giovanni Andrea Giuseppe Muti was to make the last major change to the palace when he added an entire new storey in 1702, with the crossed maces appearing in the cornice above the rusticated quoins that mark each corner. He never married, and for some time before his death in 1724 he prepared the palace for occupation by Innocenzo Bussi, whom he eventually made his heir on condition that he placed the Muti name before his own. Gabriele Valvassori worked on these improvements in 1717-19, but this was in the capacity of cabinet-maker, before he turned his hand to architecture.[12]

In view of their outstanding quality it is worth noting Bernardino Cametti's monuments to Giovanni Andrea Giuseppe and to Innocenzo's wife Maria Colomba Vincentini in S Marcello al Corso.

The only part of the interior that can ever be seen is the four ground floor rooms with stucco ceilings of 1636, entered from Piazza d'Aracoeli, but this entirely depends on whatever commercial enterprise happens to be occupying these rooms.

Palazzo Muti Papazzurri (Savorelli, Balestra)

Piazza SS Apostoli, 49

According to the inscription on the plate in Ferrerio the palace was built in 1644 by Giovanni Battista Muti Papazzurri, who was one of a family of gentleman amateur artists and was made a marchese in that year. In fact, the date that Ferrerio gives for the building is wrong, but his attribution of the

PALAZZO DE SS. MVTI DE PAPAZZVRRI LA FACCIATA CHE GVARDA SV LA PIAZZA DE SS.
Disegnato da Pietro ferrerio
APOSTOLI FV ARCHITETTVRA DEL MARCHESE GIO. BATISTA MVTI
L'ANNO. MDCXLIIII.
42

design (or at least the most recent part of it) to Giovanni Battista was repeated by Mola and it may well be correct. In that event, it is his only surviving piece of architecture.

The documents published by Antinori show that in 1612 the Maestri di Strade licensed Vincenzo Muti to build a new façade along via di S Marcello. Most of the existing façade on that side of the palace must date from the years immediately thereafter. The wide gap between the fourth and fifth bays from the left shows that there were problems in adjusting to the pre-existing buildings on the site, and the regular arches on the ground floor are clear traces of the provision that was made for shops in order to raise revenue for the development.

In 1631 a further licence was granted to authorise building on virtually all the rest of the current ground plan and the print published by G. B. De Rossi in 1635 shows the whole job completed. The 11th to 13th bays of the via di S Marcello façade were added at this time and it can be assumed that the post-1612 work had not reached as high as the mezzanine all the way, since all the existing mezzanine windows to the right of the central doorway are much smaller and more delicate than those to the left.

The Ferrerio and De Rossi prints show the Piazza SS Apostoli façade very much as it is now, but with the bizarre addition of a niche fountain with a statue of a reclining woman in the position of the first floor window immediately over the balcony. This prestige façade is indeed very small for such a large building, and the Muti Papazzurri presumably used the odd eyecatching device to give it more importance. The fountain certainly survived for some years but it is not known when it disappeared. If Giovanni Battista was indeed the architect of the 1631-38 work, it may be permissible to attribute the strange feature to the heady enthusiasms of an amateur. The cuttings in the pediments of the piano nobile windows also have a curiously finicky and amateurish quality.

Giovanni Battista and his brother were taught painting by Charles Mellin, who was a long-term guest at the palace from 1627. Two ceilings that he painted in the via di S Marcello wing remain in place.[1] They are each dominated by a single — rather ungainly — personification: that of *Glory* is cast in the mode of the mounted Marcus Curtius about to leap into the gulf, while *Fame* is a more conventional winged figure blowing a trumpet.

Claude Lorrain may well have been introduced to the Muti Papazzurri by his friend and fellow Lorrainer, Mellin, and at some time before 1635 he frescoed one of the palace rooms with landscapes on all four walls. Judging from Sandrart's rapturous description[2] this must have been a striking display of Claude's art at the time that he was discovering his vision of ideal landscape, but no trace of it now remains. Later, G. A. De Rossi, Carlo Fontana and Bizzacheri are also recorded as working on the palace, but it is now very hard to discern the results.

All these things, together with paintings that Testa executed in the garden, may have been among the casualties that the palace suffered when in 1719 the Holy See acquired it and had it modified by Alessandro Specchi, with much decoration by G. A. Soccorsi, in order to accommodate the Stuart

Opposite: Ferrerio's print of Palazzo Muti Papazzurri (Balestra) in its original form with a fountain over the entrance

pretender James III. The Stuarts continued to keep their court here until — as a plaque in the androne records — the dynasty was extinguished with the death of the Cardinal of York (Henry IX) in 1807. During the period of Stuart occupation, the palace was naturally a place of considerable social and political importance.

Palazzo Muti Papazzurri

Piazza della Pilotta, 32

According to Specchi's print of 1699, shown opposite, the architect of the palace was Mattia De Rossi. He was probably responsible for the two wings that extend from an earlier nucleus into Piazza della Pilotta. Specchi's print shows how these wings were linked at the piazza end by a grand one-storey feature consisting of an entrance set between columns, with a balustraded terrace above.

In 1909 the palace was acquired by the Holy See for the Pontificio Istituto Biblico, which still occupies it. At that time the building was drastically modified — and De Rossi's architecture virtually obliterated — by the insertion of a large library room in the cortile between the wings, and the replacement of the entrance feature by a blockish façade extending to the palace's full height.

The important feature is the galleria on the piano nobile of the north wing, which was long associated with the names of Claude and Dughet, but was recognized by Toesca in 1960 as being by Grimaldi.[1] With its three windows on each long side and a further window on the short end overlooking the piazza, it is a cheerful, light-filled space, and one of the very few surviving 17th century Roman palace rooms with landscape frescoes covering the walls. The landscapes are, in fact, in striking contrast with the riotous accumulation of eclectic features in the vault.

The iconography of the vault is built around four quadri riportati by Giacinto Calandrucci representing *Venus, Flora, Diana*, and *Diana and Endymion* — the last derived from the corresponding scene in the Galleria Farnese. Four medallions contain further references to the stories of *Venus* and *Flora*. All this is surrounded by a complex mass of decorative motifs by Grimaldi, including various allegorical figures and incorporating six feigned bronze plaques of images taken from Perrier's *Icones et Segmenta,* published in Rome in 1645. The flowers in the vases between the sections and on the herms below are universally accepted as being by Ciro Ferri, as they are very close to the painted mirrors in the galleria in Palazzo Borghese (which, incidentally, was also organised by Grimaldi).

Probably Grimaldi employed several painters on the scheme. The (heavily repainted) landscapes that fill the walls between the windows contain a range of subjects — classical buildings, torrents, crags, villages — and show the influence of Dughet, as Bartoni has pointed out.[2] At the short ends there are perspective avenues that illusionistically extend the room indefinitely. The lunettes display a more puzzling range of landscape types, with two marines that are tightly painted in the style of Tassi among others that are typically Grimaldian. Finally, the very damaged landscapes under the windows seem to be by yet another hand. The one on the north wall nearest to the entrance is, in fact, a summary paraphrase of Claude's celebrated *The Mill* in the Doria-Pamphili collection.

The date of the architecture and painting of the galleria is still unsettled. Batorska

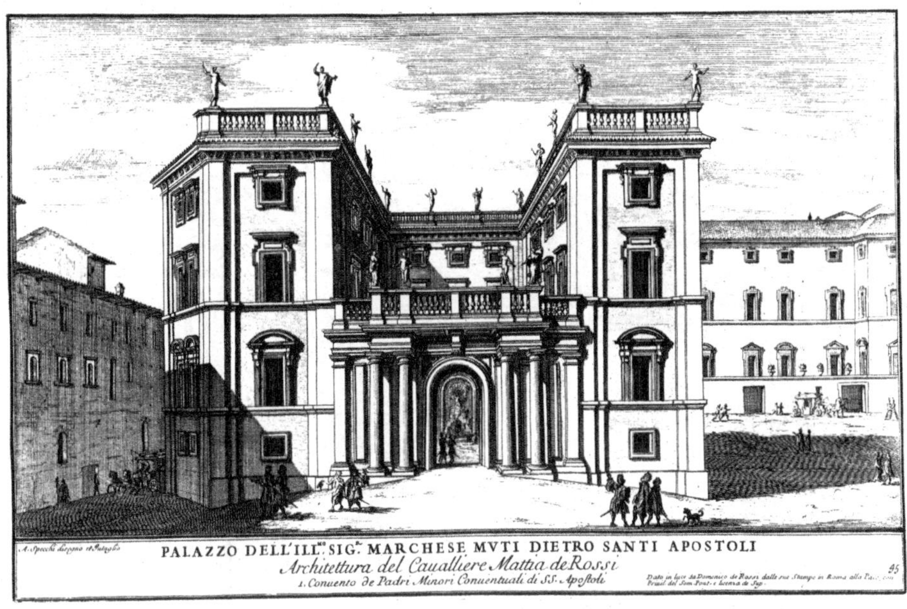

Specchi's print of Palazzo Muti Papazzurri in Piazza Pilotta showing the entrance screen that was destroyed when the area between the wings was filled in after 1909

argued that the iconography of the vault indicated a connection with a marriage, but the only one that has ever been cited in that connection is that of Pompeo Muti Papazzurri and Maria Isabella Massimo in 1660, which is much too early. Calandrucci's responsibility for the quadri riportati is put beyond doubt by Pascoli who describes how Calandrucci got the job via his master Maratta, who remained in contact with the project.[3] It is not known when Calandrucci began working with Maratta, but since he was born in 1646 and was evidently Maratta's trusted lieutenant by the time he did the work, that itself indicates a date well into the 1670s. From other evidence in Pascoli's account Guerrieri Borsoi suggests a date between 1677 and Grimaldi's death in 1680.[4] That seems extraordinarily late for the marine lunettes, which are uncannily reminiscent of Tassi's work of the 1630s. However, ten years before (in 1667-1669) Grimaldi was similarly juxtaposing retardataire marines and Bolognese landscapes in the rooms of Clement IX in the Quirinale.[5] Probably Grimaldi quite early built up a repertoire of decorative motifs and continued to recycle them without a great deal of variation throughout his career.

During the 18th century this Muti Papazzurri palace was connected by an arch with the nearby one that fronts on to Piazza SS Apostoli and, like its neighbour, it was occupied by the exiled Stuarts.

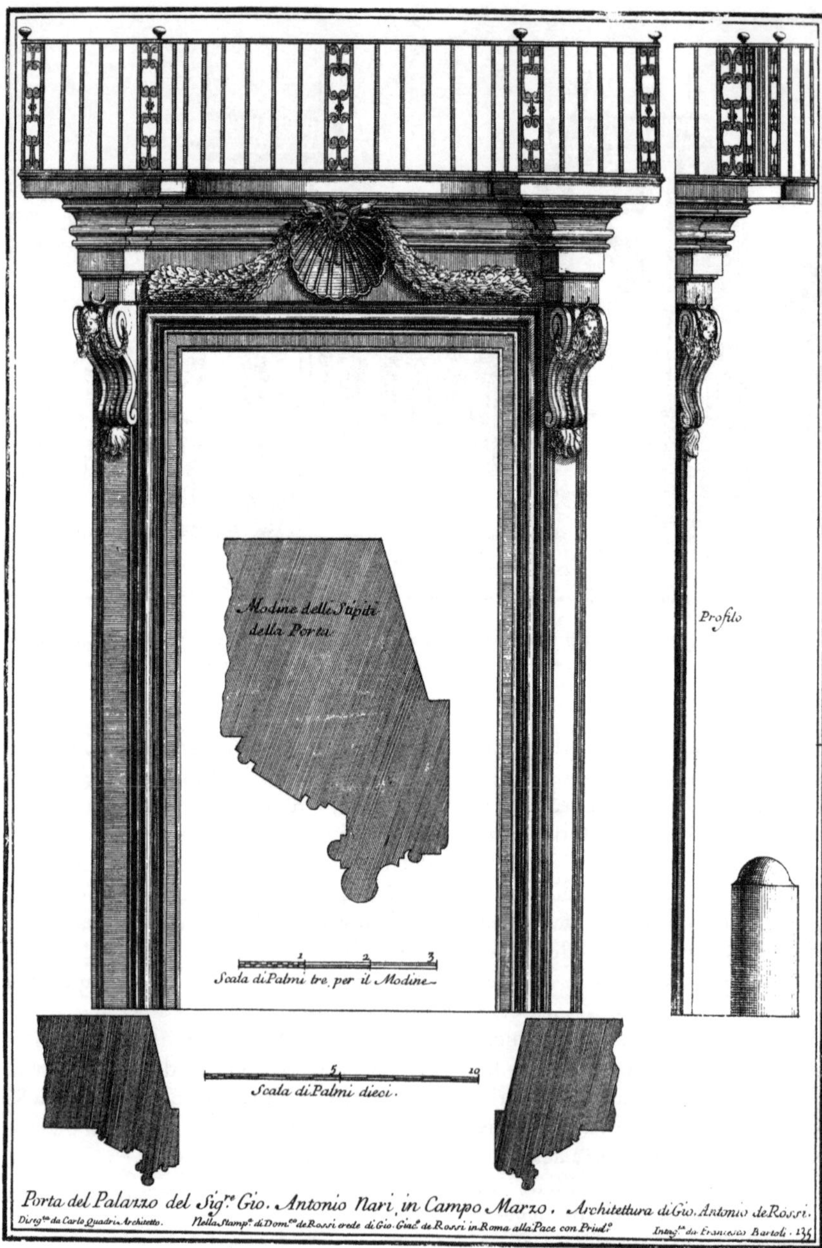
Modine delle Stipiti della Porta
Profilo
1 2 3
Scala di Palmi tre per il Modine
5 10
Scala di Palmi dieci.
Porta del Palazzo del Sig.re Gio. Antonio Nari, in Campo Marzo. Architettura di Gio. Antonio de Rossi.
Diseg.ta da Carlo Quadri Architetto.
Nella Stamp.a di Dom.co de Rossi erede di Gio. Giac.o de Rossi in Roma alla Pace con Priul.o
Intag.ta da Francesco Bartoli. 135

Palazzo Nari
Piazza S. Maria in Campo Marzio, 3

Both Pascoli and Domenico De Rossi say that the portal is by G. A. De Rossi, and Pascoli also says that he altered the staircase and the courtyard.[1] The documents published by Antinori substantiate all this.[2] The first documents signed by De Rossi for work on the palace were in 1654, the final bills for the portal were in 1659, and later that year De Rossi made his stima for work on the top part of the stairs. The palace was not painted, however, until 1666.

The portal is indeed a fine piece that is very characteristic of De Rossi's work at this period, and it provides a point of reference for other De Rossi doorway designs. As of 2010 the palace had become distressingly dilapidated.

Palazzo Nari
Via Monterone, 2

A huge, severe mid 17th century palace by Bartolomeo Breccioli, incorporating many earlier buildings. The main range with a fine cornice along via Monterone is plainly original; the four lower bays to the left are puzzling as they continue the same elevation quite faithfully; the plain flank with many openings for rimesse along via dei Nari appears to be 17th century; the rest is largely rebuilt. Note the inverted crescents of the Nari in the spandrels of the doorway, in the cornice (where they appear together with rosettes), and in the austerely imposing windows of the main front.

The salone contains Antonio Gherardi's ceiling painting of the *Story of Esther* and *Truth Triumphant over Deceit.* It was executed in 1673-74 and is not generally regarded as one of Gherardi's happier efforts.[1]

Palazzo Nuñez (Torlonia)
Via Bocca di Leone, 79

The palace was built by G. A. De Rossi for Marchese Francesco Nuñez Sanchez. The part on via dei Condotti was built in 1658-60 and extended for seven bays down via Bocca di Leone. Subsequently — but before 1680 — De Rossi extended the building by a further seven bays so that it occupied the entire isolato bounded by vie Condotti, Bocca di Leone, Borgognona and Mario de' Fiori. The windows in the first part are arranged slightly irregularly, indicating the absorbtion of earlier buildings; the second set of seven bays are evenly spaced at an uncomfortably close interval. Specchi's print (reproduced overleaf) shows rusticated quoins running the height of the building at the point where the first phase ended.

In 1804 the palace was acquired by Napoleon's brother Lucien and during the following years it was lived in by various members of the Bonaparte family. In 1842 it was bought by the fabulously rich Prince Marino Torlonia who employed Antonio Sarti to refurbish it; among other changes he privileged the long Bocca di Leone façade as the main entrance front (previously the short front on via dei Condotti had performed that function). It is now a huge, soulless block with remarkably little external character.

Pascoli recorded that both Grimaldi and Calandrucci painted rooms in the palace but there was no modern literature on them

Opposite: Door of Palazzo Nari in Campo Marzio; engraving from De Rossi's Architettura Civile

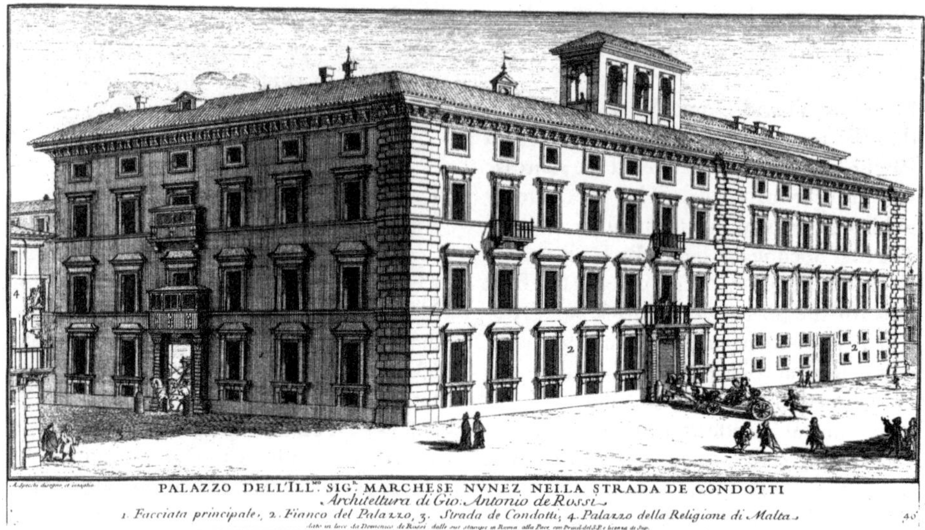

View by Specchi of Palazzo Nuñez, showing the quoins that originally separated De Rossi's first building (on the left) from his later extension

before the articles by Guerrieri Borsoi and Lodi-Fè of 1988 and 1990. The fullest account (including illustrations of all the paintings mentioned below) is in Batorska's article of 1995 but there are several discrepancies between this, Matteucci and Ariuli, and the Guide Rionali entry on the location of the rooms and the number of apartments involved.[1] Since the palace is effectively inaccessible, the following note will simply summarize the essential points from the literature.

Although the quality of Grimaldi's collaborators (who may very well have included Calandrucci in the second phase) appears to have been variable,[2] this was an exceptionally large programme (about sixteen rooms) that extended over several years. It is also notable for the subject matter of the figure scenes being almost entirely drawn from the Old and New Testaments. There are clear similarities in all this with Grimaldi's work for the Santacroce (who also employed De Rossi as their architect) and Batorska speculates[3] that Grimaldi may have had unusually close relations with both of the families.

On the piano nobile along the via dei Condotti façade there is a group of rooms with flat wooden ceilings and friezes of New Testament subjects against landscape backgrounds in the Bolognese style, all set in ornamental stucco frames. The room on the corner with via Bocca di Leone is devoted to *Scenes from the Life of John the Baptist*, the next room to the *Life of Christ* and the last to the *Life of St Peter*. Of these, the segments of the *Life of Christ* are arranged so that they each extend either side of one of the corners of the room, instead of occupying a wall each in the conventional manner. The stucco framing in this room appears very fine, contributing to an overall impression of grand sobriety that looks somewhat unusual in Grimaldi's output. Batorska accepts these rooms as being essentially by Grimaldi, and a date around 1660, when that part of the palace had just been completed, seems a reasonable assumption.

Most of the other frescoed rooms in the palace are of a totally different type, with shallow vaulted ceilings painted with a central scene flanked by subsidiary quadri riportati on the coving of the vault. The ones that are closest to Grimaldi have as their central subjects *The Baptism of Christ, Christ and the Woman of Samaria*, *Moses Defending the Daughters of Jethro* and *The Sacrifice of Manoah*, and in both the central and subsidiary segments of these there is a great deal of Bolognese landscape. All of these ceilings display the characteristic Grimaldian horror vacui, with a variety of eclectic decorative motifs. The first two feature tondi that are occupied by neat little landscape vignettes, while in the second pair the tondi contain very two-dimensional vases of flowers. Finally, there is a small Grimaldi room with an open sky composition of *Primavera and Zephyr*. All this work must have been done after the extension of the palace but before Grimaldi's death in 1680. A date in the late 1670s seems plausible.

Palazzo Ottoboni Boncompagni

Via della Vite, 7

An 18th century palace (built in 1731 according to Lombardi) on a corner site, with six bays on the Corso, immediately opposite Palazzo Peretti, which was also owned by the Ottoboni family. The ancient Arco di Portogallo crossed the Corso at this point and carried a corridor that linked the buildings either side. In 1662 it was dismantled by order of Alexander VII, as recorded in the plaque (dated 1665) at the corner of the palace.

The high ground floor mezzanine with three equal storeys above is a very good example of the way in which the architecture of palaces and apartment buildings had become virtually interchangeable by the 1730s. This was, nevertheless, the dwelling of a noble family with links to two popes, and this is advertised by the Boncompagni dragons and Ottoboni double-headed eagles in the pediments of the piano nobile windows. The strongly-moulded corner feature is divided at the level of the stringcourse, indicating that the madonella under a canopy at this point is an original feature. The extra storey above the cornice appears to be a later addition.

At street level the Corso front has been changed to accommodate shops but on via della Vite there is an exceptional group of barocchetto openings, with two fine complex doorways and two round-headed entries (probably rimesse for coaches) ornamented with 'breaking wave' volutes with a shell above. There is a third such entry on the Corso front, but no sign that there was ever a large main entrance on this prestige face of the building.

Palazzo Pallavicini Rospigliosi (Bentivoglio, Mazzarino, Pallavicini)

Via XXIV Maggio, 43

The site was important because of its closeness to the pope's palace at the Quirinale. In 1608 Cardinal Scipione Borghese, Paul V's nephew, was given the use of a small garden here, and in 1610 he began buying up neighbouring properties and arranging for church land in the area to be ceded to him. By 1612 he had obtained the whole of the present isolato.

The area was dominated by the ruins of

Palazzo Palavicini Rospigliosi in a print by Vasi. The Casino dell'Aurora is out of the picture on the raised terrace at the left side. Beyond the terrace can be seen the flank of Palazzo della Consulta

the Baths of Constantine, the last great edifice of pagan Rome. From the beginning of 1611 Scipione ordered a hectic earth-moving operation in order to make an elaborate series of gardens on three levels. Any classical sculpture found in these building works naturally went into his rapidly expanding collection. The large palace itself was started in 1613 and work proceeded rapidly, partly because the structure was built over the ancient foundations wherever possible. As the palace neared completion in 1616, however, Scipione sold the entire site to Duke Giovanni Angelo Altemps, to whom he was enormously in debt. Scipione — whose interest must have been turning at this date to the casino that he was building on the Pincio — had throughout maintained his residence in the nearby Quirinale palace and his main concern at the present palace had probably always been with the gardens, which are far more attractive than the bleak and awkwardly planned palace itself. Although the exact shares of the participants have not been disentangled, the architects involved in the project were the usual Borghese team of Flaminio Ponzio (until his death in 1613), Vasanzio and Carlo Maderno. Cigoli may be responsible for a plan for the palace that was not used and he could have had a hand in the actual work.

The site is on two levels, and originally there was also a small lower third level to the south of the palace; this is now occupied by via Nazionale. The main structures in and around the gardens are as follows.

On the upper level, that is, on the terrace

(or giardino pensile) above and to the left of the visitor as one enters the enclave from the door at 43, via XXIV Maggio:

– The **Casino dell'Aurora** (finished before 1614 and showing all the characteristics of Vasanzio's style, with a great deal of high-quality sarcophagi and other classical sculpture incorporated in the building). The ceiling painting in the central salone is Guido Reni's celebrated *Aurora*, painted between January and August 1614. The other frescoes (all completed 1614) are as follows. In the salone, on the short walls, *Triumphs of Fame and of Love* by Tempesta; on the long walls, the *Four Seasons*, works of exceptional quality by Paul Bril; and, in the central lunette and spandrels, *Putti* and *Allegorical Figures* by Cherubino Alberti.[1] In the adjoining rooms *Rinaldo and Armida* by Baglione and *Combat of Rinaldo and Armida* by Passignano.

At the opposite end of the terrace is a flight of curved and rectilinear steps (documented to Maderno, 1612) with a grotto in the reverse face. These lead down to a garden on the main level, north of the palace.

In the garden at the foot of the Maderno stairs:

– The Teatro d'Acqua, an elaborate fountain feature arranged in an exedra (1612, probably by Vasanzio).

– The Casino delle Muse, with frescoes by Agostino Tassi and Orazio Gentileschi, begun in the summer of 1611 and with Tassi's share of the work presumably completed by March 1612 when Gentileschi's daughter Artemisia made the accusation that precipitated Tassi's trial for her rape. The upper register and vault depict young women making music of all kinds amidst Tassi's quadratura setting. The *Muses* in the lower register are of lower quality.

Guido Reni's celebrated Aurora *fresco at Palazzo Pallavicini Rospigliosi. This print was made in 1787 by Raphael Morgheri and dedicated to Prince Giuseppe Rospigliosi by Morgheri and his publisher Giovanni Volpato*

Prints by Cesi of some of the pairs of putti by Guido Reni that populate the painted pergola at the Palazzo Pallavacini Rospigliosi

Still on the main level, but at the opposite (south) end of the palace, is the Loggia della Pergola (1611-1612). The feigned pergola populated by birds and animals and the five impressive landscape lunettes on the long side are by Paul Bril.* The pairs of putti that punctuate the pergola are by Guido Reni, who left Rome as soon as the work was finished, vowing never to return (though in the event the pope was to force him back within two years to paint the *Aurora*).

*The two landscape lunettes on the short wall to one's left as one faces the garden are by another hand, for which Negro suggests P. P.Bonzi as the likeliest candidate. On the other short wall, the scene of heron hunting to the left appears to be by Bril; the other is now too dilapidated to judge, but was possibly by Bonzi.[2]

On the lowest level, in a small secret garden to the south of the palace that could be reached through the Loggia della Pergola, there originally stood the Casino di Psiche (1611-1613). This building was possibly designed by Cigoli and was certainly frescoed by him with *Scenes from the Story of Psyche*, with paintings of *Apollo and Daphne* by Guido Reni on the exterior.[3] In 1875 this casino and garden were destroyed to make way for the new via Nazionale, but the Cigoli ceiling frescoes are preserved in the Museo di Roma (Palazzo Braschi), where they are displayed in the ceiling of room 12.

Duke Giovanni Angelo Altemps kept the palace only until 1619, when he sold it to Enzo Bentivoglio, who used it as a residence for his brother Cardinal Guido

Bentivoglio. Between 1623 and 1627 the Bentivoglio employed Giovanni da S Giovanni to fresco the ceilings of one room on the piano nobile and three rooms on the ground floor, immediately adjacent to the Loggia della Pergola. In these three rooms Giovanni's rather coarsely executed *Rapes of Europa, Amphitrate and Persephone* contrast with the elegant friezes that contain marines probably by Filippo Napoletano in the first two rooms and landscapes that seem close to Bonzi in the third. A nearby room has another frieze with especially sensitive but dilapidated marines in the style of Filippo Napoletano, including a rock arch that almost looks forward to the subtlety of Claude.

The palace was sold to Cardinal Mazarin in 1641, rented to the Rospigliosi from 1680, and bought by them in 1708. It later became the joint property of the Pallavicini and Rospigliosi families and was modified in 1756 to enable them to maintain separate quarters.

The Casino dell'Aurora is open on the first day of each month from 10-12 and 3-5. On these occasions one can see – though not approach – Maderno's steps at the opposite end of the terrace with, to their left, the complex pediment of the Teatro d'Acqua on the level below. The gardens and the palace (which contains one of the most famous private art collections in Italy) are not otherwise open to the public.

Vasi's view of Piazza Navona in the heat of August. The fountains have been allowed to overflow and carriages are being driven through the resulting pool to prevent the wheels warping from desiccation. Palazzo Pamphili fills the left side of the piazza as far as S Agnese

Palazzo Pamphili

Piazza Navona, 14

The original Pamphili property was at the south end of Piazza Navona (the ancient Stadium of Domitian) with its entrance around the corner on Piazza Pasquino. As the family came up in the world they bought adjoining properties and, in the late 16th century, completed a small palace with a façade on Piazza Navona itself. After Giovanni Battista Pamphili became a cardinal (in pectore 1627/published 1629) he extended the palace, employing Peparelli as his architect, and Passeri tells us that he employed Agostino Tassi to decorate some of its rooms.[1]

Giovanni Battista became Pope Innocent X in 1644 and immediately decided to buy the neighbouring buildings to the north, and to expand his own palace on their site. These plans soon developed into a more ambitious transformation of Piazza Navona into a complex that would be a memorial to his family. The main items in the project were to be a great church (S Agnese) containing the family mausoleum, linked on one side with the enlarged palace and, on the other side, with a religious college, the Collegio Innocenziano. In front of the church the obelisk from the Circus of Maxentius on the Appian Way would be incorporated in a fountain and capped with the Pamphili emblems. Most of this

Palazzo Pamphili in an engraving by Ferrerio. Borromini's gallery lies behind the Serliana window on the extreme right

ambitious scheme — in many ways reminiscent of Philip II's El Escorial in the previous century — was completed. The main exception was the family mausoleum, since in the event the pope's relatives notoriously proved too mean even to provide him with a decent burial, let alone a memorial.

The work on the palace was planned by a group of family members with the pope himself keeping a very close eye on the project and Borromini's great champion Virgilio Spada acting as the group's secretary. The pope's sister-in-law Olimpia Maidalchini and her son Camillo Pamphili were the main protagonists until Camillo fell into disfavour on his marriage to Olimpia Aldobrandini in 1647. Thereafter Francesco Maidalchini and, from 1650, Camillo Astalli were the most active family members.

The architects Girolamo Rainaldi (already aged 74 in 1644) and Borromini were involved from the beginning, and by 1645 Borromini was preparing drawings for grand new schemes. One of these embodied a huge courtyard with semi-circular ends, and others explored variations on the theme of three altane that were elaborated into towers. The decision to ignore these ambitious ideas and instead to proceed on the basis of a conservative design by Rainaldi must have been taken by the pope himself. By retaining a great deal of the earlier buildings behind his undistinguished new façade that replaced whatever front Peparelli had built, Rainaldi ensured that the rebuilding of the palace could be effectively completed between 1646 and 1650.

Borromini's hand is mainly to be seen in the two grandest rooms. The first is the palace's principal salone — named Sala Palestrina in the 19th century, when the palace was being used by the Società Musicale di Rome. This is an enormous plain white room built over a loggia between the main north and south courtyards. It was modified by Busiri Vici in the 19th century and the main surviving feature that is unquestionably by Borromini is the simple but noble stucco ceiling decoration that seems to float above the cornice.

Borromini's other contribution was the famous tunnel-vaulted gallery that runs across the entire depth of the palace at the north end, adjacent to S Agnese. Down each long side there is a series of elaborate doors and the light comes only from a Serliana window at each short end. Given that the Piazza Navona's ancestry as an imperial stadium was being emphasised by the erection of the obelisk from Maxentius's Circus, it can be assumed that the Serliana form was chosen as a reference to the emperor's box that would have occupied virtually the same spot in ancient times. But that kind of resonance with pagan imperial Rome was not the only message of the architecture. From the exterior, the gallery's Serliana appears to be contained within the architecture of S Agnese rather than that of the palace, and it is symmetrical with an identical Serliana in the Collegio Innocenzio on the other side of the church. This ambiguous merging of the statements made by the palace and the church reflects the pope's intentions for the interwoven functions of the complex. Exceptionally among the palaces of papal families, Palazzo Pamphili was seriously considered for active use as the pope's administrative headquarters for some months of the year. Although the palace was never, in fact, used in that way, the plan would have required provision to be made for the pope's private apartment, which was probably included in the church block, with the pope's bed-chamber below the southern campanile. The gallery would have acted, as it were, like a porous membrane, being part of the palace but also functioning as the antechamber to the pope's private accommodation in the church building. It must always have been a far more private space than, for example, the salone of Palazzo Barberini, which functioned as the palace's sala dei palafrenieri or guardroom.[2]

Originally the gallery was painted by Spadarino with frescoes celebrating the life of Innocent X, but the pope very soon decided to replace these and Pietro da Cortona was called in to paint the existing scheme from 1651 to 1654. It tells the story of Æneas's approach to Italy, the establishment of the Trojans in Latium, and Jupiter resolving the dispute between Venus and Juno over the fate of Æneas and the Trojan refugees. As with any display of imagery from the Æneid in a Roman palace, one of its intentions was certainly to remind the viewer of the links with ancient Rome that were claimed by the family in question. The Pamphili, in fact, asserted their descent from Numa Pompilio, Rome's legendary second king, law-giver and religious instructor.

There is a range of views about the other messages that the ceiling was intended to send. A celebrated article by Preimesberger, for example, builds up a complex web of interpretation on the basis of the Pamphili emblems, and argues for a recondite Christianising reading. With greater economy of hypothesis John Beldon Scott has explored the meaning of the Pamphili ceiling through a comparison with the earlier masterpiece by Cortona at Palazzo Barberini. He shows how the Pamphili programme illustrates the institution of impartial justice, and explains why Innocent should have wished to project that image in contrast with the unbridled self-interest of the Barberini. He also shows how the cool colouring and clear narrative style of the Pamphili ceiling embody the rationality and restraint that Innocent wanted to project, in contrast with the outpouring of poetical novelty that characterised the constructed Barberini image.

The other fresco decoration in the palace obviously cannot match Cortona's great achievement, but it is extremely interesting nevertheless. In order to create an extended enfilade along the front of the palace on the piano nobile, three rooms were retained from the earlier building works at the south end, and four new rooms similarly decorated with friezes were added to complete the sequence.

The three rooms retained from the earlier building are as follows.

Sala di Giuseppe, with a frieze by Swanevelt.

Sala di Mosè, with a frieze by the Tassi workshop, with diverse hands involved.

Sala delle Marine, with a frieze of seascapes by Tassi.[3]

The four rooms made, or remade, in the 1640s programme are:

– Sala di Bacco (the large central room over the entrance and balcony), with a frieze by Andrea Camassei, documented to 1648;

– Sala dei Paesi, with an excellent landscape frieze by Dughet;

– Sala della Storia Romana, with a frieze by Gimignani;

– Sala di Ovidio, with a frieze that is an early work by Giacinto Brandi.

Reflecting the palace's functions already described, the scheme of decoration continues into the rooms that are sited within the architecture of S Agnese. The main one of these is the vaulted Sala di Didone under the campanile, which was painted with scenes from the story of *Dido and Æneas* by Francesco Allegrini, presumably in the late 1640s. Allegrini probably also painted the Sala dei Vizi e delle Virtù immediately behind the Sala di Dido, and in 1659-1660 he returned to decorate four small rooms on the rear (west) face of S Agnese with scenes from the Old Testament. On the west face of the palace itself there are a further five decorated rooms, including one (the Sala delle Donne Illustri) signed and dated by Gimignani in 1648, and another with figures in Turkish fancy dress.[4]

As a result of Camillo Pamphili's marriage to Olimpia Aldobrandini the library of Clement VIII came to the Pamphili and a room was made for it in the Collegio Innocenziano. In 1667-1673 the ceiling of the library was frescoed with a *Triumph of Divine Wisdom* by Francesco Cozza who had previously worked for Camillo Pamphili at Valmontone.

Through the Aldobrandini marriage the Pamphili gained the great palace at the foot of the Corso and had less use for the one in Piazza Navona. In 1687 it was made available as the residence for Lord Castlemaine during his embassy to Innocent XI which was a prominent part of James II's ill-starred pro-Catholic policy. Ciro Ferri designed one of the ceremonial coaches built for this occasion (see below), and the climax of the whole affair was a banquet in the Borromini gallery, which became famous for the

The gala coach designed by Ciro Ferri for Lord Castlemaine's ceremonial embassy to Innocent XI. Above, Neptune and Britannia support the crown of England: below a marine-lion and a unicorn with attendant genii. Like the images of the trionfi on the next page, this engraving by Arnold van Westerhout comes from the commemorative volume by the painter Michael Wright that was issued in England in 1688, just as James II was about to lose his throne

Van Westerhout's engravings of two of the trionfi *made from sugar paste that adorned the table when Lord Castlemaine presented a great feast in the gallery of Palazzo Doria Pamphili during his embassy to Innocent XI in 1687*

astonishingly elaborate trionfi made of sugar with which the tables were decorated.[5] In the first quarter of the 18th century Cardinal Corsini established his library in the palace before he became Pope Clement XII and had his own family palace built in Trastevere.

The palace is now the Brazilian Embassy and is not open to the public. The gallery is quite often illuminated at night, however, and in that event one can get a tantalising glimpse of Cortona's ceiling, with *Neptune Quelling the Storm* opposite the *Trojans Landing at Latium*.

Palazzo Panizza

Piazza S Maria in Monticelli, 66

The palace, erected between 1694 and 1700, was commissioned by Giuseppe Fonseca Panizza, who already owned a derelict building on the site. The architect was Simone Felice Delino, a long-standing assistant to Carlo Fontana, who became architect to Queen Christina of Sweden and Cardinal Pietro Ottoboni. Delino — who also executed topographical prints for Falda — specialised in ephemeral displays for public functions, and the design of this complete building was an unusual undertaking for him. Although the building was designed to accommodate a single family unit (plus two shops with mezzanines), it was a purely commercial venture for renting out to the minor nobility, and a memorandum by Delino records that a consciously aristocratic style of architecture would make it easier to find tenants and increase the rental income.[1]

It is a tall building on a trapezoidal site at the end of an isolato. The heavily modelled corner mouldings stress the vertical emphasis, though the present tower-like appearance is partly due to the attic above the cornice which does not appear in Vasi's print and must be a 19th century addition. In accordance with the commercial strategy summarised by Delino, the building is virtually a compendium of the devices that characterised a noble Roman palace in the manner of G. A. De Rossi, including a fine portal with a balcony and plenty of stucco decoration over all the windows. Vasi's print shows that originally there were also further balconies over the two openings on the south east side: these doorways, under lintels decorated with fluid volutes and a mensola, are now partly blocked and split into two levels. The main stairs are ingeniously planned in triangular form to occupy a space at the back of the irregular site.[2]

As with many other palaces, the height of the ground floor mezzanines requires quite a massive entrance to reach up to the piano nobile balcony. The stucco in the entrance is a lavish, but strange, piece with a female head merging into a shell and foliage, and with two energetic lions prowling at the sides. The design of the piano nobile windows tries hard to present a noble impression, with a startlingly assertive semicircular tympanum containing a shell, together with a lintel with a central mensola and odd curlicues at the sides. The second floor windows have oak leaves below straight pediments surmounted by strapwork volutes and palmettes.

All the decorative detailing may have been done by Giovanni Francesco Zannoli, who took over the project on Delino's death in 1697 and whose father had been De Rossi's frequent collaborator.[3] De Rossi himself would doubtless have controlled the design with more finesse, but this is nevertheless a piece of minor architecture of genuine character, as well as being an exceptionally interesting example of commercial building practice at the end of the 17th century.

A view of S Maria in Monticelli by Vasi, with Palazzo Panizza immediately to the right of the church

Palazzo Patrizi (Aldobrandini)

Piazza S. Luigi dei Francesi, 37

In 1605 Olimpia Aldobrandini, the niece of Clement VIII, bought up the buildings on this site, and by 1611 she had built her palace here. The façade still displays the heraldic symbols of the Aldobrandini (the 'rastrello' and the star) in the doorway and the windows. The authorship of the — rather stiff and dry — design is hard to disentangle, as Baglione credited Carlo Maderno with it, while Giovanni Battista Mola gave it to Giacomo Della Porta. Wasserman suggested that the design could have been provided to the Maderno workshop by Maderno's un-inspired relative Giovanni Fontana, but Hibbard saw points of resemblance to the later palaces of Maderno himself and did not entirely repudiate an attribution to him.[1]

In 1642 the palace was sold to the Patrizi family who, before 1660, modified the staircase and the loggia on the court to the designs of Mola. Further work was done on the façade in 1690 (when the fourth floor and the oval ornaments above the third floor windows were probably added) and in 1747.

The palace is now the seat of the Argentine Embassy to the Holy See who have painted the façade with a pale blue/green wash said to be inspired by Pannini's depiction of the palace in the 18th century.

Palazzo Patrizi (Clementi)

Via dei Funari, 12

Built around 1580 on a trapezoid site, with balconied entrances on via dei Funari and Piazza Campitelli. The salone on the piano nobile has a frieze of the *Story of Abraham*, executed between 1626 and 1628, with narrative episodes by Giovanni da S Giovanni.[1]

There is another frieze, with landscapes and harbour scenes in the style of Tassi, in the corner room on via Delfini/via Cavaletti. Cavazzini suggests that this and the illusionistic architecture and allegorical figures in the *Abraham* frieze were probably both painted by Francesco Franchini.[2]

The building is the seat of the Soprintendenza per i Beni Architettonici e per il Paesaggio del Lazio.

Palazzo Pecci Blunt (Fani, Ruspoli)

Piazza d'Aracoeli, 3

A plain rectangular palace built by Giacomo Della Porta at the very end of the 16th century for Mario Fani, who had married Olimpia Astalli (whose family's palace, incidentally, is nearby). It passed to the Ruspoli and then the Malatesta in the 17th century, and in the 18th century it was acquired by the Pecci Blunt family, who still own it.

The otherwise good proportions of the façade are somewhat impaired by the very slight compression of the three right-hand bays, which was presumably dictated by the structure of the Albertoni palace that previously occupied the site. The fine altana with open arches appears to be original but must presumably have been rebuilt when an extra storey was added in the 19th century.

There is a loggia with 17th century landscape murals traditionally attributed to Dughet, but rejected by Boisclair and Salerno.[1]

Della Porta himself is supposed to have lived in the palace, as in 1627 did Bernardino Spada.

Palazzo Peretti (Fiano, Ottoboni, Boncompagni Ludovisi, Almagià)

Piazza S Lorenzo in Lucina, 4

A palace on this site, adjacent to S Lorenzo in Lucina, was the seat of the titular cardinal of S Lorenzo from the 13th century, when the first palace was built by the English Cardinal Hugo of Evesham (died 1287). In the period 1425-1455 Cardinals Rotomagense and Morinense rebuilt it to form one of the finest palaces in Rome according to Flavio Biondo's *Roma Instaurata*. No trace of that palace remains. The last titular cardinal to live in the palace was Alessandro Damasceni Peretti di Montalto, who occupied it together with his brother Michele Peretti, Prince of Venafro. On the cardinal's death in 1624 Urban VIII had the palace sold to the prince, as part of some complicated financial juggling described by Hibbard.[1] The prince immediately set to work to have the building rebuilt and extended to designs by Maderno. A sizeable piece of that building remains standing in via in Lucina, where the ten bays numbered 16B to 16M are substantially Maderno's original façade in his routine grand palace style. The cornice of these bays still bears Peretti emblems (lions, stars, monti, branches of pears).

In or about 1655 the Peretti disposed of the palace to Costanza Pamphili (see entry on Palazzo di Montecitorio). On her death in 1690 it passed to Marco Ottoboni, Duke of Fiano, and it stayed in the Ottoboni, later Boncompagni Ottoboni, family for 200 years. Although it was on a prime site in central Rome none of the main façades seems to have been fully completed during that period. In 1888 Prince Marco Ottoboni had the building almost completely remodelled by the architect Francesco Settimi, with new façades on Piazza S Lorenzo in Lucina, the Corso and via in Lucina. In 1898 the palace was sold, together with the Fiano collection of paintings, to the entrepreneur Edoardo Almagià.

The important thing here is the salone with a ceiling that was frescoed by François Perrier and Giovanni Francesco Grimaldi for Cardinal Francesco Peretti Montalto in 1644-45.[2] As happened also in connection with Palazzo Santacroce, Titi wrongly ascribed this work by misinterpreting a reference in Baglione, but most subsequent writers followed him in attributing the work to Baldassare Croce notwithstanding the vastly different style of that painter. Schleier was the first to propose Perrier and Grimaldi, on purely visual evidence, but even he thought that Ruggeri may also have been involved, on the strength of the received wisdom about Palazzo Santacroce.[3] It was not until Bartoni and Pierguidi published the documents that the room's true date and authorship were finally settled. We can now forget about Ruggeri and Croce, and the consequences for dating that their involvement would imply, and see that this ceiling fits neatly in Grimaldi's early development as a decorator, between the gallery in Palazzo Santacroce and the Villa Doria Pamphili. It has an importance that extends beyond Italy, because it exemplifies the type of palace decoration that Perrier and Grimaldi were to take to Paris.

Compositionally, the ceiling is basically a rather old-fashioned compartmentalised design with quadri riportati, in the tradition of the Carracci gallery in Palazzo Farnese. As always with Grimaldi there is plenty of busy decoration, but the whole thing is a degree less lavish than the essentially similar salone that he completed in Palazzo Santacroce nearly twenty years later, and it lacks the stuccoes that add a further dimension of richness to the later work. The main pictorial scheme consists of five large figurative scenes (one in the centre and one on each of the four sides), four landscapes, a series of figures of *Virtues* along the cornice, two octagons with depictions of *Eros* and *Anteros*, and four feigned bronzes with subjects that relate to the main stories. The five figure scenes are by Perrier and all the rest by Grimaldi, with the hands of assistants evident in places.[4] The general design is very characteristic of Grimaldi, and he must have had overall management of the project.

Schleier identified the subjects of the main scenes and realised that they referred to the four elements. The subjects are, in the centre, the *Chariot of Aurora* and, on the four sides, *Ceres Pleading with Jupiter for the Release of Proserpina* (Earth), *Juno asking Æolus to Scatter the Trojan Fleet* (Air), *Venus Seeking Arms for Æneas from Vulcan* (Fire) and the *Birth of Venus* (Water). There are, however, several iconographical peculiarities in the choice of the scenes and in their details. Pierguidi subjected all this to a close analysis that concluded that the subject of the cycle is not so much the four elements themselves as the idea that only alchemy can provide the key to explain the relations between the elements.[5] He also examined the significance of the Chariot of Aurora appearing in conjunction with alchemical scenes — a juxtaposition which also occurs at the Villa Ludovisi.

The four pure landscapes are given virtually the same prominence as the figurative scenes that convey the meanings just described, and Grimaldi seems to have chosen different kinds of composition and mood in order to exhibit his range as a landscape expert. The most Bolognese of the landscapes — the one with a tower and bridge — is closely based on a painting by Annibale Carracci now in the Gemäldegalarie, Berlin. Another is a shipwreck scene in the manner of Agostino Tassi. The other two appear to be attempting the kind of idealised scene of which Claude had become the acknowledged master by the mid-1640s. There does not seem, however, to be any consistent way in which the landscapes can be read as part of the overall iconography of the ceiling.[6] While subsidiary landscapes (eg in lunettes) would be nothing unusual, it is strange to find a selection of pure landscapes mixed apparently randomly with a learned mythological programme. Throughout his life, however, Grimaldi tended to use every available kind of motif in an eclectic accumulation of decorative effects.

Palazzo Perucchi (Campello)
Via Sistina, 121

A pleasing late 17th century palace with crisp window stuccoes, a double stringcourse below the piano nobile and an

The doorway of the little Palazzo Perucchi

unusual door with a shell and swags between volutes above a frieze of triglyphs and metopes bearing eight-pointed stars. The small cortile is elegantly managed, with an arcade on the entrance side and a terrace on the left. Altogether, this is a particularly assured and coherent piece of minor palace design.

The balcony and extra storey above the cornice are later additions, perhaps done in the 19th century after the palace had passed to the Campello.

Palazzo del Pio Sodalizio dei Piceni (della Naziona Picena, del Pio Sodalizio dei Piceni, Casa di Sisto V)

Via di Parione, 7

A five-bay palace of the very early 16th century. It was owned by Sixtus V who passed it on to his great-niece Flavia Damasceni-Peretti on her marriage in 1589 to Virginio Orsini, later Duke of Bracciano. After her death in 1605 the building passed to other Orsini family members who sold it in 1613 to Monsignor Castellani, who gave it in 1645 to the confraternity that is now the Pio Sodalizio dei Piceni.

During the 1590s the Orsini improved the palace by the addition of a hanging garden or terrace that has walls with blind arches and niches. The unusually complicated form of these motifs has led to their being attributed to Giacomo del Duca.[1]

The loggia that is associated with the terrace has a ceiling with frescoes depicting the *Triumph of Love* by the Cavaliere d'Arpino. Van Mander records that Federico Zuccari was commissioned to paint this at the time of the Orsini/Peretti marriage and that the existing ceiling was not done until 1593-1595. In form it is a simplified derivation of Raphael's *Psyche* loggia in the Farnesina. Puglisi and Röttgen suggest that it provided a direct model for Albani's loggia in Palazzo Verospi.[2]

Palazzo Pighini (Fusconi, del Gallo di Roccagiovine)

Piazza Farnese, 44

The Pighini family were established on this site since at least the 16th century and their palace here was traditionally attributed to Baldassare Peruzzi and Vignola. By 1705 it was due for rebuilding (possibly because of damage sustained in the recent earthquakes) but the co-owners could not agree on a common course of action. They therefore divided the palace between themselves and proceeded independantly. Count Alessandro Pighini, who wanted to rebuild and get some income from letting out apartments, moved into the wing along via Ballauri; his uncle Carlo Antonio, who simply wanted to save money and regarded the building's dilapidated state with equanimity, occupied the part fronting on to Piazza Farnese.

Alessandro proceeded with rebuilding the via Ballauri wing straightaway, with Alessandro Specchi as superintending architect. The work was finished by 1710, with fine apartments let out on the piano nobile and second floor while Alessandro himself lived more modestly in the mezzanine. Carlo Antonio lived on to 1723, rebuffing his nephew's attempts to use the law to force him to rebuild his part of the building, which ended up virtually uninhabitable. He did, however, leave his nephew his heir, so that Alessandro was able to commission Specchi to rebuild the Piazza Farnese façade, and to proceed to demolition in 1728. Specchi died in 1729 and the work was taken forward by the lesser architects Galeazzo

The west balcony of Palazzo Pighini

Tursi (d. 1731) and then Filippo de Romanis. By 1737 the work was finished, with the usual mixture of grand families renting the apartments on the main floors and a variety of humbler folk in the less desirable parts of the palace.[1]

The polish and urbanity of Specchi's work here is as different as it could possibly be from the heavy-handed and old-fashioned display of his other surviving Roman palace, Palazzo de Carolis. The via Ballauri façade extends just round the corner on Campo de' Fiori, where it still abuts on jagged unfinished brickwork; there may well have been an intention to construct a proper entrance façade here. It is restrained to the point of self-effacement, with little attempt at articulation, only the most modest accentuation of the central bays, and windows with simple architraves. The later show front facing Palazzo Farnese, on the other hand, uses many of the conventions of contemporary apartment building design in an exceptionally stylish way, with restrained shallow modelling around the crisp curvilinear balconies and ringhiere, and with the central bay privileged with decoration up the whole height of the building. Although the overall impression of elegant refinement is far from Borromini's aesthetic, there are a number of touches that do look like references to Borromini, albeit expressed in a daintier vocabulary. Note, in particular, the herms incorporated in the jambs of the central window and the canting of the outer members of the portal. The latter are knowingly canted back towards the wall, rather than away from it in Borromini's trademark motif.

The cortile contains a hanging garden on a terrace in the right (east) side but the memorable feature is the three-flight open staircase that fills the whole of the entrance wall. This is a real tour-de-force, like nothing else previously done in Rome. Each flight has less decoration than the one below, but the lowest flight — and especially the domed first-floor landing — has a prufusion of stucco that is unmistakably Borrominian. Unlike the subtle treatment of the exterior, however, the motifs are handled in a rather coarse, cumulative fashion, and it is noticeable that the rhythm of the landings and their doorways is slightly disjointed. The staircase was being built in 1732 (ie three years after Specchi's death) and, while its general conception was manifestly by Specchi, the detailed adjustments on site must have been in the hands of his successors. Part of its importance lies in its relevance for Fuga's famous double staircase at the Palazzo della Consulta, which was also begun in 1732. (See the entry on the Consulta for further discussion of this.)

Late 20th century photographs show the palace in a very dilapidated state, with the staircase in an almost ruinous condition; by 2004 it was fully restored.

Palazzo Pio di Savoia da Carpi (Orsini, Righetti)

Piazza del Biscione, 95

This site is part of the ancient Theatre of Pompey, where the Orsini clan had congregated long before the 15th century. Around 1450 the Venetian Cardinal Francesco Condulmer, who had rented the site, built a lavish palace here. The property reverted to the Orsini who improved it in the late 16th century; the only visible surviving element of this Orsini phase being the three-bay loggia that looks out over the corner with Campo de' Fiori. In 1652 the palace was bought by Prince Alberto Pio di Savoia da Carpi who commissioned Camillo Arcucci to build a new apartment and façade

Vasi's print of Palazzo Pio di Savoia da Carpi, with shops apparently using the entire ground floor of Arcucci's façade. The three-bay loggia to the right of the façade is a remnant of the 16th century Orsini palace. The palace's main entrance in Vasi's time is shown at the extreme right in an area that is now occupied by a cinema

Palazzo Pio di Savoia da Carpi. Visentini's illustration of the window design that he so strongly disliked

on the wing facing Piazza del Biscione. This was completed before 1657 when Virgilio Spada made a passing reference to it in his unsuccessful attempt to convince the Oratory that they should retain Borromini rather than Arcucci as their architect.[1] Later, the palace passed to the Righetti. Roisecco, writing in 1750, describes it as unfinished, and indeed no attempt has ever been made to absorb Arcucci's façade into the rest of the building.

The primitive little church of S Maria in Grotta Pinta (now deconsecrated) is hidden behind the left end of Arcucci's façade. It was built within some internal passages of Pompey's theatre and was originally entered from the west via an entrance in Piazza del Biscione. That entrance was blocked off by the new palace front, and the orientation of the church was reversed, so that it was entered from the east through the new façade with which it was equipped in via di Grotta Pinta.[2]

Virgilio Spada expressed grave doubts about Arcucci's grasp of planning, but even he confessed to a liking for the Palazzo Pio façade, and it is easy to see why. Although it is now marred by the addition of a heavy attic, the façade is a splendid piece, with elaborate window frames loaded with the Pio di Savoia lions and crowned eagles, which reappear together with rosettes under the cornice. As with Maruscelli's Palazzo Madama façade, the effect is gained entirely by the splendid decoration; there is no real sense of architectonic variety or rhythm.[3]

The lions dragging themselves out of the piano nobile window frames are clearly the most astonishing single motif of the whole display. Visentini characteristically selected them for especially strong censure as a most improper conceit and asked, with ponderous rhetorical irony, if they were meant to terrify the spectator.[4]

After many years as an institute for orphans, the upper floors of the palace now accommodate the Rome Center of the University of Washington (Seattle), which runs an architecture programme from this site.

Palazzo Pizzirani (Cesarini, Leoni)

Piazza di S Apollonia, 3

The palace, originally built by the Cesarini, fills a prime site immediately facing S Maria in Trastevere and it has some interesting features, though its currently dilapidated state obscures them. It appears to date from the second half of the 17th century, and is said to incorporate five earlier buildings. Before the Pizzirani acquired it in the 18th century it belonged to the Leoni, and for a few years from 1788 it was the seat of the Venerabile Conservatorio di S Giuseppe, which provided a refuge for 42 vulnerable girls under the age of 18.

The bare seven-bay façade on Piazza di S Maria in Trastevere is, in fact, the flank of the building and appears never to have had a substantial entrance. At street level all the openings are now occupied by shops and restaurants and it is not possible to make out the original arrangement, though shops could well have been present from the start. The main façade is on Piazza S Apollonia, with a massive doorway made up of a reticulated wall-plate behind pilasters supporting a square balcony on volute brackets. Via della Lungaretta, which passes in front of the palace at this point, is now unimportant, but would then have been a main route towards the Vatican. In this site the huge eagle in the lintel below the balcony would have made a strong statement of the family presence.

All the windows have simple stucco frames, with those on the piano nobile being

Vasi's view looking down Piazza S Apollonia to Palazzo Pizzirani with its huge portal. The church on the left is S Margherita. The one on the right, S Apollonia, was destroyed in the 19th century

privileged by simple straight architraves above them. The piano nobile windows are also distinguished by a strange keystone motif containing a small female head. This decoration must have been introduced between Falda's print of 1675 and Vasi's of 1758.[1] The attic above the cornice is an even later addition, though it copies the window frames and reticulated quoins immediately below, which is an unusual refinement for such extensions.

Palazzo Pizzirani

Via di Torre Argentina, 13

This palace was built for the Bussi family in the 17th century and it would originally have been a severe but well-balanced design with some real presence. In the 18th century it was acquired by the Pizzirani who (as well as placing their name over the door) added two storeys above the cornice, thereby wrecking the proportions. The balcony is modern but the two openings either side of the entrance — now occupied by shops — appear to be more or less in their original form.

Palazzo Poli

Via Poli, 54

In the 1580s Martino Longhi the Elder built a nineteen-bay palace for the Duke of Ceri in the north west part of the isolato north of the Trevi fountain, on what is now via Poli.[1] That area is now swamped by a depressing post-1870 development, and nothing is left of Longhi's building.

In 1678 the Ceri palace passed to the Conti, dukes of Poli, who employed G. B. Contini in 1712-16 to incorporate the buildings to the east and build a new façade on via della Stamperia. That façade, too, has gone, and its replacement, at via della Stamperia, 6, is a neoclassic piece of 1837 by Valadier.

There were various minor buildings between the palace described above and the Trevi fountain, and no plans had been made for dealing with the fountain since the ideas of developing the area under Urban VIII had run into the ground.[2] In 1722-23, under the pontificate of Innocent XIII (who was himself the son of a duke of Poli) the Poli family gained possession of these houses and in 1728 they obtained authorisation from Benedict XIII to incorporate the Trevi fountain into their palace. They immediately built a new wing connecting their palace to the fountain and a new façade which took the form of two symmetrical four-bay pavilions with the fountain uncomfortably sited in a recess between them. This awkward arrangement had been mandated by the planning authorities, but the drawing published by Pinto shows that the design did nothing at all to overcome the exigencies of the site. Indeed, the entire new wing — which survives under the name of Palazzo Poli, and is now occupied (together with the Valadier building) by the Istituto Nazionale per la Grafica — is quite an unimpressive piece of architecture.

In the event, the 1728 state of affairs lasted only for a few years, since in 1732 Clement XII directed that the fountain should occupy the whole breadth of the site, and the process was put in train that led to Salvi's familiar masterpiece of scenography. Salvi unified the entire area of the palace front by carrying across it a single colossal Corinthian order which completely masked the previously existing façade, though it provided windows coinciding with those of the Poli palace in three bays on each side. From the Piazza dei Crociferi side it is easy to see the quoins that mark the ends of the old front of the Poli palace that still lies behind the mass of Salvi's fountain, but nothing else of the façade is visible from the street.[3]

Palazzetto di Flaminio Ponzio

Piazza Campitelli, 6

The fine house that Flaminio Ponzio, the family architect of the Borghese, built for himself in 1600 stood at via Alessandrina, 27; it was demolished in 1932/33 when the area around the Roman Forum was being cleared.

In 1935 a new building was made in Piazza Campitelli (next to the similarly reconstituted church of S Rita) and the main components of Ponzio's façade were arranged on it. Although this is not an accurate facsimile of the original, one can still enjoy the high quality with which Ponzio's elaborate decorative motifs were executed.*

Palazzo Pulieri (Ginetti)

Via del Corso, 480-488

Originally an 18th century building and notorious as the place where the beam was fixed for the judicial torture of 'supplizio della corda'. It was completely rebuilt in the late 19th century and now has virtually no architectural interest.

*Baglione commended the palazzeto as having a 'gratiosa facciata di bei lavori compartita'[1] but Portoghesi thought that it was cold and conventional, and that it had been 'malamente ricostruito' in Piazza Campitelli.[2] Magni shows that when the building was still in via Alessandrina shops had been inserted either side of the portal but that otherwise the components of the façade were arranged more or less as they are in the reconstruction.[3]

Palazzo del Quirinale

Piazza del Quirinale

In the 16th century the Carafa family owned a villa and vigna on this sought-after, elevated site. In 1550 the Carafa leased the property to Cardinal Ippolito d'Este (the creator of the celebrated gardens at Tivoli) who turned the vigna into an elaborate garden with fountains and much antique sculpture. The existing palace was begun by Gregory XIII who employed Ottaviano Mascarino between 1583 and 1585 to expand the old villa at the north-west end of the site into a casino in characteristic 16th century villa style, with an open arcade below a loggia (which would originally also have been open but is now glazed). The two levels are connected by an oval spiral staircase with coupled Tuscan columns, which is the earliest of its kind in Rome. (The next to be built in Rome was Ponzio's at Palazzo Borghese, followed by the version by Borromini and Bernini at Palazzo Barberini; both of these may well have been intended to emphasise the papal status of the families, by reference to the famous original at the Quirinale.) The villa was surmounted by a high belvedere, the so-called torrino, which commands a complete view of Rome and is the site from which the flags of Italy and of the European Union are now flown. Mascarino also planned a forecourt for the villa, which was not built.

In 1587 Sixtus V bought the property and decided to convert it into a summer residence for the papacy, which required it to be considerably expanded. He used his regular architect Domenico Fontana to build the entire wing facing the piazza and to make a start with a new palace on the Strada Pia (via del Quirinale) to echo Mascarino's villa at the far end of the huge courtyard that was being created. The north-east wing that completed

Vasi's view of the Piazza del Quirinale before Pius VI moved the sculptures of the horse-tamers and surmounted them by an obelisk in 1786. On the left are the pontifical stables (Scuderie) begun by Specchi and completed by Fuga. On the right is the Palazzo della Consulta by Fuga, outside which an honour guard is forming up for duty. (Presumably it is the pope's coach that is shown leaving the Quirinale palace beneath Bernini's Benediction Loggia)

the courtyard was begun by Flaminio Ponzio in 1608 for Paul V. It included three state rooms and, at the end nearest the old villa, a private chapel for the pope, the Cappella dell'Annunziata, which was frescoed by Guido Reni and assistants in 1609-1610.

On Ponzio's death in 1613 Maderno took over. In 1614-15 he finished the part along Strada Pia. The entire street front of this addition was filled with two huge rooms that were needed for the Quirinale to function as a site of the papal government. These were a public chapel, the Cappella Paolina, and a room for the reception of foreign ambassadors, originally called the Sala Regia but later named the Sala dei Corazzieri because the Corazzieri regiment of papal guards used it for some of their ceremonies. Maderno also built the main door on the piazza, with statues of St Peter and St Paul by Stefano Maderno and Guillaume Berthelot, and a Madonna by Pompeo Ferrucci above the window. The enlargement and levelling of the piazza that had been envisaged but not executed by Sixtus V was also carried out by Maderno.

Urban VIII was concerned about the security of the entire complex. He had a wall built around the gardens, which by then stretched to their present extent nearly as far as the Quattro Fontane, and added the low bastion to the left of the main entrance on the piazza. He also began the work that was to grow into the Manica Lunga along via del Quirinale, by extending and heightening the low building that the Swiss guards had used as

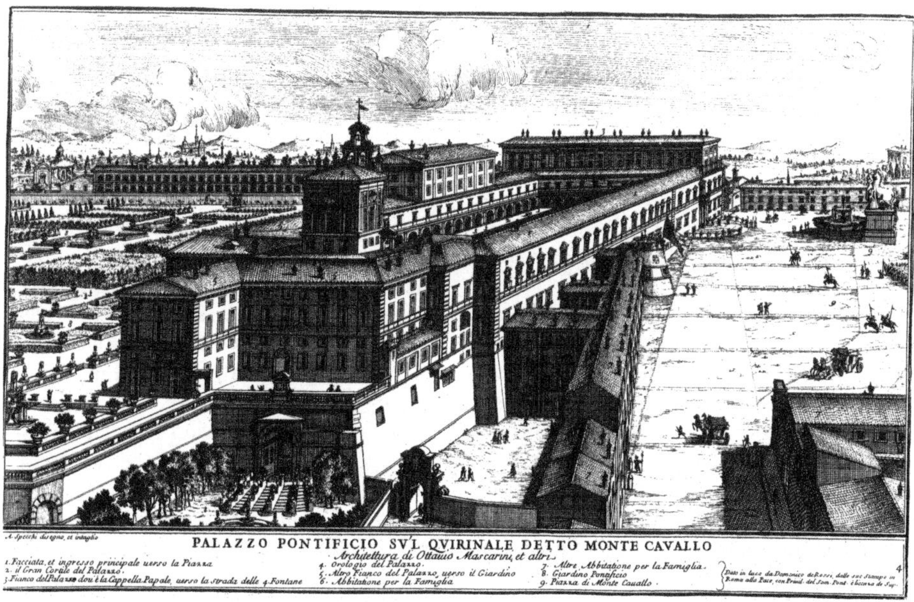

A print by Specchi that clearly displays the layout of the Palazzo del Quirinale complex. At this time the Palazzo della Consulta has still to be built in the area beyond the horse-tamers on the right. The church at the extreme left, beyond the end of the palace's Manica Lunga is S Andrea al Quirinale by Bernini

their quarters since the time of Sixtus V. The Benediction Loggia over the main entrance was added for Urban by Bernini in 1638.

In 1656 Alexander VII employed Bernini to extend the Manica Lunga as far as the entrance to the gardens in the centre of the present range.* Inside, facing the garden, Bernini constructed a double loggia, but from the outside the extension continues the previous vein of barracks-like functionalism, with no windows in the ground floor. The Manica Lunga was further extended by Specchi for Innocent XIII and completed by Fuga for Clement XII. Fuga's Palazzetto del Segretario delle Cifre at the end of the range would originally have provided an effective concluding point with its vertical emphasis, but some of that effect has been lost by the heightening of the entire Manica Lunga in 1872. From 1870 to 1944 the Quirinale was the main palace of the kings of Italy, and it now performs the same function for the president of the Republic. Both the monarchs and presidents have maintained their private apartments in the Palazzetto del Segretario delle Cifre.

The building that extends diagonally downhill from the left of the bastion on the piazza is the Palazzo della Dataria Apostolica. In its present form it was built by Busiri Vici in 1860 for Pius IX, but the part nearest the piazza incorporates a 15th

*Alexander needed this extra accommodation for his household because of his decision to make the Quirinale his normal residence.

century palace of the Maffei that was acquired by Paul V first to house his family and then to be the seat of the Cardinale Datario, which was a highly lucrative office, responsible for registering papal pensions and other concessions. At via della Dataria, 96, is the Palazzo della Panetteria. This was originally made for the family of Paul V but was rebuilt in 1766 for Clement XIII.

INTERIOR

Guided tours (unavailable on Mondays and Thursdays) can be booked online at https://palazzo.quirinale.it. In all the important rooms information sheets are available. They provide a detailed, scholarly account of everything there is to see, including the splendid discoveries that have been made in the restoration programme that has been on-going since 2001. The following account takes the course of the public visit, beginning at the north-east corner of the courtyard and going round the piano nobile in an anti-clockwise direction.

The visit begins with the three main state rooms along the north-east wing, which were entirely remodelled after 1870. They contain some of the furniture and tapestries that were then brought to the Quirinale from royal and ducal palaces in Savoy, Parma, Modena and elsewhere, but there are no survivals of the 17th century fabric until one gets to the Sala dei Pareti Piemontesi in the north-west corner. This has a frieze illustrating some of Paul V's building projects, brought to light in the recent restorations.

Unfortunately the public visit no longer includes the Cappella dell'Annunziata, the small private chapel that Flaminio Ponzio made for Paul V in the north-west corner of the courtyard, next to the Mascarino pavilion. It has a main space under an oval cupola and a rectangular presbytery, with a rich display of stucco and fresco everywhere. Guido Reni was given the commission to decorate it in 1609 and its completion in 1610 is recorded in the inscription to the left of the entrance. Although Reni employed assistants, including Albani, Lanfranco and Antonio Carracci, the entire project was evidently carefully controlled by him and much of the work is from his hand. In particular, the altarpiece of the *Annunciation*; the *Birth of the Virgin* on the entrance wall; and the *Virgin Sewing* to the left of the altar are all celebrated masterpieces. In the last two of them Reni paints with an almost quattrocento simplicity to convey the Marian imagery.

Passing across Mascarino's loggia, the visitor skirts the celebrated spiral staircase before entering Domenico Fontana's wing, which forms the main front of the palace on the piazza. In the second room, the Sala di Ercole, are the six magnificent *Stories of Æneas* painted by Corrado Giaquinto between 1733 and 1739 for a room in the villa della Regina, Turin (where photographs of the paintings now fill the original positions). The originals were brought here in 1893.[1]

GALLERY OF ALEXANDER VII

The gallery filled almost the full length of Fontana's wing. It was decorated for Alexander VII by a group of artists under the direction of Pietro da Cortona who designed a splendid unifying painted system of feigned reliefs and coupled columns with a background of sky and foliage.* Above (and illusionistically in front of) this system was

*The gallery itself was constructed, and the ceiling gilded, under the supervision of Bernini, while Cortona was in charge of the team of painters. The work took place during the plague of 1656-57 and all the painters were sequestrated in the Quirinale together with Cortona, Bernini and the pope himself. The optimistic character of the painted themes may well have been been conditioned by the circumstances.[2]

A preparatory study by Pier Francesco Mola for his fresco of Joseph Recognized by his Brethren *in the Gallery of Alexander VII in the Quirinale*

a frescoed frieze of *Scenes from the Old Testament* (plus one scene from the New Testament) by various painters. At each of the short ends of the gallery a large fresco covered the wall; these were Mola's masterpiece *Joseph Recognised by his Brethren* and Maratta's *Nativity*.

During the Napoleonic period the occupying French put much work into converting the Quirinale for Napoleon's personal occupation, though in fact he never came to use the place. One of the main modifications was to break up the great gallery into three separate rooms and to get rid of Cortona's decorative system, while retaining the frieze. Although the appearance of Cortona's work was known from surviving drawings, it was thought until recently that the decoration itself had vanished for ever. In one of the most exciting recent discoveries in Baroque art, however, it was found in 2001 that the Cortona scheme had been covered over by the French, rather than destroyed, and that much of it remained substantially intact.[3] The gallery has now been restored with the middle of the three rooms (the Sala di Augusto) displaying the Cortona scheme virtually complete (save for some sections of Napoleonic gilt patterning) and with the windows on the cortile side reopened. The first room (the Sala degli Ambasciatori) shows the Cortona scheme only on the piazza side and beneath the Maratta fresco. In the last room (the Sala Gialla) the Cortona material was too fragmentary to be permanently displayed.

The frescoes on the end walls and frieze are as follows. (N.B. One enters in the Sala degli Ambasciatori. The correct iconographical order of the paintings begins immediately on one's right and runs round the three rooms in an anti-clockwise direction.)

Sala degli Ambasciatori

End wall: *The Nativity* (Carlo Maratta);

Piazza wall: *God the Father Admonishing Adam and Eve* (Lazzaro Baldi and Gaspard Dughet); *The Expulsion from Eden* (Bartolomeo Colombo); *The Sacrifice of Cain and Abel* (Filippo Lauri and Gaspard Dughet);

Cortile wall: *The Judgment of Solomon* (Carlo Cesi); *Cyrus freeing the Jews* (Ciro Ferri); *The Annunciation* (Baldi).

Sala di Augusto

Piazza wall: *Entry into the Ark* (G. P. Schor); *Leaving the Ark* (Baldi); *Sacrifice of Isaac* (Giovanni Angelo Canini);

Cortile wall: *Victory of Joshua* (Guillaume Courtois); *Gideon* (Filippo Lauri); *David and Goliath* (F. Murgia).

Sala Gialla

Piazza wall: *Jacob and the Angel* (Schor); *The Reconciliation of Jacob and Esau* (Fabrizio Chiari); *Joseph sold by his Brethren* (Schor);

End wall: *Joseph Recognised by his Brethren* (Pier Francesco Mola);

Cortile wall: *Moses and the Burning Bush* (G. F. Grimaldi); *The Crossing of the Red Sea* (Jan Miel); *The Spies Returning from the Promised Land* (Grimaldi).

Apartment of Paul V

After the Gallery of Alexander VII one comes to a small room with a window over the main entrance, where the benediction loggia now is, and then turns left into a succession of rooms that run between the Cappella Paolina and the cortile. These rooms were intended for Paul V's own use and are decorated with Borghese emblems in the ceilings, and with friezes. Several of them have been modified considerably but the last three still have some of the painting done in 1616. Of these, the Sala del Diluvio has a frieze of *Old Testament Scenes* by Antonio Carracci; the Sala delle Virtù has a frieze with the *Cardinal Virtues* by Cesare Rossetti and landscapes in the manner of Bril; the Prima Sala di Rappresentanza has a frieze by Tassi with *Eight Scenes from the Life of St Paul.*

Cappella Paolina

The visitor emerges in the Sala dei Corazzieri, immediately by the entrance to the Cappella Paolina, which is by Maderno. It contains a high relief of the *Washing of Feet* by Taddeo Landini, sculpted in 1578 for the Cappella Gregoriana in St Peter's and brought here in 1619. The angels supporting the arms of Paul V are by Pietro Bernini (right) and Guillaume Berthelot (left). The original intention was for the chapel to be decorated with frescoes by Tassi and Andrea Commodi, who completed a bozzetto for a *Fall of the Rebel Angels* that would have filled the altar wall. In the event, the ceiling was filled with gilded stucco by Martino Ferabosco in 1616 and there was no attempt at a large fresco.

Sala dei Corazzieri

The frescoed quadratura frieze is by Agostino Tassi, Giovanni Lanfranco and Carlo Saraceni, with involvement by a team of assistants, including Spadarino, Alessandro Turchi, Pasquale Ottino and Marcantonio Bassetti. The entrance wall is by Tassi and his team while the rest is by Lanfranco and Saraceni, though all the quadratura was presumably supervised by Tassi who had notable expertise in that field.[4]

Opposite: Part of the splendid wooden ceiling of the Sala dei Corazzieri at the Quirinale, made for Paul V by Maderno. Note the Borghse emblems of the eagle and the dragon incorporated in the decoration

Vasi's view of the Quirinale gardens. The building at the extreme right is the 'Coffee House' by Fuga, the main palace fills the centre, and the Manica Lunga stretches off at the extreme left. The Pope is depicted taking the air while being shielded from the sun by a servant with a parasol

The window embrasures are by Annibale Duranti. The decoration includes the Borghese emblems of dragon and eagle, depictions of the buildings undertaken in Paul V's reign and the *Story of Moses*, impliedly casting Paul as leader of the Christian Church, as Moses was leader of the Jews. The restoration of 2005-2006 removed the heavy metope and triglyph frieze that had been added in the Napoleonic occupation, and revealed the original frieze of symbolic objects beneath.

The most striking feature is the startlingly illusionistic groups of diplomats in the exotic dress of their countries, crowded into spaces like theatre boxes, and excitedly peering down. They memorialise specific delegations that Paul V welcomed to Rome and their purpose is to celebrate his evangelical commitment and to create, as it were, a virtual image of him by reminding us that he received real delegations in the real space below.

Beyond the door by which one leaves the Sala dei Corazzieri are the Sale Rosse, not open to the public. These are two rooms with a loggia overlooking the garden, decorated by Grimaldi for Clement IX with frescoes of birds, fountains and pergolas, with a frieze containing a marine and river scenes.[5]

The greatly expanded visiting arrangements described on the official website now include a tour of the gardens. Architecturally their most interesting feature is the 'Coffee House' built in 1743 for Benedict XIV by Ferdinando Fuga.[6]

Palazzo Raggi

Via del Corso, 173

A substantial nine-bay palace on the Corso, probably of around the same date (1731) as the neighbouring Palazzo Ottoboni Boncompagni. In the 19th century it was owned by the Torlonia family who used it as the site of their bank. At street level the shop-fronts implausibly surmounted by ringhiere are all a 19th century pastiche of barocchetto motifs, but the simple rectangular portal and balcony in the seventh bay may well be original.

The design of the first storey windows mixes up-to-date and conservative idioms in an unusual way. The basic architecture of the windows is a simple stucco frame beneath an architrave supported by volute brackets, with additional volutes flat against the wall in the manner of Maderno. Within that old-fashioned armature are excellent stuccoes of female heads with swags and festoons.

The second storey windows are also unusual, with strongly plastic shells and foliage perched on top of the window frames without any further architectural component around them.

Palazzo Rocci (Pallavicini)

Via Monserrato, 25

Quite an imposing five-bay, four-storey palace that was owned by Ciriaco Rocci who had a succession of important papal appointments from 1609 to his death in 1651. Maderno worked on it, perhaps around the beginning of that period, and the windows of all except the top storey of the façade can probably be attributed to him. The present balcony is 19th century, as is the whole portal in Hibbard's opinion.[1] The court was restored in 1880.

According to Donati the staircase is in the same form as those at Palazzo Mattei di Giove and Palazzo Varese, which are squeezed into the entrance side of the cortile and open into a loggia running parallel to the façade.[2] The palace does not appear to contain anything else that reflects Maderno's involvement.

Palazzo Rondinini or Rondanini (Sanseverino)

Via del Corso, 519

From 1604 the painter Giuseppe Cesari, the Cavaliere d'Arpino built a palace for himself on this site to the designs of Flaminio Ponzio.[1] It was a substantial building of nine bays, occupying most of the frontage of the present palace. In 1744 the marchesa Margherita Ambra Rondinini bought the dilapidated building, but she probably did not start the present palace, with Gabriele Valvassori as her architect, until she had acquired adjoining property in 1749. By 1758 the architect Alessandro Dori was also involved in the project. When Valvassori died three years later at the age of 78, Dori assumed overall responsibility. The palace must have been finished soon after 1768, when it was described as nearing completion.[2]

In 1760 it was recorded that Valvassori had completed a substantial amount of the building along what is now via Angelo Brunetti, while Dori was engaged on a 'new wing' and on the staircase. Valvassori may have also built a good deal of the façade on the Corso, but Dori very probably modified this. In short, it is not clear how much of the present building represents Valvassori's intentions.[3] As it is, the palace is routinely coupled with Marchionni's Villa Albani (Torlonia) both because the two buildings were made for the display of famous collections of sculpture and because they mark, in Blunt's words, 'the end of the Baroque, as it begins to be qualified by neo-classical restraint'.[4] In fact, it is in the interiors where the resemblances between the two buildings are strongest, since both are largely determined by the common display method of incorporating classical fragments within lavish marble revetments. This has also meant that the interior of Palazzo Rondinini is one of the best preserved among the grand palaces on the Corso.

As for the exterior, the plain flatness of the wall, the restrained fenestration, the heavy string-courses and the way in which the two outer bays are demarcated by rusticated quoins all make the Rondinini palace look unadventurous and old-fashioned, in the greatest possible contrast to Valvassori's Doria Pamphili façade further down the Corso. It is very possible that a good deal of d'Arpino's palace is embedded in the present walls and that the architects were constrained, in the façade at least, by the need to incorporate the earlier work.

The outstanding feature of the façade is certainly the double entrance which leads into the courtyard through an open androne divided into three aisles by twenty columns, most of which are fine ancient pieces. (Until the early 1900s, when it was removed to the palace's library, Michelangelo's *Rondinini Pietà* now in the Castello Sforzesco in Milan was kept in the androne.) The round-headed entrances themselves have continuous roll mouldings with the outer one ending in inward-turned volutes to create a 'breaking-wave' effect, with a female head between the volutes. The exceptionally good stucco decoration of shells and oak leaves is by Giacinto Ferrari, who worked with Dori on the interior of this palace and at the Museo Pio-Clementino in the Vatican. Note the conceit of the oak sprays appearing to pass behind the keystone, with the branches reappearing at either side below the volutes.

The female heads on the keystones of the entrance are stucco casts of the Rondinini Medusa, an over life-size Roman or Hellenistic marble head that was in the Rondinini sculpture collection.[5] Goethe, whose lodgings were immediately opposite the palace in what is now the Goethe Haus, wrote rapturously that the Medusa was 'a marvellous, mysterious and fascinating work, which represents a state between death and life, pain and pleasure' and he had a cast of the sculpture in his rooms.[6] As a result of his enthusiasm the Medusa gained a tremendous cult following, and it was one of the first antique marbles to be acquired by Crown Prince Ludwig of Bavaria (himself a devotee of Goethe) for the Glyptothek that he founded in Munich. The casts in the palace entrance appear to be an original part of the structure,[7] and Goethe would have had a fine view of them from his windows. At one level the marchese Rondinini presumably incorporated them in the entrance simply to display a choice item from his collection. Since the Medusa head was an attribute of Minerva, however, his deeper intention must have been to send a message that his palace was an abode of learning where the cult of the antique was celebrated.[8]

In the wall of the cortile facing the entrance is a fountain group of *Bacchus, Venus and Apollo* with single figures disposed in three niches. The sculptures include classical components that were massively restored and worked-up at the time the palace was completed. Many more classical fragments — including some that probably came from the Cavaliere d'Arpino's collection[9]— are in the walls of the cortile, where they are set within a system of stucco panelling of geometrical shapes and obelisks. All this creates a somewhat weird effect rather like that of Piranesi's

Palazzo Rondinini: the top of one of the twin doors, with Giacinto Ferrari's stucco-work framing a cast of the Medusa Rondinini

Piazza dei Cavalieri di Malta, though a more flippant note is struck by the chic Rondinini swallows (*rondini*) perching on the obelisks.

As already noted, the interior was largely designed as a showcase for the Rondinini collection of sculpture, and it remains a very splendid affair with much gilding and rare coloured marble. The most unusual feature is probably the staircase, where the neo-classical austerity of Dori's design is set off against the refined gaiety of Ferrari's stuccoes on the landings and the vestibule, which is treated like a rococo nymphæum with seductive caryatids emerging from the walls.

On the ceiling of the gallery is a *Fall of Phæthon* by the French painter Jacques Gamelin. In the ballroom there is a Corrado Giaquinto ceiling of *Minerva Presenting Spain to Jupiter and Juno*, brought here in the early 20th century from Palazzo Santacroce in Palermo.

Since 1946 the palace has been occupied by the Banca Nazionale dell'Agricoltura.

Palazzo De Rossi

Via del Consolato, 6

A substantial seven-bay palace now sandwiched between later buildings between S Giovanni dei Fiorentini and the Corso Vittore Emanuele II. This was the Florentine area and the palace, which looks as though it dates from around the third quarter of the 17th century, does have a very Tuscan reserve about it. The round-headed doors in the outer bays are set in rusticated panels and there is more neat rustication in the form of short pilaster strips up to the sills of the first floor windows, and running up the building's full height at both ends. The piano nobile windows have plain architraves but those of the second floor are livelier, with stucco frames surmounted by stars. The cornice and frieze have lion masks, lilies and more stars. The attic above is a recent addition.[1]

The palace passed to the Panvini Rosati in the 19th century and then to the Malvezzi Campeggi who restored it in 1932, as recorded by the inscription on the via dei Cimatori façade, reading CAROLUS ALPHONSI F MALVETIUS CAMPEGGIUS PERF ET REST AD MCM XXX II.

Palazzo Ruggeri

Corso Vittorio Emanuele II, 20

Originally built for Pompeo Ruggeri by Giacomo Della Porta between 1588 and 1591 (ie immediately after Della Porta's façade for the nearby Gesù). Like its neighbour, Palazzo Celsi, it has suffered from enlargements and alterations, which in this case were carried out in the 18th and 19th centuries. Shops and a mezzanine have been inserted in the ground floor and two bays

The austere façade of Della Porta's Palazzo Ruggeri before it was mangled by later alterations. Engraving by Falda

Specchi's print of Palazzo Ruspoli seen from the Corso. This part of the palace was built in the 17th century but the elevation followed Ammannati's earlier part of the building quite faithfully

added on the right, completely wrecking the original proportions. Nevertheless, the door remains a design of noble simplicity.

The salone has a frieze illustrating the *Life of Pompey*, dated 1591 and attributed by Brugnoli to Giovanni and Cherubino Alberti. In the cortile there is a three-bay loggia with vault frescoes depicting *Fortitude, Vigilance and Prudence*. All this work is firmly within the conventions of the last years of the 16th century.

Palazzo Ruspoli (Gaetani)

Largo Carlo Goldoni, 55

One of the great Roman palaces, but mainly a somewhat conservative design of the 16th century, and with only a few features of the Baroque period.

In 1583-1586 the Florentine family of Rucellai employed Bartolomeo Ammannati to rebuild and expand a building that had been made for the Jacobilli family in the 1550s, possibly by Nanni di Baccio Bigio. In the following four years the gallery was decorated by Jacopo Zucchi, another Florentine, with an elaborate allegorical cycle on the theme of the *Genealogy of the Gods*.

In 1629 the palace passed to the Gaetani who extended it to the Corso and built the façade on that street. The architect for this was Bartolomeo Breccioli, who adopted Ammannati's elevation unchanged. In the 1640s the Gaetani also employed Martino Longhi the Younger to build the altana and a new stairway. This runs north-south in the centre of the palace betweeen the courtyard of Breccioli's new work towards the Corso and that of Ammannati's original nucleus towards the west. Longhi exploited this siting to create a light-filled stairway of imposing scale, but it is a simple design and it is not now altogether easy to understand why it should have been so universally celebrated throughout the 17th and 18th centuries. One reason may have been the steps themselves, each of which is made of one massive slab of marble. Vasi mentions them, and also the antique sculpture (now in the Vatican Museums) that decorated the space.[1]

The Ruspoli family, who still own part of the palace, acquired it in 1776 and carried out a number of modifications. Some rooms near the Corso are used for art exhibitions, but the visitor to these does not see the stairway or anything else of architectural interest.

Palazzo S Calisto

Piazza di S Maria in Trastevere, 24

The building on this site was originally the residence of the titular cardinal of S Maria in Trastevere and was expanded and rebuilt several times, notably in 1434 and 1505. In 1615 Paul V gave it, together with the church of S Calisto, to a community of Benedictine monks in exchange for their buildings on the Quirinal, which he wanted for his own projects (the papal Palazzo del Quirinale and his nephew Scipione Borghese's palace, now Palazzo Pallavicini Rospigliosi). The present palace was then built for the monks by Orazio Torriani.

Torriani's building is a severe, grand affair. It is also very old-fashioned for 1615, strictly rectilinear and with the door and all the

Vasi's view of the Piazza di S Maria in Trastevere, with Palazzo S Calisto on the left. The screen in front of the church was added by Carlo Fontana in 1702

windows on each storey emphasised by heavy reticulation. In addition to this, the quoins are reticulated, and extra quoins are inserted after the seventh and ninth bays to detach that part from the design and to emphasise the seven bays that are symmetrical around the entrance.

The portal itself is an impressive, rather naïf, piece with a good deal in common with Torriani's much more famous doorway at Palazzo Sciarra. Against a reticulated wall-plate two great volute brackets support a balustraded balcony, while between them a massive keystone displays a remarkably jolly angel. St Paul's emblem of a sword-bearing arm appears on the pedestals above the brackets, and it is repeated at the head of all the windows on the lower two floors.

The arms above the central window are those of Pius XI (r. 1922-1939) under whose pontificate the palace had its last major restoration. Before that, it had been damaged in the fighting of 1849, repaired before 1870 by Pius IX, sequestrated for use as a barracks by the new Italian State, and finally returned to the Holy See in 1907. The successive restorations have left little of the original texture, and all the sharply-cut reticulated stonework is rather reminiscent of a comfortably-established Edwardian bank.

Palazzo Santacroce

Piazza Benedetto Cairoli, 3

In the early 17th century the Santacroce family were immensely rich through the tobacco monopoly. This was their main palace, though they owned other nearby property including the building that became the Monte di Pietà. A number of important architects (Longhi, Maderno, Peparelli, De Rossi, Dori) worked on the palace over the years, but what we now see owes a lot to the changes and additions that were made in the late 19th century. These include the entire north façade facing S Carlo ai Catinari, the highly unusual fenestration above the piano nobile, the corner balconies, and two of the three portals.[1] Furthermore, the palace would not originally have looked so exposed, since it was the construction of Piazza Benedetto Cairoli that freed up its east flank. Despite all this, the palace retains an undeniably effective presence. Inside there is important work by Grimaldi.

At some time towards the end of the 16th century Martino Longhi the Elder produced a design for the palace but this was never used. In 1598-1602 Maderno worked on the rear façade and may also have done some work on the long main front, though the extent of his involvement is unclear. In 1636-40 Peparelli was employed to 'elevate the new palace and restore the old one', and it seems that by this time the 'new palace' filled the main façade from what are now the second to the fifth bays, and included the fourth side of the cortile. Peparelli added stucco decoration to some of the windows, heightened the mezzanines, added a further storey to the building, built an additional bay on the left, and carried the building further back along via degli Specchi. He also built the balconied doorway furthest to the left on the main façade, and this remained the only front entrance to the palace until the 19th century.

In 1660-63 G. A. De Rossi built along via degli Specchi to meet Maderno's earlier work on vicolo dei Catinari, and this provided space on the piano nobile for an enfilade of rooms culminating in a grand salone in the corner between the two streets. De Rossi's second phase of activity was in 1672-73 when he worked on the separate accommodation for the family's dependants on the other side of vicolo dei Catinari.

Work was still being carried out on the dependants' quarters by De Rossi's pupil Francesco Felice Pozzoni in 1697, but there is no reason to doubt that the final arrangement reflected De Rossi's intentions.[2]

The accommodation block for the dependants is a utilitarian building, and the most interesting thing about it is the famously ingenious way in which De Rossi exploited it to provide amenities and an extended sense of seigneurial space for the inhabitants of the main palace. At street level there is a wall fountain of the *Birth of Venus* at the end of a deep, narrow court precisely aligned with the palace's front and rear doorways. Thus, a person arriving at the main entrance would have seen straight across the cortile and out through the back entrance towards the pleasing vista of the distant fountain.[3] Up above street level — and almost as a visual metaphor for the stratification of social classes — provision was made for elegant life by a hanging garden on the roof of the dependants' quarters. This is reached by a bridge (built at some time between 1670 and 1672) that directly links the palace's main salone with a charming little niche fountain on the garden side.

In 1723-25 Ludovico Gregorini built along vicolo dei Catinari as far as the front of the building opposite S Carlo. In 1762-64 Alessandro Dori carried the main (Piazza Cairoli) façade to its present length, save that the last bay was left only one storey high. He also attempted to address the unusually large gap between the piano nobile windows and those of the second floor by extending the latter downwards and equipping them with ringhiere of the kind that were currently in fashion. The palace remained in that form until 1888 when the architect Luigi Tedeschi began a comprehensive restoration for Contessa Vincenza Sforza di Santafiora. One of Tedeschi's drawings of that year shows that the north façade had never been finished and that much of the building facing S Carlo was still in the form of miscellaneous structures belonging to other families. The Contessa obtained a compulsory purchase order on those buildings, however, and Tedeschi was thereby enabled to build a completely new north façade, uniform with the changes that he was making to the main front. Here Tedeschi radically altered the fenestration by removing Dori's ringhiere and inserting immediately above the piano nobile a range of square windows with stucco pediments and frames adapted from those of the second floor. It is these windows that give the Palazzo Santacroce façades their unusual rhythm, and they are an ingenious response to the problem set by the huge gap between the piano nobile and the second storey, which must originally have been caused by the need to accommodate the height of the vaults in the piano nobile. Other additions by Tedeschi were two further portals faithfully copied from Peparelli's preserved original one, and the erection on the main corner of two balconies in bombastic 19th century taste that is seriously at odds with the original fabric.

The frescoed rooms on the piano nobile consist of a gallery near the main stairway, three rooms along via degli Specchi, and the main salone in the corner of the building, which is preceded by an antesalone. For many years Titi's reading of an ambiguous passage in Baglione had been interpreted as making the Bolognese artist Ruggeri responsible for the gallery, but that idea had been increasingly questioned in the 1990s even before Ruggeri's involvement was completely ruled out by the discovery that he died in 1633. Although precise documentation is still lacking, it is now reasonably clear that both the gallery and the

Detail of Grimaldi's salone at Palazzo Santacroce

salone represent Grimaldi's work at different stages of his career. The stucco friezes and painted ceilings of the intervening three rooms are of less interest, but Grimaldi, who had longstanding ties with the Santacroce, may have worked on them also.[4]

The gallery, which is in poor condition, appears to date from around 1640 and must be Grimaldi's first major Roman room. It is constructed broadly on the same lines as the Bonzi/Cortona gallery in Palazzo Mattei di Giove and already shows many of the features that were to become Grimaldi trademarks, including landscape lunettes and female personifications along the cornice. Two of the three painted scenes along the centre line privilege the landscape background, while the main scene in the centre (*Sarah and the Angel*) appears to be by a distinctly different hand. Cappelletti suggests that Raffaele Vanni is perhaps the most plausible name for Grimaldi's collaborator here.[5]

The main salone dates from around 1660-62 and is a development of the type that Grimaldi established in the salone of Palazzo Peretti (1644-45), which in turn derived from the Carracci gallery in Palazzo Farnese. It is a splendid piece of uninhibited Grimaldian eclectisism, featuring lavish stuccoes, a central allegory of the Santacroce family, four large rectangular biblical scenes and four smaller ones in oval format, female personifications in the corners, and grisaille medallions. Both the general organisation and the style of the painting appear typical of Grimaldi; in particular, the biblical scenes are very reminiscent of Bolognese work of the first two decades of the 17th century. The unique feature of this fine room, though, is the little bridge that leads directly from one of the windows to the fountain on the roof of the servants' quarters opposite. The fountain masks the flight of steps behind it that leads up to the roof garden, and its scale is so perfectly calculated that it creates a delightfully ambiguous sense of being simultaneously part of the surrounding architecture and an item of the salone's own furnishing.

The palace is not generally open to the public. The frescoed rooms on the piano nobile are occupied by the Istituto Italo-Latino Americano. It is just possible to get a glimpse of the roof-garden fountain from street-level at the corner of vicolo dei Catinari and via degli Specchi. The large fountain at ground level is fully open to the street.

Plan of Raguzzini's apartment buildings in the Piazza di S Ignazio

Apartment buildings
Piazza di S Ignazio

The five buildings that form the piazza in front of S Ignazio were built by Filippo Raguzzini for the Jesuits in 1727-28, in pursuance of the orders contained in pope Benedict XIII's chirograph of 12 March 1727.[1] They have ever since been commonly described as constituting a 'theatre' and comparisons with the Teatro Olimpico at Vicenza and with Pietro da Cortona's remodelling of the piazza in front of S Maria della Pace have become virtually standard comments.* The Jesuits' going into the

*As Wittkower pointed out, in the 'theatre' of S Maria della Pace the church façade occupies the position of the notional stage, whereas in the Piazza di S Ignazio the church is in the position of the implied spectators and it is the dwelling-houses that form the scenic focus.[2]

Looking up to heaven in Piazza di S Ignazio

property business with such eye-catching buildings was not free from controversy; later in the 18th century Milizia was notoriously to write that these were 'ridiculous houses, shaped like bureaux'.[3] Nowadays, however, the piazza is greatly celebrated as an outstanding example of 18th century town planning.

The concave façades of the three buildings facing the church (together with the far corners of the buildings at the sides) are determined by two circles and an oval that touch but do not intersect, while the four streets that leave the piazza between the buildings take symmetrically organised outward and inward directions.[4] This makes for a rhythmic, puzzling and energetic ensemble that is hard to match in 18th century Rome, and most of the commentary that has been written about it concentrates on the highly original arrangement of the plan. What is almost as interesting, however, is that, despite the dancing, Borrominian curves of their façades these were quite modest apartment buildings, and this is perfectly reflected in their elevations. These effectively constitute a compendium of the devices that became widespread in Roman buildings for bourgeois multi-occupation, though few attained the deft, crisp elegance of Raguzzini's design. Particularly notable points are the multiple entrances, the provision of shops, the equally privileged storeys, the profusion of little iron balconies, the even distribution of stucco ornament, and the vertical 'stacking' of motifs.

Apartment building

Piazza S Lorenzo in Lucina, 31-35

The authorities of S Giacomo degli Spagnoli owned two houses here that had become dilapidated by the early 18th century. In 1714-15 Bizzacheri prepared plans for rebuilding them in a unified manner but nothing was done until 1729-33 when Camillo Paladini designed and built the present building. Although internally the accommodation was split up into smaller units right from the start, the façade appears to be completely original except for the modern shop fronts and the doorway with a balcony on the right side, which is a 19th century addition.

This is another example of how many of the best 18th century apartment buildings in Rome were built by the churches and, like the Jesuits' buildings in Piazza di S Ignazio, it displays many of the common architectural features of the type. Note, in particular, the high proportion of window area to wall; the equal importance given to the three main storeys; the most lavish stucco decoration being on the third floor (presumably as a selling point to offset the height from street level); the very numerous ringhiere distributed over the surface; the two entrances, leading to two stairs; and the vertical 'stacking' together of all the storeys in the outer bays. The strips that demarcate the outer bays have bold, flat patterns. Such strips usually carry the implicit idea of functioning as real pilasters, but here the architect has gone out of his way to block that association and to proclaim that they are purely decorative, with no structural function.

Palazzo Sciarra (Colonna di Sciarra, Carbognano)

Via del Corso, 239

Pietrangeli's study of the documents demonstrates that the palace may have been begun soon after the mid-16th century — certainly well before 1593, when it was shown as half-built in Tempesta's map. Some further work was done in 1610 when Ponzio could have been involved, though there is nothing to confirm this in the building documents. Completion had to wait until after 1630 when the Colonna replenished their finances by selling Palestrina, together with its princely title, to the Barberini. This final phase was in the hands of Orazio Torriani and lasted until 1641 when the portal was licensed.

The architecture of the façade is absolutely consistent and it appears that the later builders faithfully replicated what had been done at the outset. The only part that is an original 17th century creation is Torriani's portal, which soon achieved the status of being one of the acknowledged wonders of modern Rome. It is an astonishing bravura piece, extraordinarily old-fashioned for its date and, indeed, very loosely derived from the frontispiece to Antonio Labacco's *Libro appartenente a l'architettura* (1559).[1] There is an abundance of ornament — mascheroni on either side of the rusticated door-case, trophies in the metopes of the frieze above the door, and much enrichment of the balustraded balcony. The eye-catching feature, though, is the massive bracket in the position of the key-stone, carved with another huge mascherone with festoons flowing from its eye-sockets. (Torriani's portal at Palazzo S Calisto similarly sports an exaggerated key-stone in the centre of a rusticated door-case.)

Around 1745 Luigi Vanvitelli made for Cardinal Prospero Colonna a mirror room

The celebrated door of Palazzo Sciarra on the Corso, designed by Orazio Torriani. Engraving from De Rossi's Architettura Civile

and a library with frescoes of the zodiac by Stefano Pozzi. These extremely elegant rococo rooms remain, but otherwise most of the interior was reorganised in the 19th century. The palace has been occupied by various banks since 1898 and is now the seat of the Cassa di Risparmio di Roma. Part of it, however, is occupied by the Fondazione Roma, which has organised an exhibition space with the entrance at via M. Minghetti, 17.[2]

Palazzo Serlupi Crescenzi

Via del Seminario 113

An important precursor of the Baroque, in that the windows are placed with uneven intervals, the two outer ones being distanced from the central part, and themselves being separated by a wider interval than that employed at the centre. This was the first deliberate departure from the traditional regularity of 16th century Roman palace design. It was begun by Giacomo Della Porta in 1585 for Ottaviano Crescenzi, and passed to Francesco Serlupi (who added the Crescenzi name to his own) in the early 17th century. Building was then continued by Onorio Longhi, but the palace was never finished, only the entance bay and the four bays to the left ever being completed.

The reason why the palace was never completed was almost certainly because in 1588 — only three years after Della Porta had set to work — Ottaviano's brother Stefano bequeathed his neighbouring property to the Arciconfraternita del SS Salvatore

Print by Falda of Palazzo Serlupi Crescenzi, showing the palace as though it had been completed symmetrically around the entrance bay

under the condition that it should remain totally inalienable from them. In 1748 Marchese Girolamo Serlupi Crescenzi implicitly accepted that the palace could never be finished by creating at the end a proper formal staircase, which the building had hitherto lacked. In 1776, however, he eventually succeeded in obtaining a licence to build on the Arciconfraternita's site, but instead of extending his own palace he built a new apartment block for commercial letting. This was but one of several such buildings that the marchese owned, and indeed he lived in one of them for a period while he let out his own palace.[1]

Palazzo Sinibaldi (dei Cavalieri dell'Ordine Teutonico)

Via del Mascherone, 57

A long, low building of fifteen bays on the street that runs down towards the river past the left flank of the Farnese palace. It was originally the seat of the Knights of the Teutonic Order, catering for German pilgrims, and Vasi's print of 1754 (reproduced on p. 174) still refers to it as the palace of the 'Religione Teutonica'.

The palace was acquired by the Sinibaldi family, who used it in the 19th century as a workshop for the manufacture of woollen goods. It is now the seat of the Istituto Ecclesiastico di S Maria Immacolata, and has been in their hands at least since 1903, since that date appears on the image of the Immacolata that occupies the stucco cartouche over the entrance, where it is supported by swags of oak-leaves and a grinning mascherone.

The irregular spacing of the bays and off-centre placing of the entrance indicate the incorporation of earlier buildings. The piano nobile windows (which are uniform throughout the building) are simple rectangular frames in peperino to which stucco ornamental surrounds in late Baroque style have been attached. The top floor windows (which are also uniform throughout) have stucco frames with ornamentation carried up into the cornice.

The entrance is the most striking feature. It has a heavily reticulated wallplate surmounted by a broken pediment, within which is the stucco feature mentioned above. Blunt approvingly commented that this made 'a whole of unusual complexity'.[1] He also noted that the lower rusticated part 'might date from the 16th century' and the same comment could be made about the wooden doors, which are deeply carved with geometrical patterns.

The explanation of all this is presumably that the original building (which may very well have been of the 16th century) was quite plain and that the Teutonic Knights embellished all the windows in a single campaign. From the general appearance one could hazard a guess that this was done around the second decade of the 18th century, and the same could be true of most of the puzzling stucco decoration of the entrance. Research in the Order's archives would be needed to settle these questions.[2]

Palazzo Spada

Piazza Capodiferro, 13

This is primarily a magnificently decorated cardinal's palace of the mid 16th century, but it contains a fascinating group of illusionistic features of the Baroque period, reflecting the personality and interests of its then owner, Cardinal Bernardino Spada, who was an important figure in the Curia and the brother of Borromini's great champion Virgilio Spada.

Letarouilly's view of the cortile of the Palazzo Spada, early 19th century

The palace was built originally by Cardinal Girolamo Capodiferro, who was made a cardinal by Paul III in 1544, after he had spent three years in France as papal nuncio. Between 1547 and 1553 he carried out three further diplomatic missions to France as papal legate. The palace, which incorporated earlier Capodiferro buildings, was begun around the turn of 1548-49 and it went ahead quickly enough to permit work to start on the stucchi of the cortile by the Spring of the Holy Year 1550. The heraldic stemmi on the façade are those of Henry II of France, Paul III and Julius III.[1]

The architect was Bartolomeo Baronino of Casale Monferrato who had worked at the nearby Palazzo Farnese[2] and the extraordinarily elaborate stucchi on the façade and cortile were done by two teams of stuccoists – Giulio Mazzoni and Diego di Fiandra, and Tommaso del Bosco and Leonardo Sormani.[3] Mazzoni, together with assistants, was also responsible for the Galleria degli Stucchi on the piano nobile along the north side of the cortile. This bravura ensemble clearly derives from the Galerie François I at Fontainebleau, which Capodiferro must have seen during his diplomatic missions to the French court.

At the end of the 16th century the palace passed to the Mignanelli family, from whom it was bought by Bernardino Spada in 1632. He began by commissioning Paolo Maruscelli to enlarge the entrance vestibule in 1633-4 and to create a drive from the via Giulia to the back of the palace through the garden which was also improved at this time. In 1635 he called in the Bolognese quadratura painters Agostino Mitelli and Angelo Michele Colonna to fresco the Sala Grande or Sala di Pompeo, named after a colossal antique statue that had been acquired by Capodiferro and was believed to represent Pompey.* Among the painted figures populating the feigned balconies is a youth observing the scene through a telescope, which must be a reference to the Spada brothers' optical interests.[5] In 1644 G. B. Magno (Modanino) executed the first of Cardinal Bernardino's optical displays in the palace. This was the celebrated meridian clock, designed by Emmanuel Maignan, a French Minim of the Trinità dei Monti, which fills the corridor leading from the Sala Grande along the west side of the cortile.[6]

Maruscelli died in 1649 and Borromini, who was then retained along with his assistant Francesco Righi, was active in the palace for the next ten years. Borromini's first project (in 1650)[7] was for the piazza in front of the palace, where he proposed an elaborate painted architectural scheme on the side of Palazzo Missini-Ossoli, facing the Spada palace's main façade. The central element was a fountain, aligned with the Spada entrance, that featured a sculpture of

*This sculpture achieved great fame in the 18th century, when it was believed to be the very statue of Pompey at the feet of which Julius Cæsar was assassinated.[4]

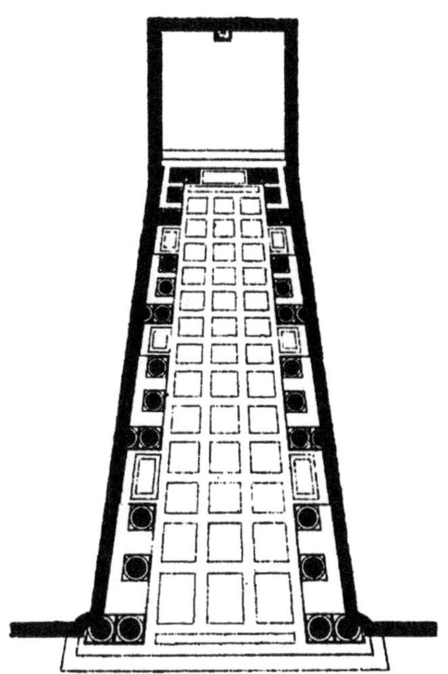

Photograph, and plan by Letarouilly, of Borromini's false perspective colonnade at Palazzo Spada

Abundance, with streams of water pouring from her breasts.[8] The implied message of the projection of Spada dominance across the open space was made explicit by the presence of the Spada arms high above the fountain. Over the following centuries the sculpture disappeared, the flow of water was adjusted to spout from a lion's head and the original antique granite basin was replaced by a strigillated sarcophagus. The present figure (which decorously folds its arms) was made by the Roman sculptor Giuseppe Ducrot as part of the restorations in 1994-1998, when some of the painted architectual surround was also recovered and restored.[9]

Borromini's most famous work at the palace followed in 1652-53. This is the celebrated false perspective colonnade in the east court, at right angles to the sight-line through the entrance towards the fountain, which can be seen from the central court through windows in the walls of the library. The colonnade replaced a painted perspective of 1642 by Magno, of which some Doric capitals were recovered and restored in the restoration of 1994-98.

Although the colonnade was of only marginal importance in Borromini's work,[10] the gigantic toy has always been regarded as a fascinating *meraviglia*. It has, however, been much altered over the years. In particular, it has lost some of its raised position in relation to the court and more light was originally admitted between the coffered sections.[11] It also originally ended in the painted representation of a garden, making a play with the real garden in the subsidiary courtyard where the viewer stood. The antique statue of a warrior (now replaced by a cast) was introduced only in the 19th century.

Borromini had already made a false perspective structure for the celebration of the Quarant'Ore in 1646 but the idea for the Spada colonnade appears to have come from an Augustinian priest, Giovanni Maria da Bitonto, who had in 1647 already executed for the Spada family something similar on a miniature scale for the high altar of S Paolo Maggiore at Bologna.

The colonnade at the palace is a puzzling construction that induces a feeling of slight disorientation and slips elusively between conventional classifications and expectations. Thus, it is not an example of adjustments made to the architecture of a 'real' and usable space to make it appear grander, as at the Scala Regia of the Vatican; nor is it a functional but patently illusionistic scenographic space, as at the Teatro Olimpico, Vicenza; nor is it a manifest 'false' perspective, with virtually no occupation of real space, as at Bramante's presbytery in S Maria presso S Satiro, Milan. It is, rather, a construction that has no practical use, that occupies a significant amount of real space, but which so arranges the components of its 8.82 metres that they appear to extend for about 35 metres. Furthermore, the mathematics of its organisation are extremely complex.*

The core function of the colonnade, along with all the other illusionistic features at the palace, was surely to add magnificence to the building.[13] There were, however, at least two sub-plots. First, the scientific and experimental aspect itself must have had a special appeal for the Spada brothers, given their intense interest in optics. Second, the colonnade also provided a peg on which to hang moralising thoughts about the deceitfulness of the senses and the illusory nature of earthly grandeur. This may, indeed, have literally been the case, since Bernardino Spada wrote just such Latin verses that may have been displayed near the colonnade itself.[14]

During the 1994-1998 restoration traces were also found of the illusionistic decoration on the palace's rear facade, which had been painted to resemble a grand display of windows under cornices, with a blue sky above. The visitor from the via Giulia entrance would thus have experienced a delicious progression of optical sensations, all calculated to convey an illusory impression of enhanced space and grandeur. It is still possible to experience something of this frisson if one stands in the centre of the main cortile, at the conjunction of the highly artificial views down the perspective colonnade to one side and across the piazza to the fountain opposite, each vista using a different technique to imply the extended reach of Spada ownership. What has been lost, however, is the further element of artifice and the *rus in urbe* associations that would have been stimulated by the painted scenography at the end of the colonnade.

Bernardino Spada, who was a very well-informed amateur of architecture, seems to have been a difficult employer, apt to change his mind and not hesitating to exploit his influential position in order to obtain second opinions from the most celebrated architects in Rome. All these characteristics were displayed in his reorganisation of the staircase that runs up to the Sala Grande at the back of the palace. This was substantially

*Prof. Camillo Trevisan has concluded that the prospettiva is not constructed according to a single consistent system, but contains elements of three different systems, viz perspectival convergence on a single vanishing point, the arrangement of the principal components in accordance with geometrical series, and individual deformation of each column on a perspectival basis.[12]

remodelled between 1658 and 1660, but as soon as the work was finished Bernardino decided that he wanted the staircase completely rebuilt in the form of two flights with a landing halfway up. Borromini unsurprisingly ceased working for Spada around this time, leaving Righi in the middle of an acrimonious dispute about the accuracy of his estimates, so that the cardinal turned to della Greca and Bernini to organise the two-flight staircase in 1660.[15] Before he left, Borromini had prepared ambitious plans for the back of the palace, with a new wing on the west side that would have been much longer and more complex than the short wing that had been built to contain the picture gallery on the east side. Those plans were dropped, and Bernardino Spada went ahead in 1660 with a project for a simplified and smaller west wing that ended in disaster when a helical staircase collapsed when it was only half-built. It is not clear to whom the cardinal may have turned to design the new wing or supervise its construction, but it was the hapless building contractor who was left to take the blame.[16]

After Bernardino's death in 1661 two further additions were made to the palace. These were the concave wall in front of the garden, built by Camillo Arcucci in 1664-7 and adorned with excellent attached stucco herms, and the terrace over the colonnade, built by Tommaso Mattei in 1700-02. There is also late 17th century decoration in several rooms.

The palace contains the Galleria Spada, which still includes much of Cardinal Bernardino's own picture collection. The Galleria is housed on the piano nobile in four rooms in and adjacent to the east wing at the back. The largest of these (the ceiling of which was painted by Michelangelo Ricciolini in 1698) was intended by Bernardino as a picture gallery right from the start.

Only the Galleria, the perspective colonnade and the cortile are open to the public. The rest of the building is occupied by the Council of State.

Palazzo di Spagna

Piazza di Spagna, 57

The basic facts are as follows. In 1647 the palace belonging to the Monaldeschi family was bought by the Spanish Ambassador, the Count of Oñate, who immediately commissioned Borromini to design a new building for the site. The following year Oñate left Rome for Naples, where he had been appointed Viceroy, and he ceded the partly rebuilt palace to the Spanish Crown. Building was resumed by the ambassadorship of the Duke of Terranova, who had the palace completed by Antonio del Grande between 1654 and 1657. The present façade, built in 1812 by Adrien Pâris when the palace was occupied by the French, retains the original tripartite entrance. The central balcony is an addition of the 1950s.

When Oñate commissioned the rebuilding he was expecting to be made a cardinal and Borromini designed for him a symmetrical building around a courtyard, with a single reception suite extending around three sides of the piano nobile. The most notable feature was the vestibule on the central axis with, to its left, a great vaulted space containing the three flights of the staircase and a large landing. This scheme did not have recent Roman precedents but it did reflect the arrangement of various royal palaces in Spain and it is quite likely that Oñate specified it for that reason. Borromini seems to have been proud of the design since, in discussing the staircase of the Oratory in the *Opus architectonicum* he (or his spokesman Virgilio Spada) wrote that he had built it with a single vault covering the whole 'come io ultimamente ho praticato nel Palazzo dell'Eccellentissimo Sig. Ambasciadore di Spagna'.

Pascoli writes that the king made Borromini a knight of the Order of St James of Compostella in recognition of his work and it is not known why del Grande was entrusted with the building in 1654, when Borromini was still available. However, it seems that del Grande was brought in with a brief to respect Borromini's general layout and to carry out the practical adjustments needed to fit the palace for use as an embassy housing an ambassador and his wife, together with the embassy staff. This meant substantial adjustment to Borromini's plans for a single reception suite, and the provision of extra accommodation in a new wing at the rear of the building, alongside via Borgognona. (The exact involvement of Borromini and del Grande is discussed by Anselmi in chapters 3 and 4 of her authoritative *Il Palazzo dell'Ambasciata di Spagna presso la Santa Sede*, where it is shown that a good deal of Borromini's arrangement of the piano nobile had been completed before del Grande's alterations.)

The vestibule may well be as Borromini left it but the staircase was rebuilt in 1899 and has lost any earlier detailing. Nevertheless, it preserves the general features of Borromini's design and something of the power of his concept may still be felt. In the vestibule, the Tuscan columns alternately linked by an architrave and separated by arches repeat the scheme of the cloister at S Carlo alle Quattro Fontane, though here the device is used to create a massively imposing effect far removed from the contemplative tone of the cloister. A factor in the vestibule's sombre power is the use of a markedly depressed arch over its central aisle. Blunt believed that this was borrowed from Sangallo's corridor on the piano nobile of Palazzo Farnese, and he also noted that the the asymmetrical jambs of the vestibule's side openings were based on that palace's entrance.[1]

The varied 17th to early 19th century decoration of the interior includes, in the audience chamber, Marco Benefial's ceiling fresco of *The Gods of Olympus* (painted in 1744, and with its nacreous colouring not one of Benefial's more attractive works). In the apartments of the ambassador are Bernini's two busts *Anima Beata* and *Anima Dannata* of about 1619.

The palace remains in use as the Spanish Embassy to the Holy See.

Palazzo della Stamperia (Cornaro)

Via della Stamperia, 7-8

This palace takes its name from the fact that it was bought in 1777 by Pius VI to accommodate the papal printing press. Most of the present building consists of the additions made by Donna Olimpia Maidalchini, sister-in-law of Innocent X, after 1647. However, these additions are just a simplified extension of the central five bay pavilion which had been built soon after 1582 by the Venetian Cardinal Cornaro.

Although Baglione and Martinelli attributed the original five bays to Giacomo Della Porta, Titi's attribution to Giacomo del Duca has been generally accepted. This part of the building does, in fact, have some very idiosyncratic features that seem far too wilful for the purist Della Porta.* One of the oddest motifs is the series of female masks

*Blunt drew particular attention to the breaking of the tops of the windows, the scrolls under the three straight window pediments, and the treatment of the blocks over the columns supporting the balcony.[1]

One of the strange masks on the façade of the Palazzo della Stamperia

under the cornice, which are continued through the 17th century addition. These masks — already shown in Franzini's print of 1643 — are, in point of fact, quite similar to those of the schematised caryatids that separate the upper storey windows in the courtyard of the Palazzo Lateranense, which is another building of the 1580s (see photograph p. 32).

The palace is now used for government offices, including an offshoot of the Presidenza del Consiglio dei Ministri.

Palazzetto Sterbini (Boncompagni)

Via del Babuino, 41

A building of eleven bays plus a two-storey belvedere. It was built by the Boncompagni, presumably around the 1740s, and passed to the Sterbini in 1822. Between 1886 and 1888 it was restored by the architect Virginio Vespignani, who added an extra storey with terrace and balustrade above the cornice.

The main door at no 41 has a lively barocchetto surround; the matching balcony in the fourth bay lacks this feature. All the other bays are equipped with identical decoration. On the ground floor there are inverted buckle motifs containing armorial emblems (a bow and quiver, and an arm holding a torch), while the top floor windows have shells. Over the piano nobile windows are busts of emperors in circular niches, which certainly constitute the building's memorable feature, and which appear to be original. The lower floor windows of the belvedere have bowler-hat tympana containing mensole.

Although there are pilaster-strips demarcating the ends of the façade and the two bays with balconies, these are not forceful enough to pull the design together, and the whole building has more the style of a casino than a full-dress palace in town.

Palazzo Strozzi (Olgiati, Besso)

Largo delle Stimmate, 26

One of several Roman palaces by Maderno that now contain no more than traces of his work. It was built for the Olgiati banking family who at some undocumented time in the first two decades of the 17th century employed Maderno to beautify it and add a new door with a ringhiera.[1] From 1630 it was rented by the Florentine Strozzi family who acquired it in 1649 and soon added a painted frieze and a ceiling incorporating their emblems to the Salone Rosso on the piano nobile.[2] In 1882 it was largely demolished and rebuilt to make way for the Corso Vittorio Emanuele II. It then passed to the Besso family who made it the seat of the Fondazioni Ernesto and Marco Besso.

Maderno worked on what was then a shallow wing along the right side of the palace and his work can perhaps be seen in the lowest two storeys of the eight bays along Largo delle Stimmate and via Cestari (though even this part may have been moved back from its original position). Everything above the piano nobile and the entire façade on the Corso Vittorio Emanuele is an 1880s construct.

Perhaps because of Baglione's specific reference to a new door, some modern writers have respectfully referred to the Largo delle Stimmate portal as being the Maderno original. However Hibbard must surely be right to dismiss both this entrance and the identical one on the Corso Vittorio Emanuele as 19th century inventions.[3]

Palazzetto 'dei Telamoni'

Via della Croce, 71

A nine-bay building, apparently of the early 17th century, that was originally a hospice, then a hospital, before becoming apartments above shops.

The remarkable feature is the pair of telamons, representing Hercules wearing the skin of the Nemean lion, that flank the door and give the building its name. They are commonly attributed to Pietro Bernini (died 1629) though there is no firm evidence for that.

Above the door is a window with semicircular tympanum and flanking volutes of uncertain date. The restrained stucco ornament of the second-floor windows appears to be of the second half of the 17th century. Everything above the cornice is a 19th century addition.

Palazzo Testa Piccolomini

Via della Dataria, 22

The entire exterior was done in 1718-19 by Filippo Barigioni, who made an exceptionally subtle job of packaging a miscellany of pre-existing buildings on a sloping site that had to accommodate a curving lane between the Quirinale palace and the neighbouring church of S Croce. The privileging of the upper storeys with stucco decoration and balconies is characteristic of the period. The elegant barocchetto tympana of the windows feature a variety of heraldic devices (eagles, crescents, rampant lions) and are of notably high quality.

Because of the site the palace presents four façades of very different scale and with very different relations to the spaces before them, and on them Barigioni used quite a limited range of stucco motifs to create completely different effects, each appropriate for its setting. Thus, in the short but conspicuous façade on Largo dei Lucchesi the window surrounds of each storey merge to produce vertical bands of stucco decoration; on the main via della Dataria façade this device is used only in the outer bays; while on the small eastern façade towards the Quirinale only four of the windows are for real, and the wall is in effect covered by abstract patterning.

Palazzo Valentini (Bonelli, Alessandrino, Spinelli, Imperiali, della Provincia)

Piazza SS. Apostoli, 119

In 1585 the Boncampagni owned the palace for some ten months before selling it to Pius V's nephew Michele Bonelli (Cardinal of Alexandria — thus Alessandrino) and in that brief period Mascarino and Martino

Ferrerio's engraving of the façade of Palazzo Valentini

Longhi the Elder made plans for rebuilding. The actual work was immediately begun for Bonelli by Fra Domenico Paganelli, whose plans were an amalgam of the Mascarino and Longhi proposals.[1] Bonelli died in 1604, by which time the main façade had been completed in standard Palazzo Farnese style, together with an undetermined amount of the side façades. Work continued under succeeding members of the Bonelli family, and there are several early references to Peparelli being the architect, though it seems unlikely that he did more than implement Paganelli's design.

In 1653 Cardinal Antonio Barberini leased the palace on his return from exile in France, and he stayed until he moved to the Barberini palace in via dei Giubbonari in 1658. At that point Felice della Greca made two alternative sets of plans for extending the palace to a new rear façade overlooking Trajan's Forum, and modifying it to accommodate Don Mario and Don Agostino Chigi, who were currently living in the palace that they leased from the Colonna in Piazza SS Apostoli. Although the acquisition of the Bonelli palace would have given the Chigi the opportunity of making a strong statement in that piazza, Alexander VII dropped the idea almost immediately and switched his attention to the Piazza Colonna area.[2]

In 1752 the Bonelli sold the palace to Cardinal Giuseppe Spinelli, a member of the Imperiali family, and most of the older surviving interior decoration belongs to this period. At the end of the 18th century the palace passed to the Valentini who in 1838 had Filippo Navone[3] build a new block at the rear, overlooking Trajan's Forum, with a façade featuring giant pilasters. The side façades linking that block to the main nucleus were designed by Louis Gabet and built between 1858 and 1874, the year after the palace had passed into the hands of the Amministrazione Provinciale di Roma. The building has been very heavily restored and does not now have much original character.

The old writers seem to have regarded the palace with more respect than its rather routine architecture now seems to merit. Its best feature is the portal — a straightforward affair of two columns and a square balcony, but successful in using sheer scale to exploit its dominant site.

Palazzo Varese or Varesi (Degli Atti)

Via Giulia, 14-21

The buildings on the site were acquired by the Milanese Monsignor Diomede Varese between 1611 and 1616 and Maderno must have built the palace for him soon thereafter. The 14-bay façade on via Giulia, with irregular spacing of windows at the right end, must have been largely dictated by the jumble of buildings that it incorporated but it is an undistinguished design in Maderno's least ingratiating manner, with severely plain windows and two simple string-courses. The portal, with a central cartouche containing a too-small head, provides the only gesture towards elegance. The Varese emblems of eagles and turrets appear in the cornice. The attic is a 19th century addition.

The entrance wall of the cortile is filled by an extraordinary four-storey loggia that rises to the full height of the building with two storeys of arcaded openings above two with flat entablatures, and with Varese eagles in the second storey. The entire airy structure, which is in the Tuscan order, must surely have been adapted from an earlier building, and it was clearly built to exploit the view down to the Tiber beyond the opposite end of the cortile where there is now a screen featuring a rusticated doorway between two niches, with a balustraded terrace above. Unfortunately, the effect has been destroyed by a large modern building that crowds against the screen and blocks the view beyond.

How much of the screen and other parts of the cortile are close to Maderno is hard to say, since there has clearly been much alteration in later periods. There is, indeed, an inscription 'Aedificata 1495 — Instaurata 1930'. Hibbard thought that there was now nothing worth attributing to Maderno in the palace except for the standard windows, and possibly the portal.[1] Nevertheless, the building remains a modest cousin of Maderno's Palazzo Mattei di Giove. This is partly due to the composition of the cortile, with a loggia on the entrance side facing a screen with a central feature set between niches; and partly due to the way in which the small square staircase is placed in a corner of the entrance side of the cortile and arranged so as to open onto a loggia running back along the line of the main façade.

Palazzo Verospi

Via del Corso, 374

The Verospi family, who came from Spain, were ennobled Romans by 1576. The palace was begun by Girolamo Rainaldi in the early 17th century for Fabrizio Verospi, who became a cardinal in 1626. It was completed in 1610 by Onorio Longhi, who is said by Baglione to have worked on the cortile, galleria and loggia.[1] In 1704/5 Alessandro Specchi carried out an extensive remodelling and the palace was again greatly altered and modernised when, after having passed through the hands of the Torlonia, it was taken over by the Credito Italiano in 1904. In the course of all these changes it lost its original cornice and altana, acquired an extra floor of accommodation, and (like most of the other palaces on the Corso taken over by banks) had the cortile filled in to provide extra office accommodation.

The important surviving feature is Francesco Albani's decoration of the vault of the loggia on the piano nobile at the rear of the building. This originally had an open arcade towards the cortile at first floor level but it is now closed in, with an entrance cut through the balustrade. The capitals of the pillars and attached pilasters are splendid affairs that embody the dogs and stars of the Verospi arms.

Albani's theme is an allegory of Time, and the formal scheme is clearly derived from Raphael's loggia in the Farnesina (though Puglisi and Röttgen suggest that Albani's immediate source would have been the Cavaliere d'Arpino's loggia (1594-95) in Palazzo Orsini, now Palazzo Pio Sodalizio dei Piceni).[2] The central panel shows *Apollo with the Four Seasons, Dawn and Dusk*; on the cove are painted *Day* and *Night* (the most impressive figure in the composition) and the gods associated with

Albani's frescoed ceiling of the loggia in Palazzo Verospi, as seen in an early 19th century etching

the days of the week — *Diana*, *Mars*, *Mercury*, *Jupiter*, *Saturn* and *Venus*. Beneath are busy little cameo-like scenes, including several lubricious ones involving satyrs, phallic herms, etc. These do not look particularly like Albani's work. The embrasures of the windows (facing on to what was originally the palace garden) are painted with grisaille figures and Northern-looking landscapes, including a tondo of a burning building and fleeing nuns that must depict the fire that took place in 1617 in the neighbouring monastery of the Convertites.

The loggia frescoes have been variously dated between 1609 and 1625. Puglisi plausibly argues that they probably formed part of work that is known to have been done for Ferrante Verospi before 1615, that only a dating of c.1611-12 would fit with Albani's account of his life and with his other known commissions, and that the window embrasure with the scene of the Convertites must have been added later.[3] As yet, however, there is no conclusive documentation.

In two neighbouring rooms are four detached parts of frescoes by Sisto Badalocchio which are all that remains from a scheme of similar period in the ground floor of the palace. They are *Mercury Presenting the Apple to Paris*; the *Judgement of Paris*; *Polyphemus and Galatea* and *Polyphemus and Acis*. These are clumsy derivations from Annibale Caracci's Farnese gallery.

Unnamed building

via degli Zingari, 55

This 18th century building was almost certainly built as an apartment building, as Lombardi says, but it has a presence that is as imposing as that of many palaces. It achieves this by using the traditional formula for a Roman palace of the previous two

The doorway of the apatrment building at via degli Zingari, 55

centuries — a rhythmic march of windows under rather massive tympana, and no attempt to articulate the wall with ringhiere or any other device except simple string-courses. The first-floor windows have deeply moulded lintels with triglyphs, creating quite a substantial architectural statement. This being the 18th century, however, there are four full storeys above the ground floor, with even the upper ones having windows of very respectable size.

The design of the windows becomes steadily simpler from one storey to the next, and the door is a notably effective composition of extreme simplicity, featuring a shell in a divided pediment that has something of the severity of the door at Palazzo del Drago (Gentili). The cornice is decorated with rosettes and stars in imitation of noble family emblems.

The shared repertory of barocchetto devices that was used in 18th century Rome for both palaces and apartment buildings usually led to an effect that was quite nervous, busy and crowded. In this apartment building the architect seems deliberately to have adopted a more reticent, aristocratic and conservative idiom in direct descent from G. A. De Rossi.

Palazzo Zuccari

Piazza della Trinità dei Monti, 14

This mansion, now the seat of the Biblioteca Hertziana, is famous as the 16th century home of the painter Federico Zuccari, and one of the most elaborate of all houses made by artists to proclaim their genius. The zoomorphic entrance and windows on via Gregoriana are the most famous feature, but Zuccari also covered the interior with frescoes. After Zuccari's death the building was heightened and extended by Girolamo Rainaldi for the subsequent owners.

The important Baroque feature is the elegantly curving covered balcony that fills the west end of the building and contributes so much to the atmosphere of the piazza. (The present compactly rounded roof of the balcony was made in 1904-06 to replace a much stranger pyramidal structure that originally extended high up the palace's wall.) As with Carlo Rainaldi's similar balcony at Palazzo Borghese, the supporting architecture of this addition makes a very assertive statement, though the balcony's function was simply to provide a place where the owners could sit in comfort while they enjoyed the spectacle beneath them.

The balcony was built in 1711 for the exiled ex-Queen of Poland, Maria Casimira, who in her ceaseless quest for recognition as a cultural trend-setter had already rented the palace for some years, employing Domenico Scarlatti as her maestro di cappella and establishing a miniature private theatre in the palace in 1708. For the staging of the operas with music by Scarlatti that were performed in the theatre in 1711 Maria Casimira obtained the services of the young Filippo Juvarra who had caused a sensation in the previous year with his revolutionary stage designs for Cardinal Ottoboni's theatre in the Cancelleria. Against that background, Körte's suggestion that Juvarra may have also designed the balcony has a certain inevitability about it, and it has often been repeated as a fact.[1]

19th century print of Palazzo Zuccari, showing the balcony with its original pyramidal roof

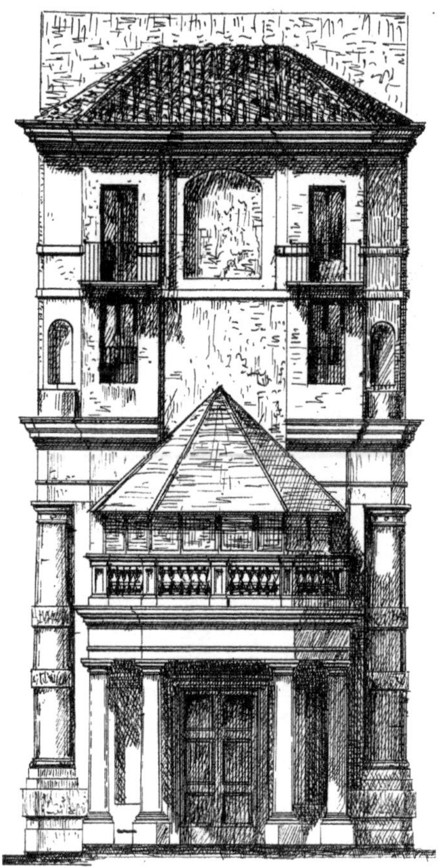

Boscarino, however, considers that the drawing attached to the planning application for the balcony does not resemble Juvarra's work and that the great architect's personal involvement is unlikely on several grounds.[2]

Elling (who believed that the work was by Juvarra) delighted in the fact that visitors to Maria Casimira's theatre entered her palace under this giant theatre box, and the idea of the co-existing internal and external theatre does have a certain ambiguity and metaphorical force. Perhaps to an even greater degree than Rainaldi's version at Palazzo Borghese, the balcony articulates the supreme self-image of aristocrats who could cast the entire outside world as a theatrical performance to be observed at their convenience.

BIBLIOGRAPHIES
AND
REFERENCES

NOTES ON CITATIONS

The general bibliography lists texts that are relevant to several palace entries. The select bibliographies for individual palaces include further texts that are relevant only to the particular building in question.

The select bibliographies use the summary format of author's name and publication date for the texts that appear in the general bibliography, and give full details of other sources. However, if the author has only one entry in the general bibliography, and no other entries elsewhere, the date is omitted. Thus Baglione's *Vite* is cited simply as 'Baglione'.

The summary format omits the details 'ed.' and 'et al.' Thus the book that appears in the general bibliography as 'Salerno, L., et al., 1973' is cited as 'Salerno 1973', and 'Frommel, C. L. & Sladek, E., eds., 2000' is cited as 'Frommel & Sladek'.

Several entries in the general bibliography relate to books of conference papers, exhibition catalogues and other kinds of edited compilation. Where individual essays from such compilations are included in the select bibliographies, the compilation is cited in summary format (eg 'in Caperna & Spagnesi, pp. 50-100').

Notes generally use abbreviated citation format and refer to texts that appear in the bibliographies, though a few notes refer to other sources, and give full citations for them. Essays from compilations are cited by the author's name and publication date.

GENERAL BIBLIOGRAPHY

Acidini Luchinat, C., 1998. *Taddeo e Federico Zuccari: Fratelli Pittori del Cinquecento*, Milan

Baglione, G., 1642. *Le vite de' pittori, scultori ed architetti dal ponteficato di Gregorio XIII del 1572 in fino a'tempi di Papa Urbano Ottavo nel 1642*, Rome

Baldinucci, F., *Notizie De' Professori Del Disegno Da Cimabue in Qua*. Successive volumes published between 1681 and 1728, Florence

Bartoni, L., 2003. 'Giovanni Francesco Grimaldi e la pittura di paesaggio nei palazzi romani alla metà del Seicento' in Cappelletti 2003, pp. 127-140

Battisti, E., 1970. 'Il simbolismo in Borromini', *Studi sul Borromini*, pp. 229-284

Beaven, L., 2010. *An Ardent Patron: Cardinal Camillo Massimo and his antiquarian and artistic circle*, London

Belli Barsali, I., 1970. *Ville Di Roma*, Milan

Benedetti, S., 1973. *Giacomo Del Duca e L'architettura Del Cinquecento*, Rome

Blunt, A., 1979. *Borromini*, London

Blunt, A., 1982. *Guide to Baroque Rome*, London. Cited here as 'Blunt *Guide*'

Boisclair, M., 1986. *Gaspard Dughet: Sa Vie Et Son Œuvre (1615-1675)*, Paris

Bonaccorso, G., 1992. 'L'opera architettonica di Giuseppe Ferroni e le vicende costruttive del convento dei Chierici Minori in Via del Lavatore' in Debenedetti 1992, pp. 149-185

Bonaccorso, G., 1994c. 'La presenza dei Chierici Minori nel rione Trevi; i casamenti di piazza Scanderbeg e via del Lavatore' in Debenedetti 1994, pp. 143-156

Borea, E., ed., 1965. *Domenichino*, Milan

Bösel, R. & Frommel, C. L., eds., 2000. *Borromini e l'Universo Barocco*, Milan

Brauer, W. & Wittkower, R., 1931. *Die Zeichnungen des Gianlorenzo Bernini*, Berlin

Briganti, G., 1962b. *Pietro da Cortona o della Pittura Barocca*, Florence

Brizzi, B., ed., 1980. *Album di Roma*, Rome

Callari, L., 1944. *I Palazzi di Roma*, third edition, Rome

Caperna, M., & Spagnesi, G., eds., 2002. *Architettura: processualità e trasformazione*, Rome

Cappelletti, F., ed., 2003. *Decorazione e collezionismo a Roma nel Seicento: vicende di artisti, committenti, mercanti*, Rome

Cappelletti, F., 2006. *Paul Bril e La Pittura di Paesaggio a Roma*, 1580-1630, Rome

Carpaneto, G., 1993. *I Palazzi di Roma*, second edition, Rome

Cavazzini, P., 1997. 'Agostino Tassi and the organization of his workshop: Filippo Franchini, Angelo Caroselli, Claude Lorrain and the others', *Storia dell'Arte*, (91), 401-431

Cavazzini, P., 2002. 'Towards a chronology of Agostino Tassi', *Burlington Magazine*, 144, 396-408

Cavazzini, P., ed., 2008. *Agostino Tassi (1578-1644): un paesaggista tra immaginario e realtà*, Rome

Chierici, G., 1957. *Il Palazzo Italiano: dal Secolo XI al Secolo XIX*, Milan

Colasanti, A., 1923. *Volte e Soffitti Italiani*, Milan

Connors, J., 1980. *Borromini and the Roman Oratory: Style and Society*, New York

Connors, J., 1989a. 'Alliance and Enmity in Roman Baroque Urbanism', *Römisches Jahrbuch der Bibliotheca Hertziana*, XXV, 207-94

Connors, J., 1989b. 'Virgilio Spada's defence of Borromini', *Burlington Magazine*, 131, 76-90

Connors, J. & Rice, L., eds., 1991. *Specchio di Roma barocca: una guida inedita del XVII secolo*, Rome

Coudenhove-Erthal, E., 1930, *Carlo Fontana und die Architektur des römischen Spätbarocks*, Vienna

Curcio, G., 1989. 'L'area di Montecitorio: la città pubblica e la città privata nella Roma della prima metà del Settecento' in Debenedetti 1989, pp. 157-204

Danesi Squarzina, S., ed., 2001. *Caravaggio e i Giustiniani: toccar con mano una collezione del Seicento*, Milan

Debenedetti, E., ed., 1985. *Committenze della famiglia Albani: note sulla Villa Albani*, Torlonia, Rome

Debenedetti, E., ed., 1987. *Ville e palazzi: illusione scenica e miti archeologici*, Rome

Debenedetti, E., ed., 1989. *L'architettura da Clemente XI a Benedetto XIV*, Rome

Debenedetti, E. 1992. *Architettura, città, territorio: realizzazioni e teorie tra illuminismo e romanticismo*, Rome

Debenedetti, E., ed., 1994. *Roma borghese: case e palazzetti d'affitto*, vol. 1, Rome

Debenedetti, E., ed., 1995. *Roma borghese: case e palazzetti d'affitto*, vol. 2, Rome

Debenedetti, E., ed., 1998. *Roma, le case, la città*, Rome

De Brosses, C., 1931. *Lettres familières sur l'Italie*, Y. Bézard, ed., Paris

Del Gaizo, V. et al., 1969. *Il Palazzo Madama: Sede del Senato*, Rome

De Rossi, D. D., 1701. *Studio d'Architettura Civile Sopra Gli Ornamenti Di Porte E Finestre Tratti Da Alcune Fabbriche Insigni Di Roma etc*, Rome

Donati, U., 1942. *Artisti Ticinesi a Roma*, Bellinzona

Donati, U., 1957. *Carlo Maderno, Architetto Ticinese a Roma*, Lugano

D'Onofrio, C., 1977. *Acque e Fontane di Roma*, Pomezia

D'Onofrio, C., 1986. *Le Fontane di Roma*, third edition, Rome

D'Onofrio, C., 1967. *Roma vista da Roma*, Rome

Elling, C., 1975. *Rome: The Biography of its Architecture from Bernini to Thorvaldsen*, Tübingen

Enggass, R., 1976b. *Early Eighteenth-Century Sculpture in Rome*, University Park, Pennsylvania

Fagiolo dell'Arco, M. & Fagiolo dell'Arco, M., 1967. *Bernini: una introduzione al gran teatro del barocco*, Roma

Fagiolo, M. & Portoghesi, P., eds., 2006. *Roma barocca: Bernini, Borromini, Pietro da Cortona*, Milan

Falda, G. B., 1665. *Il Nuovo Teatro delle Fabriche, et Edificii, in Prospettiva di Roma Moderna*, Rome. I and II 1665; III 1667-69; IV, with plates by Specchi, 1699

Falda, G. B., 1691. *Fontane*, Rome. Four volumes published under various titles from 1675. Plates in third and fourth volumes are by Venturini

Falda, G. B., 1680. *Li Giardini Di Roma: Con Le Loro Piante Alzate e Vedute in Prospettiva*, Rome

Faldi, I., 1970. *Pittori Viterbesi di Cinque Secoli*, Rome

Ferrari, G., *Lo Stucco nell'Arte Italiana: Riproduzioni in Parte Inedite di Saggi del Periodo Etrusco al Neo-Classico*, n/d, Milan

Ferrari, O. & Papaldo, S., 1999. *Le sculture del Seicento a Roma*, Rome

Ferrerio, P., *Palazzi di Roma de Piu Celebri Architetti*, Rome. I, n/d (1655); II, with plates by Falda, not before 1661. (Title of II changed to *Nuovi Disegni delle Architetture e Piante dei Palazzi di Roma dei Più Celebri Architetti.*)

Ferri, P., 1725. *Roma Ampliata e Rinovata etc*, Rome

Frommel, C. L., 1973. *Der römische Palastbau der Hochrenaissance*, Tübingen

Frommel, C. L. & Sladek, E., eds., 2000. *Francesco Borromini: atti del convegno internazionale*, Roma 13-15 gennaio 2000, Milan

Golzio, V., 1971. *Palazzi Romani dalla Rinascita al Neoclassico*, Bologna

Guide rionali di Roma, Rome. Published irregularly, and with various editors, from 1973 for the Assessorato per le Antichità, Belle Arti e Problemi della Cultura. Cited here as 'GR'

Güthlein, K., 1979. *Quellen Aus Dem Familienarchiv Spada Zum Römischen Barock*, Tübingen

Haskell, F., 1963. *Patrons and Painters: A Study in the Relations Between Italian Art and Society in the Age of the Baroque*, London

Heimbürger Ravalli, M., 1977. *Architettura, Scultura e Arti Minori nel Barocco Italiano: Ricerche nell'Archivio Spada*, Florence

Hempel, E., 1924. *Francesco Borromini*, Vienna

Hess, J., 1935. *Agostino Tassi, Der Lehrer Des Claude Lorrain: Ein Beitrag Zur Geschichte Der Barockmalerei in Rom*, Munich

Hibbard, H., 1971. *Carlo Maderno and Roman Architecture, 1580-1630*, London

Kieven, E., 1988. *Ferdinando Fuga e l'architettura romana del Settecento*, Rome

Kieven, E., 2000. 'Ferdinando Fuga (1699-1781)' in Curcio, G. & Kieven, E., eds., *Storia dell' architettura italiana: Il Settecento*, Milan, pp. 540-555

Krautheimer, R., 1983. 'Alexander VII and Piazza Colonna', *Römisches Jahrbuch für Kunstgeschichte*, 20, 193-208

Krautheimer, R., 1985. *The Rome of Alexander VII, 1655-1667*, Princeton

Lalande, J. J., 1769. *Voyage d'un François en Italie, Etc.* n/d, Yverdon

Lavin, M. A., 1975. *Seventeenth-Century Barberini Documents and Inventories of Art*, New York

Letarouilly, P. M., *Edifices de Rome moderne*, Paris. Three volumes of plates and two of text published 1840-1857. Various reprints of the plates, of which the most convenient is the reduced facsimile, Princeton, 1982

Lo Bianco, A., ed., 1997. *Pietro Da Cortona, 1597-1669*, Milan

Lombardi, F., 1992. *Roma, palazzi, palazzetti, case: progetto per un inventario 1200-1870*, Rome

Lombardi, F., 1996. *Roma. Le chiese scomparse. La memoria storica della città*, Rome

Magni, G., 1911. *Il Barocco a Roma nell'Architettura e nella Scultura Decorativa*, Torino

Mahon, D., ed., 1968. *Giovanni Francesco Barbieri detto Il Guercino, 1591-1666: Catalogo critico dei dipinti*, Bologna

Mahon, D., ed., 1991. *Giovanni Francesco Barbieri: Il Guercino, 1591-1666*, Bologna

Mallory, N., 1974. 'Carlo Francesco Bizzacheri 1655-1721' in *Journal of the Society of Architectural Historians*, 33, 27-47

Mallory, N., 1977. *Roman Rococo Architecture from Clement XI to Benedict XIV (1700-1758)*, New York

Martinelli, F., 1969. 'Roma ornata dall'architettura, pittura e scultura'. First published in C. D'Onofrio, ed., *Roma nel Seicento*, Florence

Martinelli, F., 1750. *Roma Ricercata etc*, Rome

Matteucci, A. M. & Ariuli, R., 2002. *Giovanni Francesco Grimaldi*, Bologna

Matthiae, G., 1952. *Ferdinando Fuga e la sua opera romana*, Rome

Merz, J. M., 2008, *Pietro da Cortona and Roman Baroque Architecture*, New Haven

Metzger Habel, D., 2002. *The Urban Development of Rome in the Age of Alexander VII*, Cambridge

Mola, G. B., 1966. *Breve racconto delle miglior opere d'architettura, scultura et pittura fatte in Roma et alcuni fuor di Roma*, Karl Noehles, ed., Berlin

Nevola, F. & Palmer, V., 2004. *Il Palazzo Della Consulta e l'Architettura Romana di Ferdinando Fuga*, Rome

Nolli, G. B., 1748. *Nuova Pianta di Roma*, Rome

Pane, R., 1956. *Ferdinando Fuga*, Naples

Pascoli, L., 1730. *Vite de' Pittori, Scultori ed Architetti Moderni, etc*, Rome. Vol. II 1736

Passeri, G.B., 1772. *Vite de' pittori, scultori ed architetti, che hanno lavorato in Roma, morti dal 1641 fino al 1673*, Rome

Percier, C. & Fontaine, P. F. L., 1798. *Palais, Maisons, et Autres Edifices Modernes, Dessinés à Rome / Publiés à Paris par Charles Percier et P. F. L. Fontaine en 1798*, Paris

Pierguidi, S., 2000. 'Considerazioni sulle carriere di Giovanni Francesco Grimaldi, François Perrier e Giovan Battista Ruggeri', *Storia dell'Arte*, (100), pp. 43-68

Pocino, W., 1996. *Le Fontane di Roma etc*, Rome

Pollak, O., 1909. 'Antonio del Grande, ein unbekannter römischer Architekt des 17. Jahrhunderts', *Kunstgeschichtliches Jahrbuch der K.K. Zentral-Kommission für Erforschung und Erhaltung der Kunst*, 133-161

Pollak, O., 1928. *Die Kunsttätigkeit unter Urban VIII*, Vienna

Portoghesi, P., 1964. *Borromini nella cultura europea*, Rome

Portoghesi, P., 1967. *Francesco Borromini*, Rome

Portoghesi, P., 1966. *Roma Barocca: storia di una civiltà architettonica*, Rome

Posner, D., 1971. *Annibale Carracci: A Study in the Reform of Italian Painting Around 1590*, London

Puglisi, C. R., 1999. *Francesco Albani*, New Haven

Robertson, C., 2008. *The Invention of Annibale Carracci*, Milan

Roethlisberger, M., 1961. *Claude Lorrain: The Paintings*, London

Roethlisberger, M., 1959. 'Les Fresques de Claude Lorrain', *Paragone*, 10 (109), p. 41

Röttgen, H., 2002. *Il Cavalier Giuseppe Cesari d'Arpino: un grande pittore nello splendore della fama e nell'incostanza della fortuna*, Rome

Roettgen, S., 2007. *Italian frescoes, the Baroque era, 1600-1800*, New York and London

Roisecco, Gregorio, 1739. *Descrizione Di Roma Moderna etc.* Various later editions. Rome

Romano, P., 1940. *Strade e piazze di Roma: (Piazza del Popolo)*, Rome

Rossi, Filippo, F., 1654. *Ritratto Di Roma Antica Nel Quale Sono Figurati I Principali Tempij, Theatri. ... Aggiuntovi Di Nuovo Le Vite & Effigie De'primi Re Di Essa, E Le Grandezze dell'Imperio Romano, Etc.* Various later editions. Rome

Rossini, P., 1732. *Il Mercurio Errante Delle Grandezze Di Roma, Tanto Antiche, che Moderne.* Various later editions. Rome

Russell, S., 1997. 'Frescoes by Herman van Swanevelt in Palazzo Pamphilj in Piazza Navona', *Burlington Magazine*, 139, pp. 171-177

Salerno, L., 1988. *I Dipinti del Guercino*, Rome

Salerno, L., 1977. *Pittori di Paesaggio del Seicento a Roma*, Rome

Salerno, L., et al., 1961. *Via del Corso*, Rome

Salerno, L., et al., 1973. *Via Giulia: una Utopia urbanistica del 500*, Rome

Schiavo, A., 1956. *La Fontana di Trevi e le altre opere fi Nicola Salvi*, Rome

Schleier, E., 1968. 'Affreschi di François Perrier a Roma' *Paragone*, 19 (217/237), pp. 42-54

Schleier, E., ed., 2001. *Giovanni Lanfranco: un pittore barocco tra Parma, Roma e Napoli*, Milan

Scott, J. Beldon, 1991. *Images of Nepotism: The Painted Ceilings of Palazzo Barberini*, Princeton

Scott, J. Beldon, 1997. 'Strumento di potere: Pietro da Cortona tra Barberini e Pamphilj', in Lo Bianco 1997, pp. 87-98

Spagnesi, G., 1964. *Giovanni Antonio De Rossi, Architetto Romano*, Rome

Spear, R. E., 1982. *Domenichino*, New Haven

Tessin, N., 1914. *Nicodemus Tessin d.y:s studieresor etc*, Stockholm

Titi, F., 1763. *Descrizione delle pitture, sculture e architetture esposte al pubblico in Roma etc*, Rome

Toesca, I., 1960. 'G. B. Crescenzi, Crescenzio Onofri (e anche Dughet, Claude e G. B. Muti)', *Paragone*, (125) 11, pp. 51-59

Torselli, G., 1965. *Palazzi di Roma*, Milan

Totti, P., 1638. *Ritratto Di Roma Moderna*, Rome

Vasi, G., *Delle Magnificenze Di Roma Antica E Moderna.* Ten books published 1747-1761, Rome

Vecchi, M., 1971. *Ambasciate estere a Roma*, Milan

Venuti, R., 1766. *Accurata e Succinta Descrizione Topografica e Istorica di Roma Moderna*, Rome

Visentini, A., 1771. *Osservazioni Che Servono Di Continuazione Al Trattato Di Teofilo Gallaccini*, Venice. (Facsimile reprint, 1970, Farnborough)

Waddy, P., 1990. *Seventeenth-Century Roman Palaces: Use and the Art of the Plan*, New York

Wasserman, J., 1966. *Ottaviano Mascarino and his Drawings in the Accademia Nazionale di San Luca*, Rome

Wittkower, R., 1973. *Art and Architecture in Italy, 1600 to 1750*, third revised edition, Harmondsworth

Wittkower, R., 1955. *Gian Lorenzo Bernini: The Sculptor of the Roman Baroque*, London

Zocca, M., 1927. *Architettura Minore in Italia*, Turin

SELECT BIBLIOGRAPHIES AND NOTES

Casa degli Agostiniani Scalzi

Portoghesi 1966, pp. 422-423, pls. 375-377; Bonaccorso, G., 1994a, 'La figura e l'opera di Francesco Bianchi: precisazioni su una famiglia di capomastri e architetti di origine lombarda' in Debenedetti 1994, pp. 65-89; id., 1994b, 'La casa degli Agostiniani Scalzi di Gesù e Maria in via dei Crociferi' in Debenedetti 1994, pp. 131-141; GR II, 6, p. 43

1. Portoghesi 1966, caption to pls. 375-377.
2. Bonaccorso 1994b, p. 134

Palazzo Albani (Mattei, Massimo, Nerli, del Drago)

Baglione, p. 82; Ferrerio, II, pls. 11-13; Vasi, pl. 36a; Rossi 1697, p. 686; id., 1707, p. 717; id. 1725, p. 160; Roisecco 1739, p. 134; Rossini 1750, p. 82; Martinelli 1969, p. 246; id., 1750, p. 173; Ferri 1725, p. 146; Titi, p. 300; Letarouilly, pl. 169; Wasserman 1966, p.139; Clark, A, 1975, 'State of studies: Roman eighteenth century art', *Eighteenth century studies*, IX, pp. 102-107; Delfini Filippi, G., 1985, 'Il palazzo alle "Quattro Fontane"' in Debenedetti 1985, pp. 77-116; Connors & Rice, p. 173; Beaven, pp. 237-322; GR XVIII, 2, p.25; Blunt *Guide*, p. 158

1. The Cruyl drawing is published in Blunt *Guide*, p. 235 and in Connors & Rice, p. 173. The most prominent alteration since Cruyl's day is the addition of a balcony immediately above the fountain.
2. Baglione ascribes the palace to Giacomo Della Porta but Martinelli explicitly contradicts this and says that 'la verita è che è del Cav. Domenico Fontana' (Martinelli 1969, p. 246). Blunt states that Bellori also ascribes the building to Fontana in a manuscript note (Blunt *Guide*, p. 158).
3. For a full account of Massimo's display of his collections, see Beaven, pp. 237-322.
4. Winckelmann, J. J., 1961, *Lettere italiane*, Milan, p. 151. See letters of 21 June, 1759 and 21 February, 1761.
5. Blunt notes that the small plan in Letarouilly does not correspond with that in Ferrerio, but represents the part that Albani built over the garden in Strada Felice (Blunt *Guide*, p. 158).
6. Ferri (1725), Roisecco (1739), Rossini in the *Mercurio Errante* of 1750, and the editor of the 1750 edition of Martinelli. See Delfini Filippi 1985 for various extracts.
7. Delfini Filippi 1985, p. 101
8. See the summary in GR XVIII, 2, p. 49. There is a preparatory drawing for the putti composition at the National Gallery of Scotland.
9. Pascoli, II, p. 392
10. See Clark 1975

Palazzo Albertoni (Spinola)

Baglione, p. 82; Ferrerio, II, pl. 39; Martinelli 1969, p. 247; Magni, II, pl. 35; Connors 1989a, pp. 254-259; Lombardi 1992, p. 426; GR X, 1, p. 40; Blunt *Guide*, p. 158

1. Connors 1989a, p. 253. See pp. 245-259 of this essay for a general account of the development of the Piazza Campitelli in the 17th century.

Palazzetto Alibrandi or Alivrandi (Cavalieri)

Vasi, pl. 180; Lombardi 1992, p. 318; GR VII, 1, p. 18

Palazzo Altemps

Baglione, p. 68; Ferrerio, II, pl. 18; Vasi, pl. 164; Baldinucci, vol. 5, p. 543; Letarouilly, pl. 169; Scoppola, F., 1992: 'Influssi della "Giustizia" Sistina sulla Produzione Artistica Successiva' in Fagiolo, M. & Madonna, M.L., eds. *Sisto V*, Rome, I, pp. 773-823; Scoppola, F. & Vordemann, S. D., 1997. *Palazzo Altemps*, Rome; Barroero, L. 1997, 'Giovanni Francesco Romanelli' in Lo Bianco, pp. 181-186; GR V, 1, p. 26; Blunt *Guide*, p. 160

1. Baldinucci V, p. 543. Romanelli was paid for the fresco in 1654 (Barroero 1997, pp. 184-185).

Palazzo Altieri

Ferrerio, II, pl. 38; Falda 1665, IV, pls. 28, 29; De Rossi, I, pls. 119-23; Vasi, pl. 79; Visentini, p. 33; Magni, II, pls. 56, 57; Coudenhove-Erthal, pp. 31-33; Schiavo, A., 1962, *The Altieri Palace*, Rome; Haskell, pp. 118, 161-163; Spagnesi 1964, pp. 66-72, 151-158; Marqués, M. M., 1976: 'Some Drawings by Carlo Maratta and Niccolò Berrettoni for the Altieri Palace', *Master Drawings*, XIV, pp. 51-55; Montagu, J., 1978, 'Bellori, Maratti and the Palazzo Altieri', *Journal of the Warburg and Courtauld Institutes*, (41), 334-340; Connors 1989a, pp. 229-30; Borsi, F. et al., 1991, *Palazzo Altieri*, Rome; Di Castro, D. et al., 1999, *Roma, Palazzo Altieri: le stanze al piano nobile dei cardinali Giovanni Battista e Paluzzo Altieri*, Milan; Metzger Habel, p. 138; Beaven, pp. 344-349; GR IX, 1, p. 56; Blunt

Guide, p. 160
1. Schiavo 1962, p. 74
2. See the drawing at the Albertina, Vienna, reproduced in Spagnesi, 1964, p. 177.
3. Connors 1989a, pp. 229-230
4. Metzger Habel, p. 364, n. 122
5 Elling, p. 272
6 Blunt Guide, p. 160
7. Pastor tr. Graf, 1891-1953, *History of the Popes*, London, XXXI, p. 452
8. Schiavo 1962, pp. 23-24, where precise dates are given for visits by the pope.
9. Spagnesi 1964, p. 154
10. Safarik describes the main points in Di Castro 1999, p. 122.
11. See Beaven, pp. 344-349
12. Montagu 1978, p. 334
13. Marqués 1976
14. Published, with illustrations, in Borsi 1991, pp. 177-210

Palazzetto Ansellini

Lombardi 1992, p. 166; GR IV, 7, p. 55

Palazzo Antamoro (Strada)

Falda 1691, III, pl. 28; Magni, III, pl. 27; Wittkower 1955, p. 243; D'Onofrio 1986, p. 394; Pocino, p. 260; Ferrari & Papaldo, p. 412; GR II, 5, p. 28; Blunt *Guide*, p. 160
1. D'Onofrio 1986, p. 394
2. Blunt *Guide*, p. 161, states that the door is a survivor from Strada's palace, but the present author wonders whether this is entirely convincing.

Palazzo Astalli

Pascoli, I, p. 317; Letarouilly, pl. 40; Spagnesi 1964; pp. 201-203; Pietrangeli, C., 1968, 'Il Palazzo Astalli', *Capitolium*, (XVIII), pp. 6-13; GR X, 1, p. 9; Blunt *Guide*, p. 161

Palazzo D'Aste

Lombardi 1992, p. 160; GR IV, 6, p. 22

Palazzo D'Aste (Rinuccini, Bonaparte, Misciattelli)

Ferrerio, II, pls. 28, 29; Falda 1665, I, pls. 16, 17 and IV, pl. 48; De Rossi, I, pls. 135-137; Vasi, pls. 39, 170; De Brosses, II, p. 108; Visentini, p. 27; Letarouilly, pl. 111; Salerno 1961, p. 256; Spagnesi 1964, p. 60; Wittkower 1973, p. 189; Tittoni, M. E., 1981: *Palazzo Bonaparte a Roma*, Rome; Metzger Habel, pp. 114-128; GR IX, 3, p. 94; Blunt *Guide*, p. 161
1. See Metzger Habel, pp. 114-128 for a full account of these transactions.
2. Vasi, pl. 39

Palazzo D'Aste (Pericoli, Sterbini)

Spezzaferro, L. in Salerno 1973, p. 375; Lombardi 1992, p. 341; Carpaneto, p. 47; GR VII, 2, p. 20
1. Spezzaferro in Salerno 1973, p. 375

Palazzo Avila

Carpaneto, p. 48; Lombardi 1992, p. 219; GR V, 2, p. 42; Blunt *Guide*, p. 162

Palazzo del Banco di S Spirito (Spada, Bennicelli)

Falda 1665, I, pls. 22, 23; Donati 1942, p. 186 and fig. 221; Portoghesi 1967, p. 183; Blunt 1979, p.175; id., 1983, 'Two Neglected Works by Borromini', *Römisches Jahrbuch für Kunstgeschichte*, 20, pp. 17-31; Heimbürger Ravalli, p. 275; 275; Connors 1980, pp. 273-276; GR V, 3, p. 66; Blunt *Guide*, p. 198
1. Even though the flank of the Oratory that bounded the east side of the space had been built by Borromini's rival Camillo Arcucci.
2. Though one of the prints shows a porch and shops that do not appear in the other (Connors 1980, p. 276).
3. Blunt *Guide*, p. 199

Palazzo Barberini ai Giubbonari or Casa Grande ai Giubbonari

Vasi, pl. 180; Totti 1638, p. 211; Hibbard 1971, p. 222; Porro, D., 1986, 'Lo scalone del palazzo Barberini ai Giubbonari e altre opere di Nicola Giansimoni architetto', *Studi romani*, (34), pp. 95-106; Waddy 1990, pp. 132-172; GR VII, I, p. 16; Blunt *Guide*, p. 166
1. Described in detail in Porro 1986

Palazzo Barberini

Tetius, H., 1642 and 1647, *Ædes Barberinæ Ad Quirinalem*, Rome; Ferrerio, I, pls. 7 & 8; Falda 1665, IV, pls. 17-20; Vasi, pl. 36; Skippon, P., 1732, *An account of a journey made thro' part of the Low Countries, Germany, Italy and France*, London; Tessin, p. 165; De Rossi, I, pls. 35-52, III, pls. 7, 8; De Brosses, I, p. 58; Venuti, I, p. 219; Percier & Fontaine, IV, pls. 81, 82; Letarouilly, pls. 181-186; Magni, II, pls. 42-46; Pollak 1928, I, p. 251; Brauer & Wittkower, pp. 27ff; Blunt, A., 1958b, 'The Palazzo Barberini: the contributions of Maderno, Bernini and Pietro da Cortona', *Journal of the Warburg and Courtauld Institutes*, (21), pp. 256-287; Haskell, pp. 24-62; Montagu, J., 1970, 'Antonio and Gioseppe Giorgetti: sculptors to cardinal Francesco Barberini', *The Art Bulletin*, (52), pp. 278-298; id., 1971, '"Exhortatio ad virtutem"; a series of paintings in the Barberini Palace', *Journal of the Warburg and Courtauld Institutes*, XXXIV, pp. 366-372; Hibbard 1971, pp. 80-84, 222-230; Wittkower 1973, pp. 70-73; Lavin 1975; Blunt 1979, p. 33; Brizzi, pp. 51-84; Portoghesi 1984, pp. 35-39, pls. 8-13; Magnanimi, G., 1977, 'Palazzo Barberini, la sala ovale', *Antologia di Belle Arti*, (1), pp. 29-36; id., 1983, *Palazzo Barberini*, Rome; Waddy 1990, pp. 173-272; id., 1975, 'Michelangelo Buonarroti the younger, Sprezzatura, and Palazzo Barberini', *Architectura*, (5), pp. 101-122; id., 1976, 'The design and designers of Palazzo Barberini', *Journal of the Society of Architectural Historians*, (35), pp. 151-185; Scott, 1991; id., 1997; Ferrari & Papaldo,

p. 413; Frommel, C. in Bösel & Frommel, II, pp. 96, 97; Roca De Amicis, A., 2006, 'Pietro da Cortona a Palazzo Barberini' in Fagiolo & Portoghesi, pp. 188-191; Merz, pp. 17-31; Roettgen 2007, pp. 142-157; GR II, p. 126; Blunt *Guide*, p. 162

1. Hibbard 1971, pp. 222-230 remains a lucid summary. Waddy 1990 and Scott 1991 are the essential texts of more recent years, and the present entry draws heavily on them. Chapter 2 of Haskell is probably still the liveliest general account of the personalities involved in Barberini patronage.
2. Blunt *Guide*, p. 163
3. Wittkower 1973, p. 72
4. Hibbard 1971, pp. 81-82, in 'Scipione Borghese's Garden Palace on the Quirinal' Hibbard describes the Palazzo Barberini as a 'huge, villa-like palace set back from the street in a garden on the edge of town', and draws various parallels with Maderno's earlier work in the garden of the Palazzo Pallavicini Rospigliosi (Hibbard 1964, p. 188).
5. Waddy 1990, pp. 224, 237-241
6. Ibid., p. 219; Scott 1991, p. 18
7. Waddy 1990, pp. 180-207
8. Blunt *Guide* p. 164, Merz pp. 24-25
9. Scott 1991, p. 198
10. Rumours of financial malpractice dogged Bernini for much of his life, without ever being proved beyond doubt. The present allegation was recorded by Passeri. For this, and a general account of relations between Bernini and Borromini at the time, see Connors in Bösel & Frommel, I, p. 10.
11. De Rossi attributed the windows to Borromini (De Rossi, I, pl. 41). Hibbard tentatively thought that the windows 'may even be the product of collaboration' between Borromini and Bernini (Hibbard 1971, p. 83), but Frommel goes further and sees them as the product of a completely fused and indivisible creative process (Bösel & Frommel, II, p 97).
12. Bösel & Frommel, II , pp. 97, 104
13. Manfredi in Bösel & Frommel, II, p. 102-103. Hibbard dismisses the traditional attributions of the two staircases as 'meaningless'. (Hibbard 1971, p. 82)
14. Skippon 1732, p. 667
15. Merz, pp. 17-21. Merz discusses three drawings, of which he believes two to be autograph. One of the latter had been published by Thelen. Merz totally rejects the drawn plan of a palace printed in the early editions of Wittkower's *Art and Architecture in Italy*, 1600-1750.
16. Blunt *Guide*, p. 165
17. See Merz, pp. 24-25
18. Roca de Amicis 2006, p. 190
19. Waddy 1990, p. 248; Roca de Amicis 2006, p. 190; Merz, pp. 22-24. Connors has commented that 'the Cortona portal and windows are quite intact and remarkable' (*Journal of the Society of Architectural Historians*, 57, 3, 1998, p. 321.) De Rossi's illustration of the door (De Rossi, I, pl. 52) is reproduced p. 66. For a photograph showing the original appearance of this part of the theatre, as it was in the 1920s, see p. 22 of Daolmi, D., *L'armi e gli amori*, Rome, 2001. This doctoral thesis is available on the internet at www.examenapium. it/armi.
20. Blunt *Guide*, p. 165; Blunt 1958b, p. 281. Merz, p. 25
21. That display is also available on the internet at http://galleriabarberini.beniculturali.it.
22. Scott 1991, pp. 132-134
23. See the extended discussion of this in Scott 1997
24. Barb. lat. 4360
25. Barb. lat. 4360 is printed in full as an appendix to Magnanimi 1983. The document refers to a plan that is now lost and it is not certain that the author proposed entrances on the short axis, though that seems likely as the the room was envisaged as attached to a loggia. For a possible reconstruction of the document's plan see Waddy 1990, fig.133, and for two of Borromini's preparatory drawings see ibid., figs. 146 and 147.
26. Hibbard 1971, p. 84
27. See Magnanimi 1983, p. 83 for discussion of Teti's comment, and elaboration of the philosophical themes that might be drawn from it. Magnanimi 1977 covers similar ground. Waddy concludes that the room fuses forms that were associated with the concepts of church and of dwelling (Waddy 1990, pp. 220-223).
28. See Scott 1991, p. 194.
29. Scott 1991, p. 33
30. Ibid., pp.25-26
31. Ibid., p. 96
32. Ibid., p. 53. The Daphne-like figures are Apollonian references, as are the Barberini suns.
33. These Sforza arms were overpainted by those of the Barberini, but by the 1980s the latter had been removed.
34. Scott 1991, p. 22
35. Scott 1991, p. 108
36. Montagu 1971
37. See Montagu 1970, pp. 294-295; Ferrari & Papaldo, p. 413; Magnanimi 1983, pp.136-138; Waddy 1990, pp. 257-258. The two latter include 19th century depictions of the fountain by Corot and Roesler-Franz respectively.
38. Also see above for Bernini's use of Apollonian imagery in the door leading from the salone to the oval room and in the stucco frieze of Princess Anna's salotto.
39. Waddy 1990, pp. 268-271

Palazzi Bernini

Elling, pl. 93; Lombardi 1992, pp.132,133; Carpaneto, p. 67; GR III, 3, p. 36; Blunt *Guide*, p. 166

1. For Bernini's residence at S Marta see Mormando, F., 2011, *The Life of Gian Lorenzo Bernini*, University Park, Penn, p. 320, n. 14. The plaque on the building in via Liberiana is wrong in saying that Bernini resided there until 1642.

Palazzo Boncompagni Corcos (Starinci)

Falda 1665, I, pl. 22; Uttaro, E. & Gigli, L., 2003. *Palazzo Boncompagni Corcos a Monte Giordano: Programmi e Immagini*, Rome; GR V, 3, p. 68; Blunt *Guide*, p. 169

1. Connors 1989b, p. 79
2. This is fully described and illustrated in Uttaro and Gigli 2003, on which the present entry largely relies.

Palazzo Boncompagni Ludovisi (Cerasi)

Zocca, I, pp. 68, 69; Biolchi, D., 1957. 'Il ripristino della Fontana del Babuino', *Capitolium*, (XXXII), 12, pp. 14-16; D'Onofrio 1986, pp. 132-137; Elling, pp. 303-305, pls. 114,115; Enggass 1976b, p. 155; Varagnoli, C. 1998, 'La nobiltà dissimulata, ossia il palazzo Boncompagni Ludovisi al Babuino' in Debenedetti 1998, pp. 37-59; GR IV, 3. p. 190; Blunt *Guide*, p. 169

1. Elling, p. 305
2. Enggass 1976b, p.155

Palazzo Borghese, Palazzo della Famiglia Borghese and Palazzetto Baschenis

Palazzo Borghese

Ferrerio II, pls. 22-24; Falda 1665, IV. pls. 12, 13; Vasi, pl. 69; Tessin, p. 171; De Brosses, II, p. 42; Percier & Fontaine, IV, pl. 87; Letarouilly, pls. 175, 176; Magni, II, pls. 17-21; Golzio, figs. 53-71, pls. IV, V; Hibbard, H., 1962b, *The Architecture of the Palazzo Borghese,* Rome; id., 1971, p. 141; Boisclair, M., 1976, 'La décoration des deux mezzanines du palais Borghèse de Rome', *Racar*, (3), pp. 7-28; Waddy 1990, pp. 73-128; Fumagalli, E., 1994, *Palazzo Borghese: committenza e decorazione privata*, Rome; id., 2002, 'Padre Cosimo Capuccino a Roma', in *Paolo Piazza, pittore cappuccino nell'età della Controriforma tra conventi e corti d'Europa*, Verona, pp. 189-239; Emiliani, A., 1997, *Giovanni Francesco Guerrieri da Fossombrone*, Verona; GR IV, 7, p. 7; Blunt *Guide*, p. 166

The Garden

Falda 1691, III, pls. 11,12; Hibbard, H., 1958, 'Palazzo Borghese Studies: 1, the garden and its fountains', *Burlington Magazine*, 100, 205-212; Portoghesi 1966, pls. 233-5; Ferrari & Papaldo, pp. 414-5

The Gallery

Faldi, I., 1954, *Galleria Borghese: le sculture dal secolo XVI al XIX*, Rome, pp. 16, 17; Hibbard, H., 1962a, 'Palazzo Borghese Studies: II, the Galleria', *Burlington Magazine*, (104), pp. 9-20; Batorska, D., 1997, 'Designs for the galleria in Palazzo Borghese in Rome: new proposals' *Paragone*, 48 (14), pp. 26-45; Matteucci & Ariuli, pp. 166-184

The Palazzetto Baschenis

Letarouilly, pl. 10; Athanasiou, P., 1988, 'Il cannocchiale prospettico nel palazzetto Baschenis a Roma', *Palladio*, n. s. 1, pp. 99-116; GR IV, 7, p. 42

1. The standard monograph is Fumagalli 1994 which is a fine and scholarly account of the building with the added advantage of illustrating the interior decoration very fully. It also includes the plans from Waddy 1990, which devoted a chapter to the palace. The GR entry is one of the fuller ones, and it includes the most user-friendly guide to the location of the various decorative schemes.
2. As Ponzio had been a pupil of Longhi it is quite likely that he had taken over on his master's death, which occurred before 1594.
3. Hibbard 1962b, p. 46
4. Ibid., p. 49, n. 24
5 Waddy 1990, p. 89, n. 86
6. Hibbard 1962b, pp. 48-49, n. 23
7. Waddy 1990, p. 92
8. Hibbard 1962b, pp. 66-67
9. Hibbard 1962b, p. 3
10. Waddy 1990, p. 116
11. See Faldi 1954, pp. 16-17
12. Fumagalli believes, however, that Rainaldi remained the overall director of the work (Fumagalli 1994, p. 90).
13. See Batorska 1997. As the Leipzig drawings are inscribed with titles, they provide firm identifications of the sixteen Roman rulers and the allegorical figures associated with them. That information is set out in Batorska and repeated in Matteucci & Ariuli, pp. 173-178. Batorska in fact goes beyond demonstrating Bartoli's close involvement in the Borghese gallery and argues (Batorska 1997, pp. 32, 33, 39) that the distribution of the reliefs over the vault is so close to ancient practice, and so alien to Grimaldi, that Bartoli must have designed the whole composition as well as the individual reliefs. Matteucci & Ariuli (p.173) continue to give the overall design to Grimaldi.
14. The subjects of the chapel stuccoes, completed in 1676 and also apparently designed by Bartoli, are (in the ceiling) *Religion and the Four Continents*; (around the walls) the *Four Elements*, the *Four Seasons*, *Tobias and the Angel* and *Christ with Mary and his Brothers* (Hibbard 1962a, p. 15) or *Mary and the Apostles James and John before Christ* (Ferrari & Papaldo, p. 416).
15. Waddy 1990, p. 122
16. For illustrations of the exceptional decoration of the mezzanine rooms, see Fumagalli 1994, pls. 67-81
17. Fumagalli 1994 provides a full account of all the later work, with illustrations of the Giaquinto and Costantini ceilings at Figs 117 and 1 respectively. The gabinetto is fitted up with mirrors and brackets for the display of porcelain, but as the the subject of Giaquinto's ceiling is *Religion and the Cardinal Virtues,* the room probably began as a chapel.
18. Hibbard 1958, p. 212

Palazzo della Famiglia Borghese

Ferrerio, II, pl. 25; Hibbard, H., 1962b: *The Architecture of the Palazzo Borghese*, Rome, p. 73; Connors 1989a, p. 224; Waddy 1990, pp. 108-111; GR IV, 7, p. 39

1. Connors 1989a, p. 224

2. Hibbard 1962b, p. 73
3. Connors 1980, pp.9 and 116, n. 35

Palazzo Bossi

Letarouilly, pl. 243; Spezzaferro, L. in Salerno 1973, p. 376; Lombardi 1992, p. 343; GR VII, 2, p.18; Blunt *Guide,* p. 169

1. See Blunt *Guide*, p.169 and Spezzaferro in Salerno 1973, p. 376
2. There are photographs of the cortile and stairs in Salerno 1973, pp. 376-378

Palazzo Braschi

Letarouilly, pls. 196, 197; Colasanti, pls. 188ff; Pietrangeli, C. & Ravaglioli, A., 1967, *Palazzo Braschi e il suo ambiente*, Rome; Elling, pp. 312, 313; Kirk, T., 2005, *The Architecture of Modern Italy*, New York, I, p. 76; GR VI, 1, 48; Blunt *Guide*, p. 169

1. Blunt *Guide*, p. 169
2. Kirk 2005, I, p. 76
3. Elling, p. 313

Palazzo Del Bufalo

De Rossi, I, pl. 104; Belli Barsali, p. 48; Hempel, p. 176 and pl. 117a; Blunt 1979, p. 175 and pl. 129; Lombardi 1992, p. 91; GR II, 6, p. 13; Blunt *Guide*, p. 177

1. Hempel 1924, p. 176 and ill. 117a, and Blunt 1979, p. 175 and ill. 129
2. Blunt *Guide*, p. 177. The GR entry records a traditional view that the left side of the palace dates from the 17th century and asserts that the Borromini drawing in Vienna which Blunt believed was done for the casino (Blunt 1979, p. 176) was in fact for the left door of the palace.

Palazzo del Bufalo Ferraioli (Niccolini)

Ferrerio, II, pl. 47; Titi, p. 358; Salerno 1961, p. 206; Spagnesi, G., 1963, 'Palazzo Del Bufalo-Ferraioli e il suo architetto', *Palladio*, n. s. 13, pp. 134-158; Metzger Habel, pp. 162, 170; GR III, 1, p. 22; Blunt *Guide*, p. 178

Palazzo della Cancelleria

Lavagnino, E., 1924, *Il Palazzo della Cancelleria e la chiesa di S. Lorenzo in Damaso*, Rome; Schiavo, A., 1963, *Il Palazzo della Cancelleria*, Rome; Enggass, R., 1976a, 'Baciccio: a new fresco and two "Modelli"', *Burlington Magazine*, 118, pp. 589-590; Rudolph, S., 1978, 'The "Gran Sala" in the Cancelleria Apostolica: a homage to the artistic patronage of Clement XI', *Burlington Magazine,* 120, pp. 593-601; Lombardi 1992, p. 273; GR VI, 2, p. 70; Blunt *Guide*, p. 169

1. Enggass 1976a, p. 589

Palazzo Capizucchi (Troili, Massimo, Gasparri)

Baglione, p. 82; Mola, p. 130; Falda 1665, I, pl. 32; Martinelli 1969, pp. 235, 257; Connors 1989a, pp. 251-259; Lombardi 1992, p. 426; Cantatore, F., 1993, 'Palazzo Capizucchi: trasformazioni di un isolato nella Roma di Sisto V e di Clemente X', *Quaderni dell'Istituto di Storia dell'Architettura*, (n. s. 21), pp. 39-61; GR X, 1, p. 42; Blunt *Guide*, p. 170

1. Connors 1989a, p. 253
2. See Cantatore 1993, pp. 44, 46. The family historian was Cardinal Raimondo Capizucchi.
3. Cantatore 1993, p. 46
4. Cantatore 1993, p. 48

Palazzo Capponi (Orsini, Stampa, Pediconi)

Carpaneto, p. 114; Lombardi 1992, p. 216; GR V, 3, p. 64; Blunt *Guide*, p. 171

1. For an illustration and short description of this palazzetto see Lombardi 1992, p. 215

Palazzo Capponi ('della Palma')

De Rossi, G. B., 1638, *Palazzi Diversi Nel'Alma Città di Roma*; Rome. Lombardi 1992, p.149; Papini, M. L., 2004, *Palazzo Capponi a Roma: casa vicino aAl Popolo, a man manca per la strada di Ripetta*, Rome; GR IV, 6, p. 7

1. Papini 2004, pp. 146-147 (n. 27)

Palazzo Cardelli

Ferrari, pl. CLXIV; Scano, G., 1961, 'Palazzo Cardelli', *Capitolium*, 36 (10), pp. 22-26; Spagnesi, G., 1979, *Il Centro Storico di Roma: Il Rione Campo Marzio*, Rome, pp. 55, 68; Bandes, S., 1984: 'Notes on Gaspard Dughet', *Burlington Magazine*, 126, pp. 28-33; Boisclair 1986, pp. 54, 215, 346; Ferrari & Papaldo, p. 417; GR IV, 5, p. 83; Blunt *Guide*, p. 171

1. For more about Camillo Astalli's use of Apollonian imagery see H. Langdon's article 'Claude, Apollo and the Muses', *Storia dell'Arte*, 112 (n. s. 12), 2005, esp. pp. 12-15.
2. Ferrari & Papaldo, p. 417
3. See Boisclair 1986, p. 346 for a rejection of the attribution to Dughet and an account of the landscapes' subject-matter.

Palazzo de Carolis (Simonetti, Banco di Roma)

Falda 1665, I, pl. 17; Ferri 1725, p. 116; Rossini 1732, p. 64; Magni, II, pl. 107; Salerno 1961, p. 229; Bocca, A., 1967, *Il Palazzo del Banco di Roma già De Carolis*, Rome; D'Onofrio 1986, pp. 140-145; Zanella, A., 2000, *Palazzo de Carolis*, Rome; GR IX, 3, p. 40; Blunt *Guide*, p. 177

1. See Zanella 2000, p. 18, where the chirograph is wrongly attributed to Clement IX rather than Clement XI.
2. Zanella 2000, p. 12

Palazzo Carpegna (Baldinotti)

De Rossi, I, pl 131; Spagnesi 1964, pp. 202, 203; del Gaizo, p. 82; GR VIII, 2, p. 68; Blunt *Guide*, p. 162

Palazzo Carpegna (Accademia di S Luca)

Hempel, p. 127; Blunt 1979, p. 161; Battisti, pp. 241, 242; Portoghesi 1984, pp. 181, 182, pls. 150-153; Connors 1989a, pp. 233-245; id. in Bösel & Frommel, I, pp. 7-21 and II, pp. 195-198; Kieven, E. in ibid. I, pp. 119-127; Salvagni, I., 2000, *Palazzo Carpegna, 1577-1934*, Rome; GR II, 5, 36; Blunt *Guide*, p. 171

1. Connors 1989a, pp. 233-245
2. For the roots of these messages in Ripa's emblem books, see Battisti.

Palazzo Cavallerini Lazzaroni

Salerno, L., 1964, 'Il Palazzo Cavallerini a via dei Barbieri', *Palatino*, VIII, pp.13ff; Fischer, U., 1973, *Giacinto Gimignani (1606-1681): eine Studie zur römischen Malerei des Seicento*, PhD thesis. Freiburg; Lombardi 1992, p. 376; GR VII, 1, p. 30; Blunt *Guide*, p. 171

Palazzo Celani

Lombardi 1992, p. 95; Bonaccorso 1992, pp. 161, 163, 164; id, 1994c, pp. 145-147; GR II, 2, p. 162

Palazzo Celsi (Viscardi)

Pascoli, I, p. 317; De Rossi, I, pl. 139; Spagnesi 1964, pp. 120-123; GR IX, 1, p. 86; Blunt *Guide*, p. 171

1. Pascoli I, p. 317
2. Spagnesi 1964, p. 122

Palazzo Cenci-Bolognetti (Petroni)

Vasi, pl. 135; Matthiae, p. 79; Magni, II, pl. 98; Pane, p. 116, figs. 98, 99; Wittkower 1973, pp. 252, 238; Manfredi, T., 1996, 'Il mercante e l'architetto: aspetti inediti dell'attività di Ferdinando Fuga e Alessandro Galilei da una corrispondenza commerciale tra Firenze e Roma (1733-35)', *Rivista storica del Lazio*, 4 (4), pp. 125-139; Kieven 2000, p. 545; Palmer, V., in Nevola & Palmer, pp. 52, 53; GR IX, 1, p. 36; Blunt *Guide*, p. 172

1. See Kieven 2000, p. 545. The device of tapering jambs appears in the Palazzo dei Conservatori in the six subsidary doors in the entrance loggia.
2. Wittkower 1973, p. 252

Palazzo Centini (Toni, 'dei Pupazzi')

Portoghesi 1966, pl. 307; Betti, F. 1995, 'Il palazzetto della famiglia Centini in via Capo le Case' in Debenedetti 1995, pp. 189-199; GR III, 3, p. 64; Blunt *Guide*, p. 190

1. The last two paragraphs of the present entry rely on Betti.

Palazzo Cerri (Gaucci)

Nolli, no. 655; Carpaneto, p. 137; Lombardi 1992, p. 292; GR VI, 2, p. 58

Casa dei Chierici Minori

Elling, pl. 66; Portoghesi 1966, p. 423, pls. 378-382; Lombardi 1992, p. 96; Bonaccorso 1992; id, 1994c, pp. 143-156; GR II, 5, p. 95

1. Blunt *Guide*, p. 152

Palazzo Chigi (Aldobrandini)

Ferrerio, II, pl. 14; Falda 1665, I, pls. 14, 15 and IV, pl. 27; Vasi, pl. 22; De Rossi, II, pls. 53-61; De Brosses, II, p. 47; Lefèvre, R., 1971, 'Della Porta e Maderno a Palazzo Chigi', *Palladio*, n. s. 21, pp. 151-158; id., 1973, *Palazzo Chigi*, Rome; Röttgen 2002, pp. 204, 536; Strinati, C. & Vodret, R., eds., 2001, *Palazzo Chigi*, Milan; Krautheimer 1983, p. 193; id., 1985, pp. 53-58; Merz, pp. 185-193; Metzger Habel, pp.140-142, 166-190, 213-216; GR III, 2, p. 54; Blunt *Guide*, p. 158

1. Borromini apparently wrote 'disegno di Carlo Maderno, e non com'alcuno ha creduto di Giacomo Della Porta, essendo stato fatto dopo la morte del Porta' (Lefèvre 1973, p. 96) and also 'è disegno di Carlo Maderno siccome è stato fatto dopo la morte [di Giacomo Della Porta] di sicuro' (Hibbard, p. 215).
2. Lefèvre 1973, pp. 93-99 and id, 1971, passim
3. Hibbard 1971, p. 216
4. See Merz, pp. 185-193
5. Metzger Habel, p. 213. See the next entry and that for Palazzo Valentini for summaries of the plans that della Greca had made for those sites.
6. Connors 1989a, p. 232
7. See Marino, A., 'I Chigi in città. Il palazzo barocco' in Strinati & Vodret, p. 83. Substantially the same essay is in Caperna & Spagnesi, pp. 427-436 under the title 'Palazzo Chigi, dalla Fabbrica Aldobrandini al Ministro delle Colonie'.
8. Specchi's print of 1699 (Falda, *Nuovo Teatro*, IV, pl. 27) shows a very different portal with twin Doric columns already in place on the Piazza Colonna front, but this must represent a project that was never executed. Before 1739 the Piazza Colonna entrance would have been a bare aperture in the wall, as depicted by Falda in 1665 (*Nuovo Teatro*, I, pl. 15). See Salerno 1961, p. 188 for extracts from the documents for the work done in 1739-40.
9. See Röttgen 2002, p. 204, and the essay by M. C. Guardata in Strinati & Vodret 2001, pp. 129-144
10. Hibbard 1971, p. 216
11. Ibid

Palazzo Chigi (Odescalchi)

Ferrerio, II, pl. 15; Falda 1665, I, pls. 14, 15 and IV, pl. 26; Vasi, pl. 64; Tessin, p. 176; Magni, II, pls. 52, 53; Zocca, M., in Salerno 1961, p. 243; Hibbard 1971, pp. 78, 213; Schiavo 1956, pp. 239-274; Wittkower 1973, p. 122; Waddy 1990, pp. 291-320; Metzger Habel, pp. 199-216; GR II, 8, p. 65; Blunt *Guide*, p. 172

1. Hibbard 1971, pp. 78, 213
2. Cavazzini 2008, pp. 57 & 58, and ills. 59-61
3. See Waddy 1990, pp. 304-310 for a detailed analysis of the palace's layout at this time and Metzger Habel, pp. 140-216 for a full account of the several schemes that were pursued by the Chigi.
4. Waddy 1990, pp. 317-318
5. For a trenchant analysis of the building's power see Wittkower 1973, pp. 122-123
6. The asymmetrical extension already appears in Piranesi's *Vedute di Roma* print of 1753 (Hind 26). Piranesi's *Varie Vedute* print of the palace, done

a very few years earlie, shows the central pavilion as extended by the Odescalchi, but the northern wing as only three bays.

Palazzo Cimarra

Golzio, p. 123; Elling, p. 277 and pl. 97; Connors 1989a, pp. 222, 223 and n. 37; GR I, 3, p.152; Blunt *Guide*, p. 173

1. Blunt *Guide*, p. 173
2. Connors 1989a, p. 223 and n. 37. The relevant document is ASR, Pres. delle strade, b. 50, p. 121r.

Palazzo del Cinque

Magni, II, pl. 110; Portoghesi 1966, pls. 304, 305; Mallory 1977, fig. 50; Elling, pl. 120; Bevilacqua, M., 1987, 'Un palazzo-condominio nella Roma di Benedetto XIV' in Debenedetti 1987, pp. 99-107; Curcio 1989, pp. 176-179; GR III, 2, p. 74; Blunt *Guide*, p. 173

1. Bevilacqua 1987, p. 99 and Curcio 1989, pp. 176-179

Palazzo Colonna

Vasi, pl. 63; Tessin, p. 175; De Brosses, II, p. 95; Magni, pls. 88-90; Pollak 1909, p. 135; Lavagnino, E., 1942, 'Palazzo Colonna e l'architetto romano Niccolò Michetti', *Capitolium*, XX, pp. 139ff; Agosteo, A. and Pasquini, A., 1959, *Il Palazzo della Consulta nell'arte e nella storia*, Rome; Golzio, figs. 99ff; Bandes, S., 1981, 'Gaspard Dughet's frescoes in Palazzo Colonna, Rome', *Burlington Magazine*, 123, pp. 77-88; Safarik, E. A., ed., 1999, *Palazzo Colonna*, Rome; Strunck, C., 2002, 'Le chef-d'oeuvre inconnu du Bernin: la galerie Colonna à Rome' in *Le Bernin et l'Europe: du baroque triomphant à l'âge romantique*, Paris, pp. 391-409; id., 2007, *Berninis unbekanntes Meisterwerk. Die Galleria Colonna in Rom und die Kunstpatronage des römischen Uradels*, Munich; Roettgen 2007, pp. 224-245; GR II, 8, p. 38; Blunt *Guide*, p. 174

1. Blunt notes that del Grande's drawing for the façade in the Kunstbibliotheck, Berlin was published by S. Jacob (*Italienischer Zeichnungen de Kunstbibliothek, Berlin*, Berlin, 1975, no. 365) who compares this façade stylistically with one built by the same architect for the Colonna palace at Paliano. (Blunt *Guide*, p. 174)
2. Bandes 1981, p. 78. Safarik 1999 does provide useful illustrations of the Dughet and Tempesta frescoes, and much else.
3. Pacia, A., 'Esotismo, cultura archeologica e paessaggio negli affreschi di Palazzo Colonna' in Debenedetti 1987, p. 129. For a useful discussion of all the recent scholarship, and for fine illustrations of all the frescoes noted here, see Roettgen 2007.
4. Roettgen 2007, p. 231

Palazzo della Consulta

Vasi, pl. 61; Letarouilly, pls. 29, 30, 57; Pane, p. 28, figs. 17-25; Magni, II, pls. 92-97; Matthiae, p. 70; Elling, pl. 88; Portoghesi 1966, pls. 428, 429; Borsi, F. et al., 1974, *Palazzo della Consulta*, Rome; Kieven 1988, pp. 43-47; id., 2000, p. 540; Brunetti, O., 2001, 'Fuga e i Corsini' in A. Gambardella, ed., 2001, *Ferdinando Fuga 1699-1999, Roma, Napoli, Palermo*, Naples, pp. 127-134; Nevola & Palmer passim; GR I, 4, p. 120; Blunt *Guide*, p. 175.

1. Nevola & Palmer, p. 85; Agosteo & Pasquini, p. 33; Borsi 1974, p. 208
2. See Nevola & Palmer, p. 67 for quotations of admiring comments by Rossini (in *Mercurio errante*, 1741) and Roisecco (in *Roma antica e moderna*, 1750).
3. See pp. 219-220 of Morelli's essay in Borsi 1974 for a detailed analysis of the Florentine elements in the windows and various other parts of the Consulta façade.
4. The early and final drawings are printed in Agosteo & Pasquini opposite p. 38; Borsi 1974, p.110 and Nevola & Palmer, p. 116.
5. These figures were attributed to Maini by a contemporary journalist, but the documentation for Della Valle's authorship (published in Nevola & Palmer, p. 133) is conclusive. Palmer usefully analyses the whole issue of the palace's expanded sculpture programme in pp. 132-136 of that book.

Houses at Piazza delle Coppelle, 64 and 66

Zocca 1927, I, pl. 131; Lombardi 1992, p. 363; GR VIII, 4, p. 108; Blunt *Guide*, p. 200

Palazzo Corsini (Riario)

Tessin; p. 182; Vasi, pl. 72; Percier & Fontaine, IV, pls. 84, 85; Letarouilly, pl. 192; Magni, II, pls. 99, 100; Pane, p. 58, figs. 39-6; Matthiae, p. 73; Golzio, figs. 107-10; Borsellino, E., 1981, 'Il Cardinale Neri Corsini mecenate e committente. Guglielmi, Parrocel, Conca e Meucci nella Biblioteca Corsiniana', *Bollettino d'arte*, (66), pp. 49-66; id., 1988, *Palazzo Corsini alla Lungara: storia di un cantiere*, Fasano; id., 1987, 'La decorazioni settecentesche di palazzo Corsini alla Lungara' in Debenedetti 1987, pp. 181-196; Acidini Luchinat, II, p. 143; Belardi, G., ed. 2001, *Palazzo Corsini alla Lungara: analisi di un restauro*, Savigliano; Palmer, V. in Nevola & Palmer, pp. 54, 55; GR XIII, 3, p. 70; Blunt *Guide*, p. 176

1. Borsellino 1988, p. 14
2. Blunt *Guide*, p. 176
3. Acidini Luchinat, II, p. 143
4. The grotesques were repainted and four of the repeated Riario devices were replaced by those of the Corsini by Ginesio del Barba in 1737-38 (Borsellino 1987, pp. 181-2).
5. Borsellino 1981 and id.1987, p. 186
6. Borsellino 1987, pp. 186-190
7. Ibid., p. 188

Palazzo Costaguti

Baglione, p. 166; Mola, p. 129; Titi, p. 90; Martinelli 1969, p. 240; Letarouilly, pl. 22; Lotti, L., 1961, *I Costaguti e il loro palazzo di Piazza Mattei in Roma*, Rome; GR XI, p. 56; Blunt *Guide*, p. 177

For Domenichino
Spear 1982, pp. 233-235

For Guercino
Salerno 1988, p. 157; Mahon, D. in Mahon 1968, p. 183; id. in Mahon 1991, pp. 143-144

For Mola
Tantillo, A. 1989 in M. Kahn-Rossi, ed., 1989, *Pier Francesco Mola: 1612-1666*. Milan, p. 205

For Lanfranco
Schleier, E., 'Note sul percorso artistico di Giovanni Lanfranco' in Schleier 2001, pp. 27-52, pl. 27

For Romanelli
Faldi, p. 70, ill. 265; Barroero, L., 1997, 'Giovanni Francesco Romanelli' in Lo Bianco, pp. 184-185 and ill. 147

For Tassi
Pedrocchi, A. M., 2008, 'Agostino Tassi per Monsignor Costanzo Patrizi' in Cavazzini 2008, pp. 151-168

For Dughet
Boisclair 1986, pp. 52, 53, 70

1. Many of the published descriptions of the Costaguti palace (including Lotti's 1961 monograph) are manifestly unreliable. I have found that the clearest and best documented account of the Patrizi period is Pedrocchi's 2008 essay on Tassi's involvement, and I have generally followed it here.
2. Baglione, p. 166; Pedrocchi 2008, p. 151. As explained in the present entry, it appears that none of Lambardi's work on the exterior of the palace has survived.
3. Passeri, pp. 104-105; Pedrocchi 2008, p. 151
4. Mola, p. 129
5. Carpaneto, p. 189
6. Acidini Luchinat, I, p. 135; Röttgen 2002, p. 522
7. Titi 1763, p. 91
8. Thus Pedrocchi 2008, p. 153. Röttgen agrees with Allegrini's authorship of *The Hours*, but dates it to 1624-26, which is problematic as it is the period between Costanzo's death and the Patrizi family moving out (Röttgen 2002, p. 536). Röttgen makes no mention of *Venus Arming Æneas*, even to reject it.
9. Cavazzini follows Schleier in suggesting that the quadratura in the Lanfranco room may be by Lanfranco himself, as it is simpler than that in the other rooms of the group but Pedrocchi does not follow that suggestion (Cavazzini 2008, p. 56 and Pedrocchi 2008, pp. 159,160 respectively). On the dating of the Lanfranco room, Pedrocchi's demonstration that it must have been commissioned by Costanzo Patrizi appears conclusive.
10. Cavazzini, ibid.; Pedrocchi 2008, pp. 153, 155
11. Pedrocchi 2008, pp. 159-161, ills. 165-167. Schleier 2001 (p. 42) considers that the painting was done in 1624-1626 for Monsignor Giovanni Battista Costaguti, but Pedrocchi (p. 160) explains why that cannot be right.
12 Pedrocchi 2008, pp. 156-159, ills. 163, 164. Cavazzini suggests that Filippo Franchini is the likeliest member of Tassi's workshop to have done the surround for the Rinaldo and Armida (Cavazzini 1997, p. 406). On the precise dating, while it is known that the Ludovisi *Aurora* was painted in 1622, the dates of the Patrizi and Lancellotti ceilings are not documented within the two years for which Guercino remained in Rome. Mahon believed, however, that Guercino could have completed the *Rinaldo and Armida* between arriving in Rome and starting work on the Aurora. (Mahon 1991, pp. 143-144). Certainly, the whole scheme does look like a dry-run for the great masterpiece in the Ludovisi casino.
13. Pedrocchi 2008, p. 163. For a general discussion of the ceiling see Pedrocchi, pp. 161-165 and ills. 168, 169.
14. Spear 1982, p. 233
15. Schleier 2001, p. 45
16. There is a preparatory drawing at Windsor. See Whitaker & Clayton, eds., 2007: *The Art of Italy in the Royal Collection: Renaissance and Baroque*, London, pp. 364-5.
17. Barroero 1997, p. 184
18. Boisclair 1986, p. 330. Röttgen, however, suggests a collaboration between Allegrini and Dughet (Röttgen 2002, p. 546.)

Palazzo Crescenzi (Bonelli, De Dominicis)

Baglione, pp. 364-7; Ferrerio, II, pls. 16, 17; Falda 1665, II, pl. 3; De Rossi, I, pls. 128-130; Mola, p.127; Martinelli 1969, p. 241; Titi, p. 184; Toesca, I., 1957b, 'Pomarancio a palazzo Crescenzi', *Paragone*, 8 (91), pp. 41-45; id., 1968, *Paragone*, 19 (221), p. 48; Roethlisberger 1961, pp. 89, 91; id., 1959, p. 41; id., 1969, *Paragone*, 20 (233), p. 54; Donadono, L. et al, 2005, *Il Palazzo Crescenzi alla Rotonda*, Rome; GR VIII, 4, p. 122; Blunt *Guide*, p. 177

1. Donadono 2005 not only describes the recent restoration project, but contains an essay by Marco Pupillo (pp. 15-33) that gives the first properly documented account of the palace's 16th and 17th century history.
2. Virgilio's relative Ottaviano Crescenzi employed Della Porta on what is now the Palazzo Serlupi Crescenzi during the same period.
3. See the 19th century architects' drawings reproduced in Donadono 2005, p. 38. The drawing of the via della Rotonda façade shows no indication of decorative windows on the model of those on the north side, though Vasi's plate clearly shows that these were carried round the corner for four bays. It is hard to explain this discrepancy.
4. Pupillo in Donadono 2005, p. 19
5. Id, pp. 21-23
6. Donadono, L. in Donadono 2005, p. 35. Three bays were evidently cut from the left of the Salita de' Crescenzi façade, but then the intervals were juggled so as to end up with five bays altogether.
7. Though the Crescenzi crescents on the pedestals below the original windows on Salita de' Crescenzi are included on the side facing the Pantheon but omitted on the (very slightly

earlier) via S Eustachio side.
8. Illustration, Donadono 2005, p. 38
9. Donadono, L. in Donadono 2005, p. 35

Palazzo Donarelli (Ricci)

Tafuri, M., in Salerno 1973, pp. 284-288; GR V, 4, p. 46; Blunt *Guide*, p. 178
1. Tafuri in Salerno 1973, pp. 284-288

Palazzo Doria-Pamphili

Falda 1665, I, pl. 38 and IV, pl. 21; id., 1691, III, pl. 20; De Brosses, II, p. 106; Vasi, pls. 39, 44, 66; Letarouilly, pls. 59, 60, 67; Magni, II, pls. 80-87; Colosanti, pls. 184ff; Ferrari, pls. 160ff; Pollak 1909, p. 142; Salerno 1961, p. 250; Portoghesi 1966, pls. 368-372; Frommel 1973, II, p. 88; Wittkower 1973, p. 188; Carandente, G., 1975, *Il Palazzo Doria Pamphilj*, Milan; Mallory 1977, p. 107; Krautheimer 1985, pp. 77, 85; Rodolfo, A., 1995, 'Palazzo Doria-Pamphili a via del Plebiscito', in Debenedetti 1995, pp. 313-327; De Marchi, A.G., ed., 1999, *Il Palazzo Doria Pamphilj al Corso e le sue collezioni*, Florence; Metzger Habel, pp. 222-232; Robertson, pp, 184, 185; GR IX, 3, p. 56; Blunt *Guide*, p. 178
1. For an illustration see Salerno 1961, pl. 291
2. See Krautheimer 1985, pp. 77, 85 and Metzger Habel, pp. 222-232
3. Metzger Habel, pp. 227-228
4. Ibid., pp. 231-232
5. Portoghesi 1966, p. 376 has a factual account of the façade.
6. On everything to do with Ameli's wing see Rodolfo 1995.

Palazzo del Drago (Gentili)

Callari, p. 451; Elling, p. 282, pl. 105; Lombardi 1992, p. 98; Portoghesi 1966, pl. 306; GR II, 5, p. 18; Blunt *Guide*, p. 178
1. Blunt *Guide*, p. 178

Casa del Falco (Casa di Biagio Puccini)

Portoghesi 1966, pl. 308; Lombardi 1992, p. 521; Zanella, A., 1995, 'La casa di Biagio Puccini in via del Falco', in Debenedetti 1995, pp. 353-362; GR XIV, 4, p. 66
1. In the National Museum, Stockholm, inv. 3052/1863. The drawing represents Puccini in the guise of an architect, with various arcane attributes as well as the depiction of his projected building.
2. Zanella 1995, p. 357. Fabio Barry, however, sees no need to postulate any such professional intervention (*Journal of the Society of Architectural Historians*, 55, 2, June 1996, p. 214).

Palazzo Falconieri

Ferrerio, II, pls. 30-33; Vasi, pls. 87, 88; Hempel, p. 51; Battisti, pp. 242, 243; Pollak, O., 1911, 'Die Decken des Palazzo Falconieri in Rom und Zeichnungen von Boromini in der Wiener Hofbibliothek', *Jahrbuch des Kunsthistorischen Institutes*, 5, pp. 111-141; Portoghesi 1966, pls. 1, 122-124; Wittkower 1973, p. 148; Salerno 1973, pp. 445-459, pl. III, ill. 45; Howard, E. G., 1981, *The Falconieri Palace in Rome: The Role of Borromini in its Reconstruction (1646-1649)*, New York; Connors, J., in Bösel & Frommel, I, p. 15; Thelen, H., in ibid., II, pp. 202-203; Sladek, E., 2000, 'L'architettura dei palazzi di Borromini', in Frommel & Sladek, pp. 86-97; GR VII, 3, pp. 42-55; Blunt *Guide*, p. 180
1. For this and the Falconieri family's first occupation of the palace see Thelen in Bösel & Frommel, II, p. 202.
2. Howard 1981, p. 110
3. Blunt *Guide*, p. 180
4. Wittkower 1973, p. 148
5. See Thelen 2000, p. 203 and Howard 1981, pp. 103-104.
6. See Portoghesi 1982, ill. 119
7. One of these shows the orb of the world supporting a sceptre that is interlaced with a wreath and a snake eating its own tail, and surmounted by a radiant eye; the other shows three interlaced wreaths with a radiant sun at the centre. For illustrations see Portoghesi 1966, pls. 122-124. Much of Howard's text is devoted to decoding these images and tracing their roots in 16th century emblem books.

Palazzo Farnese

Tessin, p.186; Letarouilly, pls. 115-139; Ackerman, J., 1961, *The Architecture of Michelangelo*, London, pp. 75ff; Frommel 1973, II, p. 103; Uginet, F., ed., 1980, *Le Palais Farnèse*, Rome; Dempsey, C., 1968, '"Et nos cadamus amori": Observations on the Farnese Gallery', *Art Bulletin*, 50 (4), pp. 363-374; id., 1995, *Annibale Carracci: The Farnese Gallery, Rome*, New York; Posner, I, pp. 93-108, 123-125; Barry, F., 1999, '"Pray to thy Father which is in secret": the tradition of coretti, romitorii and Lanfranco's hermit cycle at the Palazzo Farnese' in J. Imorde, ed., 1999, *Barocke Inszenierung*, Emsdetten, pp. 190-221; Witte, A. A., 2008, *The Artful Hermitage: The Palazzetto Farnese as a Counter-Reformation Diæta*, Rome; Robertson, pp. 97-181; GR VII, 2, p. 56; Blunt *Guide*, p. 180
1. Witte 2008, p. 12
2. Dempsey has pointed out that Cardinal Odoardo shared the palace with Duke Ranuccio and other members of the family, so that it is not safe to assume that the Galleria commission was entirely personal to himself. (Dempsey 1968, p. 372)
3. Witte 2008 is focused on the devotional aspect of the programme of imagery in the Camerino degli Eremiti and the Palazzetto Farnese. Barry 1999 takes a more general look at romitori and aristocratic chambers attached to churches.

Palazzo Ferrini (Cini)

Baglione, p. 156; Pascoli, II, p. 514; Martinelli 1969, p. 243; Elling, pl. 94; Lombardi 1992, p. 117; GR III, 2, p. 18; Blunt *Guide*, p. 181
1. This is according to Nolli (GR, III, 2, p.18). Blunt does not give any authority for his statement (Blunt *Guide*, p.181) that the palace was occupied by nuns from S Maria in Aquiro.

Ferrini's fortified palace at Calvi was handed over to Ursuline nuns for whom Fuga eventually designed new buildings in the 1740s. It has been asserted that Fuga worked on the Roman palace in the same period, but that could represent some confusion with the documented work at Calvi. (Those wishing to pursue the Calvi connection should consult Elizabeth Kieven's article 'Ferdinando Fuga a Calvi dell'Umbria' in *Monasterium Ursulinarum Terre Carbij: il monastero di Calvi dell'Umbria nelle carte d'archivio*, Città di Castello, 2003.)

Palazzo Galloppi (Santovetti, Volpi di Misurato)

Torselli, p. 311, Portoghesi 1966, p. 340; Mallory 1977, pp. 8-9; Connors & Rice, p.171; GR II, 1, p. 226; Blunt *Guide*, p. 181

1. See Connors & Rice, p. 171
2. See the discussion of this in Mallory 1977, pp. 8-9
3. Portoghesi 1966, p. 361

Palazzo Gambirasi

Falda 1665, 1, pl. 26; De Rossi, I, pl. 114; Spagnesi 1964, pp. 80-82; Krautheimer 1985, pp. 47-53; Roca De Amicis, A., 2001, 'Palazzo Gambirasi e Piazza della Pace: storia edilizia di un connubio difficile', *Palladio*, n. s. 13 (25), pp. 19-38; id., 2002, 'Palazzo Gambirasi e Piazza della Pace: la formazione complessa di un isolato nella Roma di Alessandro VII' in Caperna & Spagnesi, pp. 475-482; Metzger Habel, pp. 121, 292, 361, 393; Lombardi 1992, p. 222; id., 1996, p. 170; GR V, 2, p. 42; Blunt *Guide*, p. 181

1. The interaction of the demands of Alexander VII's *teatro*, the Chapter of S Maria della Pace, and the Gambirasi family is the subject of Roca de Amicis's two articles of 2001 and 2002, on which the present entry relies extensively.
2. Metzger Habel, p. 393
3. Spagnesi 1964, p. 82
4. Blunt noted that the second floor windows were unlike De Rossi's normal style, and he commented that they 'may be based on designs by Cortona to whom De Rossi ascribes them' (Blunt *Guide*, p. 181). But Domenico De Rossi ascribed all the windows of the palace to Cortona – including the very un-Cortonian windows of the piano nobile – so his testimony is of doubtful value. In truth, the clumsy format used on the second floor hardly looks worthy of De Rossi, let alone Cortona.
5. See the photographs in Roca de Amicis 2001

Palazzo Ghetti

Ghetti, F. M. A., 1973, 'La domus magna della famiglia Ghetti in via dei Giubbonari', *Lunario romano* (2), pp. 19-55; Lombardi 1992, p. 257; GR VI, 2, p. 168

1. Ghetti 1973, pp. 43-47

Palazzo Giangiacomo
and
House at via Monserrato, 102

Lombardi 1992, p. 335; GR VII, 2, p. 44; Blunt *Guide*, p. 181

Casa Giannini

Elling, p. 418, pl. 169; Bevilacqua, M., 1989, 'Casa Giannini a piazza Capranica e la tipologia, del palazzo ad appartamenti nella Roma di metà '700' in Debenedetti 1989, pp. 205-219; GR III, 2, p. 50; Blunt *Guide*, p. 243

1. Bevilacqua 1985, p. 208
2. Ibid.

Palazzo Giustiniani

Baglione, p. 130; Ferrerio, II, pls. 40, 41; Falda 1665, IV, pl. 41; Martinelli 1969, p. 243; Mola, p. 124; De Rossi, I, pls. 102, 103; Tessin, p. 174; De Brosses, II, p. 115; Percier & Fontaine, IV, pl. 21; Magni, II, pl. 27; Letarouilly, pl. 340; Hibbard 1971, p. 114; Toesca, I., 1957a, 'Note sulla storia del Palazzo Giustiniani a San Luigi dei Francesi', *Bollettino d'arte*, (4. Ser. 42.), pp. 296-308; Borsi, F. et al., 1989, *I Palazzi del Senato: Palazzo Giustiniani*, Rome; Connors, J., in Bösel & Frommel, I, p. 15; Sladek, E., in ibid., II, p. 200; Strunck, C., 2001, in Danesi Squarzina, pp. 105-111; Danesi Squarzina, S., 2001, in ibid., p. 19; Vogtherr, C. M., 2001, in ibid., pp. 139-150; GR VIII, 4, p. 54; Blunt *Guide*, p. 182

1. See Vogtherr 2001, pp. 105-111
2. See Sladek 2000
3. The old photographs reproduced in Borsi et al. 1989, pp. 60-61, show a ceiling sculpted like some of those in Palazzo Falconieri and a fancy arch with splendid Giustiniani emblems.
4. For the dating of the frescoes see Magnanami, in Borsi et al. 1989, pp. 107-118. Danesi Squarzina 2001, p. 19, states that the Giustiniani had been living in the palace for a year before they formally purchased it in 1590. The family may have influenced the iconography of the decoration even while the palace was still owned by Monsignor Vento.
5. See Strunck 2001, pp. 105-111

Palazzo Gomez (Lepri, Gallo di Roccagiovine, Silj)

Pascoli, I, p. 317; Spagnesi 1964, p. 162; Carbonara Pompei, S., 1998, 'La residenza patrizia minore alla fine del Seicento: palazzo Gomez Homen in via della Croce' in Debenedetti 1998, pp. 61-79; GR IV, 4, p. 48; Blunt *Guide*, p. 182

1. See Carbonara Pompei, pp. 61-62

Palazzo Grazioli (Gottifredi)

Ferrerio, II, pl. 51; Falda 1665, I, pl. 16; De Rossi, I, pl. 174; Titi, p. 483; Portoghesi 1966, pls. 238, 241; Krautheimer 1985, p. 30; Connors 1989a, pp. 229-230; Metzger Habel, pp.128-139; GR IX, 1, p. 72; Blunt *Guide*, p. 182

1. Metzger Habel, p. 363, n. 110
2. See Metzger Habel, pp. 128-139 for an account of Gottifredi's transactions and for an analysis of the palace's architecture.

Palazzo del Grillo (de Robilant)

Vasi, pl. 150; De Rossi, I, pls. 140, 141; Visentini, p. 40; Magni, II, pls. 108, 109 and III, pls. 26, 27; Ferrari, pls. CLII-CLXII; Portoghesi 1966, pls. 350, 351; Elling, p. 435, pls. 178, 179; Fasolo, F., 1960, *L'opera di Hieronimo e Carlo Rainaldi (1570-1655 e 1611-1691)*, Rome, pp. 251-252; Asche, S., 1978, *Balthasar Permoser: Leben Und Werk*, Berlin, pp. 21-24, 145, ills. 17-18; Lombardi 1992, p. 36; Ferrari & Papaldo, p. 422; GR I, 3, p. 48; Blunt *Guide*, p. 178

1. Blunt *Guide*, p. 178; Visentini, p. 40.
2. Fasolo 1953, p. 251-252; Blunt *Guide*, p. 178.
3. For general photographs of the garden see Elling, pls. 178, 179.
4. For a photograph of the fountain see Ferrari & Papaldo, p. 422.
5. Asche 1978, pp. 14, 21-24, and ills. 17-18. Asche also suggests that the stuccoes in the 'grotte' of the garden are probably by Permoser.
6. For a photograph of the door see Ferrari & Papaldo 1999, p. 422. The name of Carlo Rainaldi is often loosely associated with the del Grillo garden ornaments, but there is no evidence to support that beyond the very broad relationship between the del Grillo fountain and those of the Palazzo Borghese.
7. For photographs of the interior stuccoes see Ferrari, CLII–CLXII, and Portoghesi 1966, pls. 350, 351.

Palazzo Guelfi Camajani (Montauto, Rovarella, Polidori, Pericoli)

Salerno 1961, p. 209; Carpaneto, p. 270; Lombardi 1992, p. 114; GR III, 1, p. 22

1. Carpaneto 1993, p. 271

Palazzo Lancellotti

Baglione, p. 48; Ferrerio, II, pls. 48, 49; Martinelli 1969, p. 244; Visentini, p. 43; De Rossi, I, pl. 132; Vasi, pl. 108; Titi, p. 407; Hibbard 1971, p. 123; Spear 1982, pp. 96-97; Cavazzini, P., 1998, *Palazzo Lancellotti ai Coronari: Cantiere di Agostino Tassi*, Rome; id., 2008, 'La Vita e le Opere di Agostino Tassi' in Cavazzini 2008, pp. 50-56, 60-62; GR V, 2, p.12; Blunt *Guide*, p. 182

1. Cavazzini 1998 is the definitive monograph on the Palazzo Lancellotti, and I rely on it heavily, especially for the Lancellotti family background and for the remarkable fresco schemes, for which I follow Cavazzini's proposed datings. Similar material on Tassi's involvement, with useful illustrations, is in Cavazzini 2008.
2. See Spear 1982, pp. 96-97 and Cavazzini 1998, p. 26
3. Visentini, p. 43
4. All the dates in this paragraph are from Cavazzini 1998. For the Sala dei Palafrenieri and Claude see Cavazzini 1998, pp. 47, 50.
5. Such precocity would have been even more remarkable if Claude was really born in 1604/5 rather than 1600, as suggested by the documents published by Sylvestre. (Sylvestre, M., 1982: 'Claude Gelée entre Chamagne et Rome: nouveaux documents sur le peintre et sa famille d'apres les archives lorraines', *Mélanges de l'Ecole Française de Rome* (94), 929-947).

Palazzo Lante (Medici, Lante Della Rovere, Grazioli, Aldobrandini)

Marcucci, L. & Torresi, B., 1982, 'Palazzo Medici-Lante: un progetto mediceo in Roma e il "riaggiustamento" di Onorio Longhi', *Storia Architettura*, 2, pp. 39-50; Frommel, C. L., 1986, 'Papal Policy: The Planning of Rome during the Renaissance', *Journal of Interdisciplinary History*, (17), 1, pp. 56-58; Lombardi 1992, p. 369; Meccoli, M., 2003, 'Il salone dipinto di Palazzo Lante alla Sapienza', in Cappelletti 2003, pp. 187-200; GR VIII, 3, p.102; Blunt *Guide*, p. 182

1. The work to link the two buildings was licensed in 1628 (Lombardi 1992).

Palazzo Lateranense

Ferrerio, I, pl. 10; De Brosses, II, p. 321; Letarouilly, II, pl. 223; Magni, II, pls. 22-5; Schiavo, B. A., 1969, *Il Laterano: Palazzo e Battistero*, Rome; Pietrangeli, C., ed., 1991, *Il Palazzo Apostolico Lateranense*, Florence; Mandel, C., 1994, *Sixtus V and the Lateran Palace*, Rome; Cappelletti 2006, pp. 74-82; GR I, 1, p. 60; Blunt *Guide*, p. 183

1. The cycle is fully described in Mandel 1994.

Palazzo Lazzaroni (Grimaldi)

Letarouilly, pl. 54; Callari 1944, p. 447; Carpaneto, p. 267; Lombardi 1992, p. 85. GR II, 2, p. 112; Blunt *Guide*, p. 183

1. The 1853 changes were made by G. Morichini for the then owner, Benedetto Fillipani. This information, together with all other historical facts in the present entry, is from the GR account, on which both Lombardi and Carpaneto evidently rely. The GR description asserts that the palace took shape in the 17th century and that the present building is most likely due to Cardinal Grimaldi. These propositions are persuasive, as a general indication, but it is not known how much of the building was finished during the cardinal's lifetime.
2. These drawings are reproduced at GR, II, 2, p. 113.

Palazzetto Lupardi ('Casa dei Ritratti')

Zocca, I, pl. 102; Noya, C., 1994, 'Palazzetto Lupardi in via del Governo Vecchio' in Debenedetti 1994, pp. 263-273; GR VI, 1, pl. 102; Blunt *Guide*, p. 200

1. Noya 1994, p. 264
2. Ibid., p. 265
3. Ibid.
4. For an illustration of the upper window see Portoghesi 1966, pl. 302.
5. Noya 1994, pp. 264, 268

Palazzo Maccarani Odescalchi

Letarouilly, pl. 48; Lombardi 1992, p. 422; Carpaneto, p. 290; GR III, 1, p. 36

1. Reproduced in Carpaneto, p. 290

Palazzo Maccarani Savorgnan di Brazzà

Lombardi 1992, p. 85; Carpaneto, p. 292; GR II, 2, p. 142

Palazzo Macchi di Cellere (Capranica)

Lombardi 1992, p.123; Curcio, G., 1989, 'L'area di Montecitorio: la città pubblica e la città privata nella Roma della prima metà del Settecento' in Debenedetti 1989, pp. 157-204; Debenedetti, E., 1998, 'Le case della piazza e dell'antipiazza di Montecitorio: immagine pubblica e proprietà pri-vata', in Debenedetti 1998, pp. 11-35; GR III, 2, p. 76; Blunt *Guide*, p. 183

1. Curcio 1989 gives a very detailed account of the development of the piazza and its relation to other nearby projects such as that at Piazza di Pietra. Debenedetti 1998 rehearses the facts more briefly as background to a study of the social aspects of the development.
2. Curcio, op. cit., p. 160; Debenedetti, op. cit., p. 12
3. Curcio, op. cit., p. 173; Debenedetti, op. cit., p. 14
4. Curcio, op. cit., p. 174; Debenedetti, op. cit., p. 15
5. Lombardi 1992, p. 123

Palazzo Madama

Ferrerio, I, pls. 11, 12; Falda 1665, IV, pl. 10; Martinelli 1969, p. 293; Mola, p. 131; De Brosses, II, p. 115; Vasi, pl. 70; Magni, II, pls. 28-32; Portoghesi 1966, pls. 240-242; Connors 1980, pp. 107-112; id., 1989b, p. 81; Borsi, F., et al., 1994, *La Facciata di Palazzo Madama*, Rome; GR VIII, 2, p. 72; Blunt *Guide*, p. 183

1. A drawing of the old façade is reproduced in Borsi et al. 1994, p. 9.
2. See Connors 1980, pp. 107-112, for an account of Maruscelli which concludes that the architect was 'a programmatic copyist' whose quotations were 'too literal to reflect a coherent personal style'. For Connors's comments on the Palazzo Madama's influence on Camillo Arcucci, and the existence of a sumptuous, traditionalist strain of palace architecture in the 17th century, see the present entry on the Palazzo Pio di Savoia da Carpi.
3. Milizia, F., 1781: *Memorie degli architetti antichi e moderne*, Parma, p. 164; Wittkower 1973, p. 370, n. 37

Casa di Carlo Maderno

Hibbard 1971, p. 208; Donati 1942, fig. 137; GR V, 3, p. 50; Blunt *Guide*, p. 245

Palazzo Maffei (Peretti, Sannesi, Ludovisi, d'Este, Acciaioli, Marescotti, del Vicariato)

Baglione, p. 81; Ferrerio, II, pls. 20, 21; Totti 1638, p.388; Martinelli 1969, p. 245; Mola, p. 129; Roisecco, 1750, I, p. 530; Vasi, pl. 77; Titi, p. 358; Magni, II, pl. 72; Hibbard 1971, p. 25; Wasserman 1966, p. 111; Bedon, A., 1988, 'I Maffei e il loro palazzo in via della Pigna', *Quaderni dell'Istituto di Storia dell'Architettura*, (n. s. 12), pp. 45-64; GR IX, 2, p. 104; Blunt *Guide*, p. 183

Palazzo Magnani

Lombardi 1992, p. 128; GR III, 2, p. 116; Blunt *Guide*, p. 184

Palazzo Malta (del Sovrano Ordine Militare Gerosolomitano di Malta etc)

Lombardi 1992; p. 167; Carpaneto, p. 299; GR IV, 7, p. 95

Palazzo Mancini (Salviati)

Falda 1665, IV, pl. 40; Vasi, pl. 170; Salerno 1961, pp. 244-246; Schiavo, A., 1969, *Palazzo Mancini*, Rome; Russell 1997; GR II, 7, p. 69; Blunt *Guide*, p. 184

1. e.g. by Lalande, III, p. 593; Elling, p. 277; Salerno 1961, p. 245
2. It is illustrated in Salerno 1961, p. 279.
3. Russell 1997, p. 177

Palazzo Mandosi (Castelli-Mignanelli)

Carpaneto, p. 300; Lombardi 1992, p. 327; GR VII, 2, p. 90

Palazzo Manfroni

Lombardi 1992, p. 164; GR IV, 7, p. 86

Palazzo Marescotti

Lombardi 1992, p. 126; Romano, P., 1940, *Strade e Piazze di Roma*, Rome, pp. 77-80; GR III, 2, p. 106

Palazzo Maruscelli (Lepri)

Portoghesi 1966, p. 340; Bentivoglio, E. 1989, 'Palazzo Marucelli a Roma', in Debenedetti 1989, pp. 15-32; GR IV, 7, p. 103

Palazzo Massimo di Rignano (Colonna)

Falda 1691, III, pl. 27; Coudenhove-Erthal, p. 57; Lombardi 1992, p. 419; Carpaneto, p. 319; GR X, 1, p. 22; Blunt *Guide*, p. 185

1. Carpaneto, p. 319
2. Pascoli, I, p. 545

Palazzo Mastrozzi (Graziosi)

Vasi, pl. 111; Elling, p. 311, pl. 118; Blunt, A., 1958a, *Philibert De l'Orme*, London, pp. 118-122; Lombardi 1992, p. 334; GR VII, 2, p. 44; Blunt *Guide*, p. 185

1. John Ward Perkins's opinion, quoted in Blunt 1958a, n. p. 120-21.

Palazzo Mattei di Giove

Ferrerio, II, pl. 42; Falda 1665, IV, pl. 43; Vasi, pl. 78; Letarouilly, pls. 107, 108, 165, 166; Magni, II, pls. 33-5; Colosanti, pls. 171ff.; Panofsky-Soergel, G., 1967, 'Zur Geschichte des Palazzo Mattei di Giove', *Römisches Jahrbuch für Kunstgeschichte*, 11, pp. 111-188; Hibbard 1971, p. 127; Briganti 1962b, p. 160; Hess, J., 1954,'Tassi, Bonzi e Cortona a Palazzo Mattei', *Commentari*, 5, pp. 303-315; Borea, E., ed. 1965, *Domenichino*, Milan, p. 163; Spear 1982, pp. 146-7; Puglisi, pp. 7, 8, 119-121; Merz, J. G., in Lo Bianco, pp. 61-62; Cappelletti, F., 1992, 'La committenza di Asdru-bale Mattei e la creazione della Galleria nel Palazzo Mattei di Giove a Roma', *Storia dell'Arte*, 76, pp. 256-295; GR XI, 1, p. 76; Blunt *Guide*, p. 185

1. Hibbard 1971, p. 128
2. Blunt *Guide*, p. 186
3. Spear 1982, pp. 146-147; Puglisi, pp. 7, 8, 119-121

Palazzo Mellini (Cesi, Salviati, Michiel)

Vasi, pl. 133; Elling, p. 310, pl. 119; Bocca, A., in Salerno 1961, pp. 219-222; Wittkower 1973, p. 189; Hibbard 1971, pp. 206-207; Carbonara Pompei, S., 1995, 'L'architettura "temperata" di Tommaso de Marchis' in Debenedetti 1995, pp. 61-75; Curcio, G., 2002, 'Da città a metropoli: la nuova edilizia del settecento' in G. Cicucci, ed., 2002, *Roma Moderna*, IV, Rome and Bari, pp. 245-273; Lombardi 1992, p. 521; GR II, 7, p. 40; Blunt *Guide*, p. 186

1. Curcio 2002, p. 267
2. For example, Wittkower 1973, p. 189 and Carbonara Pompei 1995, p. 62.

Casa dei Merolli (Partini)

Randolfi, R., 1998, 'La palazzina dei Merolli presso S. Clemente' in Debenedetti 1998, pp. 329-325; GR XIX, I, p. 34

1. The facts on the building history in this entry come from Randolfi 1998.

Palazzo del Monte di Pietà

Baglione, pp. 99, 179-180; Titi, pl. 100; Vasi, pl. 180; Magni, I, pls. 97-99 and II, pl. 59; Hibbard 1971, pp. 218-220; Spagnesi 1964, p. 165; Schiavo 1956, p. 167; Wasserman 1966, p. 116; Portoghesi 1966, pls. 251, 252; Salerno, L., n/d, *La Capella del Monte di Pietà*, Rome; Mallory 1974, pp. 34, 35; id., 1977, p. 39; Bershad, D. L., 1977, 'Domenico Guidi: some new attributions', *Antologia di belle Arti*, I, pp. 18-23; Carta, M., 1980, 'Carlo Francesco Bizzacheri e la cappella del Monte di Pietà', *Bolletino d'Arte*, 6, pp. 49-56; id., 2000, *La cappella del Monte di Pietà di Roma*, Rome; Ferrari & Papaldo, p. 428; GR VII, 1, p. 18; Blunt *Guide*, p. 248

1. Illustrated in Hibbard 1971, pl. 89a
2. Hibbard 1971, p. 220. Blunt *Guide*, p. 249.
3. Carta 2000, p. 6.
4. Blunt *Guide*, p. 249.
5. The clearest easily available summaries of the building history are those given by Hibbard 1971, pp. 218-220, and by Carta 2000. The latter also revised earlier attributions of reliefs to the minor stuccoists who worked under Bizzacheri.
6. Enggass 1976b, pp. 51, 71
7. Ibid., pp. 50, 139
8. Ibid., p. 177
9. Ibid., p. 202
10. Ibid., p. 156
11. Carta 2000, p. 23
12. Bershad 1977, pp. 18-23; Ferrari & Papaldo, p. 428

Palazzo di Montecitorio

Falda 1665, I, pls. 14, 15 and IV, pls. 31, 32; De Rossi, I, pls. 105, 106; De Brosses, I, p. 49; Vasi, pl. 23; Magni, II, pls. 47, 48; Coudenhove-Erthal, pp. 71-78; Fagiolo dell'Arco & Fagiolo dell'Arco, no. 137; Borsi, F. et al., 1972, *Montecitorio: ricerche di storia urbana*, Rome, pp. 57-71; Braham, H. & Hager, H., 1977, *Carlo Fontana: the drawings at Windsor Castle*, London, p. 112; Krautheimer 1983, pp. 193-208; Connors 1989a, pp. 231-232; Curcio 1989; GR III, 2, p. 84; Blunt *Guide*, p. 186

1. See the documents on this episode printed in Borsi 1972, pp. 57-71
2. See Krautheimer 1983, pp. 193-208 and Connors 1989a, pp. 231-232
3. For Fontana's drawings, see Braham & Hagar 1977, p. 112. For a summary of the eventual organisation of the piazza, see the present entry for the Palazzo Macchi di Cellere.
4. Curcio 1989, p. 161

Palazzo Montoro (Chigi Montoro, Patrizi, Naro, Lepri)

Lombardi 1992, p. 337; Carpaneto, p. 349; GR VII, 2, p. 40; Blunt *Guide*, p. 186

Palazzo Muti Bussi

Via d'Aracoeli, 2

Baglione, p. 82; Vasi, pl. 116; Pascoli, I, p. 317; Letarouilly, pl. 342; Magni, II, pl. 68; Elling, pl. 96; Toesca 1960, pp. 51, 52; Spagnesi 1964, pp. 123-127; Portoghesi 1966, pl. 253; Boisclair 1986, pp. 39-40, 180-181; Connors 1989a, p. 220; Lombardi 1996, p. 282; Di Paola, R., ed. 2006, *Palazzo Muti Bussi all'Aracoeli*, Rome; GR X, 1. p. 10; Blunt *Guide*, p. 187

1. The church's Baroque façade was probably added by G. B. Contini around 1675. See Lombardi 1996, p. 282.
2. In Di Paola 2006, pp. 108-110, 113, 116. This privately published book, based on work in the Muti archives, completely supersedes all previous accounts of the Muti Bussi palace. The present entry relies on it extensively, with particular reference to Claudia Conforti's essay on the palace's architecture and to Ilaria Miarelli Mariani's analysis of the Dughet frieze.
3. Ibid., p. 115
4. Ibid., pp. 116-117
5. Connors 1989a, p. 220
6. But Marielli Mariani shows that the long sides of this stucco ceiling are modern recreations done later than 1988 (in Di Paola 2006, p. 143 and n. 50).

7. Toesca 1960, p. 52
8. Marielli Mariani in Di Paola 2006, pp. 143-150
9. As explained by Giacinta Pocci Muti Bussi in Di Paola, p. 189, such references must result from confusion with the galleria in the Palazzo Muti Papazzurri in Piazza della Pilotta, the ceiling of which is indeed largely by Calandrucci.
10. Conforti in Di Paola 2006, p. 118
11. Ibid., p. 119
12. Ibid., pp. 119 and 122

Palazzo Muti Papazzurri (Savorelli, Balestra)

Ferrerio, I, pl. 42; Titi, p. 317; Letarouilly, pl. 28; De Rossi, G. B., 1655, *Palazzi Diversi Nel'Alma Cità di Roma*, Rome, pl. 30; Wild, D., 1966, 'Charles Mellin ou Nicolas Poussin', *Gazette des beaux-arts*, 6. Pér. (68), pp. 177-214; Schleier, E., 1976, 'Charles Mellin and the Marchesi Muti', *Burlington Magazine*, 118, pp. 837-844; Torselli, p. 25; Roethlisberger 1961, I, pp. 49, 55, 90; Pantanella, R., 1995, 'Palazzo Muti a Piazza SS Apostoli residenza degli Stuart a Roma', *Storia dell'Arte*, (84), pp. 307-328; Antinori, A., 2002, 'Il palazzo Muti Papazzurri ai Santi Apostoli nei secoli XVI e XVII: notizie sull'attività di Giovanni Antonio de Rossi, Carlo Fontana e Carlo Francesco Bizzaccheri' in Caperna & Spagnesi, pp. 439-446; GR II, 8, p. 13; Blunt *Guide*, p.187

1. See Wild 1966, for illustrations
2. Roethlisberger 1961, I, p. 49

Palazzo Muti Papazzurri

Falda 1665; IV, pl. 45; Pascoli, II, pp. 312-3; Lotti, L., 1966, 'Il palazzo Muti-Papazzurri alla Pilotta', *Alma Roma*, 7, 1, pp. 20-23; Batorska, D., 1978, 'Grimaldi and the Galleria Muti-Papazzuri', *Antologia delle Belle Arti*, (7/8), pp. 204-215; Toesca 1960, pp. 51-59; Pantanella, R., 1995, 'Palazzo Muti a Piazza SS Apostoli residenza degli Stuart a Roma', *Storia dell'Arte*, (84), pp. 307-328; Bartoni, 2003; Matteucci & Ariuli, pp. 156-161; GR II, 2, p. 102; Blunt *Guide*, p. 187

1. Toesca 1960, p. 51
2. Bartoni 2003, pp.138-139
3. Pascoli, II, pp. 312-3
4. Pascoli, *Vite de' pittori, scultori ed architetti moderni, edizione critica*, Perugia, 1992, p. 755, n. 32
5. See illustrations in Matteucci & Ariuli, p. 149

Palazzo Nari

Pascoli, I, p. 317; De Rossi, I, pl. 135; Zocca 1927, I, pl. 137; Spagnesi 1964, p. 162; Antinori, A., 1991, 'Giovanni Antonio De Rossi in palazzo Nari: note sul primo borromismo', *Quaderni dell'Istituto di Storia dell'Architettura*, n. s. 14. 1989 (1991), pp. 43-54; GR VIII, 4, p. 116; Blunt *Guide*, p. 188

1. Pascoli, I, p. 317; De Rossi, I, pl. 135
2. Antinori 1989, pp. 43-45

Palazzo Nari

Mezzetti, A., 1948, 'La pittura di Antonio Gherardi', *Bollettino d'arte*, (4. Ser. 33), pp. 157-176; Pickrel, T., 1983, 'Antonio Gherardi's early development as a painter: S Maria in Trivio and Palazzo Naro', *Storia dell'Arte*, (47/49), pp. 57-64; GR VIII, 4, p. 16; Blunt *Guide*, p. 188

1. Though Wittkower thought it 'impressive' (Wittkower 1973, p. 378, n. 37).

Palazzo Nuñez (Torlonia)

Falda 1665, IV, pl. 46; Pascoli, I, p. 317; Spagnesi 1964, pp. 72-74; Guerrieri Borsoi, M. B., 1988, 'Un' aggiunta al catalogo di Giacinto Calandrucci', *Studi romani*, (36), pp. 269-282; Lodi-Fè, I., 1990, 'Un disegno di Giovan Francesco Grimaldi' in G. C. Sciolla, ed., 1990, *Nuove ricerche in margine alla mostra; da Leonardo a Rembrandt*, Turin, pp. 288-301; Batorska, D., 1995, 'Grimaldi's decorative projects in Palazzo Nuñez- Torlonia in Rome', *Paragone*, (46), pp. 42-64; id., 1997, 'Grimaldi's drawings for vault decorations in two rooms of the Palazzo Nuñez', *Master Drawings*, (35. 1997. 1), pp. 43-49; Matteucci & Ariuli, pp. 161-166; GR IV, 7, p. 97; Blunt *Guide*, p. 188

1. In particular, Batorska is alone in stating that there are two apartments at the via Borgognona end of the building and that one of these is on the second floor rather than the piano nobile, though the second floor balcony definitely supports that observation.
2. And the heavy repainting of some rooms must make analysis difficult.
3. Batorska 1995, p. 60

Palazzo Ottoboni Boncompagni

Lombardi 1992, p. 130; GR III, 3, p. 30

Palazzo Pallavicini Rospigliosi (Bentivoglio, Mazzarino, Pallavicini)

Vasi, pl. 62; Magni, II, pl. 26; Hibbard, H., 1964, 'Scipione Borghese's Garden Palace on the Quirinal', *Journal of the Society of Architectural Historians*, (23), pp. 163-192; id., 1971, p. 192; Torselli, p. 200; Golzio, figs. 197-216; Negro, A., 1996, *Il giardino dipinto del Cardinal Borghese: Paolo Bril e Guido Reni nel Palazzo Rospigliosi Pallavicini a Roma*, Rome; Di Castro, D., Pedrocchi, A.M. & Waddy, P., 2000, *Il Palazzo Pallavicini Rospigliosi e la Galleria Pallavicini*, Turin; Cappelletti 2006, pp. 143-151, 275, 276; GR I, 4, p. 124; Blunt *Guide*, p. 194

1. One of the coronets held by the putti carries the date '1614 18 Lo'.
2. Negro 1996, pp. 62-67.
3. Reni's cartoon for the figure of Apollo survives in the Fogg Museum, Cambridge, Mass. It is illustrated in Negro 1996, p. 121.

Palazzo Pamphili

Ferrerio, I, pl. 9; Falda 1665, IV, pl. 22; Wright, J. M., 1688, *An Account of His Excellence Roger Earl of Castlemaine's Embassy*, London; De Rossi, I, pls. 125, 126; Vasi, pl. 26; De Brosses, II, p. 120; Passeri, p. 111; Magni, II, p. 37; Hempel, p. 134; Montalto, L., 1956, 'Francesco Cozza nella libreria Pamphili a Piazza Navona', *Commentari*, 7, pp. 267-

302; Portoghesi 1964, p. 58; id., 1967, pls. XCV-CII; Spinosi, F., ed., 1970, *Piazza Navona: Isola dei Pamphilj*, Rome; Golzio, figs. 130-147; Blunt 1979, p. 173; Güthlein, p. 218; Preimesberger, R., 1976, 'Pontifex Romanus per Æneam præsignatus', *Römisches Jahrbuch für Kunstgeschichte*, 16, pp. 221-289; Russell, S., 1996, 'L'intervento di Donna Olimpia Pamphilj a Piazza Navona', *Bollettino d'arte*, 6. Ser. 81, 95, pp. 111-120; Russell 1997; Cavazzini 1997, pp. 413-414; id., 2002, pp. 398, 399, 403; id., 2008, pp. 78-80; Fehrenbach, F., 1998, 'Provvidenza intricata: Riflessioni sulla Galleria Pamphili' in Frommel, C. L. & Schütze, S., eds., *Pietro da Cortona; atti del convegno internazionale Roma-Firenze 12-15 novembre 1997*, Rome, pp. 108-115; Sladek, E., 2000a in Bösel & Frommel, II, pp. 177-184; id., 2000b, 'L'architettura dei palazzi di Borromini' in Frommel & Sladek, pp. 86-97; Scott 1997; Leone, S., 2004, 'Cardinal Pamphilj builds a palace: self-representation and familial ambition in seventeenth-century Rome', *Journal of the Society of Architectural Historians*, 63 (4), pp. 440-471; id., 2008, *The Palazzo Pamphilj in Piazza Navona: constructing identity in early modern Rome*, London; GR VI, 1, p. 40; Blunt *Guide*, p. 188

1. Passeri, pp. 111-2. Leone 2008, pp. 107-141, analyses the pre-papal phase of the palace: the documents establishing Peparelli's involvement are printed as an appendix.
2. There is no doubt that the Pamphili development in Piazza Navona has many characteristics of a dynastic seat, that it largely absorbs and appropriates the big new church of S Agnese, and that this presents some striking parallels with the Escorial. There is, however, continuing scholarly discussion about the project, and especially about the pope's apparent decision, late in the day, to use the palace as one of his administrative centres. See Leone 2008, pp. 283-287 for a summary of the arguments.
3. The three rooms are in the Ambassador's private part of the palace and are much more difficult to see than the later rooms along the main front, to which the Brazilian Embassy do enable scholars to have access. For the Sala di Giuseppe see Russell 1997. The Sala di Mosè frieze used to be attributed to Gimignani, but Cavazzini established Tassi as the painter of the landscape, with the other parts probably painted by Caroselli and Francesco Lauri (Cavazzini 1997, p. 413; id. 2002, p. 403; id. 2008, pp. 79-80). The Sala delle Marine frieze presents a stylistic conundrum as it appears extraordinarily old-fashioned alongside the other rooms (Cavazzini 1997, p. 414; id. 2002, pp. 399, 403; id. 2008, pp. 78, 79; Leone 2008, p. 136).
4. The 1640s friezes are fully described in Redig de Campos, 'Palazzo Pamphilj; la decorazione pittorica', in Spinosi, pp. 157-192. Susan Russell has drawn attention to the unusual privileging of the Maidalchini heraldic emblems in several of the rooms, indicating the likelihood that the famously assertive Donna Olimpia was closely involved in devising the scheme, some of which touched on themes of early Rome that were later elaborated in the Cortona gallery (Russell 1996). Russell suggests in the same article that the Sala delle Donne Illustri may well have been used by Donna Olimpia as her own audience chamber.
5. For *trionfi* generally, see Montagu, J. 1989, *Roman Baroque Sculpture*, New Haven and London, pp. 188-197

Palazzo Panizza

Vasi, pl. 112; Letarouilly, pl. 26; Lombardi 1992, p. 313; Carpaneto, p. 403; Bevilacqua, M., 1989, 'Documenti per il tardo barocco romano: casa Panizza e l'opera dell'architetto Simone Felice Delino', *Palladio*, n. s. 2, pp. 133-142; GR VII, 1, p. 38

1. Bevilacqua 1989, pp. 133, 134, 136, 138, 139
2. See Letarouilly, pl. 26, 'Plan d'une Maison située près l'Eglise S. M. in Monticelli'
3. Bevilacqua 1989, p. 136

Palazzo Patrizi (Aldobrandini)

Baglione, p. 308; Mola, p. 127; Letarouilly, pl. 20; Hibbard 1971, p. 135; Wasserman, J., 1968, 'The Palazzo Patrizi in Rome', *Journal of the Society of Architectural Historians*, 27, pp. 99-114; Vecchi, p. 47; Torselli, p. 209; GR VIII, 4, p. 74; Blunt *Guide*, p. 189

1. Mola, p. 127; Hibbard 1971, p.135; Wasserman 1968, pp. 99-108. Blunt asserted that the Aldobrandini façade was of seven bays and was reduced to four in the 19th century, but Wasserman explicitly stated that Olimpia Aldobrandini's façade was of four bays, as at present, and that is surely correct.

Palazzo Patrizi (Clementi)

Neuburger, S., 1979, 'Giovanni da San Giovanni im Palazzo Patrizi-Clementi in Rom', *Mitteilungen des Kunsthistorischen Institutes in Florenz*, 23 (3), 337-346; Cavazzini 1997, p. 401; GR XI, 1, p. 36; Blunt *Guide*, p. 190

1. See Neuburger 1979
2. Cavazzini 1997, pp. 406-409

Palazzo Pecci Blunt (Fani, Ruspoli)

Baglione, p. 82; Boisclair 1986, p. 342; Salerno 1977, III, p. 1019; Lombardi 1992, p. 419; GR X, 1, p. 20; Blunt *Guide*, p. 180

1. Boisclair 1986, p. 342; Salerno 1977, III, p. 1019

Palazzo Peretti (Fiano, Ottoboni, Boncompagni Ludovisi, Almagià)

Hibbard 1971, p. 217; Salerno 1961, p. 162; Schleier 1968; Bartoni, L. & Pierguidi, S., 2000, 'Gli affreschi di Giovanni Francesco Grimaldi e François Perrier nel salone di palazzo Peretti a Roma', *Storia dell'Arte*, (99), pp. 94-105; Pierguidi 2000; id., 2003, 'Gli affreschi del salone Peretti: il tema dei quattro elementi e la cultura alchemica', *Storia dell'Arte*, (103), pp. 41-66; Bartoni, 2003; Matteucci & Ariuli, pp. 115-116; GR III, 1, p. 82; Blunt *Guide*, p. 159

1. Hibbard 1971, p. 217
2. Bartoni & Pierguidi 2000
3. Schleier 1968
4. For a detailed discussion of this, including the possibility that Grimaldi could have been involved in one of the figure scenes, see Bartoni & Pierguidi 2000, pp. 98-99.
5. Pierguidi 2003
6. Though Matteucci & Ariuli adventurously speculate that the landscape depicting a shipwreck might refer to the scattering of the Trojan fleet by the winds released by Æolus. (Matteucci & Ariuli, p. 116).

Palazzo Perucchi (Campello)

Carpaneto, p. 409; Lombardi 1992, p. 137; GR III, 4, p. 72

Palazzo del Pio Sodalizio dei Piceni (della Naziona Picena, Casa di Sisto V)

Astolfi, C., 1940, *La presunta casa di Sisto V a via di Parione e le nozze di Flavia Peretti*, Rome; Benedetti, p. 359; Carpaneto, p. 414; Lombardi 1992, p. 286; Röttgen 2002, pp. 35-38, 276-281; GR VI, 1, p. 88; Blunt *Guide*, p. 190

1. Blunt *Guide*, p. 190
2. Puglisi, p. 12; Röttgen 2002, p. 281

Palazzo Pighini (Fusconi, del Gallo di Roccagiovine)

Roisecco 1750, I, p. 612; Titi, p. 108; Portoghesi 1966, pls. 285-7, tav. 7; Lodico, D., 1995, 'Palazzo Pighini (Pichini) in Piazza Farnese' in Debenedetti 1995, pp. 273-294; GR VII, 2, p. 88. Blunt *Guide*, p. 190

1. See Lodico 1995 for all the facts cited here on the building history.

Palazzo Pio di Savoia da Carpi (Orsini, Righetti)

Mola, p. 131; De Rossi, I, pls. 116-18 and III, pl. 79; Roisecco 1750, II, p. 41; Visentini, p. 27; Vasi, pl. 75; Titi, p. 168; Magni, II, pl. 36; Portoghesi 1966, pl. 239; Connors 1989b, pp. 81, 82; GR VI, 2, p. 150; Blunt *Guide*, p. 190

1. Connors 1989b, p. 82
2. Kristin Triff, 'The Theater in the Early Modern Era' on the King's College, London, website *The Pompey Project*, www.Pompey.cch.kcl.ac.uk
3. See Connors op. cit. for this comparison with the Palazzo Madama, and for all the material used here on Virgilio Spada.
3. Visentini, p. 27

Palazzo Pizzirani (Cesarini, Leoni)

Falda 1691, I, pl. 32; Vasi, pl. 154; Lombardi 1992, p. 482; Carpaneto, p. 416; GR XIII, 2, p. 148

1. Falda 1691, I, pl. 32 and Vasi, pl. 154 respectively. The Falda print is illustrated in Blunt, *Guide*, p. 237.

Palazzo Pizzirani

Lombardi 1992, p. 403; Carpaneto, p. 416; GR IX, 2, p. 14

Palazzo Poli

Ferrerio, I, pls. 19, 20; Pinto, J. A., 1986, *The Trevi Fountain*, New Haven and London, pp. 58-59; Lombardi 1992, p. 90; GR II, 5, p. 105

1. Ferrerio, I, pls. 19, 20
2. For the proposals under Urban VIII, see the present entry for the Palazzo Carpegna.
3. The present entry relies on Pinto 1986, pp. 58-59. For an account of how Salvi stripped out the more expensive materials from the façade but left the valueless stucco decoration in place, and how this can be seen from inside the building, see Pinto, p. 59.

Palazzetto di Flaminio Ponzio

Baglione, p. 135; Magni, II, pl. 58; Lombardi 1992, p. 439; GR XI, 1, p. 92

1. Baglione, p. 135
2. Portoghesi 1966, p. 49
3. Magni, II, pl. 58

Palazzo Pulieri (Ginetti)

Lombardi 1992, p. 152; Salerno 1961, pp. 140, 275; GR IV, 4, p. 32

Palazzo del Quirinale

Ferrerio, I, pl. 2 and II, pls. 5-8; Falda 1665, I, pl. 13 and IV, pls. 4, 5; id., 1680, pls. 5, 6; Vasi, pl. 61; Percier and Fontaine, IV, pls. 63-6; Magni, II, pls. 61-7, 91; Briganti, G., 1962, *Il Palazzo del Quirinale*, Rome; Wasserman, J., 1963, 'The Quirinal Palace in Rome', *Art Bulletin*, 45, pp. 204-244; id., 1966, p. 142; Schleier, E., 1970, 'Les projets de Lanfranc pour le décor de la Sala Regia au Quirinal et pour la Loge de Bénédictions à Saint-Pierre', *Revue de l'art* (7), pp. 40-67; Hibbard 1971, p. 194; Borsi, F. et al., 1973, *Il Palazzo del Quirinale*, Rome; Briganti, G., Laureati, L. & Trezzani, L., 1993, *Il patrimonio artistico del Quirinale: I, pittura antica; la quadreria; II, pittura antica; la decorazione murale*, Milan; Spear, R. E., 1997, *The 'Divine' Guido; Religion, Sex, Money and Art in the World of Guido Reni*, New Haven and London, pp. 152-161; Morozzi, L. ed., 1999, *Restauri al Quirinale*, Rome; Colalucci, F., 2000, *Palazzo del Quirinale; Guida alle sale aperta al pubblico*, Rome; Metzger Habel, pp. 11-62; Pasti, S. 2006, 'Pietro da Cortona e la galleria di Alessandro VII al Quirinale', in Fagiolo & Portoghesi, pp. 88-97; Roettgen 2007, pp. 68-79; Vodret, R., 2008, 'Agostino Tassi e il fregio della Sala Regia nel palazzo del Quirinale' in Cavazzini 2008, pp. 127-150; GR II, 2, 86; Blunt *Guide*, p. 191

1. Trezzani notes that the paintings were first mounted in the ceiling of a room in the royal apartments in the Manica Lunga from which they were detached in 1959. (Briganti, Laureati & Trezzani, I, pp. 88-89).

2. For an account of this episode, and of how the pope took the opportunity of seeing a great deal of Bernini and Cortona, see Barker, S., 2006, 'Art, Architecture and the Roman Plague of 1656-57', *Roma Moderna e Contemporanea*, XIV, pp. 244-246.
3. The most useful and well illustrated account of the gallery before the recent discoveries is by Trezzani in op. cit., II, pp. 191-207. For a convenient summary of the discoveries see Pasti 2006.
4. For an analysis of the contributions by Tassi's team of painters, made in the light of the recent restorations, see Vodret 2008.
5. Thus Matteucci & Ariuli, pp. 147-150. But see Trezzani in Briganti, Laureati & Trezzani, II, pp. 208-217 for the argument that only the frieze is by Grimaldi and that the open sky ceilings were executed by Cennini around 1724.
6. Mathiae, p. 39; Pane, p. 94 and fig. 73.

Palazzo Raggi

Lombardi 1992, p. 130; Salerno 1961, p. 174; GR III, 1, p. 76

Palazzo Rocci (Pallavicini)

Baglione, p. 309; Donati 1957, p. 47; Hibbard 1971, p. 207; GR VII, 2, p. 28

1. Hibbard 1971, p. 207
2. Donati 1957, p. 47

Palazzo Rondinini or Rondanini (Sanseverino)

Goethe, W. von, 1970, *Italian Journey*, tr. Auden, W. H. and Mayer, E., Harmondsworth, pp. 364-5, 490; Magni, II, pl. 73; Salerno 1961, p. 123; id., 1965, *Palazzo Rondinini*, Rome; Borsi, F. et al., 1983, *Palazzo Rondinini*, Rome; Mancinelli, M. V., 1998, 'Il Palazzo Rondinini da Gabriele Valvassori a Alessandro Dori' in Debenedetti 1998, pp. 231-257; Röttgen 2002, pp. 122-128; GR IV, 4, p. 11; Blunt *Guide*, p. 193

1. Röttgen 2002, p. 123
2. Mancinelli 1998, p. 237. However, the date 1764 appears on the fountain in the cortile.
3. Morolli in Borsi 1983, pp. 33, 35, 44
4. Blunt *Guide*, p. 193
5. Another cast of the Medusa is set over one of the doors on the second landing of the staircase in the palace.
6. Goethe, 1970, pp. 364-5
7. Salerno 1965, p. 80
8. Compare Borromini's analagous use of the Medusa head in the internal entrance at the Palazzo Carpegna.
9. Röttgen 2002, p. 124

Palazzo De Rossi

Lombardi 1992, p. 199; GR V, 4, p. 26.

1. Lombardi 1992, p. 199

Palazzo Ruggeri

Ferrerio, II, pl. 52; Martinelli 1969, p. 252; Mola, p. 227; Brugnoli, M. V., 1960, 'Un Palazzo Romano del tardo "500"', *Bollettino d'Arte*, n. s. 45, pp. 223-246; id., 1961, *Palazzo Ruggieri*, Rome; Pietrangeli, C., 1970, 'Il Palazzo del Leone Rampante', *Capitolium*, 45, pp. 25-32; GR IX, 1, p. 90; Blunt *Guide*, p. 194

Palazzo Ruspoli

Totti 1638, p. 334; Baglione, p. 346; Ferrerio, I, pl. 23; Falda 1665, IV, pl. 38; Mola, p. 129; Titi, p. 370; Vasi, commentary on pl. 68; Salerno 1961, p. 153; Pietrangeli, C., ed., 1992, *Palazzo Ruspoli*, Rome; GR IV, 7, p. 55; Blunt *Guide*, p. 194

1. Vasi, pl. 68

Palazzo S Calisto

Ferrerio, I, pl. 35; Falda 1665, I, pl. 33; Titi, p. 43; Vasi, pl. 60; Martinelli 1969, p. 246; Magni, II, pl. 72; Torselli, p. 254; Lombardi 1992, p. 480; Carpaneto, p. 101; GR XIII, 2, p. 126; Blunt *Guide*, p. 195

Palazzo Santacroce

Martinelli 1969, p. 252; Titi, p. 98; Hibbard 1971, p. 129; Sinisi, S., 1963, 'Il Palazzo Santacroce ai Catinari', *Palatino*, 1-4, pp. 13-17; Spagnesi 1964, pp. 127-130; Torselli, p. 260; Batorska, D., 1973, 'Grimaldi and the Salone Santacroce', *Storia dell'Arte*, (19), pp. 173-179; Elling, pls. 121, 177; Connors 1989a, pp. 260-267; Vicarelli, F., 1998, 'La fabbrica "dei Famigli" del palazzo Santacroce ai Catinari' in Debenedetti 1998, pp. 81-94; Ferrari & Papaldo, p. 434; Pierguidi 2000; Cappelletti, F., 2000, 'Le poche opere certe e qualche iniziale riflessione per la breve vicenda romana di Giovan Battista Ruggeri', in Bernadini, M. G., ed., 2000, *Studi di storia dell'arte in onore di Denis Mahon*, Milan, pp. 252-258; Matteucci & Ariuli, pp. 142-147; Manfredi, T., 2002, 'Palazzo Santacroce ai Catinari: continuità e trasformazione architettonica a Roma tra il XVI e il XIX secolo' in Caperna & Spagnesi, pp. 359-366; Bartoni, L., 2003, 'Giovanni Francesco Grimaldi e la pittura di paesaggio nei palazzi romani alla metà del Seicento' in Cappelletti 2003, pp. 127-140; Perri, A., 2003, 'La data di morte di Giovan Battista Ruggeri' in ibid., pp. 107-112; GR VII, 1, p. 49; Blunt *Guide*, p. 195

1. Manfredi 2002 is by far the most comprehensive published account of the building history, and the present entry draws on it heavily.
2. *Pace* the suggestion in Matteucci & Ariuli, p. 147, that the upper fountain is by Grimaldi.
3. This is very similar to the effect created by Borromini's fountain in the piazza outside Palazzo Spada. Sinisi asserts that payment documents indicate that the fountain is by Alessio De Rossi, who is known to have worked in the palace after G. A. De Rossi's time. (Sinisi 1963, p. 13). However, the fountain must at least have been planned from the time the dependants' building was started, as the deep recess that accommodates it would otherwise be inexplicable. Ferrari & Papaldo opine that the fountain dates back to Peparelli's involvement in 1636-1637 and assert that later documentation refers to it as already existing. They also point to the fountain's appearance,

which certainly looks to be of some decades before the end of the 17th century (Ferrari & Papaldo, p. 434).

4. For the date of Ruggeri's death see Perri 2003. For an analysis of the sources and a modern placing of the Santacroce work in Grimaldi's oeuvre see Pierguidi 2000, pp. 49-52 and Bartoni 2003, p. 127. For a convenient listing of the subjects see Matteucci & Ariuli, p. 142.
5. Cappelletti 2000, p. 254

Apartment buildings in Piazza di S Ignazio

Vasi, pl. 163; Milizia, F., 1781, *Memorie degli Architetti Antichi e Moderni*, Parma; Rotili, M., 1951, *Filippo Raguzzini e il Rococò Romano*, Rome; Wittkower 1973, p. 249; Portoghesi 1966, pls. 361-4; Mallory 1977, p. 22; Connors 1989a, pp. 279-293; GR III, 1, p. 22; Blunt *Guide*, p. 252

1. Rotili 1951, pp. 68, 111
2. Wittkower 1973, p. 241
3. 'Quelle ridicole case a foggia di canterani' (Milizia, F., 1781: *Memorie degli architetti antichi e moderne*, Parma, p. 202).
4. For the use of circles, rather than ovals, in the piazza's plan see Connors 1989a pp. 279-280.

Apartment building in Piazza S Lorenzo in Lucina

Acconci, A., 1994, 'La proprietà di S. Giacomo degli Spagnoli in piazza S. Lorenzo in Lucina' in Debenedetti 1994, pp. 201-215; GR IV, 7, p. 47

Palazzo Sciarra (Colonna di Sciarra, Carbognano)

Baglione, p. 135; Ferrerio, II, pl. 37; Falda 1665, IV, pl. 37; De Rossi, I, pl. 115; Titi, p. 326; Mola, p. 132; Martinelli 1969, p. 253; Letarouilly, pls. 143, 144; Magni, II, pl. 12; Salerno 1961, p. 211; Torselli, p. 265; De Seta, C., 1973: 'Disegni di Luigi Vanvitelli' in Fusco, R. D., ed., 1973, *Luigi Vanvitelli*, Naples, p. 241; Pietrangeli, C., 1986, *Palazzo Sciarra*, Rome; GR II, 6, p. 56; Blunt *Guide*, p. 195

1. Both De Rossi, I, pl. 115 and Titi, p. 326 ascribe the door to Labacco, which – as Blunt commented – is manifestly impossible.
2. The Fondazione's website (www.fondazioneroma.it) includes tantalising images of the Vanvitelli rooms, but these are currently closed to the public, and there do not appear to be any plans to open them.

Palazzo Serlupi Crescenzi

Baglione, p. 82; Ferrerio, II, pl. 55; Azzaro, B., 1987, 'Palazzo Serlupi Crescenzi', *Storia architettura*, (10), pp. 89-108; Borghese, D. 1994, 'I palazzetti d'affitto Serlupi Crescenzi tra via del Seminario e via dei Pastini' in Debenedetti 1994, pp. 169-186; GR III, 2, p. 28; Blunt *Guide*, p. 196

1. All the material in this entry about Stefano Crescenzi's will and the palace in the 18th century is from Borghese 1994.

Palazzo Sinibaldi (dei Cavalieri dell'Ordine Teutonico)

Vasi, pl. 73; Proia, A. & Romano, P., 1936, *Arenula*, Rome, p. 148; Callari, p. 470; Torselli, p. 269; Carpaneto, p. 380; Lombardi 1992, p. 327; GR VII, 2, p. 92; Blunt *Guide*, p. 196

1. Blunt *Guide*, p. 196
2. One related issue is to establish the date when the property left the hands of the Teutonic Order. The published sources are in conflict on this. Torselli and Callari follow Proia and Romano in saying that the building was sold to the Sinibaldi by 'Leopold of Austria'. The Guida Rionale, Lombardi and Carpaneto specify that the emperor in question was Leopold I (d. 1705). None of these gives the sources, however, and a sale by Leopold I would conflict with Vasi's reference to the 'Religione Teutonica' in 1754. Carpaneto further muddies the waters by commenting that Leopold I protected the Teutonic Order during the Napoleonic Wars, which in fact began almost a century after his death. The obvious explanation for all this, which would allow for the building date suggested in the present entry, is that the sale was effected not by the emperor Leopold I but by Leopold II, who reigned from 1790 to 1792. This would fit both with the troubles that the Teutonic Order experienced in the period following the French Revolution, and with Leopold II's enthusiasm for secularising the property of religious orders, as evidenced during his previous reign as Grand Duke of Tuscany.

Palazzo Spada

Ferrerio, I, pls. 32, 33; Letarouilly, pls. 243-6; Magni, II, pls. 13-16; Frommel, II, p. 61; Neppi, L., 1975, *Palazzo Spada*, Rome; Heimbürger Ravalli; Wittkower 1973, p. 148; Haskell, F. & Penny, N., 1981, *Taste and the Antique*, New Haven and London; Sinisgalli, R., 1981, *Borromini a Quattro Dimensioni*, Rome; Hunter, J., 1984, 'The architectus celeberrimus of the Palazzo Capodiferro at Rome', *Römisches Jahrbuch für Kunstgeschichte*, 21, pp. 397-403; Portoghesi, P., 1984, *Francesco Borromini*, Milan; Cannatà, R., 1991, 'Novità su Giulio Mazzoni, Leonardo Sormani, Tommaso del Bosco e Siciolante da Sermoneta', *Bollettino d'Arte*, 6. Ser. 76 (70), pp. 87-104; Cannatà, R. & Vicini, M. L., 1993, *La Galleria di Palazzo Spada: Genesi e Storia di una Collezione*, Rome; Cannatà, R., ed. 1995, *Palazzo Spada: Le Decorazioni Restaurate*, Milan; Di Battista, R., 1993, 'Trasformazioni urbane di piazza Capodiferro e piazza della Quercia a Roma', *Quaderni dell'Istituto di Storia dell'Architettura*, (22), pp. 71-80; id., 2000, 'Il progetto di Francesco Borromini per la facciata posteriore di palazzo Spada' in Frommel & Sladek, pp. 134-139; Tabarrini, M., 2008, *Borromini e gli Spada*, Rome; GR VII, 2, p. 98; Blunt *Guide*, p. 196

1. There is a convenient account of

the early history in Canattà & Vicini 1993.
2. As demonstrated in Hunter 1985.
3. See Cannatà 1991
4. For a full account of the critical fortunes of this rebarbative work, see Haskell & Penny, pp. 296-300.
5. In 1642 Colonna and Mitelli were to include a similar youth with a telescope in the quadratura scheme of the Sala di Alessandro (now part of the Museo degli Argenti) in Palazzo Pitti, Florence. As is well known, the Medici were famous as patrons of science, and especially as the protectors of Galileo.
6. A meridian clock works with a spot of reflected light rather than the shadow of a gnomon. Maignan was responsible for a similar meridian in the convent of Trinità dei Monti, where he also had executed an anamorphic mural painting of *S Francesco di Paolo at prayer in a landscape/ St John on Patmos*, which only makes sense when viewed from an acute angle and is completely illegible when seen from directly in front. This provides yet further evidence of the existence of a circle, including the Spada brothers, that was deeply interested in optical tricks and illusionism.
7. Tabarrini 2008, p. 12
8. See Tabarrini 2008, p. 11 for an illustration of Giovanni Maggi's print of the fountain.
9. J. Turner recorded in *Art News*, January 1998, p. 64 that the statue, commissioned from Ducrot by the culture ministry, had just been unveiled by Walter Veltroni.
10. See Wittkower 1973, p. 148 for a trenchant statement of the prospettiva's lack of relevance to Borromini's main concerns.
11. The design originally allowed for three windows along the right side. (Camerota, F., in Bösel & Frommel, II, p. 323) The later construction of the terrace must also have closed off light from above.
12. Prof. Camillo Trevisan's computer-aided studies of the prospettiva are published on the internet under the title *The Borromini Gallery in Palazzo Spada, Rome; Ideal regular model and deformed real model* (www.camillo-trevisan.it).
13. For an extended discussion of this topic see Connors 1979.
14. Portoghesi 1984, p. 179
15. The staircase was converted back into a single-flight configuration in 1930.
16. Since the new wing was going up at exactly the same time as the two-flight staircase, it is tempting to speculate that della Greca, and possibly Bernini, might have had a hand in both projects. See Tabarrini 2008, pp. 53-54 on this point, and Tabarrini 2008 and Di Battista 2000 more generally for the proposed developments at the back of the palace.

Palazzo di Spagna

Pascoli, I., p. 301; Pollak 1909; Hempel, p. 131; Salerno, L., 1967: *Piazza di Spagna*, Cava dei Tirreni, p. 89; Vecchi, p. 383; Anselmi, A., 2001,*Il Palazzo dell'Ambasciata di Spagna presso la Santa Sede*, Rome; GR IV, 3, p. 88; Blunt *Guide*, p. 197
1. Blunt *Guide*, p. 198

Palazzo della Stamperia (Cornaro)

Baglione, p. 82; Ferrerio, I, pl. 36; Martinelli 1969, p. 240; Franzini, F., 1643, *Descrittione Di Roma Antica E Moderna: Nella Quale Si Contengono Chiese, Monasterij, Hospedali, Compagnie, Collegij, E Seminarij*, Rome, p. 743; Titi, p. 354; Pierro, M., 1928, 'Il Palazzo della Stamperia', *Capitolium*, 4, p. 237; Benedetti, p. 226; GR II, 5, p. 57; Blunt *Guide*, p. 175
1. Blunt *Guide*, p. 175

Palazzetto Sterbini (Boncompagni)

Lombardi 1992, p. 183; Carpaneto, p. 502; GR IV, 3, p. 208

Palazzo Strozzi (Olgiati, Besso)

Baglione, p. 197; Donati 1957, p. 46; Maroni Lumbroso, M., 1962, 'Palazzo Strozzi Besso alle Stimmate', *Capitolium*, 37, pp. 542-547; Hibbard 1971; p. 206; GR IX, 2, p. 110
1. Baglione, p. 197
2. See Maroni Lumbroso 1962 for an illustration. The frieze, by Calandrucci, was destroyed in 1985 (Guerrieri Borsoi in Pascoli, *Vite de' pittori, scultori ed architetti moderni, edizione critica*, Perugia, 1992, p. 755 fn. 29.)
3. Hibbard, p. 206

Palazzetto 'dei Telamoni'

Lombardi 1992, p. 180; Carpaneto, p. 505; GR IV, 4, p. 52

Palazzo Testa Piccolomini

Elling, p. 303, pl. 116; Santese, B. M., 1983, *Palazzo Testa Piccolomini alla Dataria. Filippo Barigioni, architetto romano*, Rome; GR II, 2, 144; Blunt *Guide*, p. 199

Palazzo Valentini (Bonelli, Alessandrino, Spinelli, Imperiali, della Provincia)

Falda 1665, IV, pl. 39; Ferrerio, I, pls. 27, 28; Martinelli 1969, pp. 232, 236; Mola, p. 132; Vasi, pl. 64; Eminente, C. F., 1973, 'Dopo 100 anni radicali restauri a Palazzo Valentini', *Rassegna del Lazio*, (n. s. 20, 7), 6; Wasserman 1966, p. 93; Farina, G., 1985, *Palazzo Valentini*, Rome; Metzger Habel, pp. 192-199; GR II, 8, p. 79; Blunt *Guide*, p. 199
1. Wasserman 1966, p. 93
2. See Metzger Habel, pp. 192-199, for an account of the interest shown by the Chigi in this palace.
3. Thus Farina, but the informative placard now outside the palace says that the architect of the rear façade was G. B. Benedetti.

Palazzo Varese or Varesi (Degli Atti)

Baglione, p. 309; Spezzaferro, L. in Salerno 1973, p. 440; Hibbard 1971,

p. 207; Donati 1942, p. 97, figs. 104-107; id., 1957, p. 45; GR VII, 3, p. 34; Blunt *Guide*, p. 199

1. Hibbard 1971, p. 207

Palazzo Verospi

Baglione, p. 156; Ferrerio, II, pl. 50; Martinelli 1969, p. 253; Mola, p. 130; Titi, p. 349; Bodmer, H., 1936, 'Die Fresken des Francesco Albani im Palazzo Verospi in Rom', *Pantheon*, (18), pp. 366-369; Wasserman 1966, p. 121; Salerno 1961, pp. 175, 255; Puglisi, pp. 11-13, 125-128; Brevaglieri, S., 2001, *Palazzo Verospi al Corso*, Milan; GR III, 1, p. 72; Blunt *Guide*, p. 200

1. Baglione, p. 156
2. Puglisi, p.12; Röttgen 2002, p. 281
3. Puglisi, p. 128

Unnamed building at via degli Zingari, 55

Lombardi 1992, p. 64

Palazzo Zuccari

Körte, W., 1935, 'Der Palazzo Zuccari in Rom: sein Freskenschmuck und seine Geschichte', Leipzig; Viale Ferrero, M., 1970, *Filippo Juvarra, Scenografo e Architetto Teatrale*, Turin, pp. 54-57; Boscarino, S., 1978, 'Filippo Juvarra tra scienza e tecnica', *Restauro*, 7 (37), pp. 5, 163; Elling, pp. 279, 280; GR IV, 2, p. 102

1. Körte 1935, p. 51
2. Boscarino 1978, p. 163. For information on Juvarra and ex-Queen Maria Casimira, see Viale Ferrero 1970.

GLOSSARY

Altana: A belvedere above a building's roofline. In Rome they are permanent, roofed structures made of brick or masonry

Androne: An entrance hallway or vestibule

Avviso: A news-sheet. There were many of these forerunners of the modern newspaper in 17th century Rome.

Barocchetto: An obsolete, yet handy, word that was used to denote a specifically Roman style of architecture, derived from the Baroque, that flourished at more or less the same time as the Rococo in France.

Busselotto: An enclosed balcony. These structures were widespread throughout Rome in the 18th century.

Cardinale Nepote (or Nipote): The nephew (or other family member) of a pope, created a cardinal and enjoying a formally recognised position of great power in the Curia during the pope's reign. Some of these 'Cardinal Nephews' simultaneously held other important posts, such as Vice-Chancellor. The office was abolished in 1692.

Cortile: Courtyard

Cortile d'onore: A courtyard reserved for the use of distinguished people, implying the existence of a service courtyard elsewhere.

Di sotto in sù: The gaze of a painting that depicts its subject from below with pronounced foreshortening.

Isolato: A city block

Mascherone: Literally 'big mask'. In architecture, a carved or moulded decorative face.

Mensola: A console or substantial bracket. In barocchetto architecture the shape of a console was a common decorative motif in, for example, window pediments.

Nicchione: A large niche

Piano nobile: The main floor of a palace, where the state rooms were. This was usually the first floor, but some palaces used both the first and second floors in this way.

Piano terreno: Ground floor

Quadratura: Illusionistic painted decoration feigning an architectural construction.

Quadro riportato: Literally 'transported picture'. Painted decoration imitating a framed picture.

Rastrello: Literally, a rake. Also commonly used, albeit incorrectly, for the Aldobrandini family device of a heraldic bend with cross-bars (a 'battled bend' or 'banda doppiomerlata').

Rimessa: A coach-house. There was an enormous number of carriages in 17th century Rome, and very many palaces incorporated coach-houses.

Ringhiera: Railing. Also used for a balcony made of metal strips and bars.

Romitorio: A place that was set aside for contemplation and was usually got up in a way that made allusions to the idea of a hermitage.

Sala dei palafrenieri: Literally 'grooms' room'. The guard room of a large palace. A visitor would normally arrive here, and would be conducted onwards by a page or other functionary, according to rank.

Sala: A fair-sized room (ie one larger than a 'camera')

Salone: A big room; a hall

Salotto: A drawing-room

Serliana: A tripartite format consisting of a round-headed opening with pillars or pilasters, flanked by lower and narrower straight-headed openings. The name comes from the 16th century architectural theorist Serlio. Also called Venetian or Palladian windows

Statue parlanti: The 'talking statues' of Rome to which satirical and scurrilous verses were attached. They were the Pasquino, the Babuino, the Facchino, the Abate Luigi, the Marforio and the Madama Lucrezia.

Tondo: Round. An artwork of circular format.

Veduta: A topographical image, usually depicting some well-known tourist scene.

Vigna: A vineyard; a small country or suburban estate

INDEX OF ARTISTS

Albani, Francesco (1578-1660)
Palazzo Doria-Pamphili
Palazzo Mattei di Giove
Palazzo del Quirinale
Palazzo Verospi
Alberti, Cherubino (1553-1618)
Palazzo Albani
Palazzo Lateranense
Palazzo Pallavicini Rospigliosi
Palazzo Ruggeri
Alberti, Giovanni (1558-after 1601)
Palazzo Albani
Palazzo Lateranense
Palazzo Ruggeri
Aldrovandini, Pompeo (1677-1735 or 1739)
Palazzo Doria-Pamphili
Allegrini, Flaminio (1587-1663)
Palazzo Chigi (Aldobrandini)
Palazzo Costaguti
Allegrini, Francesco (1604-1673)
Palazzo Costaguti
Palazzo Pamphili
Ameli, Paolo Antonio (1698-1752)
Palazzo Boncompagni Ludovisi
Palazzo Doria-Pamphili
Ammannati, Bartolomeo (1511-1592)
Palazzo Ruspoli
Angeletti, Pietro (c. 1737-1798)
Palazzo Doria-Pamphili
Arcucci, Camillo (1618-1667)
Palazzo Grazioli
Palazzo Pio di Savoia da Carpi
Palazzo Spada
Baccio Bigio, Nanni di (Giovanni di Bartolomeo Lippi) (c. 1513-1568)
Palazzo Lante
Palazzo Ruspoli
Badalocchio, Sisto (1585-after 1617)
Palazzo Farnese
Palazzo Mattei di Giove
Palazzo Verospi
Baglione, Giovanni (c. 1573-1644)
Palazzo Lateranense
Palazzo Pallavicini Rospigliosi
Baldi, Lazzaro (c. 1624-1703)
Palazzo del Quirinale
Barberi, Giuseppe (1746-1809)
Palazzo Altieri
Barigioni, Filippo (c. 1680-1753)
Palazzo Albani
Palazzo Testa Piccolomini
Baronino Bartolomeo (1511-1554)
Palazzo Spada
Bartoli, Pietro Santi (1635-1700)
Palazzo Borghese
Bassetti, Marcantonio (1586-1630)
Palazzo del Quirinale
Battisti, Antonio de (active 1620s)
Palazzo della Famiglia Borghese
Palazzo Costaguti
Benaglia, Paolo (active 1720s, d. 1739)
Palazzo della Consulta
Benefial, Marco (1684-1764)
Palazzo di Spagna
Bernini, Gianlorenzo (1598-1680)
Palazzo Altieri
Palazzo Antamoro
Palazzo Barberini
Palazzo Chigi (Odescalchi)
Palazzo Colonna
Palazzo di Montecitorio
Palazzo del Quirinale
Palazzo di Spagna
Bernini, Pietro (1562-1629)
Palazzo del Quirinale
Palazzetto 'dei Telamoni'
Berrettoni, Nicolò (1637-1682)
Palazzo Altieri
Berthelot, Guillaume (c. 1580-1648)
Palazzo del Quirinale
Bianchi, Francesco (1682-1742)
Casa degli Agostiniani Scalzi
Bizzacheri, Carlo Francesco (1655-1721)
Palazzo del Monte di Pietà
Bonazzini, Giovanni Maria (active around 1610)
Palazzo Barberini ai Giubbonari
Bonzi, Pietro Paolo (c. 1576-1636)
Palazzo Albani
Palazzo Giustiniani
Palazzo Mattei di Giove
Borromini, Francesco (1599-1667)
Palazzo Barberini
Palazzo del Bufalo
Palazzo Carpegna (Accademia di S Luca)
Palazzo Falconieri
Palazzo Giustiniani
Palazzo Lateranense
Palazzo Pamphili
Palazzo del Banco di S Spirito
Palazzo Spada
Palazzo di Spagna
Boselli, Orfeo (1600-1667)
Palazzo Cardelli
Bosman, André (active around 1675)
Palazzo Borghese
Brandi, Giacinto (1621-1691)
Palazzo Pamphili
Breccioli, Bartolomeo (documented 1593, died c. 1637)
Palazzo del Monte di Pietà
Palazzo Nari (in via Monterone)
Palazzo Ruspoli
Bril, Paul (1554-1626)
Palazzo Lateranense
Palazzo Pallavicini Rospigliosi
Brozzi, Paolo (active 1670s)
Palazzo Altieri
Buonarotti, Michelangelo (the Younger) (1568-1646)
Palazzo Barberini
Buonvicini, Nicola (active 1780s)
Palazzo Altieri
Busiri Vici, Andrea (1818-1911)
Palazzo Colonna
Palazzo Doria-Pamphili
Palazzo Pamphili
Palazzo del Quirinale
Calandrucci, Giacinto (1646-1707)
Palazzo Lante
Palazzo Muti Papazzurri
Palazzo Nuñez
Camassei, Andrea (1602-1649)
Palazzo Barberini
Camassei, Giacinto (active late 1670s, d. after 1683)
Palazzo Barberini
Palazzo Pamphili

Cametti, Bernardino (c. 1669-1736)
Palazzo Boncompagni Ludovisi
Palazzo del Monte di Pietà
Canini, Giovanni Angelo (1609-1666)
Palazzo del Quirinale
Canuti, Domenico Maria (1626-1684)
Palazzo Altieri
Caporale, Francesco (active 1600s and 1610s)
Palazzo Capponi ('della Palma')
Caravaggio, Polidoro da (Polidoro Caldara) (c. 1500-1543)
Palazzo del Bufalo
Palazzo Ferrini
Carcani, Filippo (active 1670s and 1680s)
Palazzo Borghese
Carloni, Giovanni Andrea (1639-1697)
Palazzo Altieri
Caronica, Gregorio (active 1570s and 1580s)
Palazzo Capizucchi
Carracci, Annibale (1560-1609)
Palazzo Doria-Pamphili
Palazzo Farnese
Carracci, Antonio (c. 1589-1618)
Palazzo del Quirinale
Catapani, Filippo (active 1730s)
Palazzo Doria-Pamphili
Cavallini, Francesco (c. 1640-after 1703)
Palazzo Borghese
Celio, Gaspare (1571-1640)
Palazzo Mattei di Giove
Cennini, Pietro Paolo (1661-1739)
Palazzo del Quirinale
Cesari, Bernardino (1571-1622)
Palazzo Costaguti
Cesari, Giuseppe (il Cavaliere d'Arpino) (1568-1640)
Palazzo Costaguti
Palazzo del Pio Sodalizio dei Piceni
Palazzo Rondinini
Cesi, Carlo (1626-1686)
Palazzo Boncompagni Corcos
Palazzo del Quirinale
Chiari, Fabrizio (c. 1615-1695)
Palazzo Altieri
Palazzo del Quirinale
Chiari, Giuseppe Bartolomeo (1654-1727)
Palazzo Barberini
Palazzo de Carolis
Palazzo Colonna
Cigoli (Ludovico Cardi) (1559-1613)
Palazzo Braschi
Palazzo Pallavicini Rospigliosi
Cipriani, Sebastiano (c. 1660-c. 1740)
Palazzo Macchi di Cellere
Palazzo Maruscelli
Circignani, Antonio (il Pomarancio) (1560-1620)
Palazzo Altemps
Palazzo Mattei di Giove
Circignani, Niccolò (il Pomarancio) (c. 1520-after 1597)
Palazzo Barberini
Città di Castello, Matteo da (Matteo Bartolini) (c. 1530-after 1597)
Palazzo Chigi (Aldobrandini)
Claude Lorrain (Claude Gellée) (1600 or 1604/5-1682)
Palazzo Crescenzi
Palazzo Lancellotti
Palazzo Muti Papazzurri (Balestra)
Coli, Giovanni (1636-1681)
Palazzo Colonna
Colombo, Bartolomeo (active mid 17th century)
Palazzo del Quirinale
Colonna, Angelo Michele (1604-1687)
Palazzo Spada
Conca, Sebastiano (1676 or 1680-1764)
Palazzo de Carolis
Palazzo Corsini
Conca, Tommaso Maria (1735-1822)
Palazzo Doria-Pamphili
Contini, Francesco (1599-1669)
Palazzo Barberini ai Giubbonari
Contini, Giovanni Battista (1642-1723)
Palazzo Chigi (Aldobrandini)
Palazzo Macchi di Cellere
Cornacchini, Augusto (1686-1754)
Palazzo del Monte di Pietà
Cortona, Pietro da (Pietro Berrettini) (1596-1669)
Palazzo Barberini
Palazzo Gambirasi
Palazzo Mattei di Giove
Palazzo del Quirinale
Costantini, Ermenegildo (1731-1791)
Palazzo Borghese
Courtois, Guillaume (il Borgognone) (1628-1679)
Palazzo del Quirinale
Cozza, Francesco (1605-1682)
Palazzo Altieri
Palazzo Pamphili (Collegio Innocenziano)
Croce, Baldassare (1558-1628)
Palazzo Barberini
Palazzo Lateranense
De Marchis, Tommaso (1693-1759)
Palazzo Mellini
De Pomis, Antonio (active 1st quarter of 17th century)
Palazzo Chigi (Aldobrandini)
De Romanis, Filippo (1694-1742)
Palazzo Pighini
De Rossi, Ascanio (active c. 1606-c. 1630)
Palazzo Costaguti
De Rossi, Giovanni Antonio (1616-1695)
Palazzo Altieri
Palazzo Astalli
Palazzo Boncompagni Corcos
Palazzo Carpegna (Baldinotti)
Palazzo Celsi
Palazzo D'Aste
Palazzo D'Aste (in via di Ripetta)
Palazzo D'Aste (Pericoli, Sterbini)
Palazzo Gambirasi
Palazzo Gomez
Palazzo del Monte di Pietà
Palazzo Muti Bussi
Palazzo Nari
Palazzo Nuñez
Palazzo Santacroce
De Rossi, Mattia (1637-1695)
Palazzo Capizucchi
Palazzo Colonna
Palazzo Muti Papazzurri in Piazza della Pilotta
De Sanctis, Francesco (1693-1740)
Palazzo Centini
De'Vecchi, Gaspare (documented 1614, d. 1643)
Palazzo Mattei di Giove
Del Barba, Genesio (1691-1762)
Palazzo Doria-Pamphili
Del Bosco, Tommaso (1501 or 1503-1572 or 1579)
Palazzo Spada
Del Duca, Giacomo (1520-1604)
Palazzo del Pio Sodalizio dei Piceni
Palazzo della Stamperia
Del Grande, Antonio (c. 1607-1671)
Palazzo Colonna
Palazzo Doria-Pamphili
Palazzo di Spagna
Delino, Simone Felice (1655-1697)
Palazzo Panizza
Della Greca, Felice (1625-1677)
Palazzo Chigi (Odescalchi)
Palazzo Chigi (Aldobrandini)
Palazzo Valentini
Della Porta, Giacomo (1532-1602)
Palazzo Albertoni
Palazzo Altemps
Palazzo Capizucchi

Palazzo Chigi (Aldobrandini)
Palazzo Farnese
Palazzo Maffei
Palazzo Muti Bussi
Palazzo Patrizi
Palazzo Pecci Blunt
Palazzo Ruggeri
Palazzo Serlupi Crescenzi
Della Porta, Guglielmo (1500-1577)
Palazzo Farnese
Della Valle, Filippo (1697-1768)
Palazzo della Consulta
Di Fiandra, Diego (active c. 1550)
Palazzo Spada
Domenichino (Domenico Zampieri) (1581-1641)
Palazzo Costaguti
Palazzo Farnese
Palazzo Lancellotti
Palazzo Mattei di Giove
Dori, Alessandro (1702-1772)
Casa Giannini
Palazzo Rondinini
Palazzo Santacroce
Dughet, Gaspard (1615-1675)
Palazzo Borghese
Palazzo Cardelli
Palazzo Colonna
Palazzo Doria-Pamphili
Palazzo Muti Bussi
Palazzo Pamphili
Palazzo del Quirinale
Ducrot, Giuseppe (1966-)
Palazzo Spada
Fancelli, Cosimo (1620-1688)
Palazzo Borghese
Ferabosco, Martino (documented 1606, d. 1623)
Palazzo del Quirinale
Ferrari, Francesco (active through 1720s and 1740s)
Palazzo del Cinque
Ferrari, Giacinto (active 1760s and 1770s)
Palazzo Rondinini
Ferri, Ciro (1634-1689)
Palazzo Borghese
Palazzo Muti Papazzurri
Palazzo del Quirinale
Ferroni, Giuseppe (1714-1771)
Palazzo Celani
Casa dei Chierici Minori
Ferrucci, Pompeo (1566-1637)
Palazzo del Quirinale
Fontana, Carlo (1634-1714)
Palazzo Altieri
Palazzo Colonna
Palazzo Massimo di Rignano
Palazzo di Montecitorio
Palazzo Muti Bussi
Fontana, Domenico (1543-1607)
Palazzo Albani
Palazzo del Quirinale
Fontana, Gerolamo (documented 1668, d. 1701)
Palazzo Colonna
Fontana, Giovanni (1540-1614)
Palazzo Patrizi
Franceschini, Marcantonio (1648-1729)
Palazzo della Cancelleria
Fuga, Ferdinando (1699-1781)
Palazzo Cenci-Bolognetti
Palazzo della Consulta
Palazzo Corsini
Palazzo Falconieri
Palazzo Maffei
Palazzo del Quirinale
Gabet, Louis (documented 1858-1878)
Palazzo Valentini
Gamelin, Jacques (1738-1803)
Palazzo Rondinini
Garzi, Luigi (1638-1721)
Palazzo Borghese
Palazzo de Carolis
Gaulli, Giovanni Battista (il Baciccio) (1639-1709)
Palazzo della Cancelleria
Gentileschi, Orazio (1563-1639)
Palazzo Pallavicini Rospigliosi
Gherardi, Antonio (1638-1702)
Palazzo Nari (in via Monterone)
Gherardi, Filippo (1643-1704)
Palazzo Colonna
Giani, Felice (1758-1823)
Palazzo Altieri
Giansimoni, Nicola (documented 1766, d. 1800)
Palazzo Barberini ai Giubbonari
Giaquinto, Corrado (1703-1765)
Palazzo Borghese
Palazzo del Quirinale
Palazzo Rondinini
Gimignani, Giacinto (1606-1681)
Palazzo Cavallerini Lazzaroni
Palazzo Pamphili
Gimignani, Ludovico (1643-1697)
Palazzo Cavallerini Lazzaroni
Giorgetti, Gioseppe (documented 1668, d. after 1682)
Palazzo Barberini
Giorgini, Simone (documented 1677-1712)
Palazzo del Monte di Pietà
Grazioli, Carlo (active 1920s)
Palazzo Cardelli
Gregorini, Domenico (1700-1777)
Palazzo Boncompagni Ludovisi
Gregorini, Ludovico (c. 1661-1723)
Palazzo Santacroce
Grimaldi, Giovanni Francesco (1606-1680)
Palazzo Borghese
Palazzo Muti Papazzurri in Piazza della Pilotta
Palazzo Nuñez
Palazzo Peretti
Palazzo del Quirinale
Palazzo Santacroce
Guercino (Giovanni Francesco Barbieri) (1591-1666)
Palazzo Costaguti
Palazzo Lancellotti
Guerra, Gaspare (1560-1622)
Palazzo Cardelli
Guerra, Giovanni (1540/44-1618)
Palazzo Lateranense
Guerrieri, Giovan Francesco (1589-1657)
Palazzo Borghese
Guglielmi, Gregorio (1714-1773)
Palazzo Corsini
Guidi, Domenico (1625-1701)
Palazzo del Monte di Pietà
Haffner, Enrico Giovanni (1640-1720)
Palazzo Altieri
Juvarra, Filippo (1678-1736)
Palazzo Zuccari
Koch, Gaetano (1849-1910)
Palazzo del Banco di S Spirito
Lagi, Simone (documented 1620-1640)
Palazzo Barberini
Lambardi, Carlo (1554-1620)
Palazzo Costaguti
Landini, Taddeo (1550-1596)
Palazzo del Quirinale
Lanfranco, Giovanni (1582-1647)
Palazzo Costaguti
Palazzo Farnese
Palazzo Mattei di Giove
Palazzo del Quirinale
Laureti, Tommaso (1530-1602)
Palazzo Lateranense
Lauri, Filippo (1623-1694)
Palazzo Borghese
Palazzo del Quirinale
Legendre, Domenico (active 1670s)
Palazzo Giustiniani
Leoni, Ottavio (1578-1630)
Palazzo Altemps
Le Gros, Pierre (the Younger) (1666-1719)
Palazzo del Monte di Pietà
Longhi, Martino (the Elder) (1520 -1591)
Palazzo Altemps

Palazzo Borghese
Palazzo Santacroce
Palazzo Valentini
Longhi, Martino (the Younger) (1602-1660)
Palazzo Ruspoli
Longhi, Onorio (1569-1619)
Palazzo Altemps
Palazzo Ferrini
Palazzo Lante
Palazzo Serlupi Crescenzi
Palazzo Verospi
Luti, Benedetto (1666-1724)
Palazzo de Carolis
Maderno, Carlo (1556-1629)
Palazzo Barberini ai Giubbonari
Palazzo Barberini
Palazzo Borghese
Palazzo Chigi (Odescalchi)
Palazzo Chigi (Albertoni)
Palazzo Giustiniani
Palazzo Lancellotti
Casa di Carlo Maderno
Palazzo Mattei di Giove
Palazzo Mellini
Palazzo del Monte di Pietà
Palazzo Pallavicini Rospigliosi
Palazzo Patrizi
Palazzo Peretti
Palazzo del Quirinale
Palazzo Santacroce
Palazzo Strozzi
Palazzo Varese
Maderno, Stefano (1576-1636)
Palazzo del Quirinale
Magno, Giovanni Battista (il Modanino) (1591/2-1674)
Palazzo Cardelli
Palazzo Colonna
Palazzo Spada
Maille, Michel (Michele Maglia) (c. 1643-1703)
Palazzo Borghese
Palazzo del Monte di Pietà
Malescotti, Egidio (active mid 18th century)
Palazzo Lancellotti
Mancini, Francesco (1679-1758)
Palazzo Colonna
Maratta, Carlo (1625-1713)
Palazzo Altieri
Palazzo del Quirinale
Maruscelli, Paolo (1594-1649)
Palazzo Madama
Palazzo Spada
Marziani, Giovanni Domenico (active around 1630)
Palazzo Barberini
Mascarino, Ottaviano (1524-1606)
Palazzo Albani
Palazzo del Quirinale
Palazzo Valentini
Mattei, Tommaso (c. 1686– c. 1703)
Palazzo Spada
Mazzoni, Giulio (c. 1525–after 1589)
Palazzo Spada
Mazzuoli, Giuseppe (1644-1725)
Palazzo del Monte di Pietà
Mellin, Charles (1597/1600-1649)
Palazzo Muti Papazzurri (Balestra)
Meucci, Vincenzo (1694 -1766)
Palazzo Corsini
Michetti, Niccolò (1675-1759)
Palazzo Braschi
Palazzo Colonna
Palazzo Falconieri
Milani, Aureliano (1675-1749)
Palazzo Doria-Pamphili
Mitelli, Agostino (1609-1660)
Palazzo Spada
Mochi, Francesco (1580-1654)
Palazzo Braschi
Moderati, Francesco (c. 1680 – after 1724)
Palazzo del Monte di Pietà
Mola, Giovanni Battista (1585-1665)
Palazzo Patrizi
Mola, Pier Francesco (1612-1666)
Palazzo Costaguti
Palazzo del Quirinale
Montagna, Marco Tullio (c. 1594-1649)
Palazzo Borghese
Moraldi, Giovan Pietro (active around 1640)
Palazzo Doria-Pamphili
Moraldo, Giacomo (documented 1682)
Palazzo Cimarra
Morelli, Cosimo (1732-1812)
Palazzo Braschi
Morelli, Tommaso (active 1720s)
Palazzo Centini
Mormorelli, Liborio (active 1750s)
Palazzo Corsini
Palazzo Doria-Pamphili
Muratori, Domenico Maria (1661-1742)
Palazzo de Carolis
Murgia, Francesco (documented 1656/1657)
Palazzo del Quirinale
Muziano, Girolamo (1532-1592)
Palazzo Lateranense
Naldini, Pietro Paolo (1619-1691)
Palazzo Cardelli
Napolitano, Filippo (Teodoro Filippo de Liagno) (1589-1629)
Palazzo Pallavicini Rospigliosi
Nasini, Giuseppe Nicola (1657-1736)
Palazzo della Cancelleria
Nebbia, Cesare (1536-1614)
Palazzo Lateranense
Odazzi, Giovanni (1663-1731)
Palazzo Albani
Palazzo de Carolis
Ojjetti, Raffaele (1845-1924)
Palazzo Chigi (Odescalchi)
Onofri, Crescenzio (1632-after 1712)
Palazzo Colonna
Orsi, Prospero (c. 1560-c. 1633)
Palazzo Mattei di Giove
Ottoni, Lorenzo (1648-1736)
Palazzo Barberini
Palazzo del Monte di Pietà
Ottino, Pasquale (1578-1630)
Palazzo del Quirinale
Navone, Filippo (active around 1830)
Palazzo Valentini
Pacetti, Vincenzo (1746-1820)
Palazzo Altieri
Paganelli, Domenico (1545-1624)
Palazzo Valentini
Paladini, Camillo (documented 1729)
Apartment building in Piazza S Lorenzo in Lucina
Pannini, Giovanni Paolo (1691-1765)
Palazzo Albani
Pâris, Adrien (1745-1819)
Palazzo di Spagna
Parrocel, Stefano (1696-1774)
Palazzo Corsini
Passeri, Giuseppe (1654-c. 1714)
Palazzo Barberini
Passignano (Domenico Cresti) (1559-1638)
Palazzo Corsini
Palazzo Pallavicini Rospigliosi
Pécheux, Laurent (1729-1821)
Palazzo Barberini
Peparelli, Francesco (active 1626, d. 1641)
Palazzo del Bufalo
Palazzo del Bufalo Ferraioli
Palazzo Cardelli
Palazzo Cerri
Palazzo del Monte di Pietà
Palazzo Muti Bussi
Palazzo Pamphili
Palazzo Santacroce
Palazzo Valentini
Permoser, Balthasar (1651-1732)
Palazzo del Grillo

Perrier, François (1590-1650)
Palazzo Peretti
Piacentini, Marcello (1881-1960)
Palazzo Barberini
Piacentini, Pio (1846-1928)
Palazzo Capizucchi
Piazza, Paolo (1557-1621)
Palazzo Borghese
Pinturicchio (Bernardino di Betto) (c. 1454-1513)
Palazzo Colonna
Ponzio, Flaminio (1559/60-1613)
Palazzo Altemps
Palazzo Barberini ai Giubbonari
Palazzo Borghese
Palazzo Pallavicini Rospigliosi-
Palazzetto di Flaminio Ponzio
Palazzo del Quirinale
Palazzo Rondinini
Palazzo Sciarra
Pozzi, Stefano (1699-1768)
Palazzo Colonna
Palazzo Doria-Pamphili
Pozzoni, Francesco Felice (active last quarter of 17th century)
Palazzo Santacroce
Procaccini, Andrea (1671-1734)
Palazzo de Carolis
Puccini, Biagio (1673-1721)
Casa del Falco
Raffaelli, Mariano (active 1880s)
Palazzo Cardelli
Raguzzini, Filippo (c. 1680-1771)
Apartment buildings in Piazza di S Ignazio
Rainaldi, Carlo (1611-1691)
Palazzo Borghese
Palazzo Donarelli
Palazzo Mancini
Rainaldi, Girolamo (1570 -1655)
Palazzo Altemps
Palazzo Pamphili
Palazzo Zuccari
Reni, Guido (1575-1642)
Palazzo Pallavicini Rospigliosi
Palazzo del Quirinale
Retti, Leonardo (active c. 1570-1609)
Palazzo Borghese
Ricci, Sebastiano (1659-1734)
Palazzo Colonna
Ricciolini, Michelangelo (1654-1715)
Palazzo Barberini
Palazzo Spada
Righi, Francesco (documented 1649-1661)
Palazzo Carpegna (Accademia di S Luca)
Palazzo Spada
Romanelli, Giovanni Francesco (1610-1662)
Palazzo Altemps
Palazzo Barberini
Palazzo Costaguti
Palazzo Lante
Romanelli, Urbano (documented 1678)
Palazzo Barberini
Roncalli, Cristoforo (il Pomarancio) (1552-1626)
Palazzo Crescenzi
Palazzo Mattei di Giove
Rosa, Francesco (documented 1674, d. 1687)
Palazzo Centini
Rossetti, Cesare (active c. 1593–c. 1620)
Palazzo del Quirinale
Sacchi, Andrea (1599/1600-1661)
Palazzo Barberini
Salvi, Nicola (1697-1751)
Palazzo Chigi (Odescalchi)
Palazzo del Monte di Pietà
Palazzo Poli
Salviati, Francesco (Francesco de'Rossi) (c. 1509-1563)
Palazzo della Cancelleria
Palazzo Farnese
Sangallo, Antonio da, the Younger (1484–1546)
Palazzo Farnese
Sangallo, Giuliano da (c. 1443–1516)
Palazzo Lante
S Giovanni, Giovanni da (Giovanni Mannozzi) (1592–1636)
Palazzo Pallavicini Rospigliosi
Palazzo Patrizi, (Clementi)
Saraceni, Carlo (c. 1579-1620)
Palazzo del Quirinale
Sarti, Antonio (1797-1880)
Palazzo Maffei
Palazzo Nuñez
Schiratti, Tommaso (active 1580s)
Palazzo Altemps
Schor, Giovanni Paolo (1615-1674)
Palazzo Borghese
Palazzo Colonna
Palazzo del Quirinale
Soccorsi, Giovan Angelo (active around 1720)
Palazzo Muti Papazzurri (Balestra)
Soria, Giovanni Battista (1581-1651)
Palazzo della Famiglia Borghese
Sormani, Leonardo (before 1530-after 1589)
Palazzo Spada
Spadarino (Giovanni Antonio Galli) (1585-after 1653)
Palazzo Pamphili
Palazzo del Quirinale
Spägl, Andreas (active around 1718)
Palazzo della Cancelleria
Spallucci, Camillo (active around 1600)
Palazzo Barberini
Specchi, Alessandro (1668-1729)
Palazzo Albani
Palazzo de Carolis
Palazzo Galloppi
Palazzo Muti Papazzurri (Balestra)
Palazzo Pighini
Palazzo del Quirinale
Palazzo Verospi
Stanchi, Niccolò (1623 – 1690)
Palazzo Borghese
Swanevelt, Herman van (c. 1605-1655)
Palazzo Mancini
Palazzo Pamphili
Tassi, Agostino (c. 1580 -1644)
Palazzo Barberini
Palazzo Borghese
Palazzo Chigi (Odescalchi)
Palazzo Costaguti
Palazzo Lancellotti
Palazzo Pallavicini Rospigliosi
Palazzo Pamphili
Palazzo del Quirinale
Tedeschi, Luigi (active 1880s)
Palazzo Santacroce
Tempesta, Antonio (c. 1555-1630)
Palazzo Giustiniani
Palazzo Pallavicini Rospigliosi
Théodon, Jean-Baptiste (1646-1713)
Palazzo del Monte di Pietà
Tofanelli, Stefano (1752 – 1812)
Palazzo Altieri
Torrone, Angelo (active 1670s)
Palazzo Barberini
Torriani, Orazio (c. 1601-c. 1657)
Palazzo S Calisto
Palazzo Sciarra
Turchi, Alessandro (l'Orbetto) (1578-1649)
Palazzo del Quirinale
Tursi, Galeazzo (active 1720s, d. 1731)
Palazzo Pighini
Trevisani, Francesco (1656-1746)
Palazzo de Carolis
Valvassori, Gabriele (1683-1761)
Palazzo Doria-Pamphili
Palazzo Muti Bussi
Palazzo Rondinini
Vanni, Raffaele (1587-1673)
Palazzo Santacroce

Vanvitelli, Luigi (1700-1773)
Palazzo Chigi (Odescalchi)
Palazzo Sciarra
Vasanzio, Giovanni (Jan Van Santen) (1550-1621)
Palazzo Borghese
Palazzo Pallavicini Rospigliosi
Vasari, Giorgio (1511-1574)
Palazzo della Cancelleria
Venturi, Sergio (active 1620s and 1630s)
Palazzo della Famiglia Borghese
Vespignani, Virginio (1808–1882)
Palazzo Maruscelli
Palazzetto Sterbini
Vignola, Jacopo Barozzi da (1507-1573)
Palazzo Borghese
Palazzo Capizucchi
Viviani, Antonio (1560-1620)
Palazzo Altemps
Palazzo Barberini
Palazzo Lateranense
Volterra, Francesco da (Francesco Capriani) (active 1565, d. 1594)
Palazzo Cardelli
Palazzo Lancellotti
Wernle, Giacomo (1650 – 1722)
Palazzo Spada
Zuccari, Federico (1540/41-1609)
Palazzo Zuccari
Zuccari, Taddeo (1529-66)
Palazzo Farnese
Zucchi, Jacopo (1542-1596)
Palazzo Ruspoli

INDEX OF STREETS

Accademia di S Luca, Piazza dell'
Palazzo Carpegna (Accademia di S Luca)
Aracoeli, via d'
1, Palazzo Massimo di Rignano
2, Palazzo Muti Bussi
3, Palazzo Pecci Blunt
Arcione, via
70, Palazzo del Drago
Babuino, via del
41, Palazzetto Sterbini
49-52, Palazzo Boncompagni Ludovisi
Banchi Nuovi, via dei
3, Casa di Carlo Maderno
Barbieri, via dei
6, Palazzo Cavallerini Lazzaroni
Benedetto Cairoli, Piazza
3, Palazzo Santacroce
Bocca di Leone, via
79, Palazzo Nuñez
Borghese, Piazza
Palazzo della Famiglia Borghese
Bufalo, via del
8, Palazzo del Bufalo
Campitelli, Piazza
2, Palazzo Albertoni
3, Palazzo Capizucchi
6, Palazzetto di Flaminio Ponzio
Campo Marzio, via
46, Palazzo Magnani
69, Palazzo Marescotti
Cancelleria, Piazza della
1, Palazzo della Cancelleria
Capo le Case, via
3, Palazzo Centini
Capranica, Piazza
95, Casa Giannini
Capodiferro, via
13, Palazzo Spada
Caprettari, Piazza dei
70, Palazzo Lante
Cardelli, Piazza
4, Palazzo Cardelli
Carlo Goldoni, Largo
55, Palazzo Ruspoli
Colonna, Piazza
355, Palazzo del Bufalo Ferraioli
370, Palazzo Chigi (Aldobrandini)
Colonna Antonina, via
52, Palazzo del Cinque
Condotti, via dei
11, Palazzo Maruscelli
55-57, Palazzetto Anselini
68, Palazzo Malta
Consolato, via del
6, Palazzo De Rossi
Corso, via del
146-154, Palazzo Manfroni
173, Palazzo Raggi
239, Palazzo Sciarra
271, Palazzo Mancini
304, Palazzo Doria-Pamphili
307, Palazzo de Carolis
337, Palazzo Guelfi Camajani
374, Palazzo Verospi
480-488, Palazzo Pulieri
519, Palazzo Rondinini
Croce, via della
71, Palazzetto 'dei Telamoni'
78A, Palazzo Gomez
Crociferi, via dei
23, Casa degli Agostiniani Scalzi
Dataria, via della
22, Palazzo Testa Piccolomini
Dogana Vecchia, via della
29, Palazzo Giustiniani
Falco, via del
18, Casa del Falco
Farnese, Piazza
44, Palazzo Pighini
51, Palazzo Mandosi
67, Palazzo Farnese
Fontanella di Borghese, Largo
19, Palazzo Borghese
Funari, via dei
12, Palazzo Patrizi

Gesù, Piazza del
16, Palazzo Cenci-Bolognetti
49, Palazzo Altieri
Giubbonari, via dei
41, Palazzo Barberini ai Giubbonari
Giulia, via
1, Palazzo Falconieri
14-21, Palazzo Varese
97, Palazzo Donarelli
Governo Vecchio, via del
3, Palazzo Boncompagni Corcos
104, Palazzetto Lupardi
Grillo, Piazza del
5, Palazzo del Grillo
Lancellotti, via
18, Palazzo Lancellotti
Larga, via
12, Palazzo Cerri
Lavatore, via del
38, Casa dei Chierici Minori
Librari, Largo dei
89, Palazzo Ghetti
Lucchesi, Largo dei
26, Palazzo Lazzaroni
Lungara, via della
10, Palazzo Corsini
Madama, Piazza
11, Palazzo Madama
Maggio, via XXIV
43, Palazzo Pallavicini Rospigliosi
Margana, Piazza
19, Palazzo Maccarani Odescalchi
Mascherone, via del
57, Palazzo Sinibaldi
Mattei, Piazza
10, Palazzo Costaguti
Mercede, via della
11 and 12A, Palazzi Bernini
Michelangelo Gaetani, via
32, Palazzo Mattei di Giove
Monserrato, via
25, Palazzo Rocci
105, Palazzo Giangiacomo
149, Palazzo D'Aste
154, Palazzo Bossi
Montecitorio, Piazza di
33, Palazzo di Montecitorio
115, Palazzo Macchi di Cellere
Monte di Pietà, Piazza del
22, Palazzetto Alibrandi
32, Palazzo del Monte di Pietà
Monte Giordano, via di
2, Palazzo Avila
Monterone, via
2, Palazzo Nari
Montoro, via di
8, Palazzo Montoro
Navona, Piazza
14, Palazzo Pamphili
Orologio, Piazza dell'
7, Palazzo del Banco di S Spirito
Orsini, via degli
34, Palazzo Capponi
Pace, via della
8, Palazzo Gambirasi
Panetteria, Via della
15, Palazzo Antamoro
Panisperna, via
200, Palazzo Cimarra
Parione, via di
7, Palazzo del Pio Sodalizio dei Piceni
Pietra, Piazza di
26, Palazzo Ferrini
Pietro di Brazzà, Largo
86, Palazzo Maccarani Savorgnan di Brazzà
Pigna, via della
13A, Palazzo Maffei
Pilotta, Piazza della
32, Palazzo Muti Papazzurri
Plebiscito, via del
102, Palazzo Grazioli
Poli, via
4, Palazzo Poli
Quattro Fontane, via delle
13, Palazzo Barberini
20, Palazzo Albani
Quirinale, Piazza del
Palazzo della Consulta
Palazzo del Quirinale
Quirinale, via del
21, Palazzo Galloppi
Rinascimento, Corso del
44, Palazzo Carpegna (Baldinotti)
Ripetta, via di
142, Palazzo D'Aste
246, Palazzo Capponi ('della Palma')
Rotonda, Piazza della
23, Palazzo Crescenzi
S Apollinare, Via
8, Palazzo Altemps
S Apollonia, Piazza di
3, Palazzo Pizzirani
S Caterina della Rota, Piazza
91, Palazzo Mastrozzi
S Giovanni in Laterano, Piazza di
6, Palazzo Lateranense
S Giovanni in Laterano, via
122, Casa dei Merolli
S Ignazio, Piazza di
Apartment buildings
S Lorenzo in Lucina, Piazza
4, Palazzo Peretti,
31-35, apartment building
S Luigi dei Francesi, Piazza
37, Palazzo Patrizi
S Marco, via di
8, Palazzo Astalli
S Maria in Campo Marzio, Piazza
3, Palazzo Nari
S Maria in Monticelli, Piazza
66, Palazzo Panizza
S Maria in Trastevere, Piazza di
24, Palazzo S Calisto
S Pantaleo, Piazza
10, Palazzo Braschi
SS Apostoli, Piazza
49, Palazzo Muti Papazzurri (Balestra)
66, Palazzo Colonna
80, Palazzo Chigi (Odescalchi)
119, Palazzo Valentini
Scanderbeg, Piazza
85, Palazzo Celani
Seminario, via del
113, Palazzo Serlupi Crescenzi
Sistina, via
121, Palazzo Perucchi
Spagna, Piazza di
57, Palazzo di Spagna
Stamperia, via della
7-8, Palazzo della Stamperia
Stimmate, Largo delle
26, Palazzo Strozzi
Torre Argentina, Via di
13, Palazzo Pizzirani
Trinità dei Monti, Piazza della
14, Palazzo Zuccari
Umiltà,via dell'
43, Palazzo Mellini
Venezia, Piazza
5, Palazzo D'Aste
Vite, via della
7, Palazzo Ottoboni Boncompagni
Vittorio Emanuele II, Corso di
18, Palazzo Celsi
20, Palazzo Ruggeri
Zingari, via degli
55, unnamed building

ALSO FROM PALLAS ATHENE

Roman Baroque
by Anthony Blunt

Paperback, 210 x 150 mm, 128 pages, and with 98 illustrations
978 1 84368 119 9

The Baroque, for many the most thrilling architectural style ever created, was born in Rome and reached its apogee in the work of three geniuses born in the 1590's – Bernini, Borromini and Pietro da Cortona.

Perhaps the greatest student of the style was Anthony Blunt, who spent a lifetime studying and teaching the work of these architects and its importance to us now. This compact book distils the essence of his work and is an unsurpassed introduction to the Baroque in all its grandeur, drama and intellectual complexity.

In this edition buildings and architectural details are fully illustrated with contemporary engraved views and measured drawings. Many of these ravishing images have not been published since the beginning of the eighteenth century.

ALSO FROM PALLAS ATHENE

An Elephant in Rome
by Loyd Grossman

Hardback, 215 x 138 mm, 320 pages, and with 138 colour illustrations
978 1 84368 193 9

A hugely engaging read that helps explain how Rome was re-invented by the Papacy in the 17th century.
Country Life (Book of the Month)

Lively and informative. *The Sunday Times*

A fabulous read – strongly recommended. Intellect, humour and deep appreciation of the arts. *Charles Spencer*

A total delight, a brilliant vignette of 17th-century Rome, the Baroque and the Catholic church – warts and all – rolled into an erudite narrative.... with an ease of writing that is rare in art history. *Simon Jenkins*

By 1650, thanks to the twin blows of the Protestant Reformation and the Thirty Years War, Rome had lost its pre-eminent place in Europe. A new Pope, Alexander VII, fired with religious zeal, political guile and a mania for building, determined to restore the prestige of his church by making Rome once again the Caput Mundi – Head of the World. To help him do so, he enlisted the talents of Gianlorenzo Bernini, already celebrated as Europe's most important living artist (no mean feat in the age of Rembrandt and Velázquez). It was to be one the greatest artistic double act in history.

Famous as a TV presenter, Loyd Grossman has also been deeply involved in heritage and art history. His love of Rome was kindled by his first encounter with the enigmatic and strangely beautiful monument to this relationship between artist and pope: the elephant carrying an obelisk just behind the Pantheon. Written with this as a starting point, *An Elephant in Rome* is a book for those who love the sublime fascination of the Eternal City and want to understand the all too human tale of how it came to be.

ALSO FROM PALLAS ATHENE

Magick City

Travellers to Rome from the Middle Ages to 1900
by Ronald T. Ridley

Vol. 1: The Middle Ages to the Seventeenth Century 978 1 84368 067 3
Vol. 2: The Eighteenth Century 978 1 84368 139 7
Vol. 3: The Nineteenth Century 978 1 84368 140

Paperback, 214 x 141mm, each volume approx. 300 pages, and with 100-150 illustrations

The most comprehensive anthology of writings by visitors to the Eternal City ever compiled – witty, profound and endlessly entertaining.

Drawing on French, Italian, Spanish, English, German, Scandinavian and American sources, many hitherto neglected, Ronald Ridley has compiled a vivid and thought-provoking collage-portrait of Rome through the centuries, published in three elegant and richly illustrated volumes.

How did visitors arrive? Where did they stay? Did they employ guides? What were their expenses? What did they see of churches, palaces, villas and antiquities? What did they like or dislike of what they saw? What did they think of Rome in all its contemporary facets? What events did they witness? What portraits do they provide of people in Rome at the time of their visit? Excerpts from memoirs by more than two hundred visitors give a myriad fascinating insights and together provide an amazingly detailed and revealing account of Rome over nearly a millennium.

Ronald T. Ridley, professor at the University of Melbourne, was awarded the Premio Daria Borghese in 2019, and in 2022 made an honorary citizen of Italy in recognition of his contributions to the history of Rome.